DOMUS UNIVERSITATIS 1650

VERÖFFENTLICHUNGEN
DES INSTITUTS FÜR EUROPÄISCHE GESCHICHTE MAINZ
BAND 71
ABTEILUNG ABENDLÄNDISCHE RELIGIONSGESCHICHTE
HERAUSGEGEBEN VON JOSEPH LORTZ

ABRAHAM FRIESEN

REFORMATION AND UTOPIA

THE MARXIST INTERPRETATION OF THE REFORMATION AND ITS ANTECEDENTS

FRANZ STEINER VERLAG GMBH · WIESBADEN
1974

REFORMATION AND UTOPIA

THE MARXIST INTERPRETATION OF THE REFORMATION AND ITS ANTECEDENTS

BY

ABRAHAM FRIESEN

FRANZ STEINER VERLAG GMBH · WIESBADEN
1974

To Gerry

JSBN 3-515-01818-2

PREFACE

A chance remark in a class on European Intellectual History at Stanford University in the fall quarter of 1963 by the then Visiting Professor George L. Mosse on Ernst Bloch's biography of Thomas Müntzer led to a seminar paper the following quarter in Professor Lewis W. Spitz's graduate seminar in the Reformation. Subsequently published in *Church History,* this initial investigation led to a dissertation entitled "The Marxist Interpretation of the Reformation" written under the direction of Professor Spitz while a fellow at the *Institut für Europäische Geschichte* at Mainz, Germany, during the years 1965—1967. In the years since the completion of the dissertation, I have had time to explore some of the implications of the original study as well as to expand the study itself as the result of the discovery of a mass of archival material on the 19th-century historian and theologian, Wilhelm Zimmermann, whose work was so important to Friedrich Engels. This material led me to take a fresh look at the whole question of the reform of society in the early years of the Reformation, for it was the reformation of society that was also the basic concern of both Zimmermann and Marx and Engels, a concern that very naturally drew their attention to the radical attempts made to reform society in the early 16th century. As a consequence, I have added five new chapters to the beginning of the original study, while the dissertation itself has been reduced to Chapters VI, VII, VIII and IX.

Over the years I have incurred many debts. It was Professor William L. Morton, then of the University of Manitoba, who first awakened my interest in historiography. Professor Spitz at Stanford directed this interest toward the Reformation, encouraged my initial efforts, and guided the writing of the dissertation; his humane and genial guidance has accompanied the manuscript to its present form. That is not the extent of my debt to him, however; I owe him much more. I am also deeply grateful to Professor D. Dr. Joseph Lortz who generously made a two-year fellowship at his Institute (Abt. für Abendländische Religionsgeschichte) in Mainz available to me thereby permitting me to spend two years of uninterrupted work on the dissertation in a scholarly environment where I was able to present various parts of the study for critical discussion. It is to the

magnanimity manifested in the ecumencial spirit of this great Catholic
Reformation scholar that I owe the acceptance of this study, written by a
descendant of the Reformation Anabaptists, into the series of the Institute's
publications. Others have also given of their time to improve the study.
Roland Bainton and Robert Friedmann, the latter just before he died, were
both kind enough to read the original dissertation and offer suggestions for
improvement. Hans Hillerbrand read several chapters of the revised
manuscript while other segments, in somewhat different form, have appeared as essays in a number of different journals after having been presented at meetings of learned societies.

I am also indebted to all those who helped me track down the Zimmermann material. Here I must first of all mention Dr. Martin Brech, Professor at the University of Tübingen and director of the theological *Stift*
where Zimmermann himself once studied and from which he was eventually
expelled. Not only did he make all the Zimmermann materials contained
in the *Stift* archives available to me, but he also contacted many of the
libraries and archives in the area which might contain Zimmermann materials and prepared them for my coming. In this regard, Dr. Adolf Rapp,
Professor Emeritus of the University of Tübingen and author of an excellent essay on Zimmermann, was also very helpful. I should also like to
express my gratitude to the Schiller-Nationalmuseum of Marbach for
making the entire Zimmermann *Nachlass* available to me, to the Haupt-
staatsarchiv in Stuttgart for opening its archives to me, and to the Landeskirchliches Archiv, also in Stuttgart, for giving me access to its materials
on Zimmermann. Isolated letters to and from Zimmermann were made
available to me by a number of other German libraries and archives. Where
such letters have been used in this study, their sources have been duly noted.
Here I would like to express my gratitude to all these institutions; their
responses to my many letters of enquiry were invariably splendidly co-
operative.

Finally, I should like to express a more general word of appreciation to
all those who made our stay in Germany a memorable event. The Institute
for European History, Dept Abendländische Religionsgeschichte with Professor Lortz at its head, provided the focal point. Here historians and
theologians from different countries and religions persuasions labored to
interpret the Reformation in dialogue with one another. More informal
meetings took place every day over coffee, while a formal Luther-seminar
met every two weeks under the direction of Professor Erwin Iserloh of the
University of Münster and was attended by all the members of the Institute, from Professor Lortz and his Assistants down. All of the latter, Frau

Dr. Silvia Gräfin v. Brockdorff, Dr. Peter Manns and Dr. Karl Pellens, showed great concern both for our personal well-being as well as for our work and furthered both at every turn. I owe Dr. Gräfin v. Brockdorff a special word of thanks for her expert help in seeing the manuscript through the printers and for her help in reading the proofs. Two friends at the Institute, Dr. Friedhelm Krüger and Dr. Helmut Feld, both of whom were living in Tübingen with their families when I arrived there in the fall of 1970 to persue my Zimmermann studies, added to the pleasure of living in Mainz and made my evenings in Tübingen, after the archives had forced me out into the cold night, most pleasant. Added to these were the many pleasant hours spent at the home of my mother's uncle, Abraham Braun, and his daughter, Irmgard. Last, but most importantly, I should like to express my gratitude to my wife Gerry who not only helped me in my research while at the Institute but who also typed the first draft of the dissertation while we were still in Germany, a typing that was interrupted only by the birth of our son Eric. Her love, encouragement and help, which have accompanied me throughout the many transformations of the manuscript, have been a constant source of strength. It is to her that I dedicate this book.

Financial help for this study has come from the Canada Council and the *Institut für Europäische Geschichte* in Manz, Germany. These grants made possible the writing of the dissertation in Germany. A Summer Faculty Fellowship as well as a major research grant from the University of California at Santa Barbara made possible the first major revisions in the study and the research trip to Germany in the fall of 1970.

It is with regret that I must admit that none of the above share in the responsibility for the book's many shortcomings; that responsibility lies with me alone, a responsibility I shall attempt to bear with as good grace as possible.

Abraham Friesen
Santa Barbara, California
September 1973

CONTENTS

INDRODUCTION

The interpretation of the Reformation has long been plagued by partisan polemics of one kind or another. Catholics have attacked reformers and humanists; humanists have turned against Catholics and Protestants; while defenders of the Magisterial Reformers have attempted to discredit Catholics, humanists, and Reformation radicals alike. And just at the moment when the Ecumenical Movement, in conjunction with certain other influences, began to intrude a more irenic tone into Reformation scholarship, another interpretation — that of the Marxists — has arisen to oppose the emerging consensus between Protestants and Catholics. Indeed, so radical are the differences between Marxist and non-Marxist interpretations of the Reformation that there seems to be no way in which the two can be reconciled. But if they cannot be reconciled, they can at least be explained. It is in this latter sense — as an attempt to explain the Marxist interpretation of the Reformation — that this study wants to be understood. For it is only by understanding that we can hope to come to grips with it.

In order to attempt such an explanation, it was necessary to begin with the Reformation debate concerning the reform of 16th-century society itself. For, the more one reads the Marxist literature on the Reformation, the more apparent it becomes that the Marxists have taken the side of Thomas Müntzer and the peasants in this debate against Luther and the established authorities. Thus, to be able fully to explain the Marxist interpretation, several questions needed to be answered: 1) what was the nature of the Reformation debate? 2) what were the presuppositions behind the various arguments? 3) how did this debate influence the interpretations of the events in question? 4) and why have the Marxists chosen to side with Müntzer and the peasants? It is these questions which have largely determined the format at least of the first part of the present study.

Since the 1841—43 three-volume history of the Peasants' War written by the Young Hegelian, Wilhelm Zimmermann, which formed the sole factual foundation upon which Engels built his 1850 reinterpretation, plays such a pivotal role in this study, the opening chapter delineates, in miniature, the Young Hegelian rejection of Luther and attraction to Müntzer and the peasants. Chapter II attempts to set this phenomenon into its

larger perspective, a perspective which also helps to explain the irreconcilability of the Reformation debate between Luther and Müntzer described in Chapter III. The immediate interpretations, which have had
implications for all subsequent interpretations and which resulted largely
from these debates, are then traced in Chapter IV.

Part II begins the process all over again, but for a later interpretation
of the same events, with a chapter that traces Zimmermann's intellectual
development and the historical frame of reference which determined his
interpretation of the Peasant's War. Against this background, Chapter VI
attempts to explain Zimmermann's interpretation.

Three chapters on the main outlines of the Marxist interpretation of the
Reformation follow: Chapter VII deals with Engels-reinterpretation and
the revisions of some of his immediate followers; Chapter VIII is primarily
devoted to a discussion of the dilemma in the Marxist historiography of
the Reformation caused by the concept of the *frühbürgerliche Revolution;*
and Chapter IX stresses the recent attempts to reconcile all the disparate
elements of this interpretation. A concluding chapter of a critical nature
brings the study to a close.

No attempt has been made to try to include mention of all the Marxist
studies on the Reformation. Rather, I have been concerned to trace the
antecedents of, and the major developments within, this interpretation.
Indeed, some of the studies I originally discussed in my dissertation, "The
Marxist Interpretation of the Reformation," submitted to Stanford University in September of 1967, out of which this study grew, had to be
omitted here because with the discovery of the archival material on Zimmermann the manuscript took on a scope much broader than I had envisioned in my dissertation. For it was only after reading this material
that the Joachist tradition from Müntzer to Marx became apparent to me
and could be used as the unifying element of the entire study.

In her recent study on *Prophecy in the Later Middle Ages. A Study in
Joachimism* (Oxford, 1969), which I saw only after my own manuscript
had been completed, Marjorie Reeves remarks: "A prophet foretells the
future: he can also create it. For the historian the history of prophecy contains the delicate problem of the interplay between word and action. Are
prophecies fulfilled because of their far-seeing diagnosis or because of the
response they evoke in action? The historical significance of Joachim lies
in the dynamic quality of certain key ideas which he proclaimed," (p. 135).
The present study adds a further dimension to this phenomenon, for it is
the study of the interpretation of a certain period of history, which was
itself strongly affected by this prophetic element, by prophets who inter-

preted that past from the perspective of the prophetic future. And it was Joachim's "third status" of history — that era of complete freedom — which, in one way or another, has constituted this prophetic future. Hence the title of this study — *Reformation and Utopia: The Marxist Interpretation of the Reformation and its Antecedents.*

PART I: THE REFORMATION DEBATE

Chapter I

TWO REFORMATIONS

AN DEN UNGENANNTEN

Du, dessen Name ich nicht nenne,
Weil stündlich ihn mißbraucht die Welt,
Nach dessen Wiederkunft ich brenne,
Wie liegt so brach dein Ackerfeld!

Sie streiten seit viel hundert Jahren,
Ob je du anfiengst oder nie,
Ob du zum Himmel aufgefahren —
Doch dich, ach dich vergessen sie.

Sie klammern sich an deine Wiege,
An deinen Kreuzesstamm und Tod,
Sie färben deine edeln Züge
Mit deinem Blut ach düsterroth.

Doch keiner strebt, dich zu erreichen,
Zu thun, was du als Mensch gethan,
Den Göttern braucht man nicht zu gleichen,
Drum beten sie als Gott dich an.

Es will mir fast das Herz verbrennen,
Seh ich, o du der Menschheit Licht,
Wie sie, die stets nach dir sich sehnen,
Fast Alles sind, nur Menschen nicht.

Weltsegnend gingst du unverdrossen
Hin, wie die Sonne, still und groß,
Bis purpurn, von der Nacht vergossen,
Dein Blut, wie ihr's, zur Erde floß.

Was ich anbete, ist dein Leben,
Du großer Mensch im Gottesschein,
Mein Glaube sey, dir nachzustreben,
Wie du zu wirken und zu seyn.

This poem, written by Wilhelm Zimmermann in 1839, is an important statement of Zimmermann's interpretation of Christianity and in large part determined the interpretation of the Reformation he presented in the first edition of his history of the 1525 German Peasants War. His rejection of this interpretation in the early 1850's then also strongly influenced the revisions he made in the second (1856) edition.

1. STRAUSS AND LUTHER

During the months of July to December of 1857 and into January, 1858,
David Friedrich Strauss, author of the notorious *Leben Jesu* written in the
passion of his youth during the years 1835—36, began to read Luther with
the intention of writing his biography. He had just completed a study of
Ulrich von Hutten and the Heidelberg historian and literary critic, Georg
Gottfried Gervinus, suggested that a biography of Luther would be a suit-
able sequel.[1] Indeed, such a study would have fitted well into the total
scheme of the Reformation which Strauss had himself described to a friend
some months earlier. There he argued that the Reformation era had been
preoccupied with a most momentous task, a task which could be, and had
been, viewed from various perspectives. It could, he stated, be perceived
as a cultural task: the destruction of medieval barbarism through the study
of the Ancients. This had been the view of Erasmus. The new life, Erasmus
believed, would spread like a zephyr, quietly and gently, the way that
warm air melts ice and brings forth the budding tree. But, Strauss asked,
where else could this warmth come from than from the sun itself. The sun,
however, or the animating center of any culture was religion. Grasped
at its profoundest point, therefore, the cultural task was a religious task.
This, he continued, had been Luther's view: the extirpation of the abuses
within the ecclesiastical hierarchy, abuses which had come to rest like an
ominous cloud between the cultural sun and a stunted humanity. But the
perpetrators of these abuses were living men who held political power
and had become ensconced in powerful institutions. Would such men,
Strauss asked rhetorically, have allowed themselves to be disenfranchised
without further ado by that mild cultural zephyr or even that religious
sun? Never! One would much rather have to confront such men on the
firm ground of reality, with the tangible weapon of material opposition.
In the last analysis, therefore, Strauss reasoned, the task was a political
task; and since the hierarchical pressure came from outside the country,
a national task as well. This had been Hutten's view of the matter. Thus
even though Strauss conceded that Erasmus's view had been the most re-
fined and Luther's the most profound and fervent, yet Hutten's had been
the most practical and concrete; indeed, it had encompassed the other two
perspectives as well since Hutten had been permeated by the humanistic
ideals of Erasmus and deeply stirred by Luther's religious fire.[2]

---

[1] See the letter of David Friedrich Strauss to Moriz Rapp, July 9, 1856. *E. Zeller*,
ed., Ausgewählte Briefe von David Friedrich Strauss (Bonn, 1895), p. 369.
[2] Strauss to Käferle, March 10, 1856. Ibid., p. 350.

But whereas Strauss had been attracted by the Erasmian humanism and the humanistic politics of Hutten, already in the earliest stages of his work on Luther he commented that the smell of theology went against his grain.[3] Nor did Strauss's repugnance of the Lutheran theology subside. By December 3, after having immersed himself in the secondary literature of his subject and concluding that nothing of substance had yet been written on Luther, he still complained that he had not really entered into the spirit of his work because

"der Widerwille vor dem theologischen Geschmack des Stoffs ist zu groß."[4]

Strauss's aversion had a very specific focus. Already on November 9 he wrote to his friend, Moriz Rapp, that

"Um nun aber Luther zu begreifen, muß man seine Rechtfertigungslehre und die inneren Kämpfe, die ihn dazu führten, sich deutlich machen, sich in dieselben hineinleben."[5]

This, he complained, was not easy, at least not for him.

"Zunächst sind mir diese Gemüthszustände widrig und das Resultat derselben, die Rechtfertigungslehre, erscheint als Unsinn."[6]

It was this doctrine of justification, he wrote Friedrich Theodor Fischer on December 24, which kept him from really coming to grips with Luther.

"Denn so wie er liegt, ist er etwas rein Irrationales, ja Scheußliches. Ergänzung oder vielmehr Ersetzung der eigenen Gesetzerfüllung durch die — und obenein das Leiden — eines Andren!"[7]

Nor could he overcome his antipathy to Luther's doctrine of justification, even though by January 3, 1858, he had begun to read Luther's own writings.[8] Finally, on January 29, he could take it no longer and wrote Rapp:

"Mit meinen Arbeiten ist seit meinem letzten Brief gleichfalls eine Krisis eingetreten. Nachdem ich mich ein Vierteljahr lang bemüht hatte, mich in den Luther hineinzulesen und mir Appetit zu einer Arbeit über ihn zu machen, habe ich es zuletzt als vergeblich aufgeben müssen. Ich sehe ein, daß Hutten der äußerste Punkt ist, bis zu welchem ich mich der Reformation nähern kann; über ihn hinaus beginnt das Theologische, zwischen welchem und mir eine unübersteigliche Kluft ist und bleibt."[9]

---

[3] Strauss to Rapp, July 9, 1856. Ibid., p. 369.
[4] Strauss to Friedrich Theodor Vischer, Dec. 3, 1857. A. Rapp, ed., Briefwechsel zwischen Strauss und Vischer, II (Stuttgart, 1953), 127.   [5] Zeller, Ausgewählte Briefe, p. 373.
[6] Ibid.   [7] Rapp, Strauss-Vischer Briefwechsel, II, 131.
[8] See his letter to Vischer, Jan. 3, 1858. Ibid., p. 136.
[9] Zeller, Ausgewählte Briefe, p. 383.

Somewhat later he gave a more detailed reason for turning from Luther.

"Ich verehre den großen Befreier mit inniger Dankbarkeit; ich bewundere seine
Mannhaftigkeit, seinen überzeugungstreuen Muth; ich fühle mich angezogen durch
so manche Züge voller, gesunder Menschlichkeit, die sein Leben wie seine Schriften
bieten: aber Eines ist, was mich innerlichst von ihm scheidet, was mir, klar vor-
gestellt, jeden Gedanken einer biographischen Arbeit über ihn unmöglich macht.
Ein Mann, bei dem Alles von dem Bewußtsein ausgeht, daß er und alle Menschen für sich grundverdorben, der ewigen Verdammnis verfallen waren, aus
der sie nur durch das Blut Christi und ihren Glauben an dessen Kraft erlöst werden können — ein Mann, dessen Kern dieses Bewußtsein bildet, ist mir so fremd,
so unverständlich, daß ich ihn nie zum Helden einer biographischen Darstellung
wählen könnte. Was ich auch sonst an ihm bewundern und lieben möchte: dieses
sein innerstes Bewußtsein ist mir so abscheulich, daß von Sympathie zwischen
mir und ihm, wie sie zwischen dem Biographen und seinem Helden unerläßlich ist,
niemals die Rede sein könnte."[10]

Strauss's flirtation with Luther is evidence that a great gulf existed between his own theology and that of his Lutheran heritage, a gulf that had
been brought about by a "second reformation" in German theology. Strauss
himself was very much aware of this, as we have seen, and described its
essence in the introduction to the 1864 edition of his *Leben Jesu*. The
struggle during the Reformation, he remarked here, had been between what
had then appeared intolerable and the Bible. This intolerable had pertained
wholly to the doctrine and practice of the Church, and the Bible had provided what had at that time seemed a satisfactory substitute. The sifting,
therefore, had been relatively easy, for the Bible had still been viewed as
the unquestioned treasure of revelation and salvation to the people. Now,
however,

"ist auch das, was dem Protestanten damals noch geblieben war, die Bibel mit
ihrer Geschichte und Lehre, von dem Zweifel in Anspruch genommen, in ihr selbst
soll eine Scheidung vorgenommen werden zwischen dem, was für alle Zeiten wahr
und verbindlich, und dem, was nur in vorübergehenden Zeitvorstellungen und
Zeitverhältnissen begründet, für uns unbrauchbar, ja unannehmbar geworden
ist."[11]

And reason and experience were to be the criteria to be applied as the
yardstick of the truth of the Bible. By this standard a considerable part of
that which had passed under the name of Christianity had become absolutely intolerable. For Strauss part of this was obviously Luther's doctrine

---

[10] *Strauss*, Gesammelte Schriften, I (Bonn, 1876), 41, edited by *E. Zeller.*
[11] *Strauss*, Das Leben Jesu, für das deutsche Volk bearbeitet, I (Bonn, 1904), VI.

of justification with its concept of the divinity of Christ, its concomitant belief in His atonement for the sins of mankind, and His subsequent resurrection from the dead.

Here was a reformation more drastic than Luther's, as Strauss himself clearly saw. Here was a total change in the perspective on religion, for the very documents upon which Luther's Christian faith rested had come under the critical eye of the historian[12] and had been found wanting. Here was manifested a transition from revealed religion to philosophy: no longer the superiority of revealed religion over philosophy or even their juxtaposition. Here revealed religion was subordinated to philosophy, the humanistic philosophy of the Young Hegelians.[13]

2. CHRISTIANITY AND THE YOUNG HEGELIANS

Strauss's own earliest work on the life of Christ had been motivated by the desire to free mankind from the remaining fetters of an outdated orthodoxy to the liberty of a new humanism. As such, it fitted well into his Hegelian dialectic, for by criticising the "truth" of the past one inevitably rose to a higher truth until one reached the ultimate unity of all truth. But although Strauss's work was revolutionary in its effect, it was not as original as has sometimes been assumed. Perhaps the best assessment of his critical work, as Brazill has remarked, a judgment concurred in by Karl Barth as well as his own teacher, Ferdinand Christian Baur,[14] was made by Strauss's contemporary, Eduard Quinet.[15] Quinet argued that Strauss had merely brought together a number of disparate strands of German thought since Kant and welded these together.

"If this work had been the product of the thought of one man, so many minds would not have been alarmed by it at once. But, when it is seen as the mathematical consequences of almost all the work accomplished on the other side of the Rhine during the last half century, and that each had brought a stone to this sad sepulcher, learned Germany trembled and fled before its work."[16]

As Brazill comments:

---

[12] For an assessment of Strauss's ability as an historian, see *K. Barth*, From Rousseau to Ritschl (New York, 1959), pp. 364—365.

[13] See *W. J. Brazill*, The Young Hegelians (New Haven, 1970). One of Luther's main objectives had been, of course, precisely the opposite: the freeing of theology from philosophy. See *W. Link*, Das Ringen Luthers um die Freiheit der Theologie von der Philosophie, 2nd ed. (Darmstadt, 1969).

[14] *P. C. Hodgson*, The Formation of Historical Theology. A Study of Ferdinand Christian Baur (New York, 1966), pp. 75—76.

[15] *Brazill*, The Young Hegelians, p. 98.   [16] Quoted in ibid.

"There was nothing unique in Strauss' book; there was only the union, perhaps long implicit, of separate developments in the study of philosophy, history and biblical criticism."[17]

But in spite of the fact that much of the work of the Young Hegelians was negative and critical in character — and from their perspective it had to be since they argued that the archaic forms of intellectual life had to be destroyed before new forms could arise — they did have a positive program. This consisted primarily in a renewed humanism. As can be seen from the introductory poem by Wilhelm Zimmermann, a classmate of Strauss and Vischer both at the theological preparatory school at Blaubeuren and the University of Tübingen, as well as the author of an epoch-making three-volume history of the German Peasants' War written in 1841—43,[18] this humanism encompassed even Christ. But in the process of humanizing Christ, man took on god-like characteristics. Already Hegel had been accused by some of his contemporaries of having deified man, but he was able to fend off his accusers by retorting that the latter had not followed his reasoning.[19] His followers, however, and especially the Young Hegelians, were uninterested in retracing Hegel's intellectual pilgrimage; their interest lay solely in the final outcome of his thought. This Hegel postulated as a kind of Kingdom of God on earth to be realized by the gradual eradication of the dichotomy between a transcendant God and an imperfect world through the spirit of God which worked its will in the world and manifested itself with ever-increasing clarity in the history of the world. With the full realization of God's spirit in the world, all opposites would be suspended.[20] This implied, of course, the eventual union of God and man and the consequent perfectibility of man.

"For the Hegelian of the right the unity of God and man occurred in the unique form of Jesus; for the Hegelians of the left [the Young Hegelians], the unity of God and man occurred in all humanity through a progressive historical development. The Young Hegelians (Brazill continues) were not Christians, they were humanists. And that humanism, the product solely of Hegel's influence, formed their essential unity and divided them from the Hegelians of the right."[21]

---

[17] Ibid.

[18] W. *Zimmermann*, Geschichte des großen deutschen Bauernkrieges, 3 vols. (Stuttgart, 1841—1843). Zimmermann's history shall figure prominently in this study since it was the only one used by Friedrich Engels for his Marxist reinterpretation.

[19] *J. Gebhardt*, Politik und Eschatologie. Studien zur Geschichte der Hegelschen Schule in den Jahren 1830—1840 (München, 1963), pp. 54—62.

[20] See especially the following: *Barth*, From Rousseau to Ritschl, pp. 268—305; *K. Löwith*, Meaning in History (Chicago, 1949), pp. 54—62; and *F. Heer*, Hegel (Frankfurt a. M., 1955), pp. 7—61.   [21] *Brazill*, The Young Hegelians, p. 53.

Consequently, in Young Hegelian thought, Christ became merely the man who had achieved the greatest awareness of God and had thus become the most god-like person in history. The goal of history, however, was that everyone should achieve this same awareness, for only then could the earthly utopia arrive.

It is from this vantage point that the introductory poem by Zimmermann takes on meaning. He complains that the world has misunderstood Christ's purpose. Theologians quarrel over whether Christ was co-eternal with the Father, whether or not he rose from the dead; people venerate His crib and the cross on which He died, and glory in His blood. In all this, however, they miss the essential point and forget that Christ was a man: no one tries to emulate His work on earth. Because men feel they cannot emulate Christ, they have begun to venerate Him as God. This, however, keeps them from striving to scale the heights of His humanity. Zimmermann, therefore, and with him all the Young Hegelians, vow to go beyond this position:

> "Was ich anbete, ist dein Leben,
> Du großer Mensch im Gottesschein,
> Mein Glaube sey, dir nachzustreben,
> Wie du zu wirken und zu seyn."

This, then, was the essence of Christianity as enlightened by the Hegelian philosophy. As Zimmermann put it only one year after his *Bauernkrieg* came off the press:

"Die Pfaffenreligion hat durch die moderne Wissenschaft tödtliche Streiche erhalten, und sie wird an ihren Wunden für die Gebildeten bald so gut als verröchelt und verendet haben. Aber während dieselbe Wissenschaft selbst den letzten Faden, der den Menschen an eine höhere Welt bindet, den Unsterblichkeitsglauben mit eiskaltem Hohn entzweischnitt, wenigstens für sich entzweischnitt, und das göttliche Kind mit dem Bade ausschüttete, wendet sich das Herz der Zeit wieder der Religion, ihrem ewigen Geiste, zu, als einem unabweisbaren Bedürfnis, einer Religion jedoch, die den Himmel nicht blos im Jenseits sucht und hofft, sondern praktisch ihn in's diesseitige Leben hineinzieht. Im Mittelpunkt des Materialismus und des Gemeinen muß das Ideale und Höhere von selbst aufgehen, und die Selbstsucht der Gegenwart muß von der Liebe, das Geld von dem Geist überwunden werden, für welchen der Geringste unter den Brüdern nicht blos, wie jetzt, Mittel ist, sondern Selbstzweck."[22]

This Kingdom of God on earth was to be achieved through the teachings of a Christianity purified by the Young Hegelians. According to Zimmer-

[22] W. *Zimmermann,* "Der Roman der Gegenwart und Eugen Sue's Geheimnisse," Jahrbücher der Gegenwart, II (Tübingen, 1844), 214.

mann, in lectures given in Heilbronn early in 1838, these teachings could
be summed up as follows:

"1. Gott ist nur Liebe u. Güte, und gleich gnädig *gegen Alle.*
2. Die Menschen sind eins mit ihm.
3. Der Geist lehrt uns, daß wir *Gottes Kinder sind.* Röm. 8, 14 ff. Grim Vorr. 47.
4. Das 1. Gebot für d. Menschen ist die Liebe zu Gott, die sich durch Erfüllung
seines Willens — des Guten — bethätigt.
Dieses 1. Gebot fordert ferner, da *alle* Menschen gleichmäßig Kinder Gottes u.
also auch *Brüder* u. *gleich* sind, daß jeder den Nächsten (anderen) liebe, *wie sich
selbst.*
Nichts gilt als der *Glaube,* der durch die *Liebe thätig* ist. Gal 5, 6. d. h. d. Glaube
ist die innere *Ueberzeugung,* das Gefühl der *Wahrheit,* mit dem seine göttl. Lehre
die Gemüther ergreift.
Grundidee = das *Reinmenschliche.*"[23]

3. ZIMMERMANN AND THE PEASANTS' WAR

Aside from this "second reformation" which turned the Young Hegelians
away from the Lutheran theology of the Reformation, there was, however,
something about the early sixteenth century that invited a comparison with
the late eighteenth and early nineteenth centuries. Both were periods of
intense intellectual speculation and social turmoil, though the intellectual
speculation at least of the Young Hegelians, as we have seen, was at opposite poles from that of Luther. What attracted them then was the revolutionary atmosphere of the time, or, in the case of David Friedrich Strauss,
the humanism of the period, a combination very similar to their own time,
or so at least they thought. More specifically, the more radical were attracted to the German Peasants' War of 1525 because they saw similarities between their own struggles and the social revolution attempted by the
peasants during the Reformation. Arnold Ruge, for example, Young Hegelian political radical and editor of the unofficial Young Hegelian journal,
the *Hallische Jahrbücher,* as well as joint editor with Karl Marx of the
Deutsch-Französische Jahrbücher during 1843, remarked that

"unser Leben steht abermals an einem jüngsten Tag, wie er mit dem Christentum
und der Reformation hereinbrach."[24]

---

[23] *W. Zimmermann,* "Vorlesungen über Deutsche Geschichte," Zimmermann Nachlaß
(Schiller Nationalmuseum, Marbach), in manuscript form without pagination. These lec-
tures were in all probability given early in 1838, for on March 16th of that year Eduard
Mörike, the Swabian poet and friend of Zimmermann, wrote to Hermann Kurz, asking:
"Was wissen Sie von Zimmermann's Vorlesungen?" *K. Fischer* u. *R. Kraus,* eds., Eduard
Mörikes Briefwechsel, II (Berlin, 1903), 274.
[24] Quoted in *W. Neher,* Arnold Ruge als Politiker und politischer Schriftsteller (Hei-
delberg, 1933), p. 74.

Zimmermann was more specific than this. Writing to Gervinus, from whom he desired, and received, a favorable review of his *Bauernkrieg*, he remarked:

"Ich wollte meinem Volke ein Buch in die Hand geben, das eine seiner denkwürdigsten Begebenheiten der Wahrheit getreu und würdig erzählen, und das von interessantem Bezug auf seine Gegenwart wäre: hängt doch die grosse Bewegung von 1525 mit der neusten Strebung und Gährung innig zusammen, wenn auch nicht das Gestern, doch wie das Vorgestern mit dem Heute. Die bedeutungsvollsten Klänge, so manichfaltig sie durch die Gegenwart sich ziehen, sind sie nicht dieselben, welche durch das erste Jahrzehnt der Reformation rauschten? Es sind dieselben Saiten, die angeschlagen werden, und der sie spielt, ist ein und derselbe Geist."[25]

This revaluation of the revolutionary aspects of the sixteenth century first began under the influence of the French Revolution. Roughly to the time of the Enlightenment, the Peasants' War, and it is this that shall concern us primarily in this study, had been seen as a side-issue of the theological Reformation, resulting from the religious struggles of the period. The French Revolution, however, for the first time pointed clearly to the social causes of revolutions and, by so doing, pointed the way to the reinterpretation of past revolutions in the light of what was happening in France. Thus the theological issue, already partially ignored, or misinterpreted because of a changed theological perspective,[26] was ignored still more because interest came to be focused on the revolutionary tendencies of the age. It was natural, therefore, when viewed from this perspective that the Peasants' War should become the pivotal event of the Reformation era and the religious conflict a side-issue.

Since most of the historians who wrote on the Peasants' War of 1525 between 1789 and Engels' pamphlet of 1850 viewed the past through the eyes of the present, it is not too surprising to find the early stages of a reinterpretation of the period beginning about 1790. The first steps in this direction were cautious and hesitating, but the influence of the Enlightenment and the French Revolution became increasingly apparent in the different aspects of a new interpretation being produced. More and more this new perspective was imposed upon the history of the sixteenth century until Zimmermann came along in 1841—43 and placed all the various

[25] Zimmermann to Georg Gottfried Gervinus, Jan. 12, 1844. In the Universitätsbibliothek Heidelberg, Heid. Hs. 2529 Nr. 450.

[26] See also the comment by Barth on Strauss's hostility to Luther: "Speaking in this way he [Strauss] had in fact, with the hostile acumen, seen what the historian as a rule either cannot or will not see, but he was not himself a historian." From Rousseau to Ritschl, p. 265.

strands together, much as David Friedrich Strauss had done in his *Leben Jesu*, while at the same time adding a few insights of his own, to form a new and coherent interpretation which captured the imagination of many of his contemporaries.

The reaction to the French Revolution was therefore an important factor in the new interpretation of the Reformation; but this reaction was not always the same and the differences are reflected in the German historiography of the Peasants' War from 1790 to Zimmermann's time. Georg Sartorius,[27] professor of history at Göttingen, friend of Goethe and the early phase of the French Revolution, writing in 1795, decried previous histories of the Reformation and the Peasants' War for their theologically polemical nature. His own history of the Peasants' War was written because he had noted a marked similarity between the factors that had caused the religious and social upheavals of the 16th century and those that had caused the French Revolution in his own day. Sartorius did not glorify the Peasants' War as Zimmermann was to do later; rather, he used it to demonstrate that people, brought up in ignorance and suppressed by equally ignorant and despotic lords, rise in revolt when incited by *Schwärmer* and radicals. If one could only enlighten the rulers to allow the common man to become educated and gain a measure of freedom, then this same man would not fall prey to the blandishments of the fanatics. Enlightenment, therefore, was not responsible for revolution; tyranny and ignorance were. On the contrary, enlightenment was the only means by which *that* progress could be fostered which history had made ever since man had begun to use his rational faculties.[28]

Neither, aside from a few exceptions, did the immediate successors of Sartorius glorify revolution. Georg Theodor Strobel, writing in the preface to his biography of Thomas Müntzer in the same year as Sartorius, also felt himself motivated to write by the events of the French Revolution. The restless and turbulent days in which he lived had turned his attention to the unhappy days of 1525, to the time when so many regions in Germany had been so terribly devastated and depopulated. His fervent prayer was that these unhappy days might soon pass and peace and quiet once again descend upon his fatherland. Only then could progress be assured.[29]

This trend, to see a marked similarity between the Peasants' War and the French Revolution, continued on. Like Sartorius and Strobel, most

---

[27] *G. Sartorius*, Versuch einer Geschichte des deutschen Bauernkrieges (Frankenthal, 1795).   [28] Ibid., p. 10.
[29] *G. Th. Strobel*, Leben, Schriften und Lehren Thomae Müntzers, des Urhebers des Bauernaufstandes in Thüringen (Nürnberg & Altdorf, 1795), p. VII.

writers wanted to use the comparison to warn against extremism and party fanaticism, and to call for more humane relations between reasonable and enlightened men. Revolution never had and never would bring improvement and progress; these would come only through enlightened education and the creation of more equitable relations among men. Thus Paul Streif hoped that his study of Thomas Müntzer and the Peasants' War would not only serve to entertain, but would also teach those who glorified the past in order to promote revolution in the present that new and better conditions would not necessarily arise from the ashes of revolution like a phoenix. Progress came slowly and by peaceful means.[30]

There was, however, another line of interpretation which also had its source in the period of the French Revolution: this combined a justification of the Peasants' War, a justification of revolution, with an ever-increasing glorification of Thomas Müntzer. Karl Hammerdörfer, for example, writing in 1793, expressed the opinion that Müntzer's name would have been honored by history, along with those of Stauffacher and William Tell, had the former's revolution been successful. Müntzer's revolution being abortive, however, misfortune had overtaken him in the form of an executioner's axe. The consequent condemnation by posterity stood in marked contrast to the homage paid Luther's name, upon whom good fortune had deigned to smile. Sometimes, was the profound reflection of Hammerdörfer, one could only blush for shame at seeing history so abused.[31]

Although both Strobel and Leo von Baczko[32] began a cautious revision of the "Müntzer-legend," they both expressly rejected Hammerdörfer's interpretation. Nevertheless, this interpretation bore fruit in the short Müntzer biography by Georg Carl Treitschke of 1811. Treitschke professed to find in Müntzer, partly veiled and partly revealed, the ideas of the Enlightenment and the French Revolution. For this reason he believed that Müntzer's contemporaries, caught in the confines of their own time, had failed to appreciate the latter's genius. Not until later, in the period of the Enlightenment, had men begun to recognize the true greatness that was Müntzer's.[33]

Zimmermann not only fell heir to this intellectual heritage, but he also used the histories of this period as the foundation for his own interpretation of the Peasants' War. Many of the explicit interpretations contained

---

[30] *P. Streif,* Thomas Müntzer oder der Thüringische Bauernkrieg (Leipzig, 1836), p. VI.

[31] *K. Hammerdörfer,* Geschichte der Lutherischen Reformation (Leipzig, 1793), p. 57.

[32] *L. von Baczko,* "Thomas Müntzer," Geschichte und Politik, II (1804), 1—71.

[33] *G. C. Treitschke,* "Thomas Müntzer," Archiv für Geographie, Historie, Staats- und Kriegskunst (April—Mai, 1811), 204—205.

in the above studies were taken over by him and other implicit ones made explicit. But there is one major difference between Zimmermann and his forerunners which sets him apart from these and makes his work much more significant: Zimmermann, perhaps because he was the first since the Enlightenment and the French Revolution to view the Peasants' War in its totality and within the context of his Hegelian philosophy, was also the first to place all the events into a new and meaningful context toward which the others seem to have striven. But before we can go into that interpretation in any detail, we must first examine the nature of the sixteenth-century conflict regarding the problem of reform and revolution and the impact this had upon the immediate interpretation of the period as well as tracing in greater detail the change in perspective which made possible Zimmermann's interpretation.

Chapter II

THE INTERPRETIVE FRAME OF REFERENCE

1. THE MARXIST ATTRACTION TO MÜNTZER

This love-hate relationship in favor of Müntzer and against Luther manifested in the writings of Zimmermann and Strauss respectively is also one of the hallmarks of the Marxist interpretation of the Reformation. More importantly, however, it points to a basic similarity between the religious radicals of the 16th century and such 19th-century radicals as Marx and Engels who, like Strauss and Zimmermann, had themselves originally been Young Hegelians. This basic similarity is primarily one of goals and derives ultimately from the common Old Testament character of their thought.

It was the 19th-century Russian anarchist Michael Bakunin who first called Marx a "modern Moses."[1] Perhaps "secular" Moses would have better expressed what Bakunin had in mind. In any case, Bakunin was apparently pointing to the astonishing similarities between certain Jewish Old Testament ideas and those of Marx, though the latter were in a totally secularized and supra-national context. Ernst Bloch, the 20th-century Jewish Marxist "philosopher of hope," undoubtedly had the same similarities in mind when he wrote in 1949:

"Ein Ende des Tunnels ist in Sicht, gewiß nicht von Palästina her, aber von Moskau; — ubi Lenin, ibi Jerusalem."[2]

It is these similarities that Arnold Künzli stressed in his 1966 "psychographie" of Marx as well when he stated:

"Alle unsere Untersuchungen führten letztlich immer zu der Erkenntnis, daß Marx in seinen Vorstellungen vom kommunistischen Endzustand ohne Klassen, ohne Staat, ohne Partei, ohne Institutionen, ohne Gewalt, ohne Konflikte, von etwas Irrationalem bestimmt wurde, dessen er sich nicht bewußt war, das ihn aber mit der unerbittlichen Gewalt des Numinosen in seinem Bann hielt. Wir

---

[1] See *A. Künzli*, Karl Marx, Eine Psychographie (Wien, 1966), p. 198.
[2] *E. Bloch*, Freiheit und Ordnung (Frankfurt a. M., 1969), p. 165. First published in 1949.

haben die These aufgestellt und zu begründen versucht, daß diese irrationale, numinose Macht, die Karl Marx' Wesen prägte, das ihm wohl wesentlich von seiner Mutter tradierte und von ihm in der Auflehnung des jüdischen Selbsthasses ins Unbewußte verdrängte Judentum war, und das heißt die biblische Botschaft, wie sie vor allem im Alten Testament verkündet wird."[3]

This repressed heritage surfaced again in Marx's thought. It is Künzli's thesis, therefore, that Marx's classless communistic society is nothing less than a secularization of the eschatological Jewish Kingdom of God on earth; that the proletariat is the elect nation which will inaugurate this kingdom; that God's role in history is taken over by the dialectical forces of historical materialism; and that Marx himself wanted to lead his elect nation, like a "modern Moses," into the Promised Land by showing the proletariat, at least theoretically, how all this was to be accomplished.

All of this is of extreme importance for an understanding of the Marxist interpretation of the Reformation, for that era had its own Old Testament prophet in the person of Müntzer who wanted to be another Daniel to the princes and who signed his threatening letters to the Dukes of Mansfeld, "Thomas Müntzer mit dem Schwert Gideons." For, like Marx, he too wanted to establish the Kingdom of God on earth. Indeed, as we shall argue in the next chapter and as Johann Rühel already remarked in his letter to Luther of May 26, 1525, Müntzer was so imbued with Old Testament concepts that when Philip of Hesse confronted him after his arrest he argued solely from the Old Testament. Rühel put it this way:

"Ich höre aber, daß sich der Landgraff des Evangelions nicht geschämet, sich mit Münzer in einen hefftigen streit damit begeben. Münzer hat das alte Testament gebraucht, der Landgraff aber sich des neuen gehalten, sein neues Testament auch bey sich gehabt und darauß die sprüche wieder Münzern gelesen."[4]

If one compares these two Old Testament types, one finds the greatest of similarities in their thought. The point of departure for both is an eschatological one: the hoped-for Kingdom of God on earth, that is the communistic classless society. Both will be inaugurated by the elect: in Müntzer's case, by his followers; in Marx's case, by the proletariat. In both instances, the elect cooperate with a supra mundane force guiding history: God in the case of Müntzer, and the dialectical forces of historical materialism for Marx. The elect are enabled to do this because they have been initiated into the secrets of the historical dialectic; in Müntzer's case

---

[3] *Künzli*, Karl Marx, p. 798.

[4] *D. Martin Luthers* Werke. Kritische Gesamtausgabe. Briefwechsel 3. Band (Weimar, 1933), 511. (Hereafter cited as WA, Br., and his writings as WA.)

because God has revealed these to him; in Marx's case because he has discovered the scientific laws of historical progress. Since this is so, both feel compelled to play the role of prophet, for only through them will the Kingdom of God be established on earth. These similarities in their intellectual paradigms — and they will become even more apparent later — make it clear why Müntzer has become the hero of the Marxist interpretation of the Reformation.

But, as Heinrich Heine remarked in his "Französische Zustände," if one takes a position for Müntzer (and Heine did, stating that Müntzer had been right and Luther wrong), one is forced into opposition to Luther.[5] This has its ultimate *raison d'être* in Luther's differing view of society. For not all men have believed in the perfectibility of society, and Luther, Müntzer's greatest adversary during the early years of the Reformation, was one of these. From his New Testament perspective of the radical separation of the spiritual from the temporal realms — the spiritual realm being the ideal realm of perfection and the temporal realm being the real realm of imperfection — it appeared impossible that a Kingdom of God could ever be established on earth. Consequently, in his polemic with Müntzer, a polemic that culminated in their differing attitudes to the German Peasants' War and Müntzer and the peasants' demand for the reformation of 16th-century Christian society, these two paradigms of society came into conflict, a conflict that has colored most if not all subsequent interpretations of these events.

2. THE SOURCES OF A DUAL APPROACH TO CHRISTIAN SOCIETY

These conflicting paradigms have a long history and go back to the biblical story of creation and the subsequent fall of man. Their source is to be found in the tension that exists in the Judeo-Christian tradition between the concept of a Creator-God who is the "Wholly Other" and a creature-man tainted by the sin of Adam. For one of the earliest promises given by God to Adam was the promise of reconciliation. But how was reconciliation to be achieved, and once achieved, would it take away the taint of Adam's sin from mankind? In other words, would reconciled man become god-like and human society perfect, or would such perfection not be achieved on earth in spite of the reconciliation?

It will be argued here that these conflicting views have been expressed primarily in two paradigms — those of the Old and the New Testaments. There have, of course, been variations of these basic themes; but beneath

---

[5] *H. Heine*, Werke und Briefe, IV (Berlin, 1960), 516.

the often fascinating, and therefore diverting, embellishments of the variations the groundswell of the theme can invariably be detected. These basic themes are clearly delineated in Oscar Cullmann's *Der Staat im Neuen Testament*. According to Cullmann, it would be a superficial understanding of the problem to assume that the relationship of the State to Christianity was the same as it had been in Judaism. Cullmann argues, rather, that the problem is totally different, for Christianity expressly rejected the Jewish theocratic ideal as satanic. The New Testament or Christian ideal, Cullmann continues, is an entirely different one.

"Das Evangelium weiß nichts von einer Konfusion zwischen Gottesreich und Staat, wie sie für das theokratische Ideal des Judentums charakteristisch ist. Im Gegenteil, es widersetzt sich dem theokratischen Ideal des Judentums mit der gleichen Schärfe, mit der es dem Totalitätsanspruch des römischen Staates gegenübertritt. Das Judentum wird vom römischen Staat verfolgt, weil es ein eigenes politisches theokratisches Programm hat. Das trifft aber für das entstehende Christentum gerade nicht zu."[6]

But as Cullmann indicates and the history of Christianity demonstrates only too clearly, the Old Testament theocratic ideal was not entirely given up in post New Testament times. Thus one can find both positions espoused by Christian thinkers at different times. For the purposes of this study, the views of St. Augustine will serve to form the one pole of this argument while the other will be exemplified by the views of Joachim of Fiore. The two are brought together, however, in Joachim's writings, for, as the originator of a view contrary to St. Augustine's, Joachim could not but begin with the great Father of the Church. In evolving his theology of history, Joachim was at times uneasily aware of the basic antagonism existing between himself and St. Augustine, yet he attempted to minimize this antagonism at every turn and portray his position as essentially orthodox.[7] In spite of this, the antagonism is clearly apparent.

a) St. Augustine

St. Augustine's views were themselves to a large extent crystallized in opposition to and polemic against the chiliastic visions of history in the early Church.[8] In contrast to these, he saw Christian history from the vantage point of the cosmic struggle between God and Satan, a conflict reflected in the antagonism between the *Civitas Dei* and the *Civitas*

---

[6] *O. Cullmann*, Der Staat im Neuen Testament (Tübingen, 1956), p. 6.

[7] *H. Grundmann*, Studien über Joachim von Fiore, 2nd ed. (Darmstadt, 1966), pp. 95—97.

[8] Ibid., p. 74. See also *H. A. Deane*, The Political and Social Ideas of St. Augustine (New York & London, 1963), p. viii; and *Löwith*, Meaning in History, p. 167.

Terrena. These two cities are "not identical with the visible church and state but are two mystical societies constituted by two opposite species of man."[9] The *Civitas Dei* is an ideal and timeless entity embodying all the elect, whereas the *Civitas Terrena* is the city of sinful man on earth. What is of decisive importance for St. Augustine in the *Civitas Terrena* is that God has, through Christ, broken into time to effect the redemption of man and his reconciliation to God. But not of all men; only those predestined to salvation. Nor does the Christian Church, which has come into existence as a result of this redemptive act, constitute a miniature *Civitas Dei* on earth, for the Church, according to St. Augustine, remains the *ecclesia permixta*, containing both the "wheat" and the "tares." As such, it belongs to neither city, yet it signifies the *Civitas Dei* and, insofar as it contains the elect, is the *Civitas Dei peregrinans.*

According to St. Augustine, therefore, the Church as a temporal phenomenon has no essential history, for it manifests no development toward perfection or any other temporal goal. In the words of the renowned Reformation Augustinian, Martin Luther, the Christian, who has been saved through faith in the redemptive act of God, as long as he is *peregrinans* here on earth, is *simul justus et peccator:* totally saved, yet while on earth still a sinner, for his salvation will only be completed in heaven. In spite of this, the Christian Church is as perfect an institution as one will ever find on earth, and is better or worse to the extent to which it appropriates Christ. Christ, therefore, is the decisive historical factor for the Church and with His death and resurrection salvation is complete; anyone who believes participates fully in this salvation no matter at what point in history he has lived. The only growth that the Church can participate in here on earth is a growth in numbers, not in perfection.[10]

b) Joachim of Fiore

The opposite position has often been asserted against this view. Whether by revolutionary means, or by divine intervention and the establishment of the millenial Kingdom of God on earth, or whether by means of historical evolution of one form or another, the protagonists of change have posited the possibility of a perfect human society, or at least the possibility of a better human society. And it has been particularly at those points in time when the tension between the real and the ideal has become painfully apparent that these protagonists have arisen to advocate drastic remedial measures. As Arnold Ruge pointed out, there have been essen-

---

[9] *Löwith*, Meaning in History, p. 169.

[10] See *Grundmann*, Joachim von Fiore, pp. 73—76, and *Löwith*, Meaning in History, pp. 166—173.

tially three major periods in the history of Western Civilization in which this tension has reached crisis proportions: the period beginning with the emergence of Christianity and ending with the decline and fall of the Roman Empire, a second period beginning with the 12th century and culminating in the Reformation, and a third period beginning prior to the French Revolution and lasting beyond the Revolutions of 1848. The chiliasts of the early Christian period found their greatest adversary in St. Augustine at the height of the first crisis. The 12th century ended with another chiliast, though one of an evolutionary bent, Joachim of Fiore. The chiliastic tendencies emanating from his theology of history found their greatest adversary during the crisis years of the Reformation in the neo-Augustinian Luther. And it was in Hegel's and Marx's thought that the chiliastic tendencies of the 18th and early 19th centuries reached their clearest expression. The failure to achieve any meaningful reforms after 1848, however, may have caused Hegel and his disciples, too, to fall into rapid eclipse.[11]

Whereas St. Augustine was content to accept the tension between the ideal and the real in temporal society, Joachim of Fiore was not. Nor did Joachim view the history of the Church from the same perspective. Beginning with the typological exegetical method current in the Middle Ages, which referred all the Old Testament "types" to Christ, Joachim began to reinterpret the history of the Christian era. Applying the concept of the Trinity to the divisions usually postulated in world history in his day, the *ante legem, sub lege,* and *sub gratia* periods, Joachim emerged with a new scheme. From this perspective, the differences between the *ante legem* and the *sub lege* eras tended to become blurred, for Joachim viewed the era before Christ as a single entity — the period of God the Father. The *sub gratia* era remained that inaugurated by Christ, but it was followed by a third era, that of the Holy Spirit. Aside from this, Joachim also argued that a distinct parallel existed between the history of the Israelites as a nation in the Old Testament and the history of the Christian Church beginning with the New Testament and extending into his own time. Particularly in his commentary on Jeremia[12] it becomes clear to what extent Joachim forces the history of the Church into the grand outlines of

---

[11] This may well account for Hegelianism's rapid decline after 1850, a phenomenon K. *Barth* remarked upon in his From Rousseau to Ritschl: "That is what is astonishing. That Hegel, at all events outwardly, should temporarily at least appear to have been put so much in the wrong by the events of history; that is the amazing fact," p. 269.

[12] H. *Grundmann,* "Kirchenfreiheit und Kaisermacht um 1190 in der Sicht Joachims von Fiore," Deutsches Archiv für Erforschung des Mittelalters, XIX (1963), 353—396.

his Old Testament scheme. The early period of Church history, from Christ to Constantine, he argues, coincides with the history of Israel prior to Saul, for in both periods God rules directly over these entities. The period of the Old Testament history from Saul to the Babylonian Captivity coincides with the period of Church history from Constantine to the end of the Byzantine era, for now both come under secular rulers. And the last period of Israel's history, the period beginning with the Babylonian Captivity and ending with the birth of Christ, coincides with the period of Christian history since Charlemagne. This last period had not yet ended in 1200, two years before the death of Joachim.[13]

Nevertheless, the turning point, or the end of the last era of the Church, was close at hand, for Joachim, who counted some forty-two generations in the era of God the Father — allowing approximately thirty years for each generation — argued that the era of the Son would last about the same length of time. Such a reckoning would establish the decisive turning point in the year 1260. Although Joachim did not emphasize the date,[14] he did stress the fact that the world was about to enter into an era of great change through which the last of the three eras, that of the Holy Spirit, would be inaugurated.

There is, of course, a strong evolutionary progression in Joachim's scheme; nor are there any decisive breaks between the various eras. The three stages overlap, with the second beginning before the first has run its course. Similarly, the third age is already underway in the second, beginning with St. Benedict, but visibly inaugurated by the Cistercian order to which Joachim himself belonged.

"The ideal Cistercian community, self-sufficient, steeped in renunciation and mystic joy, possessed truly the 'libertas perfecta a curis mundi.' To Joachim's eyes, this was the final solution of all political, social, economic, and religious problems, the 'curae mundi' that accounted for all the evils and the unhappiness of man."[15]

This view was not unique to Joachim, for others, too, believed that the Cistericans were bringing about

"the beginning of a radical transformation of the whole religious and social order of the time"[16]

---

[13] Ibid., pp. 361—367.

[14] *Grundmann*, Joachim von Fiore, p. 52.

[15] G. *La Piana*, "Joachim of Flora: A Critical Survey," Speculum, VII (1932), 273. See also particularly *F. Seibt*, "Utopie im Mittelalter," Historische Zeitschrift, 208 (1969), 555—594.

[16] *La Piana*, "Joachim of Flora," p. 273.

by the rapid spread of their movement. Yet Joachim was the first to anchor this hope in a theology of history.

Although Joachim hesitated to draw the obvious conclusion his theology of history led to, the conclusion that Christ could not have been the ultimate answer to the problem of the reconciliation between God and man since the era of Christ and the New Testament covenant was to be superseded by the third covenant of the Holy Spirit,[17] he nevertheless drew a fairly detailed picture of this third age under the aegis of the Holy Spirit. If the era of God the Father had been characterized by the law, and that of Christ by grace, the era of the Holy Spirit would be characterized by the progressive moral perfection of man through a new spiritual life. The three elements of this *perfectio* would be *contemplatio, libertas,* and *spiritus.* In this age, the Church as an institution would become superfluous and gradually die, for everyone would be his own priest. Then the words of St. Paul,

"that now we know and prophecy only in part, but when that which is perfect is come, that which is in part shall be done away!" (1 Kor 13, 12)

will come true.[18] Obviously, Joachim was not willing to accept the tension that existed between an increasingly corrupt Church and the ideals of Christianity harbored in his own order.

What began as a prophetic look into the future by means of an exegesis of the Book of Revelation on the part of Joachim soon turned into a movement with strong chiliastic overtones. It is not necessary to trace this development in any detail here; this has been done elsewhere.[19] Nevertheless, it is important to note that beginning with the Spiritual Franciscans various groups began to see themselves in the role assigned by Joachim to the Cistercians and believed themselves to be living at the beginning of the age of the Spirit. According to Ernst Benz,

"Dieses Bewußtsein spricht sich in der oft wiederholten Behauptung aus, daß mit dem Auftreten des hl. Franz und seines evangelischen Ordens, in der Periodeneinteilung der symbolistischen Geschichtstheologie der Joachiten gesehen, mit dem Anbruch der sechsten Epoche der Kirchengeschichte, die Weltzeit der Kirche abgelaufen ist und ein ganz neues Weltalter anbricht."[20]

---

[17] *Grundmann,* Joachim von Fiore, pp. 102—103.

[18] *Löwith,* Meaning in History, p. 148.

[19] See especially *E. Benz,* Ecclesia Spiritualis. Kirchenidee und Geschichtstheologie der Franziskanischen Reformation (Stuttgart, 1934).

[20] *E. Benz,* "Die Kategorien des eschatologischen Zeitbewußtseins," Deutsche Vierteljahrsschrift für Literaturwissesnchaft und Geistesgeschichte, 11 (1933), 201.

Immediately such an assertion was made, the representatives of the old and new ages were destined to come into conflict; and, indeed, the Spiritual Franciscans did come into conflict with the whole ecclesistical edifice of their day. And so did all the other groups who came to see themselves as that nucleus ordained to inaugurate the new age. But the old order did not immediately pass away, and those who based their opposition to it on Joachim's teachings were declared heretical, as were aspects of Joachim's own system.[21]

3. MÜNTZER AND THE JOACHIST TRADITION

That Joachim's teachings were widespread during the later Middle Ages and could be found in most parts of Europe has long been known. That they formed a substantial element of the Taborite wing of the Hussite movement has also repeatedly been pointed out.[22] Here, however, it is important to test the argument that Joachim's ideas strongly influenced those of Thomas Müntzer, for if such a connection can be established the quarrel between the neo-Augustinian Luther and the Joachite Müntzer would take on much broader dimensions and significance than has hitherto been assigned to it and would fit into the classic dichotomy we have been tracing. Perhaps the best place to begin such an enquiry is with the recent study by Ruth Kestenberg-Gladstein in which the writer deals primarily with the Wirsberger heresy and the polemic against it in and around Erfurt in the last half of the 15th century. The Wirsbergers, a Joachite sect, emerged during the 'sixties in the neighborhood of Eger, just inside the Bohemian border. Their ideas, similar to those laid down in the "Pikard Articles" of the Taborites, seem, however, to have been more directly influenced by Joachist and pseudo-Joachist thought, as the Erfurt *Questio* of 1466, in which their ideas were discussed, reveals.[23] In this *Questio*, Joachim's "third status" came particularly under fire.

Kestenberg-Gladstein argues that the question of the "third status" came up for a solemn university disputation in 1466 for several reasons. First, because Joachist concepts were widespread in the region, coming from the Wirsbergers as well as from Hussite ideas imported from Bo-

---

[21] *Grundmann*, Joachim von Fiore, pp. 13—17.

[22] See especially *R. Kestenberg-Gladstein*, "The 'Third Reich.' A Fifteenth-Century Polemic against Joachim, and its Background," Journal of the Wartburg and Courtauld Institutes. 18 (1955), 255—257; and *H. Kaminsky*, "Chiliasm and the Hussite Revolution," Church History, XXVI (1957), 43—71. (Hereafter this journal will be cited as CH.)

[23] *Kestenberg-Gladstein*, "The 'Third Reich,'" p. 257.

hemia more directly as the result of the city's commercial and other relations with that country. (Aside from harboring Joachist visions of the
"third Reich," she also points out that it should be remembered that Thuringia was the region in which the legend of the Emperor Frederick kept
resurfacing in a particularly tenacious fashion.) Secondly, and perhaps
more importantly, these ideas fell upon more fertile ground here than
elsewhere because the contrast between rich and poor was more apparent.[24]
In any case, the Erfurt *Questio* is proof of the fact that Joachist ideas were
a live issue in Thuringia during the latter half of the 15th century, and
their influence must surely still have been strong by the time Müntzer
appeared on the scene and began to preach in Zwickau in 1522. Indeed,
this influence may have motivated the Zwickau Prophets, those spiritualist
weavers who so strongly influenced Müntzer as we shall see later, as well.[25]

But there are more tangible connections. In 1516, Lazarus Sardia published Joachim's commentary on Jeremia. In 1519, Simon de Luere followed this with the publication of Joachim's *Concordia novi ac veteris
Testamenti.*[26] Other works were published in 1527, but these would have
come too late to influence Müntzer who was executed in 1525. We have
Müntzer's own testimony of 1523 that he had read Joachim's Jeremia
commentary, but he qualified the importance of this study for his own
thought. Writing to Hans Zeiss, the commissioner of Allstedt, on December 2, 1523, he remarked:

"Ir solt auch wissen, das sie dise lere dem apt Joachim zuschreiben und heissen sie
ein ewiges evangelion in grossem spott. Bey mir ist das gezeugnis abatis Joachim
groß.[27] Aber meine leer ist hoch droben, ich nym sie von im nicht an, sundern
vom ausreden Gotis, wie ich dan zurzeit mit aller schrift der biblien beweisen
wil."[28]

Müntzer's apparent qualification may not be as significant as it at first
seems, especially if one sees him, as he must have seen himself, as already
living in the age of the Spirit and therefore communicating directly with
God. For was this not precisely what Joachim had predicted?

---

[24] Ibid., p. 258.

[25] See especially *P. Wappler*, Thomas Müntzer in Zwickau und die "Zwickauer Propheten", 2nd ed. (Gütersloh, 1966).

[26] *Grundmann*, Joachim von Fiore, pp. 193—194.

[27] *E. W. Gritsch*, Reformer without a Church: The Life and Thought of Thomas Müntzer
(Philadelphia, 1967), p. 107, in quoting this passage, leaves out the preceding sentence,
which makes it easier for him to deny Joachist influence on Müntzer's thought.

[28] *G. Franz*, ed., Thomas Müntzer, Schriften und Briefe (Gütersloh, 1968), p. 398.
(Hereafter cited as Schriften und Briefe.)

Other tangible evidence of Joachist influence, or, at the very least, similarities in thought, can be pointed to. In the fall of 1524, fresh from his expulsion out of Mühlhausen, Müntzer arrived in Nuremberg where he had his most notorious pamphlet against Luther published, his "Hochverursachte Schutzrede," through the good offices of his friend Hans Hut. The printer, Johann Herrgott, had also printed some of Andreas Carlstadt's writings and appears to have been an ardent adherent of the Reformation radicals. Albrecht Kirchhoff, who scoured the archives for traces of Herrgott in 1877, said the following of his relationship to Müntzer:

"Man ist vielmehr berechtigt anzunehmen, daß er [Herrgott] ein aufrichtiger Anhänger Thomas Münzer's war und sich mit vollem Herzen der socialistischen Bewegung angeschlossen hatte, ihr seine geschäftliche Thätigkeit mit Bewußtsein widmete, ja, daß er sogar von seinen Zeitgenossen den hervorragenderen Führern jener Bewegung beigezählt wurde."[29]

It was this same Herrgott who, in 1526, just after the bloody suppression of the Peasants' War, wrote a pamphlet entitled "Von der neuen Wandlung eines christlichen Lebens,"[30] and personally circulated it in Zwickau and the surrounding region, agitating to keep the revolutionary spirit alive.[31] But he was captured and executed at Leipzig one year later for his trouble.

The opening paragraph of Herrgott's pamphlet is a classic statement of the Joachist view of history:

"Es seynd gesehen worden drey wandlung / die erst hat Gott der Vater gehalten mit dem alten Testament / Die andere wandlung hat Gott der Sohn gehabt mit der welt ym newen Testament / Die dritt wandlung wird haben der heylig geist / mit dieser zukünfftigen wandlung von yrem argen do sie yetzo ynnen seynd."[32]

The title itself is symptomatic of Joachim's prophetic vision: the transformation (neue Wandlung) of the Christian life to a new morality.

Only recently Ferdinand Seibt has compared this pamphlet to Joachim's vision of the future age, contained in a document known as the *Liber Figurarum* reprinted by Herbert Grundmann in 1950,[33] as well as to the

---

[29] *A. Kirchhoff,* "Johann Herrgott, Buchführer von Nürnberg und sein tragisches Ende 1527," Archiv für Geschichte des deutschen Buchhandels, I (1878), 27.

[30] Published in *A. Götze u. L. E. Schmitt,* Aus dem Sozialen und Politischen Kampf. Flugschriften aus der Reformationszeit, 20 (Halle/S., 1953), 53—64.

[31] *Kirchhoff,* "Johann Herrgott," pp. 29—34.

[32] *Götze u. Schmitt,* Aus dem Sozialen und Politischen Kampf, p. 53.

[33] *H. Grundmann,* Neue Forschungen über Joachim von Fiore (Marburg, 1950), pp. 85—121.

better known *Utopia* of Thomas More,[34] and demonstrated the remarkable similarities between the three. In any event, Herrgott's little pamphlet also has striking similarities to, and, according to Kirchhoff, certainly mirrors dependencies upon, Müntzer's ideas. His argument for a democratic communistic Christian society in which the new man will appear has its counterpart in Müntzer's thought as well as in Joachim's monastic ideal. It may well be that Müntzer's elect band of followers, his *Bund*, was to play the same role in changing society as Joachim's monasteries were to do earlier.[35]

But there is yet another angle from which the Joachist influence can be observed, an influence which leads to what Jürgen Moltmann has termed the "Reich-Gottes-Theologie" of the 17th century with its chiliastic overtones. The pivotal person here, as far as the connection with Müntzer is concerned, is Martin Cellarius, the young friend of Philip Melanchthon who was won to the radical cause of Müntzer and the Zwickau Prophets by Marcus Stübner in 1522, as Paul Wappler pointed out some time ago.[36]

In 1581, Giacopo Brocardo, born in Venice and educated there as an Aristotelian humanist, found himself and his theology condemned by the French National Synod of the Calvinist Church. It accused him of being a fanatical chiliast and declared his prophetic interpretation of the Scriptures to be a "profanation de l'Ecriture Sainte."[37] Because of this condemnation, Brocardo was also expelled from the Calvinist Netherlands when he sought sanction there. Nevertheless, he was welcomed in Bremen where he had his most important works published and where he came to know intimately the "second reformer" of the city, Christoph Pezel. Through Pezel's good offices, his ideas also found acceptance and strongly influenced the "Reich-Gottes-Theologie" of Johannes Coccejus, Bremen's leading theologian. This was first pointed out by F. A. Tholuck in his book, *Das Akademische Leben im 17. Jahrhundert*. Tholuck quoted a letter of 1703 from the late 17th-century Spiritualist, Friedrich Breckling, to Johann Heinrich May, professor of theology at the University of Giessen, which stated in part that

"Coccejus hat das Meiste und Beste aus des Jacobi Brocardi *mysterio interpretationis in Genesin, prophetas et apocalypsin,* der in *thesi* sehr trefflich schreibt, aber

---

[34] *Seibt,* "Utopie im Mittelalter."
[35] This whole complex of problems needs investigation.
[36] *Wappler,* Thomas Müntzer und die "Zwickauer Propheten," p. 65.
[37] *J. Moltmann,* "Jacob Brocard als Vorläufer der Reichs-Gottes-Theologie und der symbolisch-prophetischen Schriftauslegung des Johannes Coccejus," Zeitschrift für Kirchengeschichte, LXXI (1960), 112.

in applicatione ad sua tempora bisweilen *a scopo Dei* abirrt; und weil Brocardus bei den Reformierten in Verdacht ist, so hat er dessen Lehre und Prophetiam fortgepflanzt und seinen Namen verschwiegen, wie es auch Gürtler tat."[38]

In a recent study,[39] Delio Cantimori placed this same Brocardo into the intellectual world of Joachist ideas surrounding Savonarola and his disciples. This, according to Moltmann, is amply confirmed by Brocardo himself:

"Als seine Quellen gibt Brocard immer wieder Joachim von Fiore, dessen Schriften er ausführlich zitiert, und Savonarola, den er für den 'Elia der Endzeit' hält, an."[40]

But, as far as Brocardo was concerned, there was another great exponent of this tradition, and that person was none other than Martin Cellarius, whom he called "der tiefste Denker der Reformation."[41] A little below Cellarius in importance, Brocardo placed Wolfgang Capito and Martin Bucer, both reformers in Strassburg, the former strongly influenced by Cellarius as Bucer himself admitted.[42] The influence of Joachist ideas on Brocardo can therefore be seen as coming together from two different sides: from the writings of Joachim directly, and more indirectly through the writings of Cellarius, influenced by Müntzer and the Zwickau Prophets. This double lineage tends to confirm the supposition that Müntzer's ideology was influenced by Joachist thought, or, at the very least, ran along similar lines.

But even though one might still dispute Müntzer's dependence upon Joachim of Fiore and the Joachite tradition (and the question obviously calls for further investigation),[43] what follows in the next chapter will make clear that he fits into that category of people who, like Joachim and Marx, were unwilling to tolerate the tensions in society and felt compelled to resolve these tensions in one way or another. In this respect he was as different from Luther as Joachim was from St. Augustine who argued that there would always be more or less severe tensions between the ideal and the real in temporal society. Given these opposite views

---

[38] Quoted in ibid., p. 111.

[39] *D. Cantimori,* "Visione e speranze di un ugonotto italiano," Revista storica Italiano (1950), 199 ff. See also Moltmann, "Jacob Brocard," p. 113.

[40] *Moltmann,* "Jacob Brocard," p. 115.

[41] Ibid., p. 116.

[42] See Bucer's letter to Zwingli of April 15, 1528, cited in ibid., p. 116, note 16: "Cellarius, der durch und durch von dem wiedertäuferischen Geist beseelt ist, hat durch seinen allzu langen und vertrauten Umgang unseren Capito ganz eingenommen."

[43] See also *M. Reeves,* The Influence of Prophecy in the later Middle Ages: A Study in Joachism (Oxford, 1969), pp. 490—491.

regarding the perfectibility of society, particularly 16th-century Christian society, it should be clear that Müntzer and Luther would clash over the issue of how best to reform 16th-century Christendom. It is to this clash that we must now turn, not only in order to confirm or deny our suppositions, but also to lay the foundations for the Marxist interpretation of the Reformation. For, because the Marxists wish radically to restructure capitalistic society, they have focused, in their historical studies, on precisely these attempts at revolutionary reform in other periods.

CHAPTER III

THE GERMAN PEASANTS' WAR AND REFORMATION CONCEPTS OF REFORM

1. THE CONCEPTUAL FRAME OF REFERENCE

The conflict between the proponents of these Old and New Testament paradigms of society in 16th-century Germany, whose pivotal event appears to have been the 1525 Peasants' War, constitutes one of the central themes of the Reformation era. This same conflict has also played a decisive role in all subsequent interpretations of the period, for it enters into a most crucial problem of that troubled time — the problem of the reform of the Church in what was nearly universally thought to be a Christian society.[1] Since it was Luther who first broke with the medieval paradigm of the Christian society, one should probably consult him at the outset of this chapter.

Luther returned to the theme of the reform of the Church time and again, and, after 1525, usually in connection with a denunciation of his arch-enemy, Thomas Müntzer. His expositions on this topic are remarkably uniform, but perhaps his most enlightening statement on it is contained in his commentary on the Sermon on the Mount. Here he remarked:

"Hierauff zu antworten mustu jmer das heubtstuck mercken, das Christus seine predigt für seine Christen allein thut und wil sie leren was sie für leut sein sollen widder den fleischlichen wahn und gedancken, so da zumal auch noch jnn den Aposteln steckte, das sie meineten, er würde ein new regiment und keiserthum anrichten und sie drein setzen, das sie regiereten wie die herrn und jre feind und böse welt unter sich brechten, wie denn allzeit fleisch und blut wündschet und sucht am Euangelio, das es herschafft, ehre und nutz habe und nichts leiden durffe. Darnach auch der Bapst getrachtet und solch regiment zu wegen bracht hat, das sein wesen ein lauter weltliche herschafft ist worden und so gefürchtet, das jm alle welt hat müssen unterthan sein.

Also sehen wir jtzt auch, das alle welt am Euangelio das jre suchet und soviel rotterey daher entstehen, die nichts anders jm sinn haben, denn wie sie sich auff-

---

[1] The problem has usually been seen from the perspective of the relation of the Reformation to revolution. See especially W. *Stolze*, Bauernkrieg und Reformation (Leipzig, 1926).

werffen und zu herren machen und andere dempffen, wie der Müntzer anfieng mit seinen bawern und jm nach andere sich auch beweiset haben. Da zu werden auch die rechten Christen damit angefochten, wenn sie sehen das so übel zugeht jnn der welt, auch jnn jrem eigen regiment, das sie gerne wolten selbs drein greiffen und walten. Aber es sol nicht sein und sol niemand dencken das uns Gott wolle so lassen regieren und herschen mit weltlichem recht und straffe, Sondern der Christen wesen sol gar davon gescheiden sein, das sie sich nichts damit bekömern noch zuschaffen haben, sondern die denen es befolen ist lassen dafür sorgen, wie man sol güter aus teilen, handeln, straffen, schützen x. und lassen gehen wie sie es machen, wie Christus leret 'Gebt dem Keiser was des Keisers ist', Denn wir sind jnn ein ander hoher wesen gesetzt, welchs jst ein Götlich, ewig reich, da man der dinger keines bedarff so jn die welt geboren, sondern ein jglicher für sich jnn Christo ein herr ist beide über Teuffel und welt x. wie anders wo gesagt jst.”[2]

This is a most significant passage for an analysis of the intellectual frame of reference into which the arguments of the various groups involved in the question of reform, and particularly in the Peasants' War, must be placed. In the first instance, it points clearly to the fact that the social and the religious problems of the time come together in the then current concepts of the Christian society. As long as the two — the social and the religious realms — were viewed as essentially one, reform in the one realm must affect the other. When there were reforms attempted in both simultaneously, reforms, be it said here, which led to the religious revolution of the Reformation and the abortive social revolution of the Peasants' War, interaction was inevitable. Therefore, it is on the concept of the Christian society that the problem of reformation and revolution must focus.

It is important to note further that Luther placed the Apostles' misinterpretation of Christ's concept, a misinterpretation based on an Old Testament understanding of the Kingdom of God, into the same category as that of the popes, Müntzer, the peasants, and other sects; the last being in all probability a reference to the Münsterite Anabaptists in particular, or the Anabaptists in general. All of these had attempted to establish an earthly Kingdom of God, whereas Christ had called for a spiritual kingdom. This "mixing" of the two realms, as Luther termed it, had led to confusion and no end of trouble.

Aside from his reference, if reference it was, to the pacifistic Anabaptists, Luther was essentially correct in this judgment. Certainly there were differences between the Old Testament concept of the Kingdom of God on earth and those of the papacy, Müntzer, the peasants, and the sects;

---

[2] WA, 32, 388—389.

nevertheless, the fundamental judgment remains sound. In one way or another, all of these tried to establish a visible Christian society to which
everyone could belong. This is true of the Old Testament concept,[3] as
well as of the medieval ideal of the *Corpus Christianum* and Müntzer's
Kingdom of God.

In the Old Testament, the Hebrew nation was looked upon as God's
chosen people, His elect. The ideal form of government for this chosen
people was to be a theocracy with God, through His spiritual representative, the sole ruler. Because of this, the laws were given to Moses on
Mount Sinai by God Himself, and their observance was the Hebrew
nation's part of its covenant with God. Through the voluntary fulfillment
of the Decalogue, it became possible for virtually every member of the
nation to achieve salvation. For although man was deemend to have fallen
from his former purity, yet the possibility of renewal was postulated. This
implied, of course, that a godly society could be achieved in the temporal
realm, or, at the very least, that such a society could be initiated already
here on earth. But the failure of the Hebrew nation to live up to this ideal,
a failure graphically illustrated in God's statement to Samuel when that
nation chose a king — "Hearken to the voice of the people in all that they
say to you; for they have not rejected you, but they have rejected me from
being king over them,"[4] — points to the tension that existed between the
Old Testament ideal of the Kingdom of God on earth and its all-too-
human reality. It is for this reason that the Old Testament prophets were
continually castigating the Israelites for not living up to their covenant
with God.

The similarities between the Old Testament concept of the Kingdom of
God on earth and the medieval ideal of the *Corpus Christianum* are great
indeed. In the *Corpus Christianum*, as in the Old Testament concept, the
political boundaries of the Holy Roman Empire were considered coexten-
sive with the religious boundaries of the Roman Catholic Church. Thus,
whereas the major confrontations in the Old Testament took place between the prophets and the kings, those in the *Corpus Christianum* took
place between the popes and the emperors.[5] The ideal of the *Corpus Christianum*, too, required that all its members live good Christian lives. In
reality, however, only a minority did. The same tension had existed in

[3] See particularly *J. Bright*, The Kingdom of God (New York, 1953).
[4] 1. Samuel 8:7. Quoted from the Revised Standard Version (New York, 1953), p. 291.
[5] See particularly *W. Ullmann*, The Growth of Papal Government in the Middle Ages
(London, 1955), and the literature cited by *L. W. Spitz*, "The Impact of the Reformation
on Church-State Issues," in *A. G. Huegli*, ed., Church and State under God (St. Louis,
1964), pp. 59—112.

the Old Testament covenantal relationship. Whereas those not reaching the ideal in the Old Testament were castigated by the Hebrew prophets and encouraged to mend their ways, those in the *Corpus Christianum* should have been above reproach in Christ. The reality, however, was still very much the same. Consequently, over the years, the Church institutionalized the means of grace and the sacrament of penance and made it possible, in this way, for every member of the *Corpus Christianum* to attain to salvation. The process, begun here on earth, was continued in purgatory until each individual was acceptable before God. The tension in the temporal realm, however, remained, and over the years the cry for moral reformation within the *Corpus Christianum*, in head and members, gained in momentum. The desire for moral reform can be seen in all walks of life: it came from the Conciliarists, from the Brethren of the Common Life, and from the humanists as well as from the masses. And it was this tension between the ideal of the *Corpus Christianum* and the reality of 16th-century society which led to the unrest during the time of the Reformation.

It is within this intellectual frame of reference that the dispute concerning the nature of reform took place during the Reformation. This is true of the Catholic Church as well as of Luther, the peasants, Müntzer and the others. In some, as in the peasant articles, this frame of reference is more implicit than explicit; nevertheless, it is most certainly there. Already in the *Reformatio Sigismundi*, for example, although the author begins with the lament that,

> "Gehorsamkeyt ist tod,
> gerechtigkeyt leyt not,
> nichts steht in rechter ordenung,"[6]

he still proceeds to speak in terms of "jung und alt, alle gemein christenheyt, nyemant ausgenomen."[7] But precisely this "gemein christenheyt," this *Corpus Christianum*, stood in need of being reformed in head and members:

"Almechtiger got, schöpffer himels und ertrichs, gib krafft und thu genad, gib weysheyt zu einem erkennen und zu vollbringen nach dem allerseligsten statten und ein ordennung zu haben geystlichs und weltlichs stats in der dein heyliger name und gotheyt bekennet werde; wan dein zorn ist offen, dein ungenade hat unns begriffen; wir geen als dye schoff on hirten, wir gen an dye weyde an urlaub."[8]

---

[6] *H. Koller*, ed., Reformation Kaiser Siegmunds (Stuttgart, 1964), p. 50.
[7] Ibid., p. 78.   [8] Ibid., p. 50.

Here, then, lies the problem: on the one hand, everyone was a Christian in the *Corpus Christianum*, but on the other hand, this Christian society stood in dire need of reformation from top to bottom.

That there were inequities in this Christian society even the illiterate peasants were aware. But before the advent of Luther and his "evangelical" teaching and German translation of the Bible, the peasant was essentially at a loss as to how to reform society. He argued, as did the authors of the articles of the *Bundschuh* in Hegau, 1460, that the lords were violating the "old law."[9] Others, especially the Piper of Niklashausen, went further and argued that all earthly government be abolished.[10] And for still others the example of Switzerland loomed large.[11] Yet because the official teachings of the Roman Catholic Church tended to support the hierarchical *status quo* in Church and State, the peasant reasoning remained somewhat vague and disparate.

All this was changed with the advent of Luther's teachings and his translation of the Bible into German. Some of the peasant articles, it is true, still argued in the same vein,[12] but with the articles of the Baltringen and Memmingen peasants of 1524 it becomes very apparent that the peasants have begun to equate the reformation of the *Corpus Christianum* with the implementation of Luther's evangelical teachings which they now term "God's law."[13] Increasingly they argue that the demands they make on the established authorities in Church and State are based on the Scriptures, and only if it is demonstrated to them that they are not, are they willing to cease and desist from them.[14]

From the majority peasant point of view of 1524, therefore, it is quite clear that the new Lutheran Gospel, equated by them with the "pure Word of God" contained in the Scriptures, has become the divine law to be applied in reforming the *Corpus Christianum*. For their part, they are willing, at least so they reiterate at every occasion, to abide by the decisions of this law.[15] It was, of course, obviously to their advantage to do so, and equally disadvantageous to the ruling classes to do so. Therefore, while Luther was fashioning new wineskins into which to pour his new wine, the peasants were obviously pouring that new wine into the same old wineskins. This situation made Luther's teachings truly revolutionary, and it was precisely this that Luther objected to.

[9] *G. Franz*, ed., Quellen zur Geschichte des Bauernkrieges (Darmstadt, 1963), p. 62. Numerous other examples could also be cited. (Hereafter cited as *Franz*, Quellen.)
[10] Ibid., p. 63. [11] Ibid., pp. 12, 73, 81, and other instances.
[12] Ibid., pp. 96—97, 101—102.
[13] Ibid., pp. 152—154. A classic example is "Die Memminger Dörfer an den Rat von Memmingen," of 14th Feb., 1524, ibid., p. 168. [14] Ibid., pp. 170—171. [15] Ibid., p. 174.

2. LUTHER AND THE REFORM OF THE CHURCH

Luther broke with this intellectual frame of reference and returned to what he considered to be the New Testament example. As can be seen from the introductory quotation from his commentary on the Sermon on the Mount, Luther rejected the attempt to establish a temporal Kingdom of God on earth and spiritualized the "true church" out of existence, contenting himself with tolerating the "wheat" and the "tares" in his local congregations. His speculations concerning the *ecclesiola in ecclesia*[16] never ripened into reality, and, indeed, his Augustinian anthropology combined with his theology of the "bondage of the will" to make it virtually impossible for him to localize the "true church." And if one could not localize the elect, and was forced to spiritualize them into another realm, then the two realms must forever remain apart even though the Christian remained a member of both realms as long as he lived. Indeed, the very fact that this Christian continued to be *simul justus et peccator* for Luther made it impossible for him to envision a "pure church" at all; for, in spite of the fact that the believer was totally justified through faith in Christ, he still remained a member of the temporal realm and, as such, a sinner on the road to perfection. That perfection, however, would never be achieved on earth.

This being the case, the temporal realm could not be governed according to any "laws" drawn from the Gospel, which, in fact, proclaimed only grace, but had to be governed according to the laws of reason.[17] Nevertheless, Luther fully expected the Church, and in particular the individual Christian, to be a leaven in society for the amelioration of wrong.

It is this theory of the two realms or kingdoms that Luther himself singled out as being the key to the understanding of his writings against the peasants, and, we might add, against Müntzer as well. The failure of the peasants to realize this should not deter us, for Luther complained that all his contemporary critics, even close theological allies, had failed to see that this was the key despite the fact that he had written often and extensively concerning it.[18]

---

[16] "Deutsche Messe und Ordnung Gottesdiensts," WA, 19, 75.

[17] "An die Rathsherren aller Städte deutsches Lands, dass sie christliche Schulen aufrichten und erhalten sollen," WA, 14, 9—53.

[18] "Den andern, die durch dise verfuret odder sonst so schwach sind, das sie meyn buchlin nicht mugen mit den spruchen Christi vergleichen, sey dis gesagt. Es sind zweyerley reich, Eyns ist Gottis reich, das ander ist der wellt reich, wie ich so offt geschrieben habe, das michs wundert, wie man solchs noch nicht wisse odder mercke, denn wer dise zwey reichs weys recht von eynander zu scheyden, der wird sich freylich yn meynem buchlin nicht ergern." "Ein Sendbrief von dem harten Büchlein wider die Bauern," WA, 18, 389.

Anyone who reads Luther's great Reformation pamphlets cannot help but be impressed with the fact that Luther envisioned a spiritual renewal within the Church through the effective working of the Word of God. Therefore he could say with conviction in his "Eine treue Vermahnung zu allen Christen, sich zu hüten vor Aufruhr und Empörung," that

"Wilche meyne lere recht leszen und vorstehen, die machen nitt auffruhr. Sie habensz nit von myr gelernet."[19]

God was the great mover in human history and the spiritual renewal would come through His Word; it was a spiritual battle and should remain such.[20] Yet despite the fact that Luther was convinced God would accomplish the reform through His Word, he still felt compelled to instruct the rulers as well as the populace at large in their duties. Reform was permissible if initiated in an orderly manner by the duly constituted authorities; indeed, in his "An den christlichen Adel deutscher Nation" he called on the emperor and the princes to take the initiative in this reform should the ecclesiastical authorities fail to do so.[21] The common man, however, was to refrain from inciting to revolt or initiating reforms on his own. Only at the behest of his ruler was he to act.[22]

Luther realized clearly enough that the reforms he asked for in the Church would have social consequences; in fact, it was precisely the Church's involvement in the affairs which belonged rightly in the realm of the temporal kingdom he polemicized against.[23] Yet he most certainly did not expect the Church to give up its influence in the temporal realm; this influence, however, should be relegated strictly to spiritual concerns.[24] Therefore, when he advised the princes to reform the Church in this manner — and they could only have removed the Church from its usurped influence in the temporal realm, not induced it to exercise its spiritual influence, for only God could accomplish this — Luther believed he was merely telling the princes to take back what rightly belonged to them and the temporal realm in the first place.[25]

Luther, therefore, believed himself to be involved in a spiritual battle whose purpose it was to bring the Church back to its spiritual function, a function, however, which was to be carried out in the temporal realm.[26] The Christians, who as members of the spiritual realm also belonged to

---

[19] WA, 8, 681.   [20] WA, 8, 683.   [21] WA, 6, 404.   [22] WA, 8, 680.
[23] "An den Christlichen Adel," WA, 6, 409, and 415.   [24] Ibid.   [25] Ibid., p. 409.
[26] F. Lau, Luthers Lehre von den beiden Reichen (Berlin, 1952), p. 18, has correctly stated that, "Die Frage nach dem geistlichen Regiment ist aber die Frage nach Luthers Kirchenverständniss."

the temporal realm, were to exercise the ethics of the Sermon on the Mount
in the secular realm unless they had a direct or indirect command from
God to do otherwise because of their office, as for example, the princes.[27]
The Christian should not, therefore, mix the two realms to the extent that
he attempt to justify temporal advantages with Christian teachings. This
would be to seek selfish ends through a hypocritical adherence to God's
Word, an affront God would not tolerate. In the realm of the social, therefore, the Christian had no right to make demands, which were natural and
reasonable in themselves, on the basis of the Gospel, for the Gospel taught
that the Christian should sooner suffer an injustice than demand justice.[28]

3. LUTHER AND THE PEASANTS

According to Luther, the peasants were attempting to do precisely this
in their Twelve Articles; they were using Scripture to justify their demands for social and material improvement.[29] Luther had no reason to
quarrel with these demands; in the secular realm they might well be just
and should be granted.[30] Yet in the spiritual realm they could not be demanded. If the peasants were to insist on these demands and proceed to
revolution in order to attain them, then Luther asked that they stop pre-
tending to be Christians,[31] for he was not willing to see the Christian
teachings adjusted to accommodate the social demands of the peasants.
Despite this fact, Luther would have been pleased to see the princes meet
the demands of the peasants.[32] Indeed, Christian princes would do so of
their own accord. Rather than adjust the Christian teachings so that they
could be made to justify the demands of the peasants, Luther asked both
peasants and princes to allow their Christian principles to regulate their
social actions.[33] Both Christian prince and Christian peasant had their
God-ordained function even in the temporal realm which was to benefit

---

[27] Ibid., p. 35.   [28] "Ermahnung zum Frieden," WA, 18, 314.   [29] Ibid., pp. 307—324.

[30] To the princes he said: "Dazu ym welltlichen regiment nicht mehr thut, denn das
yhr schindet vnd schatzt, ewrn pracht vnd hochmüt zu furen bis der arme gemeyne man
nicht kan noch mag lenger ertragen." Ibid., p. 293; and to the peasants: "Hieraus ist nü
leichtlich auff alle ewr artickel geantwortet, Den ob sie gleich alle naturlich recht vnd
billich weren ..." Ibid., p. 319.

[31] Ibid., p. 316, and again p. 322.   [32] Ibid., pp. 298—299.

[33] To the princes he remarked: "Wolan, wyl yhr denn vrsach seyt, solchs gottes zorns,
wirds on zweyffel auch vber euch ausgehen, wo yhr euch noch nicht mit der zeyt bessert ..." Ibid., p. 294. In his "Wider die räuberischen ... Bauern," he put it positively:
"Aber die oberkeyt, so Christlich ist, vnd das Evangelion leydet, der halben auch die
bawren keynen scheyn widder sie haben, soll hie mit furchten handeln, und zum ersten
die sachen Gott heym geben vnd bekennen, das wyr solchs wol verdienet haben." Ibid.,
p. 359.

their fellow Christian.[34] But precisely because neither the princes nor the peasants were willing to allow their Christian principles to regulate their social actions, or better still, because neither were Christians, for their social actions betrayed their non-Christian character, Luther asked both to solve their differences on a non-Christina level.[35]

Between his "Ermahnung zum Frieden" and his notorious "Wider die räuberischen ... Bauern," Luther had heard of the peasant excesses at Weinsberg and other regions. He had personally attempted to stem the tide of revolt in his own back yard and had been rebuffed. He had observed how the *Mordpropheten* had "duped" the peasants into demanding social equality on the basis of Christian principles, especially in Thuringia. Not only, therefore, had the peasants not given up their claim to social justice on Christian principles, under cover of these very principles they had also robbed, plundered, and devastated the property of others and indulged in wanton slayings. In so doing they had not only sacrificed their just position in the temporal realm with regard to their demands, for Luther strongly believed that it was the duty of heathen and Christian magistrates alike to suppress revolution,[36] but they had also, and this was of much graver concern to Luther, proven themselves to be worse than heathens since they had misused God's Word to cover their selfish desires.[37]

As has been pointed out, Luther was concerned with a spiritual renewal, therefore his "revolution" was primarily on the spiritual plane. But the ecclesiastical forces of his day had become so hedged about with temporal powers and so ensconced in the world as feudal landlords that Luther's spiritual revolution could very easily cause a social upheaval. One need only mention the problem of the secularization of church property in this regard to become fully aware of this possibility. Yet, as far as Luther was concerned, these were only consequences in the temporal realm of his spiri-

---

[34] "An den Christlichen Adel," WA 6, 409. In his "Ermahnung zum Frieden," however, he had to admonish the princes. "Ich hett wol ander artickel widder euch zu stellen, die gemeyn Deutschland vnd regiment betreffen, wie ich than habe ym buch an den deutschen adel, dawol mehr angelegen were. Aber weyl yr die habt ynn den wind geschlagen, müst ihr nü solche eygen nutzige artickel horen vnd leyden, Und geschicht euch eben recht als denen nicht zu sagen ist." WA, 18, 298.   [35] Ibid., p. 329.
[36] See Luther's "Eine treue Vermahnung," WA, 8, 679, as well as "Ermahnung zum Frieden," WA, 18, 303 and 306. Revolution by the masses was perhaps the worst thing that could happen in the temporal realm as far as Luther was concerned. See also *P. Althaus,* Luthers Haltung im Bauernkrieg (Basel, 1953), p. 24.
[37] The above discourse may well explain Luther's stand in the Peasants' War; it in no way justifies the extremes of his last pamphlet, however. Indeed, one should find very few historians or even theologians who would condone them. See, for example, Lau's criticism in his Luthers Lehre von den beiden Reichen, p. 47, note 110.

tual revolution, consequences which would not have occurred had the Church not wrongly become bound up in temporal concerns. Despite his intemperate and often abusive language against the Church of his day, and his incitement to established government to take the initiative in the spiritual revolution should the ecclesiastical powers fail to do so, Luther clung to the belief that God's Word would accomplish the task by itself and physical force would not be necessary.[38] Therefore, as he himself said, he was no revolutionary in the political sense of the word. As a matter of fact, when social revolution did come, he turned against it as no one else did. In the spiritual realm, however, he most certainly was a revolutionary, but not everyone was able to keep the two kingdoms as neatly divided as he was, or wanted to.

The peasants, who were concerned primarily with the temporal realm, most assuredly did not understand Luther's theory of the two realms, nor did they care to separate the one from the other. They were first and foremost concerned with the application of Luther's new theology to their present needs.[39] And Luther's accusation that they were misusing God's Word to justify selfish ends certainly had its kernel of truth. Yet, seen from the peasant perspective which did not really understand Luther's "otherwordly" reasoning,[40] the latter's revolution must have appeared very similar to the one they envisioned. Were they not both for the secularization of Church lands, only for different reasons? Did they not both want to see the Church removed from its ties with things all too temporal? Did they not both call down God's judgment upon the ecclesiastical and secular lords alike? Yet from their point of view Luther justified his own revolution but condemned theirs.

Luther did more, however. In his role as spiritual scourge in an age all too godless, Luther moved about the social realm with virile words of condemnation. Thus, for example, in his "Ermahnung zum Frieden," he told the princes:

"Denn das sollt yhr wyssen, lieben herrn, Gott schaffts also, das man nicht kan, noch will, noch solle ewr wueterey die lenge dulden. Yhr müst anders werden und Gotts wort weichen, Thut yhrs nicht durch freundliche willige weysze, so

---

[38] This must be seen in the context used above, that Luther believed the princes to be entitled to "free" the Church from its wordly ties, for the Church had usurped these in the first place.

[39] *J. Lortz*, Die Reformation in Deutschland, vol. 1, 3rd ed. (Freiburg i. Br., 1949), pp. 159—175 for a description of motives in the Reformation.

[40] "Aber die Gegenfrage! Gewiß, die Bauern beriefen sich zu Unrecht auf Luther. Die Rechtfertigung ihrer Forderung aus der reformatorischen Lehre sind die erste weltgeschichtliche Fehldeutung der Ansichten Luthers." Ibid., p. 333.

must yhrs thün, durch gewelltige vnd verderbliche vnwesze, Thüns disze bawrn nicht, so mussens andere thun, Und ob yhr sie alle schlugt, so sind sie noch vn-geschlagen, Gott wird andere erwecken, Denn er will euch schlagen vnd wird euch schlagen. Es sind nicht bawren, lieben herrn, die sich widder euch setzen, Gott ists selber, der setzt sich widder euch, heymzusuchen ewr wueterey."[41]

But the pamphlet was directed against both princes and peasants. Any peasant reading this passage could not have found a better justification for his revolt, for Luther had called it the judgment of God on the princes. Yet to the peasants he counselled reasonable compromise, if not outright Christian submission. Luther's dialectic must most assuredly have passed well over the heads of his peasant readers.

If Luther viewed the religious and social problems of his day through the eyes of his theory of the two kingdoms, the peasants, as has been noted, viewed them from the point of view of the *Corpus Christianum,* in which everyone was Christian, although in need of reformation. Since this society was Christian, Christian equality should apply. The artificial social and ecclesiastical hierarchy which had been established did not really have a "Christian" basis, although the established Church sought to justify it. Therefore, the peasant demand that "divine law" be made to apply in this Christian society had its justification. Hence the misunder-standing must not all be laid at the peasant door. Certainly they misunder-stood Luther, but Luther also misunderstood their motives, or perhaps bet-ter, rejected their interpretation as wrong because he saw the problem from the perspective of his theory of the two kingdoms. Whereas all men were Christian in the *Corpus Christianum,* though in need of reform, Luther told the peasants: "Denn es nicht muglich ist, das so grosser hauffe alle-sampt rechte Christen seyen vnd gute meynung haben."[42] A further cause for misunderstanding had been Luther's belief that the whole peasant movement had been instigated by the *Mordpropheten,* particularly by Tho-mas Müntzer.[43]

4. MÜNTZER AND THE REFORM OF CHRISTENDOM

This Thomas Müntzer, at first attracted to Luther's new theology, be-gan rapidly to become disenchanted when he realized that the latter's teach-ings were not leading to any major reform of late medieval Christian society, and, indeed, that Luther had discarded the ideal of a Christian society he still clung to. After Luther's "rediscovery" of the Bible, how-ever, Müntzer could no longer argue for such a society on the basis of

[41] WA, 18, 294—295. [42] "Ermahnung zum Frieden," WA, 18, 292. [43] Ibid., p. 296.

scholastic theology, for he too had accepted the Scriptures as normative in matters of the Christian faith. Rather than fasten on the New Testament for his paradigm of the Christian society as Luther did, however, Müntzer turned to the Old Testament which suited his purpose much better. It is for this reason that his view of the ideal Christian society has great similarities with those of the *Corpus Christianum* and the Old Testament concept of God's chosen people.

Because, as we have seen, it is impossible to view man as totally depraved and incapable of good within this context, Müntzer rebelled against Luther's anthropology[44] with its concomitant views of grace and the separation of the two realms.[45] Drawing on the medieval mystical tradition with its Neoplatonic overtones,[46] Müntzer asserted that everyone in the "gemeyne christenheyt" was potentially an "elect"[47] since his soul, which was akin to God and receptive to the working of the Holy Spirit, could be turned inward toward God and away from the "creatureliness" which impinged upon it from without. If, however, everyone is potentially an "elect," then it is once again possible, if wrong theologies, like Lutheranism and Catholicism, are removed from the scene and man shown the correct way to God, that a Kingdom of God can be erected on earth. Hans-Jürgen Goertz is undoubtedly correct when he remarks that Müntzer's view of the salvation process is much more complex than that of the vulgar Catholicism of his day and the moralism preached by the *Devotio Moderna* and the Christian Humanists;[48] nevertheless, it must be stressed in the context of Luther's thought that, in the final analysis, Müntzer does preach a "law" rather than a "gospel," for Christ's sacrifice is not really essential to man's salvation in his scheme.[49]

Since this is the case, Müntzer can argue that there is essentially no difference between the Old and New Testaments, if only one reconciles them properly.[50] As a matter of fact, however, the Old Testament fits better into

[44] "Das hast du mit deinem fantastischen verstandt angericht auss deinem Augustino, warlich ein lesterlich sach, von freyem willen die menschen frech zu verachten." "Hochverursachte Schutzrede," *G. Franz*, Schriften und Briefe, p. 339.

[45] For the importance of Luther's doctrine of grace in the context of his views concerning the two realms, see *F. E. Cranz*, An Essay on the Development of Luther's Thought on Justice, Law, and Society (Cambridge, Mass., 1964).

[46] See *H.-J. Goertz*, Innere und Äußere Ordnung in der Theologie Thomas Müntzers (Leiden, 1967), pp. 92—121.

[47] See especially Müntzer's letter to Christoph Meinhard, May 30, 1524. Schriften und Briefe, pp. 402—404; also *Goertz*, Innere und Äußere Ordnung, p. 48.

[48] *Goertz*, Innere und Äußere Ordnung, p. 128.   [49] Ibid., p. 132.

[50] "Dann es muss die kunst Gottis betzeugt werden aus der heyligen biblien in einer starcken vorgleichung aller wort, die in beyden testamenten clerlich beschriben stehn, 1. Cho. 2 ..." "Protestation," Schriften und Briefe, p. 228.

his scheme of things than the New, and Müntzer, therefore, draws heavily upon it in order to justify his concept of the Kingdom of God.[51] He takes, as his point of departure, the Christendom of his own day which he knows to be in desperate need of reform.[52] Nevertheless, God is still the ultimate ruler of this Christian society,[53] and the people still God's people. Many things, however, have blinded the people from seeing correctly God's way of salvation, one of the worst being the practice of infant baptism[54] which allowed the "wheat" and the "tares" to exist side by side in the Church. Nor has the gospel been preached in Christendom since because of the rationalizations of the Roman Catholic priests, and, more recently, of the Lutherans: the former because of their ceremonies,[55] and the latter because of their doctrine of cheap grace.[56] Now, however, in the end times,[57] God has awakened a new Daniel, a new prophet, to declare to princes, people, and false prophets alike the correct road to salvation.[58] If this road is followed, Christendom will really become the Kingdom of God on earth.

Roman Catholics, Lutherans, and "godless" princes,[59] therefore, had either to be won over to Müntzer's cause or else, when and if they refused, to be destroyed, for in their opposition to Müntzer these ultimately opposed God and the realization of His Kingdom on earth. The duty of the "Christian" prince, consequently, was not merely to maintain the peace in the secular realm,[60] but to do away with the "godless" who hindered the propagation of the "true" Word of God[61] and actively to further the cause of God's Kingdom. When, therefore, the princes could not be won, Müntzer began to preach their destruction by the "elect" whom he equated more and more with the "common man" eager to accept his new teachings

---

[51] "Welche [Lutherans] vorfluchen das alte testament, disputiren vil aus Paulo von werken, verschumpiren das gesetze aufs eusserlichste und haben dennoch nicht die meynung Pauli, solten sie auch zuprasten." Müntzer to Christoph Meinhard, May 30, 1524. Schriften und Briefe, p. 403.   [52] "Ausgedrückte Entblössung," ibid., p. 286.

[53] See especially Müntzer's letter to Albrecht von Mansfeld, May 12, 1525. Ibid., p. 469.   [54] "Protestation," ibid., p. 227.

[55] Ibid., p. 230.   [56] "Ausgedrückte Entblössung," ibid., p. 306.

[57] Ibid., pp. 310—311; see also: "Fürstenpredigt," ibid., p. 255.

[58] "Fürstenpredigt," ibid., p. 257.

[59] As far as Müntzer was concerned, of course, all those opposed to his teachings were godless, for they hindered the elect from realizing the voice of God in their innermost soul.

[60] "Dann sie haben euch genarret, das ein yeder zun heyligen schwuer, die fursten seindt heydnische leuthe yres ampts halben, sie sollen nicht anders dann burgerliche einigkeyt erhalten." "Fürstenpredigt," Schriften und Briefe, p. 257.

[61] Ibid., pp. 258—259.

if only given the opportunity through the destruction of the false prophets and the godless princes.[62]

Müntzer's concept of the Kingdom of God on earth also led him to view the Scriptures and the activity of the Holy Spirit from the vantage point of the Old Testament. Thus, a cardinal tenet of his faith was that the Bible was a dated revelation of God given at a specific time in history by particular men inspired by the Holy Spirit. It was not, however, the final revelation of God to man, for according to Müntzer, the Holy Spirit continued to communicate with men in progressive revelation. A dichotomy therefore existed for Müntzer between the "inner" and the "outer" Word of God: the "outer" Word being Scripture and the "inner" Word referring to the continual revelation of the Holy Spirit. At times he referred to Scripture as the "dead" Word, and to the voice of the Holy Spirit as the "living" Word. In contrast to Luther and the other reformers, who asserted that the function of the Holy Spirit with regard to Scripture was merely to elucidate its meaning since the fullness of revelation had come in Jesus Christ, Müntzer believed that the Holy Spirit was still alive in the hearts of men everywhere and could lead them to a true faith in Christ without recourse to the Scriptures.[63] This Spirit was also continually revealing new insights to men, and to Müntzer it had revealed the imminent inauguration of the Kingdom of God on earth.

Under the concept of the Kingdom of God on earth, Müntzer seems to have envisioned a kind of utopian Christian-communistic society. Communistic ideas drawn from the Bible were, of course, not strange to medieval society. The organization of the monasteries was to a large extent based on these ideas. The Hussite movement, and particularly the Taborite wing of that movement, harbored these ideas.[64] The fact that Müntzer went to Bohemia in 1521 and issued his famous "Manifesto"[65] there, thus identifying himself with the entire Hussite movement and trying to portray himself as its new leader, demonstrates that he was strongly influenced by these ideas, as were the Zwickau Prophets.[66] Thus the communistic idea

[62] "Das arme volck kan vor der vergifft der gotlosen in sich nit kummen. Es stehet ein yeder noch raussen vorm tempel und erwartet, wenns doch wil einmal gut werden." "Ausgedrückte Entblössung," ibid., p. 293. And again in his "Hochverursachte Schutzrede," ibid., p. 333.

[63] "Ausgedrückte Entblössung," ibid., pp. 277—278. See also C. Hinrichs, Luther und Müntzer (Berlin, 1952), p. 48.

[64] See N. Cohn, In Pursuit of the Millenium (New Jersey, 1957), pp. 217—236.

[65] Schriften und Briefe, pp. 495—505.

[66] Cohn, Millenium, p. 252, feels that the Taborite influence was decisive for both Storch and Müntzer who were both in Bohemia at one time or another. See also P. Wappler, Thomas Müntzer und die "Zwickauer Propheten", pp. 29—30.

was not a new one and there seems to be no reason, therefore, to discount Müntzer's confession that "omnia sunt communia, und sollten eynem idern nach seyner notdorft ausgeteylt werden nach gelegenheyt."[67]

Lydia Müller believed that it was from Thomas Müntzer and his disciple, Hans Hut, that the Hutterites had received their idea of a community of goods in the fellowship of believers.[68] Carl Hinrichs, in his penetrating study, *Luther und Müntzer,* believed that this idea of a community of goods in the fellowship of believers, Müntzer's *Bund,* had indeed been an integral aspect of the latter's thought.[69] Müntzer's confession at his trial, therefore, that all goods should be held in common, was only a logical expression of his thought and not something forced from him under torture.[70] But this was a community of goods based on the biblical example in the Book of Acts.[71] Only in a society in which a community of goods existed could men live together in brotherhood and love and thus create the conditions necessary for the revival of that purity which had existed in the Apostolic Church and which was a necessary precondition for the establishment of the Kingdom of God's elect here on earth.[72] Thus it was not primarily a new social order that Müntzer desired, but rather a new church which needed this social order to be able to come into being.

This new social order, so necessary for the church, had, however, implications which were truly revolutionary for the society of Müntzer's day. Müntzer divided society into two camps: the elect and the godless. The elect were those who had taken the oath to accept and follow the precepts of the Word of God as understood by Müntzer and had joined the latter's *Bund;*[73] the godless were those who actively opposed it. Although no one was to be barred from this *Bund* because of his social status, any prince who should wish to join was to be considered equal with the rest of the

---

[67] G. *Forell,* "Thomas Müntzer, Symbol and Reality," Dialog reprint, II (Winter issue, 1960), p. 11. Müntzer may also have been influenced in his communistic thinking by Plato's Republic which he had read. See "Ausgedrückte Entblössung," Schriften und Briefe, p. 290.

[68] L. *Müller,* Der Kommunismus der Mährischen Wiedertäufer (Leipzig, 1927), pp. 74—76.

[69] *Hinrichs,* Luther und Müntzer, p. 20.   [70] Ibid.

[71] Even Melanchthon stated in his "Die Historia Thomä Müntzers, des Anfängers der Thüringischen Aufruhr ...," "Er lehrte auch, dass die Güter gemein sein, wie in Actis Apostolorum geschrieben steht, dass sie die Güter zusammengethan haben." *Luther,* Sämtliche Schriften, XVI (St. Louis, 1899), 164.

[72] *Hinrichs,* Luther und Müntzer, p. 21. According to Müntzer himself, riches and honor were the greatest deterents to faith. See "Ausgedrückte Entblössung," Schriften und Briefe, p. 282.   [73] *Hinrichs,* Luther und Müntzer, p. 21.

members.[74] The princes who refused to join the assembly of the elect and actively opposed it were to be exterminated,[75] for as long as such princes ruled over the people as they did, suppressing and tyrannizing them and thereby keeping them from realizing God's calling and the working of the Holy Spirit in their lives, the Kingdom of God would not be established on earth.[76] If, however, the princes joined, they were to use their swords to promote the new society by destroying the godless, at which point they might even be granted some form of power or at least honor in it.[77]

Thus Müntzer at first welcomed, even wooed, members of the feudal ruling class into his *Bund*. His denunciations of those princes who refused to join his *Bund* were not based on the fact that they had *merely* oppressed the people;[78] rather, he denounced them because they had opposed God and His Kingdom and had kept the poor from hearing the true gospel. His society, therefore, was not limited to the poor, no matter how difficult it might be for the "camel to pass through the eye of a needle," but it was limited to the elect who had the assurance of salvation, although at times it almost appears as though Müntzer believed that only the lower classes could belong to the elect.[79]

According to Müntzer, this new society would be inaugurated by God when the time was ripe. And it was this moment in God's historical dialectic which the Holy Spirit had revealed to him. Since, however, the existing hierarchy in Church and State had rejected his proposals for peaceful reform, Müntzer was gradually forced to the conclusion that the coming of the Kingdom of God on earth would have to be effected by means of

[74] See the letter of Hans Zeiss, Schösser in Allstedt, to the Elector Frederick of Saxony, May 7, 1525, in which he wrote concerning the nobles allowed into Müntzer's *Bund*. *Franz*, Quellen, p. 516. See also Zeiss to Christoph Meinhart of May 5, 1525. Ibid., p. 512.

[75] See Müntzer's letter to the Duke of Mansfeld, May 12, 1525. Ibid., pp. 519—520. That these last threatening letters are not *Übersteigerungen*, as some would have it, but represent integral aspects of Müntzer's thought, is shown by the parallel passages from his "Fürstenpredigt," Schriften und Briefe, p. 259; and his last pamphlet, "Hochverursachte Schutzrede," ibid., p. 330.

[76] See Müntzer's letter of April 26 or 27, 1525, to the people of Allstedt. Schriften und Briefe, p. 455. The same theme was sounded already in his "Ausgedrückte Entblössung," ibid., p. 275.

[77] L. H. Zuck, "Fecund Problems of Eschatological Hope, Election Proof, and Social Revolt in Thomas Müntzer," F. H. Littel, ed., Reformation Studies (Richmond, 1962), p. 244.

[78] H. Böhmer, "Thomas Müntzer und das jüngste Deutschland," Gesammelte Aufsätze (Gotha, 1927), p. 199.

[79] See the letter of Zeiss to Christoph Meinhart of May 5, 1525. *Franz*, Quellen, p. 512; the statement of Hans Hut, ibid., p. 523; and numerous passages in Müntzer's "Ausgedrückte Entblössung."

a war against the godless. In this war, God would do the fighting. Yet Müntzer did not expect God to act entirely on His own, but rather through the agency of His elect. Consequently, he envisioned the establishment of the Kingdom of God on earth in the same light as Israel's conquest of the Promised Land. Regarding the latter, Müntzer stated:

"Sie haben das lant nicht durch das Schwerdt gewonnen, sonder durch die krafft Gottis, aber das schwerdt war das mittel, wie uns essen und trincken ein mittel ist zu leben."[80]

Therefore, no matter how small or how poorly armed the forces of the elect might be, God would give them the victory.[81]

5. MÜNTZER AND THE PEASANTS

Because of the similarities between the peasant aims and the aims of Müntzer, the former could see in Müntzer, and Müntzer in the peasants, kindred spirits. In the attempts of both the peasants and Müntzer to attain the ideal Christian society here on earth, the Gospel of Christ had, in one way or another, to be construed as a new law.[82] If one would only consent to live by this new "divine law," as the peasants would have it, then just conditions could be established on earth. They themselves were willing to abide by such a law, and their hope was that the nobles and ecclesiastical princes could be persuaded to do the same. Similarly, Müntzer believed that if only he were allowed to propagate his teachings with the consent of the authorities, teachings which, moreover, the populace hungered for, moral reform could be achieved and the Kingdom of God set up. All those who remained obdurate and opposed Müntzer's teachings, or, in the case of the peasants, all those who would not accept the "divine law," which these had discovered in Luther's new doctrines, as normative would eventually have either to be coerced or exterminated. The logic used here is similar to that used by the medieval Church to justify the execution of heretics. In the latter case, the heretic was considered a cancerous sore which had to be cut out of the Christian body before it contaminated adjacent members. Similarly, Müntzer and the peasants argued that those who opposed them hindered the erection of the Kingdom of God and had to

---

[80] "Fürstenpredigt," Schriften und Briefe, p. 261.

[81] "Gideon hett eynen solchen festen, starcken glauben, das er mit im ein unzelige grosse welt durch dreyhundert man überwant." "Ausgedrückte Entblössung," ibid., p. 273. And in this connection as well: "O, allerliebsten bruder, wozu erinnert uns diss evangelion anderst, denn das der glaub mit alle seynem ursprunge helt uns unmüglich ding für." Ibid., p. 288.

[82] See especially W. *Joest*, "Das Verhältnis der Unterscheidungen der beiden Regimente zu der Unterscheidung von Gesetz und Evangelium," *H.-Horst Schrey*, Reich Gottes und Welt: die Lehre Luthers von den zwei Reichen (Darmstadt, 1969), pp. 196—220.

be dealt with. Müntzer, in the final analysis, was much more ruthless in this regard than most of the peasants, for his concept of the Kingdom of God was more radical than theirs. Nevertheless, they both seem to have had very similar àims, at least outwardly. Yet Müntzer went far beyond these outward aims to the regeneration of man; and well he might, for he was the theologian.

It was these outward similarities which made it possible for Müntzer to use the social turmoil of his day for his own ends. Since the peasant cause seemed also to be his cause, he was willing to join the insurgents. In the end, however, he realized that they had not had similar goals, for the insurgents had indeed fought merely for selfish ends whereas he had fought a holy war for holy ends. This is brought out clearly in his last letter to the citizens of Mühlhausen after the failure of the revolt. Here he accuses his followers of not really understanding what he had been preaching about, and, instead of seeking the glory of God and the welfare of Christianity, they had sought to satisfy their own selfish desires. Because of this, they had failed to achieve their objectives in the war, or, more correctly, God had not allowed them to achieve these objectives.[83]

In spite of the similarity of their aims, Müntzer's influence in the Peasants' War was not as great as some have imagined. There is no doubt that he did establish a *Bund*,[84] a kind of secret society, but this *Bund* could not have had a broad base in Germany.[85] It seems to have been confined to Mühlhausen and the surrounding district, but here it apparently drew large crowds of people.[86] The purpose of the *Bund*, however, was not

---

[83] Schriften und Briefe, p. 473. Johann Rühel commented as follows on this letter which he sent to Luther on May 26, 1525: "Schicke euch hierinne Thomas Münzers Bekänntnüsse, so er zu Heldrungen gethan, Darzu copie der schrifft auss seinem gefängnüss an die von Mühlhausen, und wiewohl dieselbige von den wiederwärtigen alss eine Wiederrufsschrifft gedeutet, ist sie doch im Grunde bey mir eine Stärckung seines furhabens, will allein den Bauern zumessen, dass sie auss dem, dass sie ihren eignen nutz zu sehr gesucht, der unfall und straff troffen. Ich besorge, man sage, was man wolle, es sey ein *desperat mensch*." WA, Briefe, 3, 510.

[84] Hans Zeiss wrote to Duke John of Saxony about it on July 28, 1524. *Franz, Quellen*, p. 486; the chronicler of Mühlhausen mentions it in his Chronicle, ibid., p. 501; Müntzer also confessed that the had formed a *Bund*. See his "Bekenntnis und Widerruf," Schriften und Briefe, p. 548.

[85] Even the Marxist, *M. Bensing*, Thomas Müntzer und der Thüringer Aufstand 1525 (Berlin, 1966), p. 107, has conceded that Müntzer's purpose had been "das er wolle das land uff 10 meyl weges umb Molhawsen eingenommen haben und das land zu Hessen und mit den fursten und herrn verfaren, wye oben angezeyt."

[86] Time and again Zeiss speaks in his dispatches to the Saxon princes of the crowds drawn by Müntzer and his accomplices, especially Heinrich Pfeiffer. See also the documents relating to Müntzer in *Walter Peter Fuchs*, Akten zur Geschichte des Bauernkriegs in Mitteldeutschland, vol. II (Jena, 1942).

primarily to foment revolution, it only did so when the Kingdom could
not be inaugurated peacefully. Its main purpose was to form a nucleus of
the elect which would eventually inherit the earth after the godless had
been destroyed.[87] Thus, while admitting that Müntzer was an effective
agitator in his limited sphere of activity, it must be vigorously denied that
he masterminded the whole peasants' revolt from his lair in Mühlhausen.
Particularism was far too rampant among the peasants for this and most of
the peasants, especially those from southern Germany, had much more
limited and less utopian goals than Müntzer. It is therefore not surprising
that the peasants, in their Twelve Articles, appealed to the Magisterial
Reformers like Luther, Melanchthon, and Zwingli for support and did not
even mention the name of Thomas Müntzer. Even by Müntzer's own
confession it is known that he had no influence outside his own particular
local area.[88] And, in the end, not even here did everyone choose to follow
him.[89] Nevertheless, his teachings did act as a catalyst to crystalize the
discontent of the peasants in parts of Thuringia; for although the revolt
was already well under way here by the time Müntzer returned from
southern Germany in early 1525, his ideas provided the insurgents with
a "myth" to strive after and his revolutionary rhetoric served to encourage
their revolutionary ardor.[90]

6. THE ANABAPTISTS AND THE PEASANTS' WAR

No doubt exists as to the involvement in the Peasants' War of Thomas
Müntzer and the peasants, as well as Luther, although on opposite sides.
Such is not the case with respect to the Anabaptists, implicitly placed in the
same category as the peasants and Müntzer by Luther. Here Luther was
in error, at least insofar as he judged all Anabaptist groups by the Münsterite example. For, to begin with, the majority of the Anabaptists were
pacifistic.

---

[87] *Hinrichs*, Luther und Müntzer, pp. 18—20.

[88] See his own confession, Schriften und Briefe, p. 544; also *G. Franz*, "Die Entste-
hung der 'Zwölf Artikel' der deutschen Bauernschaft," Archiv für Reformationsgeschichte,
XXXVI (1939), 197. (Hereafter this journal will be cited as ARG.) See also the latter's
Der deutsche Bauernkrieg, 4th ed. (Darmstadt, 1956), p. 110, and Valentine Lötscher,
Der deutsche Bauernkrieg in der Darstellung und im Urteil der Zeitgenössischen Schwei-
zer (Bern, 1948), pp. 118—125.

[89] The Mühlhausen chronicler relates that when Müntzer was about to move against
the princes at Frankenhausen, many of the citizens of the city would not follow him
and others had already deserted him. *Franz*, Quellen, p. 501.

[90] See also *A. Waas*, Die Bauern im Kampf um Gerechtigkeit 1300—1525 (München,
1964), pp. 232—233.

The confrontation between the two positions, that is between Müntzer and the peaceful Anabaptists, took place already before the Peasants' War in September of 1524. In his famous letter of that month to Thomas Müntzer, Conrad Grebel, the leader of the Swiss Anabaptists, wrote:

"dess Huiufen bruder schribt du habest wider die fürsten geprediget dass man sy mit der funst angriffen solte / ist ess war / oder so du krieg schirmen woltest / die taflen / dass gsang / oder anderss so nit in clarem wort fundist / alss du disse gemelten stuk nit findest So ermann ich dich by gmeinem heil unser allen wellist darvon abstan und allem gutdunken ietz und hernach / so wirst du gar rein werden der unss sunst in andren artiklen bass gefälst den keiner in disem tütschen ouch anderen länderen."[91]

Theoretically, therefore, at least the leaders of the Swiss Anabaptists had no intention of advocating any kind of social revolution, never mind becoming implicated in revolution.[92]

But what about their followers? Undoubtedly, Anabaptism cannot have played a causative role in the Peasants' War, as perhaps Thomas Müntzer's teachings did in Thuringia,[93] because the movement only became more than a conventicle after the first adult baptism in January of 1525.[94] At the most, one can speak only of an involvement in the Peasants' War. Even at that, Anabaptism appeared in Basel and Bern only after the Peasants' War and not during or even before it; and in the entire region, Zollikon excluded,[95] only some thirty peasants appeared in court before 1527 accused of being Anabaptists.[96] Paul Peachey has pursued the problem and come to the conclusion that the only place where Anabaptism intermingled with the Peasants' War was in Hallau, close to the scene of the peasant uprising on the Swiss-German border. In February, 1525, one of the Zurich group, Hans Brötli, came into the region to win converts to Anabaptism.[97] When the authorities in neighboring Schaffhausen demanded the surrender of Brötli, the peasants rose to defend him, yet in the former's letters to Zollikon there is nothing to indicate that Brötli became involved in the

---

[91] Conrad Grebel and friends to Thomas Müntzer, September 5, 1524, Quellen zur Geschichte der Täufer in der Schweiz, vol. I (Zurich, 1952), 20, edited by *Muralt* and *Schmid*. (Hereafter cited as Quellen, Schweiz.)

[92] Ibid., p. 21.   [93] For this it arrived too late.

[94] *P. Peachey*, Die soziale Herkunft der Schweizer Täufer in der Reformationszeit (Karlsruhe, 1954), p. 55.

[95] Zollikon was the home of the first Anabaptist congregation. See *F. Blanke*, Brüder in Christo (Zurich, 1955).   [96] *Peachey*, Die soziale Herkunft, p. 55.

[97] It is true that the Zurich Anabaptists also advocated the abolition of the small "tenth." This may well have played into the hands of the revolting peasants, although *J. F. G. Goeters*, Ludwig Hätzer (Gütersloh, 1957), p. 32, does not believe so.

peasant movement, although he was impressed by the poverty of the peasants. The latter must, however, at least have believed Brötli and the Anabaptists to have been on their side and therefore protected him.[98] Only in one instance did an Anabaptist actually confess to having participated actively in the Peasants' War.[99] It is clear, however, and Peachey admits as much time and again, that the radical doctrines of the Anabaptists, which in essence upset the social order of the time, added to the turmoil in the hearts and minds of many suffering under real or imagined burdens. But their actual participation in the Peasants' War was negligible, which is all the more impressive since Anabaptism in Switzerland experienced its greatest expansion precisely during and shortly after the social upheaval of 1525.

What about Anabaptism in other regions? It is a well-known fact, of course, that Balthasar Hubmaier in Waldshut did not share the opinion of his Zurich friends concerning the "sword" and that, as a result, Waldshut joined the peasants in their war against the Hapsburgs.[100] Hubmaier and Waldshut, however, constituted a minority opinion in this regard, and it is interesting to note that two Anabaptists in this group refused to participate in the conflict. Jakob Gross[101] and Ulrich Teck were consequently forced to leave Waldshut, but the Peasants' War had made the participation of Anabaptists in war a burning issue in Waldshut.[102] The example of Waldshut demonstrates quite explicitly that the division for or against the sword rested largely with the personal convictions of the Anabaptist leaders. Nor does Hubmaier seem to have changed his views on the subject after the defeat of the peasants and his forced departure from Waldshut. Quite the contrary, we find him arguing against Hans Hut, the former part-time associate of Müntzer turned pacifist, that one must fight on the side of the authorities if they so require.[103] Thus neither Hubmaier's posi-

---

[98] *Peachey*, Die soziale Herkunft, pp. 55—63.   [99] Ibid., pp. 63—64.

[100] See *Franz*, Bauernkrieg, p. 103; *G. Williams*, The Radical Reformation (Philadelphia, 1962), pp. 64—68; and *T. Bergsten*, Balthasar Hubmaier, Seine Stellung zu Reformation und Täufertum (Kassel, 1961), pp. 277—301.

[101] Toward the end of 1526 Gross was captured in Strassburg where he confessed: "Sey von Waltshut kommen und abschieden müssen umb das willen, dass er nit haben wollen zu den buren gen Zell zu ziehen ... Sagt auch, was der oberkait zustehe, das (woll) er halten und für sein person wider kein oberkait nie willens zu setzen, etc.; wolle wachen, hüten, harnisch anlegen, den spies in die handt nehmen: des sper er sich gar nit; aber die leuth zu todt zu schlagen, dass sey in keim gebott gots geschriben." *M. Krebs* und *H. G. Rott*, eds., Quellen zur Geschichte der Täufer, VII. Band, Elsass, I. Teil (Gütersloh, 1959), p. 64.

[102] *G. Westin*, introduction to Balthasar Hubmaier Schriften, *G. Westin* and *T. Bergsten*, eds. (Gütersloh, 1962), p. 28.   [103] Ibid., p. 40.

tion nor that of the Swiss Anabaptists with regard to the sword was influenced in the least by the defeat of the peasants.[104]

We cannot pursue the problem in any detail here, but a general summary shall be attempted. The farther away from Zurich one looks, the later the Anabaptists appear on the scene.[105] Hence the crucial conjunction of Peasants' War and Anabaptism took place in Switzerland and upper Germany. Toward the end of 1526, for example, Anabaptism came into the region of the Tyrol,[106] but already in 1525 Georg Blaurock and Felix Mantz, both Swiss Anabaptists, had begun to win adherents here.[107] Eduard Widmoser, who turned his attention to this region, asserted that the Anabaptists had sooner pacified the populace than incited it to revolt.[108] The same was certainly true of southern Germany, as a perusal of the Anabaptist documents[109] and Claus-Peter Clasen's study shows.[110]

The picture changes the farther north one moves into central Germany and down the Rhine, however. This was not least of all due to the intellectual climate in these regions which Anabaptism encountered. Central Germany, of course, had been influenced by Müntzer, and his ideas remained behind to haunt the hopeful minds of men for some time after his death. In 1526, Hans Hut, the former friend and associate of Thomas Müntzer, was baptized by Hans Denck in Augsburg.[111] Upon rebaptism, Hut returned to Franconia and southern Thuringia late in 1526 where he preached for a time.[112] But the leading figure in the Anabaptist movement in central Germany was Melchior Rinck, also a former disciple of Müntzer, who was particularly effective in winning converts to the Anabaptist

---

[104] It should be stated in this connection as well that Ludwig Hätzer's biographer, Goeters, has denied that the former had been implicated in the Peasants' War. *Goeters, Ludwig Hätzer*, pp. 55—56.

[105] See especially W. *Schäufele*, Das Missionarische Bewußtsein und Wirken der Täufer (Neukirchen Vluyn, 1966), pp. 15—37.

[106] E. *Widmoser*, "Das Täufertum im Tiroler Unterland," unpublished doctoral dissertation, University of Innsbruck, 1948, p. 34, pointed out that: "Der Tiroler Bauer kehrte sich jedoch von den fremden lutherischen Predigern ab, weil er in ihnen die Anstifter der Gewalttätigkeiten und Greuel des Aufstandes zu sehen glaubte. Die 'dürren' Predikanten, die von außen ins Land kamen, wurden nach dem furchtbaren Ende des Bauernkrieges immer weniger."   [107] Ibid., p. 36.   [108] Ibid., p. 35.

[109] Only very isolated and unrewarding references are made to the Peasants' War in the various volumes of the recently edited Anabaptist documents (Quellen zur Geschichte der Täufer.)

[110] C.-P. *Clasen*, Die Wiedertäufer im Herzogtum Württemberg und in benachbarten Herrschaften (Stuttgart, 1965).   [111] *Williams*, The Radical Reformation, p. 162.

[112] J. S. *Oyer*, Lutheran Reformers against Anabaptists (The Hague, 1965), p. 48.

cause in parts of Hesse and Thuringia.[113] Although both Hut and Rinck converted to Anabaptism, substantial remnants of Müntzerian ideas remained, especially in the radical chiliasm of Hans Hut.[114] But not only did both Hut and Rinck come from a somewhat Müntzerian background, Denck, who baptized Hut and probably Rinck as well, may also have been influenced by Müntzer.[115] This factor undoubtedly made the transition from revolutionary chiliasm to spiritual Anabaptism easier. It might not be amiss to recall in this connection Müntzer's last letter to the citizens of Mühlhausen where he rejected revolution as a means of inaugurating the Kingdom of God on earth for the future. Hut may have gone through a similar experience even before he met Denck and was baptized by him. This chiliasm, however, still remained revolutionary, only now God would be the initiator of revenge, not the elect.

The same radicalization of Anabaptist teachings is apparent the farther one moves down the Rhine. J. F. Gerhard Goeters has pointed to the presence of Sacramentarian views in this region as the cause for this pheno-

---

[113] *Williams,* The Radical Reformation, p. 435. It is probable, although there seems to be no conclusive evidence for the assumption, that Rinck was brought into the Anabaptist fold by Hans Denck who also baptized Hut. See *R. Weiss,* "Die Herkunft der osthessischen Täufer," ARG, 50 (1959), 1/2, 7.

[114] The argument as to whether Hut was a revolutionary chiliast and to what extent he remained bound to Müntzer's ideas despite his rebaptism, has been debated long and vigorously. The attempt by *H. Klassen,* "The Life and Teachings of Hans Hut," The Mennonite Quarterly Review, XXXIII (1959), 3, 171—205, and 4, 276—305 (hereafter this journal will be cited as MQR), to make Hut into a pacifist and to emphasize his break with Müntzer is not convincing. *G. Rupp,* "Thomas Müntzer, Hans Huth, and the 'Gospel of all Creatures,'" Bulletin of the John Rylands Library, 43 (1960/61), 492—519, argues for a close relationship of ideas between Hut and Müntzer even after the former's conversion, p. 162. *J. M. Stayer,* "Hans Hut's Doctrine of the Sword; an attempted Solution," MQR, 39 (1965), 3, 181—191, argues that Hut's theme of eschatological revenge could just as easily have ended in another Münster had other factors been equal. See also the last in this series: *R. Friedmann,* "The Nicolsburg Articles, a Problem of Early Anabaptist History," XXXVI (1967), 4, 392—409 who sees Hut as a chiliast, but not as politically seditious.

[115] See especially *G. Bäring,* "Hans Denck und Thomas Müntzer in Nürnberg 1524," ARG, 50 (1959), 145—181. In a personal letter to this author, Robert Friedmann emphatically rejected Bäring's speculations, and *W. Fellmann,* in his introductory biography to the writings of Hans Denck, Hans Denck Schriften, vols. II & III (Gütersloh, 1956 & 1960), stated: "Thomas Müntzer kam kurz darauf nach Nürnberg, seine Schriften sind ebenfalls bei Höltzel gedruckt worden. Ob es zu einer persönlichen Berührung mit Denck kam, wie viele annehmen, läßt sich durch die Quellen nicht belegen. Auffallend bleibt, daß beim späteren Prozeß der Rat Denck mit Müntzer nicht in Beziehung bringt. Mit Hans Hut, der damals Müntzer nahestand, ist Denck jedoch in Nürnberg zusammengetroffen, ja er scheint ihn beherbergt zu haben." Vol. II, p. 10. The similarities of language between Denck and Müntzer, which Fellmann pointed to in his edition of Denck's writings, may therefore go back to their common heritage of German mysticism.

menon.[116] In Hesse the same is true, where, in certain regions, the influence of Melchior Hoffmann was strongly apparent.[117] Thus, according to Goeters, Anabaptist apostles from the Netherlands arrived in Münster in January of 1534 and baptized the Sacramentarians of that city.[118]

Therefore, the essential problem that faces us with regard to Anabaptism and the Peasants' War the farther we are removed from Zurich is whether or not, and this is especially true of Thuringia, the revolutionaries of 1525 joined the Anabaptist movement once it was brought into their region by wandering apostles. In Thuringia and Franconia, as we have seen, two former followers of Müntzer who had joined the Anabaptist movement returned to preach the new teachings in the regions of Müntzer's greatest influence. How did these newly won converts to the Anabaptist movement look back upon the Peasants' War when confronted by the authorities? A number of such confrontations have been recorded for us.[119] One of the questions asked was whether or not the Peasants' War had been a godly war.[120] Of some fifteen questioned, seven had participated in the war but none asserted that it had been godly. One, indeed, stated that the uprising had been made for "temporal reasons" and had therefore been unjust; had it been made for the sake of the Gospel, however, he did not know whether it would have been just or not.[121] A number of others claimed that they had been misled by two men named Adam Craft and Heinrich Rab and had never really understood what it had all been about. They were unanimous, however, in rejecting revolution for the future.[122] On the other hand, there were men like Hans Römer, Müntzer's companion on the latter's trip to Nuremberg, who had been baptized by Hans Hut but considered Müntzer his father and who, together with his band of followers, planned the destruction of Erfurt, only to be discovered before the plan could be implemented. Yet Römer admitted members to his group only through baptism and upon the promise of living a good Christian life and refraining from revolution.[123] Obviously, the two movements had merged here and caused not a little confusion.

---

[116] *J. F. G. Goeters*, "Die Rolle des Täufertums in der Reformationsgeschichte des Niederrheins," Rheinische Vierteljahrsblätter, 24 (1959), 3/4, 224.

[117] *R. Weiss*, "Herkunft und Sozialanschauungen der Täufergemeinden im westlichen Hessen," ARG, 52 (1961), 163, and 186.

[118] *Goeters*, "Die Rolle des Täufertums," p. 224.

[119] *G. Franz*, et al., Urkundliche Quellen zur Hessischen Reformationsgeschichte, Wiedertäuferakten 1527—1626 (Marburg, 1951).

[120] No. 28, August, 1533: "Verhör der Wiedertäufer zu Sorge bei Hersfeld," ibid., p. 64.   [121] Ibid., p. 67.

[122] In how far they really meant this must remain a matter of speculation. Ibid., pp. 64—72.   [123] *Oyer*, Luthers against Anabaptists, pp. 96—97.

The evidence, therefore, demonstrates that few, if any, of the pacifistic Anabaptists were involved in the Peasants' War. Indeed, their theology of the two kingdoms, as Robert Friedmann has termed it,[124] postulated a break between the "world" and the "church" equally as radical as that of Müntzer. However, their concept was combined with other ideas to rob it of its revolutionary tenor. One of these, of course, was their theology of martyrdom[125] which postulated a persecuted church as the only true church of Christ. This idea was necessarily combined with a pacifistic attitude toward the ruling authorities who might well be the persecutors. Therefore, there could be no compromise between the "believers' church" and the "wordly" temporal authorities, and all "good" Anabaptists refused to serve as temporal authorities in whatever capacity.[126] Nonetheless, the Anabaptists did strive to achieve a church "without spot or wrinkle," and insofar as they did, they drew close, once more, to Müntzer and the peasants.

7. MÜNTZER, THE PEASANTS AND THE ANABAPTISTS

If one were, then, to divest Müntzer of his revolutionary potential, as he himself did after the defeat of the peasants, one would have to accept the coexistence of "Christians" and "unbelievers," as the Anabaptists did. The Kingdom of God, which Müntzer wanted to inaugurate through the sword of the elect, would then have to await the pleasure of Christ's return, when the saints would become victors with Christ. Therefore the eschatological, as well as the pacifistic elements, separated Müntzer from the Anabaptists.

If it is correct that Hut rejected revolutionary tactics at the same time as Müntzer, that is after the battle of Frankenhausen where Müntzer and the peasants were defeated, which Hut witnessed, then only the eschatological element would remain to separate him from the Anabaptists. And this seems, indeed, to have been the case. But pacifistic chiliasm could be tolerated in Anabaptism, as Hut's example makes clear. Here, then, must have been the meeting ground between the two groups, a meeting ground which gave occasion for grave misinterpretation during the Reformation era.

If one accepts this as the intellectual background against which the Peasants' War was fought, then it becomes amply clear why Luther rejected

---

[124] R. Friedmann, "The Essence of Anabaptist Faith," MQR, XLI (1967), 1, 5—24.

[125] E. Stauffer, "Märtyrertheologie und Täuferbewegung," Zeitschrift für Kirchengeschichte, 52 (1933), 545—598.

[126] See especially H. J. Hillerbrand, Die politische Ethik des oberdeutschen Täufertums (Leiden, 1962).

the arguments of the peasants and of Müntzer, as well as those of the Anabaptists later on. It also becomes obvious why the peasants and Müntzer
could mistake each other for allies, and why some peasants could at least
sympathize with the Anabaptists. It may be said further that although the
peasants did not understand Luther's theory of the two realms, and for
that reason applied his teachings to their social condition, Müntzer understood it only too well, but rejected it because he approached the problem
from an entirely different perspective.

CHAPTER IV

THE PEASANTS' WAR AND REFORMATION POLEMICS

1. THE EMERGENCE OF THE CATHOLIC INTERPRETATION

Eyn warhafftig spruch alhie erklert
Was luther hat furgenommen mit seinem schreiben
Das hatt pfeiffer begunst mitt predigen zu treiben
Thomas muntzer mitt der vffruhr angefangen
Hans hergott mit seynem trewmbuch begangen
Baltzar do durch die widdertewffrey gestifftet
Zwingel die Sacramentarier vorgifftet
Seine gemeine schwermer alles Gots dienst verwustet
Vnd ander gutwergk seynner gebot vernichtet
Alle sundt vnd laster frey zu vbenn gelehret
Gotliche schrifft: wahrheit vnd gerechtigkeit verkeret
Widder die ware Christliche kyrche geschnettert
Ihren glauben vnd religion gelestert
Solche fruchte kommen, aus der luttrischen schrifft
Noch wil man nicht erkennen seyn hellische gifft.

Peter Sylvius, Leipzig 1527.

The conflicting intellectual paradigms which determined Reformation attitudes toward the reform of late medieval Christendom to a great extent also determined the nature and direction of Reformation polemics. These polemics centered largely around the Peasants' War, for it was here, as we have seen, that the ideas of reform came into sharpest conflict. And it should therefore not be surprising to find that these same polemics have exerted a major influence upon the subsequent interpretations historians have given to the era.

From the Catholic perspective — the ideal of the *Corpus Christianum* — of course, the only reform necessary was a moral reform, if the necessity of reform was conceded at all. Certainly they did not deem it necessary to substitute an entirely new theological system for the existing one in order to resolve the tension between the ideal and the all-too-human Christian society of their day, as Luther proposed to do. Indeed, some years after the initiation of Luther's reformation it became apparent to many,

Luther included, that even the Lutheran alternative did not lead to the resolution of this tension. For, although Luther did expect his followers to live a more moral Christian life, their actions confirmed his belief that one could not, in the final analysis, determine whether a person was a Christian merely by his public actions.

Luther's theology, however, was aimed at the Christian's life in the spiritual realm. Therefore his "freedom of a Christian man" applied only in this realm, as did the equality implicit in his doctrine of the priesthood of all believers. When these ideas were brought to bear upon the medieval concept of the *Corpus Christianum*, however, they acquired a decidedly revolutionary potential, as we have had occasion to note in the previous chapter. These revolutionary implications were welcomed by the peasants who felt themselves oppressed by the *status quo* in Church and State, but they were vehemently rejected by the Catholic Church which, viewing Luther's teachings from the same perspective, had a vested interest in that *status quo*.

It is these two factors — the concept of the *Corpus Christianum* and the rejection of the revolutionary implications of Luther's theology when applied to that concept — that are essentially responsible for the Catholic interpretation of Luther as foisted upon the world primarily by Johannes Cochläus.[1] This view, whose main outlines had already become apparent before Cochläus, appears to have been the nearly universal Catholic reaction to Luther after the Peasants' War, for it was this war which seemed to confirm their worst suspicions of Luther's teachings.[2] It was probably Hieronymus Emser who first projected this Catholic image of Luther into sharper focus and expressed in no uncertain terms the latent Catholic suspicions in his "Auf Luthers grewel wider die heiligen Stillmess. Antwort" of July, 1525.[3] Here Emser collected innumerable passages from Luther's writings which appeared to him seditious of law and order and concluded from these that Luther was to blame for the entire peasants' revolt.[4] Emser's tract was quickly followed by that of Cochläus on Luther's *Bauern-*

[1] *I. Cochlai*, Commentaria Ioannis Cochlaei, de Actis et Scriptis Martini Lutheri Saxonis (Mainz, 1549).

[2] "Die Papiste gaben dem Luther vnd seiner leer die schuld / der hett disz feür anzündt / vn darnak die oberkeit an sy gehetzt zu stechen / hawen / morde. x. vnd sy beredt / damit das himelreich zuverdiene. Zuletst / als es allenthalb pran / hab er wid wollen loschen / da es nit mer halff. Daher / so man an etliche orten da des Luthers leer gepredigt war / an die predig leütet / pflegt ma zusage / da leüt ma die mordt glocke." *Franck*, Chronica, p. cclxxiij. And in the margin is written: "Luther wirt vom Ecken Cocleo x. die schuld gebe der pauren auffrur."

[3] See *A. Herte*, Die Lutherkommentare Johannes Cochläus (Münster, 1935), p. 175.

[4] Ibid., p. 176.

schriften[5] with the same accusations. Even Erasmus — and this is significant for the humanist view of the Christian society, the *respublica christiana* — accused Luther in his *Hyperaspistes* of 1526 of causing the social turmoil of the previous year with his German pamphlets couched in their incendiary language, and singled out Luther's teaching on the "freedom of a Christian man" for special attack.[6] Indeed, so well did this and other Erasmian passages fit into the argumentation of Cochläus that they were used by the latter,[7] as well as Johannes Janssen[8] some three hundred years later, to lend prestige and credence to their point of view.

The picture of Luther that emerged from this Catholic perspective of the *Corpus Christianum*, particularly as it related to the Peasants' War, was that of a revolutionary-turned-reactionary. For, according to Cochläus — and it was his description that became normative for subsequent generations of Catholic scholars well into the twentieth century[9] — although Luther had been primarily responsible for the Peasants' War, when he began to sense that the peasants could impossibly win the war, he turned against them and went over to the side of the princes, calling on these in the most intemperate language to slay the insurgents as so many mad dogs. Then, while the princes wallowed in peasant blood and Luther's own prince, Frederick the Wise, was barely dead, Luther, in apparent unconcern for what was transpiring, married a runaway nun and indulged the sexual lusts he, as well as his wife, Catherine von Bora, had foresworn in their respective oaths of celibacy and chastity.[10]

---

[5] Ibid., pp. 176—177.

[6] *Erasmus,* Werke, vol. IV (Darmstadt, 1969), p. 241. Edited by Werner Welzig.

[7] See *Herte,* Die Lutherkommentare, p. 29 ff.

[8] *J. Janssen,* History of the German People at the close of the Middle Ages, vol. IV (New York, 1966), pp. 152—153. Translated from the German edition of 1876 by A. M. Christi.

[9] See *A. Herte,* Das katholische Lutherbild im Bann der Lutherkommentare des Cochläus, 3 vols. (Münster, 1943).

[10] Already in August of 1525, in response to Luther's "Wider die räuberischen ... Rotten der Bauern," Cochläus stated the following: "Ist es aber nit hochlich vnd hertzlich tzu erbarmen, das der stolz vnd trotzig munch, so er dz arm volck durch so vill bucher vnd mancherley anretzung tzu solchem auffrur vngeluck vnd verterben gebracht hat, nach dem er syhet, das die Bawrn vnterliegen, auff das er gnade fynde bey den Fursten, vbergibtt er nit allein leib vnd seel der armen vnd yemerlich verfurten Bawrn dem Teufel vnd ewigentodt, sonder schilt vnd schmehet auch die todten auff's aller vnerlichst. Vnd das man mag mercken vnd erkennen, das er in solchen iamer vnd blutvergiessen hertzliche freud habe, hat er in kurtz, do der iamer am grosten was, ein Jungs weib offentlich tzu der ee genomen, triumphyrt, vnd hochzeyt gehalten, das doch ist nit alleyn wider seyn geschworne eyd treuw vnd hulde, die er seiner Oberkeit vnd Got selbs gelobt vnd gethan hat, sonder auch wider gemeine ordnung der gantzenn Christenheit." Quoted in ibid., I, 178—179.

This Catholic image of Luther held its own well into the twentieth century. For, although such Catholic scholars as M. Dannenmayr, C. Schmalfus, and A. Michl began, in some respects, to take a less jaundiced view of Luther as a result of Enlightenment influences, a view which led to the recognition of positive religious characteristics in the Reformer on the part of nineteenth-century Catholic scholars like J. J. I. Döllinger, J. A. Möhler, and J. D. Allzog, the basic Catholic portrayal of Luther, particularly insofar as it pertained to the Peasants' War, changed little. But even these revisionistic tendencies in Germany were snuffed out by the growing confessional strife in the latter half of the nineteenth century and forced, particularly Döllinger, to retreat to the older, more uncompromising Catholic position, a position clearly manifested in the studies of Janssen, H. Denifle, and H. Grisar. A second revisionistic trend set in once again, however, at the turn of the century, beginning with the work of Sebastian Merkle and culminating in the magisterial study of the Reformation by Joseph Lortz. It was in the last study that the first substantial revisions in the Catholic image of Luther as it related to the Peasants' War were made.[11]

2. SIMILARITIES TO THE PEASANT PERSPECTIVE

The similarities between this interpretation and that of the peasants with regard to Luther's actions during the peasant uprising are striking although the value judgments, at least in the initial stages of Luther's supposed metamorphosis, are totally different. Like Cochläus, the peasants, too, believed Luther at first to be on their side. Their application of Luther's new theology to their social condition, as well as their appeal to him in connection with the justness of their cause, all point in this direction. According to Kurt Uhrig, Luther's teachings nourished the growing self-confidence of the German peasant in the early years of the Reformation and led him to view himself as *the* supporter of the Lutheran Reformation.[12] When, however, Luther turned against them in his "Wider die räuberischen ... Bauern," the peasants soon became disillusioned, and his ultimate support of the princes' cause seemed only to confirm what they had already begun

[11] On the Catholic historiography of Luther and the Reformation since Cochläus, see the folowing: *Herte, Das katholische Lutherbild; Hubert Jedin,* "Wandlungen des Lutherbildes in der katholischen Kirchengeschichtsschreibung," Wandlungen des Lutherbildes, ed. by *Karl Forster* (Würzburg, 1966), pp. 79—101; *Johannes Hessen,* Luther in katholischer Sicht, 2nd ed. (Bonn, 1967); and *Richard Stauffer,* Luther as seen by Catholics (Richmond, Virginia, 1967).
[12] *K. Uhrig,* "Der Bauer in der Publizistik der Reformation bis zum Ausgang des Bauernkrieges," ARG, XXXIII (1936), 70—125, and 165—225.

to suspect — that he had turned his back on them and left them to a desperate fate. It is obvious that many peasants now turned from Luther,[13] either submitting sullenly to the emerging Lutheran state church, espousing radical Anabaptist doctrines, or even returning, as in the case of Mühlhausen and some other regions, to the Catholic fold. As far as the peasants were concerned, therefore, although Luther at first seemed to favor their reform movement, he began to take on the appearance of a reactionary once the peasants attempted to implement his teachings in the temporal realm. They, too, argued that Luther must obviously have forseen the peasant defeat, and, before it was too late, gone over to the side of the victorious princes. What else then could Luther be in the eyes of the peasants but a revolutionary-turned-reactionary? The only difference between the peasant position and that of the Church was that whereas the Church rejected Luther and his seemingly revolutionary teachings because they appeared to undermine the established authorities in Church and State, the peasants welcomed and tried to implement them. Their view of Luther, therefore, was essentially the same as that of the Catholic Church.

3. MÜNTZER'S POLEMIC AGAINST LUTHER

The crucial polemical confrontation of the Reformation era with regard to the reform of late medieval Christendom, however, took place between Luther and Thomas Müntzer. Unlike the Church and the peasants, Müntzer did not accuse Luther of inciting to revolution and therefore would not have accused him of becoming a reactionary after the revolt, had be lived longer. For Müntzer, perhaps better than any of Luther's other contemporaries, understood the latter's position only too well and therefore rejected it.

It seems that Müntzer viewed himself as standing somewhere between the Catholic and Lutheran extremes from the very beginning, for already in his "Prague Manifesto" of November, 1521, he rejected both positions.[14] His own position vis-a-vis these two extremes is clarified particularly in two passages where he brings the Catholics and the Lutherans together: in his letter to Hans Zeiss of December 2, 1523, and in his "Protestation"

---

[13] See the famous letter of June 4, 1525, from Hermann Mühlpfort, Bürgermeister of Zwickau, to Stephan Roth of Wittenberg in which the former remarked: "Doctor Martinus ist pei dem gemeinen Volk und auch pei Gelarten und Ungelarten in grossen Abfall, achten sein Schreiben von sehr unbestendik." *Franz*, Quellen, p. 583. See also Luther's reply to Nicolas Amsdorf of May 30, 1525, where Luther stated: "Gratia et pax! Novam gloriam mihi nuntias, mi Amsdorfi, quod adulator Principum vocer, quales mihi glorias his annis Satan multas concitavit." WA, Briefe, 3, 517.

[14] Schriften und Briefe, p. 497.

of the following year. In these passages, Müntzer on the one hand rejects
the Catholic position because it has subverted the true faith by its emphasis upon ceremonies[15] and a pernicious concept of good works.[16] On the
other hand, he rejects the Lutheran position because it has done away with
even the right kind of good works.[17] The Lutheran teaching, he remarks
elsewhere, does not want to have anything to do with works and tends
completely to the freedom of the flesh.[18] It would appear, therefore, that
Müntzer's fundamental criticisms are based, once again, on his desire to
reform the Christendom of his day: the Catholics, who placed their trust
in ceremonies and the wrong kind of works, remained unconcerned about
the reformation of society, while the Lutherans, emphasizing faith to the
detriment of good works, freed the flesh to works of evil even more than
the Catholic teachings.

It is Müntzer's concern with the reformation of the society of his day,
therefore, which motivates most of his criticism of Luther and his teachings.[19] Luther, as we noted previously, although he may have broken with
the medieval concept of the *Corpus Christianum* theoretically, did not do
so on the practical level. His concept of the *ecclesiola in ecclesia,* expressed
in 1526, never ripened to maturity and he finally contented himself with a
Volkskirche in which the "wheat" and the "tares" were retained. It is this
attitude that Müntzer rejects already in his "Prague Manifesto" of 1521
where he proclaims that the time has come to separate the "wheat" from
the "tares," for the harvest is at hand. Only when such a separation has
taken place will the "new apostolic church" arise, first in Bohemia and
from there spread to the rest of Christendom.[20] But the classic passage in
which these ideas are elaborated is found in Müntzer's "Protestation." Here,
in his comparison of the "pure" apostolic church with the "corrupt" church
of his own day, he puts his finger, once again, squarely on the coexistence
of the "wheat" and the "tares" within the Church as the source of the

---

[15] "Protestation," ibid., pp. 229—230.

[16] Müntzer to Hans Zeiss, Dec. 2, 1523. Ibid., p. 398.

[17] "Wir alle mussen den fuzsstapfen Cristi nachfolgen, mit solchen gedangken gerustet
sein, do hilft kein glosse zu der menschen, die mit synlicher weisse die werkheiligen
uberwunden nach yhren bedunken, so die werlt nach hocher vergiftem glauben dan die
andern mit tolpelischen werken." Ibid.

[18] "Ir lere will gantz und gar nicht inss werck denn zur freyheyt des fleyschs."
"Ausgedrückte Entblössung," ibid., p. 306. See also Luther's remark in his letter to the
Saxon princes of July, 1524: "Denn sie halten (Gott lob) uns doch für ärgere Feinde
denn die Papisten." WA, 15, 215.

[19] See also Müntzer's remark concerning the end of the "fifth kingdom" and the
necessity of reform in Christendom in his "Fürstenpredigt." Schriften und Briefe, p. 255.

[20] Ibid., p. 504.

Church's corruption. It had been in order to avoid precisely such a situation that the early Church had admitted only mature men and women who had been given extensive instruction in the faith. As time went on, however, holy signs had come to supplant the inner as well as the outer reality of the faith.[21] This substitution of ceremonies for the reality of the Christian faith and action had led to the baptism of infants with the inevitable result that all Christians had become spiritual children. As a consequence, all semblance of reason had left the Church.[22] And because the Church had come to rely increasingly upon the ceremonies and pernicious works, God had blinded the German nation more than any other and had allowed it to espouse the greatest of errors. All of this had come about as the result of an "unvorstandener tawffe."[23]

It was this situation in the Catholic Church that Müntzer wanted to change, and when Luther's innovative theology failed to do so he turned against him as well. We have already noted that whereas he criticized the Roman Catholics for their reliance upon ceremonies and pernicious good works, he turned on the Lutherans because of their sola fideism. That mere faith was not enough, is one of his recurring themes: one had to become conformed to Christ in action as well.[24] The process by which the individual "elect" came to this conformity with Christ has a great deal of similarity to the way in which the "pure apostolic church" would be erected in society. One does not come easily to the Christian faith, he tells his readers in his "Protestation," as the "scribes" would have us believe. It takes much more than merely believing what Christ has said.

"Nein, lieber mensch, du must erdulden und wissen, wie dir Got selbern dein unkraut, disteln und dorner aus deinem fruchtbaren lande, das ist aus deinem hertzen, reutet ... Nim ein ebenbilde, wenn man sagt, Cristus hats alleine ausz-gericht, ist vil, vil zu kurtz. Wenn du das heubt mit den glidern nicht verfassest, wie mochtestu dann seinen fusztapffen nachfolgen?"[25]

Just as these evils must be uprooted in the human heart before faith can blossom, similarly — and the truth of this grows on Müntzer — those who hinder the elect from following God, the oppressive princes, the false Catholic and Lutheran prophets, must be uprooted from society before the elect of God can realize their potential and form the new apostolic church.

[21] "Protestation," ibid., pp. 227—228. [22] Ibid., p. 229. [23] Ibid., p. 230.
[24] "Von dem gedichteten Glauben," ibid., p. 224. "Protestation," ibid., p. 227: "... das die ausserwelten sollen und mussen christformig werden und mit mancherley leyden und zucht Gottis werck in achtung haben."
[25] "Protestation," ibid., pp. 233—234. See also his "Fürstenpredigt," ibid., pp. 250—252.

Those, therefore, and Luther is among them, who mislead the people into a false sense of security either in ceremonies, pernicious works, or salvation by faith alone, are hindering the creation of the new apostolic church. Luther, in particular, makes broad the narrow way leading to salvation[26] and takes away the restraints placed on the flesh.[27] In essence, Luther is really denying the power of God to change mankind.[28] At the same time, however, he also denies that man has a free will and, consequently, the power to change himself, thus leaving him in a hopeless dilemma.[29]

Aside from the personal aspect of salvation, Müntzer's major criticism of Luther has to do with the latter's conception of the prince's role in bringing about the reformation of society. Unlike Luther, Müntzer does not view the prince as belonging merely to the temporal realm. In his "Fürstenpredigt" he tells the Saxon princes that those who have told them that they are

"heydnische leuthe yres ampts halben, sie sollen nicht anders dann bürgerliche einigkeyt erhalten"

are making fools of them.[30] Their duty entails much more than this; Müntzer makes this amply apparent when he tells the princes that they need a new Daniel to lead them. This new Daniel is none other than Müntzer himself whose theology should be accepted by the princes as the only correct one. Their first duty, then, is to do away with those who are hindering the spread of his gospel, for it is they who are keeping the new apostolic church from coming into being.[31] Furthermore, should there still be some who will not accept Müntzer's teachings once this has been done, then the princes are forcefully to separate the "wheat" from the "tares." The princes are not, in the manner of Luther, to leave this to the power of God, for God will not do it without their swords. Nor does a godless man, who hinders that others hear the "true" gospel, have a right to live; such a man must die.[32] For the elect are a holy people who have the duty to destroy the godless — a command Christ did not rescind in the New Testament.[33]

Müntzer was obviously polemicizing directly and at times indirectly against Luther's view of the prince's obligations. According to the latter, it was the duty of the populace, with rare exceptions, to be obedient to the rulers ordained of God. The Christian had no right of rebellion even if the prince turned out to be a tyrant. Only God could judge the ruler.

[26] Ibid., p. 239.
[27] "Ausgedrückte Entblössung," ibid., p. 306.
[28] Ibid., pp. 268—269.
[29] "Hochverursachte Schutzrede," ibid., p. 339.
[30] "Fürstenpredigt," ibid., p. 257.
[31] Ibid., p. 258.
[32] Ibid., pp. 336—337.
[33] Ibid.

Furthermore, the princes belonged to the temporal realm where law and reason must prevail but where Christian teachings could not be used to justify legal, social, economic or other demands on either side. It would, of course, have pleased Luther had the "Christian" princes exercised their Christian principles in the temporal realm. If they did not, however, and Luther conceded that Christian princes were "rare birds," there was virtually nothing the populace could do about it except to suffer the consequences according to the ethics of the Sermon on the Mount and leave the punishment to God. It is at this point that Müntzer becomes most critical of Luther.

Particularly in his "Hochverursachte Schutzrede" Müntzer takes a strong exception to these teachings.

"Schäme dich, du ertzbube, wiltu mit der irrenden welt heuchlen zuflicken, Luce 9., und hast alle menschen wöllen rechtfertigen. Du waist aber wol, wen du solt lestern, die armen münch und pfaffen und kaufleüth können sich nit weren, darumb hast du sye wol zu schelten. Aber die gotlosen regenten soll nyemandt richten, ob sye schon Christum mit füssen treten. Dasz du aber den pawrn setigst, schreibst du, die fursten werden durch das wort Gotes zu scheytern gen, und sagest in deiner glosz uber das newlichiste kayserlich mandat: Die fürsten werden von dem stul gestossen. Du sichst sye auch an vor kaufflewth. Du soltest deyne fürsten auch bey der nasen rucken, sy habens woll vil höher dann villeicht dye andern verdienet, was lassen sye abgen? An iren zynsen und schynderei etc.? Doch das du die fürsten gescholten hast, kanstu sy wol wider muts machen, du newer pabst, schenckest in klöster und kirchen do sein sy mit dir zufryden. Ich rath dirs, der pawer möcht sonst zufallen."[34]

And somewhat later on he accuses Luther even more forcefully of ingratiating himself with the princes.

"Über deinem rhümen möchte einer woll endtschlaffen vor deiner unsynnigen torheyt. Dasz du zu Worms vorm Reich gestanden pist, danck hat der Teütsch adel, dem du das maul also wol bestrichen hast und hönig gegeben, dann er wenethe nit anderst, du würdest mit deinem predigen Beheymische geschenk geben, clöster und stifft, welche du ytzt den fürsten verheyssest. So du zu Worms hettest gewanckt, werest du ee erstochen vom adel worden, dann losz gegeben, weysz doch ein yeder. Du darffst warlich dir nit zuschreiben, du woltest dann noch ein mal dein edels blut, wie du dich rhümest, darumb wagen, du geprauchest doselbst mit den deinen wilder tück und lyste. Du liessest dich durch deinen rath gefangennemen und stellest dich gar unleydlich. Wer sich auff deyne schalckheyt nit verstünde, schwür woll zun heyligen, du wärest ein frümmer Mertin. Schlaff sanfft, liebes fleisch!"[35]

[34] Ibid.   [35] Ibid., p. 341.

It is apparent from these and other passages[36] that Müntzer believed Luther really to be on the side of the princes at least from the time of his confrontation with Charles V at the Diet of Worms. All his gestures of good will to the peasants had, therefore, to be construed as acts of duplicity. The implication that Luther's theology was the result of his desire to play "the new pope" thus comes to the fore in Müntzer's writings time and again.[37]

It may well be that Müntzer did not understand Luther's doctrine of the two realms; it is evident, however, that he saw its implications vividly enough. These he rejected, and he did so precisely because they did not fit into his pattern of the Kingdom of God on earth. In this latter society — once the "tares" were removed from the "wheat" — Christian equality should pertain, for Christ was to be its lord.[38] If, then, the princes "trampled on Christ with their feet" and hindered the spread of the "true" Christian faith, they themselves were to be uprooted by the people to whom power would be given. For the princes are not lords of the sword, but its servants, and therefore cannot do as they please: they are to administer justice.[39] The responsibility for an uprising, should it occur, would not lie with the peasants, but with the princes, for these had not been willing to put an end to their evil, unchristian practices.[40] Yet not even this is Müntzer's chief complaint against the princes. Because they are unwilling to stop oppressing the populace at large, the peasants did not have the time to learn to read, to study the Scriptures for themselves, thus allowing the "true" Christian teachings to take hold in their lives and usher in the new apostolic church. Therefore the princes are equally guilty with the Catholic and Lutheran theologians for the inability of the Kingdom of God to be established on earth. Consequently, a new Daniel must call for their destruction, a destruction which God wills, for the end times are upon us and God's historical dialectic means to usher in the new era whether man likes it or not.

4. THE FORMULATION OF THE LUTHERAN INTERPRETATION

Müntzer's execution at the hands of the princes on the 27th of May, 1525, coupled with the defeat of the peasant movement made it possible

---

[36] See Müntzer's letters to the Eisenacher, May 9, 1525, ibid., p. 463, and his letter to Graf Albrecht von Mansfeld, May 12, 1525, ibid., p. 469.

[37] See also "Hochverursachte Schutzrede," ibid., p. 340.

[38] See his letter to the Eisenacher, May 9, 1525. Ibid., p. 340.

[39] "Hochverursachte Schutzrede," ibid., pp. 328—329, as well as his letter to Hans Zeiss, July 22, 1524, ibid., p. 416.   [40] Ibid., p. 416.

for the victors to put the insurgents in an odious light and to write the history of the uprising in their own way and to their own advantage. For anyone, and there were some, who would defend the vanquished could certainly no longer do so openly. Furthermore, both Luther and Müntzer viewed the victory of the princes as a judgment of God — judgment for Müntzer and the insurgents and justification for Luther and the established authorities. Thus the history of the Peasants' War written by Luther, Melanchthon and their followers was colored both by the years of polemic between Luther and the radicals as well as by the confident Lutheran assumption that Müntzer's defeat was an act of God's judgment. And if an act of God's judgment, then Müntzer must have been working in opposition to God as he had been working in opposition to Luther. The peasant defeat of 1525, therefore, could only tend to confirm Luther's earlier suspicions of the radicals, suspicions which had begun with Melanchthon's letter to Luther at the Wartburg concerning the disconcerting theories of the Zwickau Prophets who had come to Wittenberg in December of 1521.

These initial suspicions, first expressed in Luther's reply to Melanchthon's letter to him at the Wartburg, written January 13, 1522, came more and more to be confirmed in Luther's mind as time went on. His letters to Spalatin of January 17, 1522, May 29, 1522, September 4, 1522, August 3, 1523, as well as those to Nicolas Hausmann of March 17, 1522, and Christoph Hofmann toward the end of 1522, manifest an increasing concern on the part of Luther over the teachings of the Saxon radicals and the trouble which might result from them. In his famous letter to the princes of Saxony of July, 1524, these fears are expressed in no uncertain terms. Luther, of course, saw the struggle in cosmic terms as the struggle between God and Satan. It was this setting which allowed him to see Müntzer's defeat as a victory of God over Satan, but already in the above letter to the Saxon princes it is strongly suggested that Müntzer is at least an unwitting tool in the satanic strategy, if not an outright willing one. Nevertheless, as long as the confrontation between himself and Müntzer remains a verbal one, no attempt should be made to restrain Müntzer, for in the cosmic struggle for the souls of men, some must fall, be injured and die, in order that the truth be known. If, however, the devil at Allstedt should, as he threatens to do, proceed to acts of insurrection, then the authorities must intervene.[41]

But within only one month Luther was already warning the Mühlhausen city fathers against Müntzer, for in the intervening period he had be-

[41] Luther to the princes of Saxony, July 1524. WA, 15, 210—214.

come convinced of the revolutionary potential of the latter's teachings. Müntzer, he remarked, was a false prophet, a wolf in sheep's clothing who was out to foment trouble. His actions in Zwickau and Allstedt had demonstrated what kind of tree he was for the fruit of it was murder, insurrection, and the spilling of blood. His spirit could not be the spirit of God.[42]

Whereas the Catholics accused Luther of fomenting the peasants' revolt, a charge which was given substance by the peasants' own interpretation of Luther's teachings and their subsequent appeal to him, Luther placed the blame for the peasant unrest on Müntzer and the *Mordpropheten*. The foundations for this accusation were laid in the above-mentioned letter to the princes of Saxony. Aside from arguing that Müntzer was the tool of satanic forces, Luther here accused him of attempting to establish an earthly kingdom, the very kind of kingdom that Christ, in the presence of Pilate, had rejected.[43] The social consequences of such a goal were quite clear to Luther.

"Ja wenn das recht were, das wyr Christen sollten kirchen brechen und so stürmen wie die Juden, So wollt auch hernach folgen, das wyr müsten leyblich tödten alle unchristen, gleych wie den Juden gepotten war, die Cananiter und Amoriter zu tödten, so hart, als die bilder zu brechen. Hie mit würde der Alstettisch geyst nichts mehr zuthun gewynnen denn blut vergissen, und wilche nicht seyne hymlische stym höreten, musten alle von yhm erwürget werden, das die ergernis nicht blieben ym volck Gottes, wilche viel grösser sind an den lebendigen unchristen denn an den hültzen und steynern bilde."[44]

The command to execute the Cananites had, however, Luther continued, been given to a nation chosen by God to be His people, a nation which God had delivered from Egyptian bondage amidst signs and wonders. Yet no such supernatural confirmation of Müntzer's election had been forthcoming. In spite of this, Müntzer had the audacity to expect everyone to believe in his election merely because he continually asserted it. But while asserting that election, he became increasingly involved in social revolution contrary to every command of Christ.[45]

---

[42] Luther to the city fathers of Mühlhausen, Aug. 21, 1524. WA, 15, 238—240.

[43] Luther to the princes of Saxony, July, 1524. WA, 15, 212.

[44] WA, 15, 220.

[45] WA, 15, 220. Luther restates this interpretation of Müntzer's ideological position and its kinship to the Old Testament in a number of passages after the revolt. We have already noted the classic reference to it in his commentary on the Sermon on the Mount. This is reiterated in a sermon of October 29, 1531: "Und hiemit leret er uns, das wir Christen uns solchs kriegs, so die welt furet und treibt, nichts uberall annemen sollen und nicht thun, wie unser Teuffels Propheten, Müntzer sampt seiner rotterey thaten,

It is during this critical period as well that Luther begins to link the teachings of the *Mordpropheten* in a causative way to the increasing social unrest amongst the peasants. As early as his letter to the princes of Saxony, where he argued that Müntzer's goal was the destruction of the established authority, Luther posed the ominous question:

"Was sollt der geyst wol anfahen, wenn er des pöfels anhang gewünne?"[46]

And only one month later he tells the Mühlhausen city fathers that Müntzer is sending messengers into the surrounding regions to win the populace over to his cause. These messengers do not enter by the front door, but move stealthily from place to place shunning the light of day and open confrontation as much as possible. They argue that all who hear and accept their teachings are God's elect, while those who reject them belong to the reprobate and deserve to die.[47]

The conviction that Müntzer, or at least men filled with his spirit, are at the bottom of the social unrest is first expressed in general terms in his "Ermahnung zum Frieden" written in response to the peasants' Twelve Articles. Here, addressing the peasants, Luther remarked:

"Der halben ist meyne freundliche bruderliche bitte lieben herrn vnd bruder, sehet ia zu mit vleis, was yhr macht vnd gleubt nicht allerley geysten (!) vnd predigern,

die das Regiment angriffen, Welchs gehört fleisch und blut untereinander zu, das ist: menschen gewalt, krefften und weisheit, herrschafft und regiment auf erden, Wir aber sollen gerust sein widder ander feinde den jrrdische, welche mit uns kempffen umb ein ander leben, reich, land und herrschafft, da es gilt ewig leben odder tod, himlisch reich odder hellisch fewr, ..." WA, 34, I, 386. Or again in a sermon of January 1, 1532: "Ideo *sol mans unterscheiden.* Quisque videat, quid sibi deus praeceperit x. Sic Muntzer fecit, qui legerat in Regum libris: David eduxit gladium et occidit impios, Iosua 31, hoc verbum habens fur zu et dicebat: et nos oportet Reges et principes x. quia David et patres, qui bellarunt in vetere testamento dederunt exemplum. Das *mangelt yhm,* quod verbum dei non recte discernebat." WA, 36, 11. This theme is sounded again in his commentary on Galatians, WA, 40, I, 118; his lectures on Genesis, WA, 42, 531; and his sermons on the Gospel of Matthew, WA, 47, 450 and 561, as well as his sermons of the year 1539, WA, 47, 794. An interesting comment on the Old Testament aspect of Müntzer's thought is also made by Johann Rühel in his letter to Luther of May 26, 1525, where he describes for Luther Müntzer's post-Frankenhausen confrontation with Philip of Hesse. ". . . Münzer hat das alte Testament gebraucht, der Landgraff aber sich des neuen gehalten, sein Neues Testament auch bey sich gehabt und darauss die sprüche wieder Münzern gelesen ..." WA, Briefe, 3, 571.

[46] WA, 15, 212.

[47] Luther to the city fathers of Mühlhausen, Aug. 21, 1524. WA, 15, 239. And in his commentary on Psalm 82 of 1530 he blamed the whole Peasants' War on this insidious propaganda. "Hette man den Müntzer, Carlstat und yhre gesellen nicht so lassen schleichen und kriechen ynn frembde heuser und kirchspiel, da hin sie niemand gesand, auch keinen befelh hatten, so were alles das grosse unglück [the Peasants' War] wol verblieben ..." WA, 31, I, 210.

Nach dem der leydige Satan itzt viel wilder rotten geyster vnd mordgeyster, vnter dem namen des Euangeli hat erweckt vnd damit die wellt erfullet."[48]

And somewhat further on:

"Da sehet, lieben freunde, was yhr fur prediger habt, wie sie ewre seele weynen, Ich sorge, es seyen etliche mordpropheten vnter euch komen, die durch euch gerne wollten herren ynn der wellt werden, darnach sie nu lengest gerungen haben, vnd fragen nicht darnach, das sie euch furen ynn fahr leybs, gutts, ehre vnd seele, beyde zeytlich vnd ewiglich."[49]

These general statements become much more specific after the outbreak of the Peasants' War, for in the interim Luther had become convinced that Müntzer and his ilk bore the sole responsibility for the uprising. Thus his statement to the princes in his "Wider die räuberischen ... Bauern:"

"Dabey man nu wol sihet, was sie ynn yhrem falschen synn gehabt haben, und das eyttel erlogen ding sey gewesen, was sie unter dem namen des Euangeli ynn den zwelff artickeln haben furgewendet, Kurtz umb, eyttel teuffels werck treyben sie, Und ynn sonderheyt ists der ertzteuffel, der zu Mölhusen regirt [Müntzer] und nichts denn raub, mord, blutvergissen anricht, wie denn Christus Johan. viij. von yhm sagt, das er sey eyn morder von anbegynn."[50]

Indeed, Luther's conviction that Müntzer was the archdemon who had fomented the entire peasants' revolt was so strong that he wrote to Johann Rühel on May 4, 1525, exclaiming:

"Dasz sie [the peasants] aber nicht Münzerisch sollten sein, das glaube ihnen ihr eigen Gott und sonst niemand."[51]

The peasants' resort to violence also convinced Luther that the former had in reality been hypocrites who had attempted to use the Word of God as a facade, an excuse behind which to hide their evil intentions. In his "Ermahnung zum Frieden" he warned them concerning this, saying:

"Darumb sage ich aber mal, Ich lasse ewr sachen seyn, wie gutt vnd recht sie seyn kan, weyl yhr sie aber selbs wollt verteydingen vnd nicht gewallt noch vnrecht leyden, mugt yhr thun vnd lassen, was euch gott nicht weret, Aber den Christlichen namen, den Christlichen namen sage ich, den lasst stehen, vnd macht den nicht zum schanddeckel, ewrs vngedultigem, vnfridlichem, vnchristlichem furnehmens."[52]

Then, once the fighting had broken out, he wrote in his "Wider die räuberischen ... Bauern:"

---

[48] WA, 18, 301.   [49] WA, 18, 308.   [50] WA, 18, 351.
[51] WA, Briefe, 3, 482.   [52] WA, 18, 314.

"Zum dritten, das sie [the peasants] solche schreckliche, grewliche sunde mit dem Euangelio decken, nennen sich Christliche bruder, nemen eyd und hulde und zwingen die leutte, zu solchen greweln mit yhnen zu halten, da mit sie die aller grosten Gottslesterer und schender seynes heyligen namen werden und ehren und dienen also dem teuffel unter dem scheyn des Euangelij, daran sie wol zehen mal den tod verdienen an leib und seele."[53]

Equally, if not more momentous than the peasants' resort to violence for Luther's interpretation of Müntzer and the peasants was their defeat which Luther regarded as a sign that God had vindicated his cause.[54] His earlier assumptions concerning Müntzer had been proven correct; it was not God's spirit that had spoken through Müntzer, but the spirit of sedition and revolt, the spirit of self-glorification, the spirit of Satan. Where, now, were all of Müntzer's boasts, his confident assumption that he and his followers constituted God's people and that God therefore would do battle for them? Where all the boasts he had hurled in Luther's and the princes' faces during the past year? If anyone who had witnessed the defeat of Müntzer and the peasants did not see an open and apparent judgment of God in this event and turn from his seditious ways as a result, he was beyond redemption. Nevertheless, let this event be a warning to those who have eyes that they may cease and desist from similar revolutionary intentions lest they too come under the judgment of God. Let them recognize that anyone who advocates the establishment of a kingdom of God on earth by revolutionary means is nothing but a false prophet whose teachings are to be rejected.[55]

Obviously, Luther understood Müntzer's ideological position and the consequences deriving from it prior to the Peasants' War, but he remained somewhat undecided precisely what to do about it. He recognized the similarities Müntzer's views had with the Old Testament Jewish concept of the Kingdom of God on earth, but he argued that Christ had rejected that concept. Nevertheless, Luther did posit one condition under which even he might be persuaded to accept Müntzer's and the peasants' position. Writing in his letter to the princes of Saxony, Luther remarked that God

[53] WA, 18, 358.

[54] See his letter to Johann Rühel of May 23, 1525, in which he makes the following comment on the peasants' defeat: "Es ist Gottes vrteyl: Qui accipit gladium, gladio peribit. Das ist trostlich, das der geyst an den Tag komen ist, damit hynfurt die bauren wissen wie vnrecht sie haben, und villeicht yhr Rotterei lassen odder weniger werden." WA, Briefe, 3, 507—508. See also the opening sentences to Luther's "Eine schreckliche Geschichte und ein Gericht Gottes über Thomas Müntzer." WA, 18, 367.

[55] "Eine schreckliche Geschichte," WA, 18, 373.

had confirmed His choice of the Hebrew people by manifest signs and wonders;

"Aber diser geyst hat noch nicht beweyset, das da Gottes volck sey, mit eynigem wunder, da zu rottet er sich selbs, als sey er alleyn Gottes volck, und feret zu on ordenlich gewallt von Gott verordenet und on Gottes gepott, und will seynem geyst gegleubt haben."[56]

He says nearly the same thing to the peasants in his "Ermahnung zum Frieden:"

"Sollt yhr nu bestehen mit ewrem furnemen, vnd habt doch beyde gottlich vnd Christlich recht ym newen vnd allten testament, auch das naturliche recht, widder euch, so musset yhr eynen newen sonderlichen befehl von Gott auff bringen, mit zeichen vnd wunder bestettiget, der euch solchs zuthün macht gebe vnd heysse."[57]

Neither Müntzer nor the peasants, however, produced any such signs and wonders, although after the war Luther asserted that Müntzer had boasted he would catch all the bullets of his enemies in the sleeve of his coat.[58] Yet Luther believed a sign from heaven had been given — the peasant defeat — which convinced at least him that God could impossibly have been on the side of Müntzer and the peasants.

The peasants' resort to revolution, then, coupled with their defeat at the hands of the princes convinced Luther of the rightness of his cause. His view that the affairs of men were directed by God left him little alternative but to espouse this position. Indeed, it is a position that Müntzer would undoubtedly have taken had his forces been victorious. In the preface to his "Eine schreckliche Geschichte," therefore, Luther could vent an exulting cry of vindication:

"Gnad und fride. Diss offenbarlich gericht des ewigen Gottes und schrecklich geschicht, so er hatt lassen gehen uber und widder die lere und schrifft und rotten Thomas Muntzer, des mördischen und blut gyrigen propheten, hab ich lassen ausgehen, zu warnen, zu schrecken, zu vermanen alle die ienigen, so itzt auffrur und unfrid treiben und zu trost und stercke aller der, so solchen iamer sehen und leyden mussen, auff das sie greyffen und fülen, wie Gott die rottengeyster und auffrürer verdampt und willens ist, mit zorn zu straffen, Denn hie sihestu, wie disser mordgeyst sich rhümet, Gott rede und wircke durch sie und sey seyn Göttlicher wille und thut, als sey es alles gewonnen mit yhm, Und ehe er sich umbsiehet, ligt er mit ettlich tausent ym drecke. Hette Gott aber durch yhn geredt, solchs were nicht geschehen, Denn Gott leuget nicht, sondern hellt fest uber seym

---

[56] WA, 15, 220.   [57] WA, 18, 304.   [58] "Eine schreckliche Geschichte," WA, 18, 373.

wort, Nu aber Thomas Muntzer feylet, ists am tage, das er under Gottes namen durch den teuffel geredt und gefaren hat."[59]

It is this mood of confidence, that God has vindicated their cause, that is largely responsible for the tone of the broadside attributed to Melanchthon which played such a determining role in the interpretation of those tumultuous times down to the time of the French Revolution, *Die Historia Thomä Müntzers, des Anfängers der Thüringischen Aufruhr, sehr nützlich zu lesen*.[60] The author must obviously have been a close associate of Luther's, for all the strands of Luther's arguments are woven into a coherent whole, and all his suspicions accepted as confirmed by what is taken to be God's judgment of the peasant cause. The defeat of the peasants, therefore, by confirming all of Luther's latent suspicions about Müntzer and the peasants, plays as crucial a role in determining the ultimate Lutheran interpretation of these events as it played in determining the Catholic interpretation of Luther which also emerged immediately after the Peasants' War had run its course.

Aside from Luther's writings on Müntzer, which were apparently widely circulated,[61] and various tracts and letters of Müntzer himself, the author of the above pamphlet must also have had access to Müntzer's confession, or at least have had first hand information about it. This information quite probably came to him via Luther who was kept informed by Johann Rühel. Besides providing Luther with a detailed account of Müntzer's last days in his letter of May 26, 1525, Rühel stated:

"Schicke euch hierinne Thomas Münzers Bekantnusz, so er zu Heldrungen gethan, Darzu copie der schrifft ausz seinem gefängnusz an die von Mühlhausen."[62]

We need not here go into the details of Melanchthon's delineation of Müntzer as given in the *Historia*. Suffice it to say that Müntzer was portrayed as a fanatic possessed of an evil spirit who had fomented the Peasants' War. But it did not stop here. Müntzer was further depicted as the advocate of a form of communism which he was plotting to establish by means of professional revolutionaries sworn to do his bidding. His goal was the egalitarian communistic Kingdom of God on earth which would be inaugurated shortly.

[59] WA, 18, 367.
[60] *Luther*, Sämtliche Schriften, XVI, 160—173.
[61] For example, a certain Joachim Ruwe wrote to Herzog Ernst von Braunschweig on June 20, 1525: "Ich schicke I. F. G. ock [...] de bekanntnisse Thomas Munters und wes Martinus darup geschreven, wes ock Munter in seiner fengnisse an de van Molhusen geschreven." Akten zur Geschichte des Bauernkrieges in Mitteldeutschland, ed. by O. *Merx*, G. *Franz*, and W. P. *Fuchs* (Jena, 1942), II, 497. (Hereafter cited as *Fuchs*, Akten des Bauernkrieges.)   [62] WA, Briefe, 3, 510.

Luther and Melanchthon's view of Müntzer undoubtedly also colored
their evaluation of Anabaptism.[63] Luther's view can be gleaned from three
of his writings against the Anabaptists: his "Sendbrief wider etliche Rottengeister," "Vorrede auf Justus Menius Buch 'Vom Geist der Widertäu-
fer,'" and his "Kurzes Bekenntnis vom heiligen Sacrament wider die
Schwärmer."[64] The closest he comes to tracing the origin of Anabaptism
is in his "Sendbrief." Here he lumps all the various radical groups under
one category. Two characteristics, he asserts, are manifested by all of them:
they all glory in the possession of the Spirit, and all despise the sacraments.
Manifested first by Thomas Müntzer, these characteristics are common to
all *Schwärmer* and *Rottengeister*. Nor is there any difference between the
spirit of Anabaptism and these other radicals, for he remarks that it is
true that the spirit of Anabaptism is one with the spirit of the Enthusiasts.
In fact, this is also the spirit of the Zwinglians, for, no matter how loudly
Zwingli might contend that he is an enemy of Anabaptism, the fact remains that with regard to baptism and the sacraments, the same spirit
resides in both parties. In the final analysis, however, the entire lot comes
directly from the devil who is constantly seeking to undermine God's Word.
And in his "Bekenntnis" he lists all those affected by this heresy: the
Enthusiasts and enemies of the sacraments, Carlstadt, Zwingli, Oecolam-
padius, Schwenkfeld, and all Zwingli's followers in Zurich.

Melanchthon had a somewhat different criterion by which he judged
who was to be categorized as an Anabaptist, but on the problem of their
origin he was in agreement with Luther. His great concern was with sedition and insurrection, and it was this he focused upon.

"Habent autem Anabaptistae multas alias notas, quibus declarant, quo Spiritu
agantur . . . Est et hoc dogma impium, quod exigunt, ut Christiani conferant totas
facultates in commune, de qua re obiter hic dicemus. Est enim et hoc dogma de
communicandis facultatibus una inter seditionum faces, quas fanatici isti spargunt
in vulgus. Ego non minus pro seditiosis habendos censeo, qui publicas et receptas
leges de rerum divisione improbant, quam illos qui prorsus negant fas esse Chri-
stiano gerere magistratus."[65]

The above was written in 1528 and makes obvious allusions to his *Historia* where Müntzer was portrayed as the revolutionary who used the

---

[63] For a fuller treatment of their view, see *J. S.* Oyer, "The Writings of Luther against
the Anabaptists," MQR, XXVII (1953), 1, 100—110, and *Oyer*, "The Writings of
Melanchthon against the Anabaptists," ibid., XXVI (1952), 4, 259—279.

[64] See *Oyer*, "The Writings of Luther against the Anabaptists,," pp. 100—110.

[65] *P. Melanchthon* "Adversus Anabaptistas Indicum," Melanchthons Werke, *R. Stup-
perich*, ed., I (Gütersloh, 1951), 291.

communistic ideal to incite the masses to revolt. A definite link therefore
existed between Müntzer and the Anabaptists. When the Anabaptists drove
out the ruling powers in the city of Münster in 1534 and set up the revolutionary "New Jerusalem," Melanchthon was only confirmed in his suspicions.

Already in a letter to Myconius of February, 1530, Melanchthon had
noted that the entire species of Anabaptists owed its origins to Storch and
his followers.[66] In the final analysis, all Anabaptists were the same, for,

"etiam qui minimum habent vitii, tamen aliquam partem civilium officiorum
improbant."[67]

Their piety he considered a mere sham, for, given the opportunity, they
would invariably show their true colors as the group at Münster had.[68]
John Oyer therefore concluded that Melanchthon had

"viewed Anabaptism as one long line of aberration from true Christianity. The
sporadic outbursts of the Münster Kingdom and the Müntzer led Peasants' War
were to be expected when false teachings were afoot."[69]

There is, then, little to choose between Luther and Melanchthon on the
problem of the origin of Anabaptism. Both see it beginning with the
Schwärmer and proceeding in a direct line from Müntzer, Carlstadt,
Zwingli, Münster, to the Anabaptists. Whereas Luther later differentiated
between the pacifistic and revolutionary Anabaptists,[70] Melanchthon always felt that the one was as bad as the other, and, given the opportunity,
even the peaceful Anabaptists would erupt in another Münster. For, had
not the Münsterites at first paraded as peaceful Anabaptists?

5. BULLINGER'S CONTRIBUTION

The second focal point of conflict was in Zurich between the Zwinglians
and the Anabaptists, or the Swiss Brethren, as Harold S. Bender has
termed them.[71] Zwingli had little to say about the origins of Anabaptism,
for he knew that they had come out of his own camp. He did have the
dubious good fortune, however, of being followed by Heinrich Bullinger,
who was not only his spiritual successor, but also his son-in-law, and it
was Bullinger who created the most influential and lasting theory regarding
the origins of Anabaptism.

---

[66] Corpus Reformatorum Melanchtonis Opera, *C. G. Bretschneider*, ed., II (Halis,
Saxonum, 1835), 17.　　　[67] Ibid.
[68] Melanchthon, "Verlegung etlicher unchristlicher Artikel, welche die Wiedertäufer
vorgeben," Sämmtliche Schriften, XX, 1709.　[69] Oyer, "Melanchthon," p. 277.
[70] *Oyer*, "Luther," p. 108.　　　[71] *H. S. Bender*, Conrad Grebel (Goshen, 1950).

In his earlier works, there is no indication of Bullinger's later theory concerning the origins of Anabaptism, but by 1560 it had been developed and explicitly stated in his *Der Widertöufferen vrsprung, fürgang, Secten, etc.*[72] But perhaps his most succinct statement of the theory appears in his *Reformationsgeschichte.*

"Von anfang der Töuffery und Töufferen hab ich wytlöuffig geschrieben in meinem ersten getruckten Buch wider Töuffery. Dorumm ich hie nu kurtze verzeichnis thun wil. Daniden in Saxen, an der Saal, entstundet ettlich unrüwige geister imm Jar Christi 1521 und 1522. Under welchen die fürnemmen warend Nicklass Storck, der pfyffer, Melchior Ringg, und Thomas Müntzer. Da aber hieuor in dieser history gemeldet, wie sich Müntzer, hie offhin in dise Landts art gethan, und da zu imm Grebel, Mantz und andere unrüwige geister kummen, und den widertouff, usz dem Müntzer gesogen haben. Den habend sy ouch Zurich angelhept zu tryben und leeren."[73]

Thus Bullinger accepted but made more explicit the theory concerning the origins of Anabaptism which Luther, and particularly Melanchthon, had formulated earlier.

Bullinger's purpose was to vindicate Zwingli and Zurich, for with the spread of the Lutheran notion that the Reformed Church was in essence just another branch of the radical tendencies derived from the Zwickau Prophets, Bullinger had become increasingly irritated and had begun to look for an avenue of escape. Eventually some of the writings of Melanchthon, in which the latter traced the origins of Anabaptism to the Zwickau Prophets and Müntzer, came into his hands. Here was the theory he had sought; it would remove the stigma from Zurich and place it back into the Lutheran camp where Melanchthon himself had found it.[74] The Reformed Church could then pose as the church which had fought the accursed Anabaptist heresy from the very beginning, a heresy brought into Switzerland by Thomas Müntzer, the arch-heretic himself, and espoused there by Grebel and Mantz out of spite to Zwingli because he had denied them the chairs in Greek and Hebrew respectively in his school.[75]

6. SEBASTIAN FRANCK'S DISSENTING ASSESSMENT

Not everyone accepted this theory, however, for already in 1536 Sebastian Franck had presented a more cautious appraisal. He argued that the Anabaptists had arisen "gleich in vnd nach der auffrur der bauren."[76] Nor

---

[72] H. *Fast*, Heinrich Bullinger und die Täufer (Weierhof, Pfalz, 1959), pp. 89—132.

[73] H. *Bullinger*, Reformationsgeschichte (Frauenfeld, 1838), p. 237.

[74] *Fast*, Bullinger und die Täufer, pp. 92—98.

[75] *Bullinger*, Reformationsgeschichte, pp. 237—238.   [76] *Franck*, Chronica, p. cxciiij.

did he consider them to be Spiritualists, Luther's criterion for lumping them all together. Rather, he remarked that they had grown out of a new biblical literalism. And, although he bemoaned their eccentricities and innumerable divisions, he stated categorically that

"Ich bsorgt mich vor keim volck weniger einer auffrur / wann ich Bapst / Keyser vnd der Türck selbs wer dann vor disem."[77]

There was one exception he pointed to, however, and that was Hans Hut.

"Alleyn in Johanne Hutten etwan jrem vorsteher ist ein buchstabischer eifer gewesen / der hat ausz Mose vnd den Propheten genummen / vnd gmeynt sy werden wie Israel als Gotteskinder die Gottlosen auszreüten müssen / ab er nit ehe dann sy Gott darzu fordere vnd anschicke."[78]

But, Franck continued, few followed Hut in this regard; rather, they nearly universally condemned his opinion as erroneous, for they argued that the Old Covenant had been superseded by the New Covenant of Christ. Therefore, Old Testament examples like Moses were no longer relevant. As a matter of fact, Franck remarked, they took the New Testament so literally that they refused to swear an oath or go to war.[79]

Franck, however, was somewhat vague as to their relationship to Müntzer. Early in his section dealing with the Anabaptists he named the following as their leaders: Balthasar Hubmaier, Melchior Rinck, Hans Hut, Hans Denck, and Ludwig Hätzer. Müntzer's name was conspicuously absent.[80] He mentioned Müntzer only once in this part of his study, and that in the following context:

"Etlich halten vil auff die schrifft / als auff Gottes wort / fussen nur zuuil auff den buchstaben / tragen bücher mit jnen wa sy gehn vnd stehn. Dargegen sagen die anderen / weil wir bücher haben / so sei noch kein Christus vorhanden. Dise halten auch nit vil auff alle eusser predig vnd schrifft / meynen wir müssen all on mittel von Gott gelert werden. Auch dz die schrifft nit Gotts wort sey / vnd man on dise wol gleübig vnd selig werden mög. Sihe Joan. Denck artickel / Item Ludwig Hetzers / Thome Müntzers, etc."[81]

Nevertheless, he argued, in another context, that the Anabaptists attempted to excuse Müntzer's participation in the Peasants' War with the argument that he had been forced into that situation. They considered Müntzer, he continued, a God-fearing man who had tried to stop his followers from rebellion.[82] And, indeed, Müntzer was still supposed to have

[77] Ibid., p. cxcviij.   [78] Ibid.
[79] Ibid., p. cxcix.   [80] Ibid., p. cxciij.   [81] Ibid., p. cxcv.   [82] Ibid., p. clxxxviij.

a large following of secret adherents in Thuringia, but these were not Anabaptists. Nor had Müntzer ever baptized, although he had rejected infant
baptism and preached adult baptism. Perhaps he died too soon to have
instituted adult baptism, Franck concluded.[83]

7. THE POSITION OF THE ANABAPTISTS

What about the Anabaptists themselves? How did they see their relationship to Müntzer and Münster? Neither in the *Hutterite Chronicle*[84] nor in
the writings of Menno Simons[85] is there any mention made of Müntzer
or the Zwickau Prophets. On the other hand, neither do the names of
Grebel and Mantz come up in the writings of Menno Simons. They do
loom large in the *Hutterite Chronicle*, however, where Grebel and Mantz
are revered as the spiritual fathers of the Hutterites.[86] The group which
both the *Chronicle* as well as Menno Simons repudiate with some vehe-
mence are the Münsterite Anabaptists.

The Hutterites had their own view of where these fanatics came from,
for, although the two preachers who had come to Münster first had been
Lutherans, and Jan van Leyden, who had joined them later, had been a
Dutchman who had taught and practised adult baptism, the Münster debacle had been the work of the devil.[87] Later, after they had been accused
of being kindred spirits of the Münsterites, the *Chronicle* came up with
an emphatic denial.[88] There were no similarities between themselves and
those of Münster.

Menno Simons, of course, was caught in the very midst of the Münster
scandal. And though he wrote, in his first tract against "The Blasphemy
of John of Leiden" (1535) just shortly after his conversion, that Leyden
had been a "false teacher (who) desert(ed) the pure doctrine of Christ
and beg(an) to trafic in strange doctrine,"[89] no one believed his disclaimers.
Throughout his life, therefore, Menno was concerned to remove the stigma
of the Münster uprising from the Anabaptist name. Thus, time and again,
and especially in his 1552 "Reply to False Accusations," he confronted
his accusers.

We do not like to reprove and judge those who are already reproved and judged
of God and man; yet since we are assailed so fiercely with this matter and without basis in truth, therefore we would say this much in defense of all of us —

[83] Ibid.
[84] *R. Wolkan*, ed., Geschichtsbuch der Hutterischen Brüder (Wien, 1923).
[85] *M. Simons,* Complete Works (Scottsdale, Penn., 1956), edited by *J. C. Wenger.*
[86] *Wolkan,* Geschichtsbuch, pp. 34—36.   [87] Ibid., pp. 107—108.
[88] Ibid., p. 407.   [89] *M. Simons,* Complete Writings, p. 33.

that we consider the doctrine and practice of those of Münster in regard to king, sword, rebellion, retaliation, vengeance, polygamy, and the visible kingdom of Christ on earth a new Judaism and a seductive error, doctrine and abomination, far removed from the Spirit, Word and example of Christ. Behold, in Christ Jesus we lie not.[90]

The stress on the New Testament is clearly apparent here, as it was in Franck's description, and the attempt to establish the Kingdom of God on earth labelled as a "new Judaism and a seductive error." Therefore, Menno Simon's view of Münster, too, was determined by his rejection of the Old Testament paradigm of the perfect Christian society.

The voices of the peaceful Anabaptists were drowned out in the general turmoil of the period and its resulting repression, however. After all, their protestations of peace were but a shameful cover-up. Nor did they have any lasting base from which to propagate their views. As a result, the views of Luther and Melanchthon, especially as modified by Bullinger, came to carry the day. For the interpretation of Müntzer, Melanchthon's *Historia* became normative, while for an interpretation of Anabaptism, it was Bullinger's *Wiedertöufferen Ursprung* that played this role.[91]

[90] Ibid., p. 547.
[91] For a Marxist perspective on the subsequent "Lutheran" interpretation of Müntzer, see *Max Steinmetz.* "Das Müntzerbild in der Geschichtsschreibung von Luther und Melanchthon bis zum Ausbruch der französischen Revolution," Habilitationsschrift, University of Jena, 1956.

PART II: THE MARXIST INTERPRETATION

CHAPTER V

ZIMMERMANN'S INTELLECTUAL FRAME OF REFERENCE

1. ZIMMERMANN AND THE JOACHIST TRADITION

It would be alien to the purpose of this study to pursue the interpretation of the Reformation which resulted from Luther's, Melanchthon's, and Bullinger's views of the events described above any farther, for although these views certainly carried the day and came to be incorporated in the Protestant tradition, it is not this tradition that the Marxists have chosen to follow. Indeed, since Luther's theory of the separation of the two realms was primarily responsible for his, Melanchthon's, and the subsequent Protestant interpretation of the Peasants' War as it related to the broader question of reform, Marx, who most certainly did not share this view with Luther, could not have accepted the interpretation of events which resulted from it either. It was only when he and Engels found a study which interpreted the Peasants' War from the perspective of a paradigm similar to the concept of Müntzer's Kingdom of God on earth that they could formulate their own interpretation. Such a study was Zimmermann's history of the German Peasants' War. Therefore it is much more important for our study that we seek to understand the paradigm that determined Zimmermann's interpretation than that we trace the historiography of the Reformation from Luther to Zimmermann. This paradigm, which had been present since the days of Joachim of Fiore, but which, from its very inception, had been under the shadow of heresy, passed through a process of secularization by the time it emerged in Hegel and the Young Hegelians.

In the introduction to his *Studien über Joachim von Fiore*, Herbert Grundmann noted that Alois Dempf had, in 1925, called for an investigation into

"das stille Weiterwirken des Evangeliums aeternum [of Joachim] vom dritten Reich ... bis Hegel."[1]

---

[1] *Grundmann,* Joachim von Fiore, p. 6, note 1.

Although Grundmann approved of the idea and made some references to such a continuity in his own study, he still believed that, given the present (1927) state of Joachite scholarship, it was too early to attempt an investigation of this magnitude. Zimmermann, writing some eighty years earlier, was totally uninhibited by any such caution and in a few bold strokes sketched the outlines of precisely this development from the medieval mystics to Hegel, under whose influence he himself wrote.

"Die philosophischen Bestrebungen dieser Zeit," he remarked in his *Geschichte der deutschen Nationalliteratur* dedicated to Gervinus, "sind freilich noch weit zurück, wenn auch verhältnismäßig nicht so weit als die geschichtlichen. Das erstere sieht man schon daraus, daß es die Mystiker sind, welche man die Erzväter der deutschen Spekulation genannt hat und nennen muß, denn auf diese Mystiker laufen die Anfänge einer selbständigen, in deutschem Boden wurzelnden Philosophie zurück."[2]

He justified the above statment by drawing attention especially to three German thinkers and briefly elucidating their importance for this philosophical tradition: Tauler, Böhme, and Johann Albrecht Bengel. Of Tauler he remarked:

"Dieser geistvolle Mönch hat nicht nur in seiner Zelle Wahres und Hohes geschaut. und die Reinigung und Erleuchtung des Geistes als den Weg zur Vereinigung des Menschen mit Gott gepredigt, also eine geläuterte Religion angebahnt; sondern er ist auch als Redner und Sprachschöpfer für deutsches Geistesleben bedeutend."[3]

Böhme he called "der sogenannte deutsche Philosoph" and drew attention particularly to the pantheistic aspects of his thought.

"Schon da er als Knabe das Vieh hütete, ging in seiner Seele der Gedanke auf an die innige Verbindung zwischen Natur und Gott, er hatte Gesichte, und versenkte sich tief in das Göttliche."[4]

He then proceeded to relate Böhme's importance for the philosophy of his own day.

"Aber die neueste Zeit hat ihn [Böhme] zu Ehren gebracht. Deutschlands größte Weltweise haben bekannt, daß sie dem Schuster manchen Blick in die Natur und in die götlichen Dinge abgelernt haben, und sie haben in der That noch mehr von ihm gelernt und herübergenommen, als sie sagen, besonders Schelling."[5]

This union of God and man Zimmermann saw combined with a "modern" view of history by Johann Albrecht Bengel in the early eighteenth century. Although Bengel's vision had been somewhat clouded,

---

[2] W. *Zimmermann*, Geschichte der prosaischen und poetischen deutschen Nationalliteratur (Stuttgart, 1846), p. 94.   [3] Ibid., p. 95.   [4] Ibid., p. 129.   [5] Ibid., p. 130.

"so hat er doch vieles von dem Geist seiner Zeit und vieles von dem Verlauf des folgenden Jahrhunderts richtig angeschaut und vorausgeschaut. Und was Andere aus der Erkenntnis der Weltgeschichte [Hegel?], welche ja selbst die fortwährende Offenbarung Gottes ist, erkannten und erkennen: das machte er sich klar an dem geschriebenen Worte der Offenbarung, das ihm die Ahnungen seines Geistes wiederspiegelte."[6]

Bengel had proclaimed, Zimmermann continued, that the more the Spirit revealed itself on earth,

"desto mehr werde das römische Pabstthum gedemüthigt werden, und die Könige, die sich dadurch nicht warnen, sondern sich noch immer 'von dem Thier und dem falschen Propheten' (dem Pabstthum und der jesuitischen Politik) verführen lassen, werden im Kampfe mit Christus, d. h. dem wahren Geiste des Christenthums untergehen."[7]

The final outcome of this process would be that

"das nach Ausscheidung des Zeitlichen bleibende Ewige des Christenthums, das ewige Evangelium, ein heiterer, heiliger, einträchtiger Gottesdienst; es werden seyn gesunde, fruchtbare, friedliche Zeiten, eine überschwengliche Fülle des Geistes; noch wird es Regenten und Obrigkeiten geben, aber sie werden mit den Regierten als mit ihren Brüdern umgehen, und Alles, was menschlicher Vorwitz, Pracht und Schwelgerei daneben eingeführt haben, wird nicht mehr seyn."[8]

Had this not been a study of German literature, Zimmermann would undoubtedly also have included, indeed begun, his lineage with Joachim of Fiore, for it was he, Zimmermann argued in his *Bauernkrieg*, who had exercised the greatest influence on Thomas Müntzer. In this study, written just prior to his history of German literature, Zimmermann remarked that Müntzer, after he had become alienated from the theology, indeed from the very Christianity of his time, had steeped himself in medieval mysticism.

"Werke von Mystikern des Mittelalters waren es, die jetzt seinem Verstand und Herzen die meiste Nahrung boten. Vorzüglich waren es Geschichten von Männern und Frauen, die sich göttlicher Gesichte und Unterredungen rühmten, oder denen sie nachgerühmt wurden; am unverkennbarsten übte der Calabrese Abt Joachim, der Prophet des zwölften Jahrhunderts Einfluss auf ihn (Vom getichten Glauben)."[9]

It was not the visions that Zimmermann stressed as having been important for Müntzer, however; rather it was Joachim's theology of history.

---

[6] Ibid., p. 320.   [7] Ibid.   [8] Ibid., p. 321.
[9] *Zimmermann*, Bauernkrieg, I (1841—1843), 55.

"Es werde das Zeitalter des Geistes kommen, und mit ihm die Liebe, die Freude und die Freiheit, alle Buchstabengelehrsamkeit werde untergehen und der Geist frei hervortreten aus der Hülle des Buchstabens, seine Form etwas Vergängliches, Vorübergehendes, das Evangelium des Geistes sei das ewige Evangelium. Mit diesem werde die Verheissung des Herrn in Erfüllung gehen, dass er noch Vieles zu verkündigen habe, was die Menschen seiner Zeit noch nicht fassen konnten, und dass der Geist ihnen diess einst verkünden und sie in alle Wahrheit leiten werde. Dann werde eine Gemeinschaft von Brüdern auf Erden seyn, von Spiritualen, Söhnen des Geistes, denen die heilige Schrift nach ihrem geistlichen Sinne das lebendige Wasser sei, jene Schrift, die nicht mit Tinte und Feder auf Papier geschrieben worden, sondern durch die Kraft des heiligen Geistes in dem Buche des menschlichen Herzens. Die Organe, durch welche bisher das Göttliche den Menschen nahe gebracht worden sei, Priester und Lehrstand werden aufhören, die Söhne des Geistes bedürfen einer solchen Vermittlung nicht mehr, der Geist werde ihr Lehrer seyn, die innere Offenbarung die Stelle der äusserlichen Autorität vertreten, die Religion eine rein innerliche, eine unvermittelte Gottesanschauung seyn, alle Mysterien ganz offenbar, und die Weissagung des Propheten Jeremias (31, 33, 34) erfüllt, dass Gott selbst der Lehrer aller sein, und allen sein Gesetz in ihr Herz schreiben wolle; sich offenbare, werde alle irdische Hohheit zu Schanden werden."[10]

It is quite apparent that three aspects of this intellectual tradition are stressed by Zimmermann: first, that history is progressive, more specifically the progressive revelation of God; secondly, that there is the possibility of a union of God and man; and, thirdly, putting the first two together, that as history progresses, and it progresses because God and man draw ever closer together, there is the possibility, no, more than that, the certainty and inevitability of the perfect society on earth — the Kingdom of God itself.

2. THE INFLUENCE OF FERDINAND CHRISTIAN BAUR

Were Zimmermann's views of history as well-known as those of Marx and Engels, it would be unnecessary to discuss them here. This is not the case, however, for in spite of the fact that his history of the Peasants' War has frequently been republished (and that as late as 1952) and more often cited, few scholars have attempted to penetrate the mind behind the history itself. Hence, the attention Zimmermann has received, such as it is, has been devoted primarily to a discussion of his history of the Peasants'

[10] Ibid.

War.[11] But this, undoubtedly his most influential piece of work, and the one that shall hold our attention here as well for the simple reason that Engels depended solely upon it for his own study, cannot be understood in isolation; it must be seen within the context of his total activity. For history is not merely the story of man; rather it is the story of man as related by himself. This adds a certain dynamic to history, but also a fallible human element. And in Zimmermann's case, this human element, which he himself eventually recognized to be present, must be sought in his intellectual frame of reference.

Balthasar Friedrich Wilhelm Zimmermann was born to what he himself referred to as "ganz unbemittelte"[12] parents in the employ of the Württemberg court on January 2, 1807. Because of this poverty, Zimmermann was at first to learn a trade. But his intellectual promise was recognized by his mother's brother who prevailed upon the parents to allow the boy to acquire a classical education.[13] Thus at the age of eleven, Zimmermann entered the Stuttgart *Gymnasium*. It was here that he encountered the noted Swabian poet Gustav Schwab who first awakened his love of poetry, history and Antiquity.[14] It was here, too, that the intellectual vistas first began to open to Zimmermann and where he made exceedingly rapid progress in his studies. Stimulating as his encounter with Schwab was, it was through the devoted efforts of another teacher, a gentleman named Keim, that a solid basis for Zimmermann's future education was laid.

"Keim," wrote Zimmermann's wife in the early 1860's, "legte den Grund zu dem, was aus Z. geworden ist, namentlich auch durch Bücher, welche er ihm theils lieh theils schenkte."[15]

---

[11] See especially: *H. Barge,* introduction to the 1939 edition of Zimmermann's Bauernkrieg, 2 vols. (Naunhof & Leipzig, 1939); *W. Blos,* introduction to the 1891 Volksausgabe of Zimmermann's Bauernkrieg (Stuttgart, 1891); *W. Blos,* introduction to his Florian Geyer (Berlin, 1921); *E. Guggenheim,* Der Florian Geyer-Stoff in der deutschen Dichtung (Berlin, 1908); *H. Hausherr,* "Wilhelm Zimmermann als Geschichtsschreiber des Bauernkrieges," Zeitschrift für Württembergische Landesgeschichte, X (1951), 166—181; *M. Lenz,* "Florian Geyer," Vom Werden der Nation (München & Berlin, 1922), pp. 161—192; *A. Rapp,* "Wilhelm Zimmermann," Schwäbische Lebensbilder, VI (Stuttgart, 1957), 266—285; *G. Schilfert,* "Wilhelm Zimmermann," in *J. Streisand,* ed., Die deutsche Geschichtswissenschaft vom Beginn des 19. Jahrhunderts bis zur Reichseinigung von oben (Berlin, 1963), pp. 170—184; and *E. Stemmer,* "Wilhelm Zimmermann, Sein Leben und seine Dichtung," unpublished Ph. D. dissertation, University of Tübingen, 1921.

[12] *Zimmermann* to Ignaz Hub, April 28, 1845. Zimmermann Nachlass, 27, 500.

[13] In all of Zimmermann's own biographical notes this is pointed out, but in the brief biography written by his wife in the early 1860's the following is stated: "Auf seine eigene Veranlassung kam er in das Stuttgarter Gymnasium, in die niederste Klasse ..." Ibid., Z 1030. In all probability, however, Zimmermann is to be believed over his wife in this instance.   [14] *Stemmer,* "Wilhelm Zimmermann," p. 16.

[15] *L. Zimmermann,* "Wilhelm Zimmermann," Zimmermann Nachlass, Z 1030.

Indeed, so precocious was Zimmermann that when he entered the Lutheran theological preparatory school at Blaubeuren[16] in October of 1821 at the age of 14, along with such other future Swabian luminaries his own age as David Friedrich Strauss, Gustav Pfizer, poet, historian, and younger brother of the Swabian Liberal, Paul Pfizer, the theologian, Christian Märklin, the poet and humorist, Julius Krais, the later philosopher of aesthetics at the universities of Tübingen and Zurich, Friedrich Theodor Vischer, and Gustav Binder who gained prominence as an educator and administrator, he was unanimously recognized as the intellectual leader of the class.[17] From the beginning, Zimmermann ranked first academically in his class as well, a position he retained the full four years at Blaubeuren.[18] This leadership, combined with an enthusiastic and gregarious personality, enabled Zimmermann to exercise a considerable and beneficial influence upon his classmates.[19]

At Blaubeuren, Zimmermann came under the guidance of two particularly outstanding teachers, Friedrich Kern and Ferdinand Christian Baur, both later appointed to the faculty of theology at the University of Tübingen where he and his friends continued to study under them. It was during these years that Zimmermann, who was Baur's favorite pupil because of his dedication, his advanced understanding of, and exceptional receptivity for the beauty and grandeur of Greek civilization, Baur's area of special interest, was strongly influenced by the ideas of Baur.[20] This influence comes to the fore already in a poem that Zimmermann recited at the end of his last year at Blaubeuren to the assembled student-body on the day of the class's departure from the school, a poem which Strauss later called

"ein herrliches Gedicht . . . Wenn ich mich des Gedichts erinnere, das er am Morgen unseres Abschiedstages von Blaubeuren vortrug, worin er in beredten, vom tiefsten Eindrucke begleiteten Worten die Summe unserer dortigen Entwicklung zog: so steht Zimmermann wieder in der ganzen Bedeutung vor mir, die er damals für den Kreis seiner Mitschüler hatte."[21]

---

[16] The school had originally been a monastery founded by the Counts of Tübingen as early as 1095. However, the building in which Zimmermann and his friends attended school was erected between 1466 and 1502. When Tübingen became Protestant in 1534, the monastery was turned into a Lutheran school, and in 1817 into a preparatory school for future Württemberg Lutheran theologians. For a contemporary description of the examinations by which students in Württemberg were selected for Blaubeuren where they received four years of instruction at the expense of the state, see D. F. Strauss, "Christian Märklin. Ein Lebens- und Charakterbild aus der Gegenwart," Gesammelte Schriften, X (Bonn, 1878), 184—186.   [17] Ibid., p. 194.

[18] See the Blaubeuren "Personal-Buch des königl. Seminars in Blaubeuren," in the library at Blaubeuren which begins with Zimmermann's class.

[19] Strauss, "Christian Märklin," p. 194.   [20] Ibid.   [21] Ibid.

It is apparent from the content of this poem that Baur's interpretation of Antiquity — and especially of Plato — was a major influence upon Zimmermann and his comrades. Adolf Rapp, who quoted portions of it, remarked that it consisted of nineteen stanzas

"mit Sprachgewalt, edlem Schwung, überströmender Empfindung dessen, was dies Blaubeuren ihnen gewesen, auch seine Landschaft, Homer, die Antigone, Vergil, Geschichte und Philosophie, in der Platon lehrt, daß die wahre Wirklichkeit die ewigen Ideen sind, zu denen aus der vergänglichen Sinnenwelt die Seele den Weg zu finden hat, dann die (von Baur erschlossene) Religionsgeschichte, die ausmünde in des Heilands reine Gotteslehre."[22]

History, therefore, had a purpose and a goal for Zimmermann already at this early point in his life, for he remarked further:

"Ein heiliger Wille hält der Welten Zügel;
Das Gute steht, des Bösen Plan zerreißt."[23]

Baur's influence on Zimmermann is confirmed by his wife in her biographical sketch of her husband written in the early 1860's:

"Im Jahr 1821," she wrote, "wurde er in das filologische Seminar zu Blaubeuren aufgenommen. Hier hatte er namentlich den nachmals als Theologen so berühmt gewordenen Professor Dr. Chr. *Baur,* den Stifter der sogenanten Tübinger Schule, vier Jahre lang zum Lehrer, der sich ebenfalls besonders seiner annahm und den größten Einfluß auf ihn hatte."[24]

This influence must now be more clearly delineated if at all possible, for it would appear that the relationship which had existed between Baur and Zimmermann in Blaubeuren was disrupted at the university. Had this not been the case, one could expect to find at least some correspondence between the two later, especially after Zimmermann turned to Baur's own field of interest and produced his four-volume history of the Christian Church a few years before Baur died.[25] But no such correspondence exists,[26] nor is there any mention of Baur's name in any of Zimmermann's letters seen by the author. Nevertheless, the influence of Baur's ideas on those of the mature Zimmermann is amply apparent.[27]

[22] *Rapp,* "Wilhelm Zimmermann," p. 267.   [23] Quoted in ibid.
[24] Zimmermann Nachlass, Z 1030.
[25] *Zimmermann,* Lebensgeschichte der Kirche Jesu Christi, 4 vols. (Stuttgart, 1857—1859). Indeed, Zimmermann asked the Heidelberg theologian, K. B. Hundeshagen, to write the preface to this study.
[26] See the breakdown of Baur's correspondence in *E. Barnikol,* "Der Briefwechsel zwischen Strauss und Baur," Zeitschrift für Kirchengeschichte, 73 (1962), 77—78.
[27] *Rapp,* "Wilhelm Zimmermann," p. 267. *G. Müller* holds the same to be true for Strauss: "Die Bedeutung der Schulzeit in der Blaustadt kann nicht hoch genug angesetzt werden." Identität und Immanenz. Zur Genese der Theologie von D. F. Strauss (Zurich, 1968), p. 39.

In his recent book, *The Foundation of Historical Theology. A Study of Ferdinand Christian Baur*,[28] Peter C. Hodgson makes numerous references to Baur's Blaubeuren lecture manuscript, "Geschichte des Alterthums," as well as to one of his earliest published works, *Symbolik und Mythologie, oder die Naturreligion des Alterthums*. The last appeared in 1824—25 while Baur was still at Blaubeuren and dealt with a topic he apparently also lectured on there.[29] These documents are of the greatest importance for an analysis of Zimmermann's historical viewpoint, for, as Hodgson himself remarks, many of Baur's historical

"categories and conceptions appear quite early in [his] career,"[30]

a remark Hodgson makes with reference to Baur's "Geschichte des Alter-thums" which he taught only at Blaubeuren. According to Hodgson, Baur's earliest pronouncements on the historical process demonstrate his dependence upon both Schleiermacher and Schelling. In his argument that the proper content of history is the story of man rather than of nature and things, he is evidently dependent upon Schleiermacher; and in his belief that history as a whole is the revelation of divine providence, a remark that came from Zimmermann's pen in his *Geschichte der deutschen National-literatur* as well, he is clearly dependent upon Schelling.[31] Baur elaborated on the latter idea in his *Symbolik und Mythologie*:

"Ist die Weltgeschichte überhaupt, in ihrem weitesten und würdigsten Sinne, eine Offenbarung der Gottheit, der lebendigste Ausdruck der göttlichen Ideen und Zwecke, so kann die, da überall, wo geistiges Leben ist, auch Bewußtseyn ist, als Einheit desselben, nur als die Entwiklung eines Bewußtseyns angesehen werden, welche zwar nur auf eine der Entwiklung des Bewußtseyns analoge Weise zu denken ist, aber mit dem beschränkten Maßstabe desselben nicht gemessen wer-den darf."[32]

Already the dilemma that faces the historian in the above context be-comes apparent; for if history is to be "in its widest and most worthy sense, . . . a revelation of Divinity," then this Divinity must reveal itself, since it is intangible spirit, through the human consciousness. Consequently, Baur is forced to argue, and in this he is already in agreement with Hegel, al-though he read him only after the publication of Strauss's *Leben Jesu* in

---

[28] (New York, 1966).   [29] *Müller*, Identität und Immanenz, pp. 39—40.
[30] *Hodgson*, Baur, p. 169.   [31] Ibid., pp. 145—146.
[32] Quoted in ibid., p. 146. (*F. C. Baur*, Symbolik und Mythologie, Stuttgart 1824, Bd I, V.)

1835,[33] that the historical process is also, and above all, the story of the development of the consciousness of the divine in mankind. As Hodgson remarks:

"In some of his early writing, Baur describes the relation as that between divine being and human consciousness. The divine idea has its truth in itself, implicitly; but it becomes true for history, for human consciousness, by means of the 'constant correlation of ideal and real'. The real 'mediates the *consciousness* of the idea'. Human consciousness, in other words, is the historical reality by which the idea is manifested."[34]

History, therefore, is the result of the interaction between divine ideas and human awareness or realization of these ideas. At the same time, however, history is also the revelation of divine providence, which means that it is, in large measure if not totally, determined by God. And here, of course, lies the crux of the problem: if Divinity, which is pursuing its goal in history, is realized in history only through human subjectivity, how much freedom of action does man have in shaping his own destiny? Baur attempted to resolve this dilemma by arguing that there is a congruence between "divine and human freedom, between idea and manifestation," but, as Hodgson points out, this congruence "tends to evaporate into an identity in which only the necessity of the divine prevails."[35]

But since Baur assumes that a congruence exists between divine idea and human manifestation, between divine providence and human freedom, he is the more able to plead a relatively strong case for objectivity in historical research. In order to bring any kind of meaning to this objective research, however, the historian must explicate history's overriding meaning from such research. This distinction is made already in Baur's lecture manuscript, "Geschichte des Alterthums," where history is divided into three categories: into

"a 'purely objective' method, appropriate to annals and chronicles, which treats events in their simple sequence, without developing connections or involving the reflection of the writer; a 'pragmatic' method which treats the connections between events according to the laws of causality; and a 'philosophical' method, which shows that historical events are manifestations of a ruling idea, which serves as the basis of the inner continuity and meaning of the historical process."[37]

It is this last category Baur accepts as the highest form of historical writing and into which he places himself in his *Symbolik und Mythologie:*

---

[33] At least this is the conclusion reached by Hodgson, pp. 22—30, and most other Baur scholars.   [34] Ibid., p. 147.   [35] Ibid., p. 149.   [36] Quoted in ibid., p. 161.   [37] Ibid., p. 162.

"Den bekannten Vorwurf der Vermengung der Philosophie mit der Geschichte
fürchte ich dabei nicht: ohne Philosophie bleibt mir die Geschichte ewig todt und
stumm."[38]

It is then the less surprising to find Baur arguing further that history
must be constantly rewritten, and that from the latest philosophical perspective.[39] And, of course, from his own philosophical perspective, first
influenced by Schelling and then by Hegel, this latest, and therefore at
the moment only viable, philosophical perspective had as its fundamental
axiom that history was essentially the work of the eternal Spirit. The historian's duty, therefore, was to discover "the eternal thoughts of the eternal
Spirit, whose work history is" in history.[40]

The culmination of this historical process, as Zimmermann already remarked in his Blaubeuren poem, would be the establishment of "des
Heilands reine Gotteslehre." This remark, as well as the lines from his
poem,

> Ein heiliger Wille hält der Welten Zügel;
> Das Gute steht, des bösen Plan zerreißt.

demonstrate that Zimmermann had thoroughly absorbed Baur's views by
the time he left Blaubeuren in 1825. And these views prepared him, as
they did Strauss and Vischer, for an enthusiastic reception of the Hegelian
philosophy once they were exposed to it. That the transition was relatively
easy is manifested by the fact that Baur himself became a Hegelian for a
time after 1835.

3. ZIMMERMANN'S ASSOCIATION WITH WILHELM WAIBLINGER

Zimmermann completed his studies at Blaubeuren in 1825 and immediately enrolled, as was the custom for students coming from Blaubeuren
and its three sister institutions, in the faculty of theology at the nearby
university as a *Stiftler*,[41] one year before Baur and Kern were appointed. It
was the death of Ernst Bengel, grandson of the more renowned Johann Albrecht Bengel and the leading theologian in the Tübingen faculty at the
time, together with the somewhat dubious promotion of a Professor Wurm
from the same faculty to become Dean of Nürtingen in 1826, which made

---

[38] Quoted in ibid., p. 163. *(Baur,* loco cit. Bd I, XI.)
[39] Ibid.   [40] Quoted in ibid., p. 164.
[41] This was the term applied to all who lived in the so-called "Tübinger Stift," the
residence, but more than that, for state supported theology students and a few others.
For a good description of the Stift and its institutions, see *R. von Mohl,* Lebenserinnerungen (Stuttgart & Leipzig, 1902), pp. 97—103.

these appointments possible.[42] Since the course of studies for *Stiftler* was strictly prescribed — in this first year Zimmermann attended classes in the Psalms, history, anthropology, geometry, Classical Literature, mathematics, Acts of the Apostels, and Isaiah[43] — no member of Zimmermann's class got to hear Bengel. Nor did Baur and Kern arrive until one year later, thus there were virtually no outstanding teachers in the philosophical and theological faculties at Tübingen during that first year, or, for that matter, aside from Baur, for the rest of Zimmermann's sojourn at the university.[44] Had there been someone on the faculty to stimulate Zimmermann, he might not have been so attracted to, and, according to Strauss, negatively influenced by Wilhelm Waiblinger.[45]

Waiblinger, an intimate friend of Eduard Mörike since 1821, both of whom were studying theology at Tübingen when Zimmermann arrived there, had manifested marked literary talents at a very early age. Already at seventeen, while still studying at the Stuttgart *Obergymnasium* under Gustav Schwab, Waiblinger published a novel entitled *Phaeton*. This led to his association with men of the calibre of an Uhland, a Matthisson, a Dannecker and others. In his first Tübingen years, Waiblinger apparently cut so impressive a figure that he seemed the very embodiment of the proverbial young genius. Steeped in a romanticism derived from the writings of Byron and endowed with an insatiable appetite for adventure, Waiblinger was constantly generating grandiose literary projects, few of which he ever brought to fruition. It was his unstable character, however, which was his undoing. His all-too-early fame fostered a vanity that fed an increasingly inflated ego, while his earlier creative imagination turned more and more to flights of wild fantasy. Vacillating between periods of intense creativity and passionately hedonistic love affairs, Waiblinger could also move from the most abject remorse over these illicit affairs to utter callousness regarding them.[46]

By the time Zimmermann met him in 1825, Waiblinger's reputation was already more than a little tarnished because of a particularly scandalous

---

[42] See particularly *A. Hausrath*, David Friedrich Strauss und die Theologie seiner Zeit, I (Heidelberg, 1876), 31—33.

[43] A list of classes Zimmermann attended at Tübingen is contained in the files relating to Zimmermann in the Landeskirchliches Archiv, Stuttgart.

[44] *Strauss* described their transition from Blaubeuren to Tübingen as follows: "Nirgends fanden wir einen Baur oder Kern wieder: wir fühlten uns im Punkte des Unterrichts zurück statt vorwärts gekommen, und damit auch in der Stimmung gedrückt statt gehoben." "Christian Märklin," p. 203.   [45] Ibid., p. 194.

[46] See *H. Maync*, Eduard Mörike. Sein Leben und Dichten, 5th ed. (Stuttgart, 1944), pp. 70—71.

affair he had had with a certain Julie Michaelis. Zimmermann was nevertheless strongly attracted to him, asserting in a letter to Ignaz Hub as late
as 1845 that Waiblinger had been his daily companion during that first
year at Tübingen.[47] This attraction probably rested on Waiblinger's apparent geniality and literary prowess, both characteristics Zimmermann
also manifested. According to Strauss, Waiblinger's influence on Zimmermann was considerable and tended to encourage the latter's already un-
healthy striving for the genial and the spectacular. That this influence was
extensive is confirmed by Zimmermann himself in his short story, *Das
Modell*. Here — and it is clear he is speaking of Waiblinger — he remarked:

"Ich hatte ihn auf der Universität kennen gelernt, er war mein Landsmann, und
nannte sich in Rom, seinen teutschen Namen in's Italienische ändernd, Gibello.
Er war ein ganzes Jahr mein täglicher, fast einziger Gesellschafter, und hatte ein
großes Gewicht über mich, ob ich gleich heute noch nicht begreife, wodurch. Sein
ganzes Aeußeres, vor allem das aschfarbene Gesicht, darin die wilde Glut der
rollenden Augen, das hämische Lächeln um den Mund, der stolze freche Hohn,
womit er Heiliges und Unheiliges ansah, waren keine Eigenschaften, die geeignet
waren, Liebe und Zutrauen zu erwecken. Sein ganzes Wesen hatte etwas Unheim-
liches, Unreines, nicht unähnlich jenem Mephisto, wie ihn Göthe in seinem größten
Gedichte bezeichnet hat, und doch zog er mich an, er war mir lange Zeit unent-
behrlicher Geselle, und riß mich fort von Freude zu Freude, mein ächter Mephi-
stopheles."[48]

Although this relationship lasted only one year since Waiblinger, who
was expelled from the *Stift* in early 1826, left for Italy shortly thereafter
where he died in 1830, the effects remained behind to haunt Zimmermann
for a long time to come. For he himself acquired many of the very characteristics he attributed to Waiblinger in the passage just quoted. As late as
1852, Vischer, who had been Zimmermann's closest friend, wrote the following in a letter to the latter after their friendship had been disrupted
by something Zimmermann had done in Frankfurt during the days of the
Frankfurt parliament:

"Ich sage dir lieber gleich so viel, daß es nicht politische Differenz ist; diese an
sich hätte mich nicht persönlich verstimmt. Aber zusammengenommen mit einigen
Pfaffen, die du mir persönlich versetztest, erzeugte die politische Differenz das
böse Blut. Erinnere dich z. B. was du mir hinwarfst, als ich bei der Abstimmung
über das Reichsoberhaupt im schwersten inneren Kampfe in der Paulskirche auf

---

[47] Zimmermann Nachlass, 27, 500.
[48] *Zimmermann*, Das Modell (Stuttgart, 1834), pp. 22—23.

u. abging. Dies u. Aehnliches sprach eine Fülle der Selbstgewißkeit aus, die ich, als schlichtes Menschenkind zweifelnd u. im Dunkeln suchend, (obwohl über die Falschheit mancher Richtungen, Parteibeschluß etc. nicht im Dunkeln) — als eine Form des Geistes überhaupt haßte. Es war ein Genialitätswesen darin, das ich — ich muß jetzt offen seyn — als eine fremde, in deinem Geiste seit der Waiblingerschen Zeit festgesetzten Pflanze verwünschte."[49]

It was this disdain for the opinion of others and the conviction that he alone was right that became characteristic, as Vischer pointed out, of Zimmermann's action after 1825. And this was undoubtedly due to Waiblinger's influence. This attitude permeates much of his writing to 1850, especially his histories of the Peasants' War and German literature. That it quickly alienated many people, even, eventually, close friends like Vischer and former teachers like Baur and Schwab, becomes only too evident from a letter of Schwab written to Zimmermann in 1843.[50] It was this same characteristic that brought him into trouble in the *Stift* and led to his eventual expulsion from there on April 27, 1829.

4. CONTACT WITH HEGEL

One other event at Tübingen is of considerable importance for an understanding of Zimmermann's intellectual frame of reference as well as his character. This has to do with the nature of his encounter with Hegelian ideas at the university. We have already noted that a peculiarity of Baur and his students, especially of those who had studied under him at Blaubeuren, was their easy transition to Hegelianism. Eduard Zeller, Baur's son-in-law and close friend of Strauss, as well as the latter's sometime student, explained this phenomenon in the following way:

"Es ist eine für die ganze weitere Entwicklung der protestantischen Theologie nicht unwichtige Tatsache, daß Strauss sowohl als Baur, daß also die beiden Begründer der neuen, von Schwaben ausgehenden Richtung der theologischen Forschung durch Schleiermachers Schule hindurchgingen, ehe sie in der Hegelschen ihren Schwerpunkt fanden."

While the two schools of thought went their separate ways in northern Germany, Zeller continued,

"gingen sie hier von Anfang an in eine Strömung zusammen, sie befruchteten und ergänzten sich gegenseitig: von Schleiermacher lernte man die Religion in ihrer

---

[49] Vischer to Zimmermann, Nov. 9, 1852. Zimmermann Nachlass, 55, 417. According to Waiblinger's Die Tagebücher 1821—1826 (Stuttgart, 1956), p. 318, Zimmermann's name is one of the last entries in Waiblinger's diary.

[50] Gustav Schwab to Zimmermann, June 5, 1843. Zimmermann Nachlass.

Eigentümlichkeit verstehen, die theologischen Vorstellungen in ihrer geschichtlichen Bestimmtheit fassen, zergliedern und prüfen; von Hegel fand man sich durch seinen aufs Ganze gerichteten Blick, durch die Strenge seiner dialektischen Entwicklung, durch die lockende Aussicht gefesselt, alle Dinge aus ihrem innersten Grunde zu begreifen, in allem Sein und Geschehen die einheitliche, mit dialektischer Notwendigkeit sich vollziehende Offenbarung der Idee zu erkennen. Strauss konnte sich der Anziehungskraft dieses Systems um so weniger entziehen, da es nur die folgerichtige Fortbildung dessen war, dem er bisher gehuldigt hatte, des Schellingschen."[51]

There are in this development strongly romantic overtones. Though this romantic influence is perhaps more marked in Zimmermann's intellectual development than in that of Baur and Strauss, an influence that came to Zimmermann largely through Waiblinger and his *Byronschwärmerei*, it is present in the others as well. The influence exerted by Romanticism, combined with an attraction to Schelling's philosophy, led back to a fascination for mystics such as Jakob Böhme during this time, as Strauss, who was particularly drawn to the occult in his earliest Tübingen days, himself remarked.

"So eben erst aus der Dumpfheit und unsteten Träumerei der Periode zwischen dem Knaben- und Jünglings-Alter zu festerem Selbstbewusstsein gediehen, glaubte ich eben in dieser Unmittelbarkeit des Gefühls die Warheit zu besitzen, und konnte nicht einsehen, wozu alle die Umstände und misstrauischen Vorkehrungen, womit Kant an das Erkennen der Dinge herantritt ... In solcher Stimmung, wie musste Schelling's intellectuelle Anschauung, Jakob Böhmes unmittelbarer Blick in die Tiefen der Gottheit und Natur, mich ansprechen und begeistern!"[52]

This more romantic approach to religion was not too far removed from the theological position known as *Supranaturalismus* which ruled in the faculty of theology at the time. Ernst Bengel, its leading exponent, was also the leading light of the faculty. Yet as a student of Kant's philosophy, he brought strongly rationalistic overtones to his interpretation, especially of biblical miracles. With his death in 1826, however, the theology of Schleiermacher began to supersede the older school. And it was Baur who introduced this new theology to Tübingen immediately he was appointed.[53]

If Schelling was the philosopher of Romanticism, Schleiermacher was in many ways its theologian. He asserted that there were two cardinal aspects to any religion: first, the subjective religious emotion prompted in man

---

[51] Quoted in *M. Leube*, Die Geschichte des Tübinger Stifts (Stuttgart, 1954), pp. 584—585.
[52] *D. F. Strauss*, "Justinus Kerner," Hallische Jahrbücher, 2 (January 2, 1838), 9.
[53] *Hodgson*, Baur, p. 17.

by the objective reality of God; and, secondly, the human attempt to express this emotion in rational terms. The first constituted the essence of
religion; the second merely the verbalized reflection of this essence. Yet
it was the latter that resulted in the creation of dogma. Dogma, consequently, could change from generation to generation and place to place
depending upon the number of variables in the human equation. No one
formulation could therefore be absolutely correct, although one could
discern higher and lower forms of religion. This view was to influence
Zimmermann considerably, as a reading of his treatment of Joachim of
Fiore makes only too apparent.[54]

It was at this juncture that Zimmermann and his friends came upon
Hegel. Strauss, once again, recalled the importance, particularly of Hegel's *Phänomenologie,* for their development.

"Während der Verstand in die schärfste dialektische Schule genommen wurde,
boten sich dem Geiste die tiefsten Ahnungen, der Phantasie die überraschendsten
Ausblicke; die ganze Weltgeschichte zog in neuer Beleuchtung an uns vorüber;
Kunst und Religion in ihren verschiedenen Formen tauchten an ihrer Stelle auf,
und dieser ganze Reichtum an Gestalten ging aus dem Einen Selbstbewußtsein
hervor und wieder in dasselbe zurück, das sich damit als die Macht aller Dinge
kennen lernte."[55]

And it was Strauss's talented classmate Zimmermann who really stimulated their interest in Hegel.

"Hegel war damals in Tübingen noch so gut wie unbekannt; Schneckenburger,
[a *Repetent* in the *Stift*] der sein Zuhörer in Berlin gewesen war, brachte ihn
zuerst ausführlicher auf das Katheder, und unser alter Blaubeurer Freund, Zimmermann, in dem Alles schneller als in uns Uebrigen aufging und wieder ab-
welkte, pries, höhnisch absprechend über unsere damaligen Heroen, unter welchen
wir freilich neben Schleiermacher auch Twesten, neben Schelling Franz Baader an-
gestellt hatten, Hegels Encyclopädie als das Buch der Bücher, mit dessen Studium,
der 'Arbeit im Begriff', er mehr als einmal seinen abendlichen Durst nachdrück-
lich zu begründen wusste. Mit richtigem Takte wählten wir nun aber zu unserer
Lectüre nicht die Encyclopädie, welche in ihre aphoristischen Haltung dem An-
fänger mehr nur Schlagworte als wirkliche Ausschlüsse geben konnte, sondern
die uns gleichfalls von Zimmermann gerühmte Phänomenologie."[56]

In later days Zimmermann himself liked to think back with a certain
pride in the role he had played in making Hegel known at the university.
Thus, in his letter to Ignaz Hub of April 28, 1845, he remarked:

---

[54] See, for example, his Lebensgeschichte der Kirche Jesu Christi, III (Stuttgart, 1859),
458—459.   [55] *Strauss,* "Christian Märklin," p. 224.   [56] Ibid., pp. 223—224.

"In Tübingen studierte ich mehr Geschichte u. Poesie als Theologie, aber viel Philosophie, besonders Hegel: ich war der erste, der in Tübingen Hegel studierte, und diesen Landsmann erst hier aufbrachte und bekannt machte."[57]

What he never recalled, however, was a related incident which occured in the *Stift* as early as February 17, 1827, that is, late in his third semester at the university. During that semester, Zimmermann along with the rest of the class was called upon to write an essay "Über das Wesen des Bösen in psychologischer u. metaphysischer Hinsicht, nebst Berücksichtigung der wichtigsten philosophischen Theorien." The *Repetent* who read the essay remarked in the report submitted to *Ephorus* Jäger, the head of the *Stift*, that, aside from a few introductory remarks of a poetic and aesthetic nature on Genesis IV, Zimmermann had followed the Hegelian speculation,

"welche so weit Ref. vergleichen konnte rein u. verbatimus abgeschrieben ist."[58]

The incident caused a furor in the *Stift*.

Jäger, commenting on the report, wrote that the *Repetent* had sent him Zimmermann's essay and accused the latter of plagiarism. This accusation, he remarked, was not quite correct since Zimmermann had himself referred to Hegel in the essay, and must have told Jäger that

"weil er einmal ganz in diesen hineingerannt ist sich nicht von seinen Worten losmachen konnte."[59]

In the meantime, Jäger continued, he had sternly reprimanded Zimmermann, warning him against repeating such a *jurare in verba magistri*, and had told him to rewrite the essay independently of Hegel.

Toward the end of his comments, Jäger requested that his colleagues in the faculty of theology check into the matter as well. Only Kern, Zimmermann's former Blaubeuren teacher, seems to have done so, however. His notes, appended to those of Jäger, offer further insight into Zimmermann's character. Kern suggested that the latter had become involved in similar escapades earlier and that he, Kern, hat tried to reform him. But that had proven a hopeless venture. What was more, Kern argued that the passages taken from Hegel were indeed an outright plagiarism and not only, or merely, a *jurare in verba magistri*. But what irked Kern even more, was the fact that Zimmermann's passages on Genesis IV were taken verbatim from lectures he had given at Blaubeuren![60]

This incident is not only of considerable importance for an understanding of Zimmermann; it will serve to confirm later findings as well. Here,

---

[57] Zimmermann Nachlass, 27, 500.
[58] Semi-annual report written on Nov. 8, 1827. Stiftsakten.　　[59] Ibid.　　[60] Ibid.

however, it demonstrates only too clearly Zimmermann's facile nature and
the fact that he was not always careful as to how he used his materials.
Further, his encounter with Hegelian ideas took place well before Schnek-
kenberger began to lecture on Hegel in his class on the "Geschichte der
neuesten Philosophie" during the winter semester of 1828—29.[61] Consequently, Zimmermann may well have been solely responsible for intro-
ducing Strauss and his other friends to Hegel, as he asserted in his letter
to Ignaz Hub. Since the incident caused a not inconsiderable furor in the
faculty of theology, Baur must certainly have become aware of it, being
close to Kern as he was. On the one hand, the incident must surely have
pained him not a little since Zimmermann had been his favorite pupil
in Blaubeuren; but on the other hand, one is tempted to think that he
should have begun to wonder now, and particularly later when Strauss
and Vischer began to steep themselves in Hegel as well, what it was about
Hegel that so attracted the brightest of his former students. Under these
circumstances, could he have refrained from reading Hegel until 1835,
after the appearance of Strauss's *Leben Jesu?* Whatever the case may be,
one thing is certain: Zimmermann had discovered that intellectual perspective which he not only found most satisfying intellectually, but which he
considered to be the only correct one. It is no wonder, then, given his dis-
position, that he should speak so disparagingly of the intellectual heroes
of his classmates, heroes which had till then also been his own.

5. ZIMMERMANN'S EMERGING PHILOSOPHICAL PERSPECTIVE

Although Zimmermann himself remarked to Ignaz Hub, as we have just
seen, that he had studied a great deal of philosophy at the university,
especially that of Hegel, and in spite of the fact that he could on occasion
deride his earlier intellectual heroes, the influence of former philosophical
systems remained. Indeed, as Zeller remarked, the transition from Schleiermacher and Schelling to Hegel was relatively easy, especially if one had
approached the former through Baur's perspective. In a sense, Hegel was
the capstone to all of these, his philosophy the end product of a development in which the others stood. Nor is it insignificant that Schelling, Hegel,
Baur, Zimmermann, and Strauss were all Württembergers standing in the
same intellectual tradition and all, at one time or another, students in the
Tübingen theological *Stift*. It is therefore instructive, in view of Zimmermann's own philosophical-religious synthesis, to read the reports written
by the *Repetent* Stirn on two further essays that Zimmermann wrote in

---

[61] See *Müller*, Identität und Immanenz, p. 45.

the *Stift*. The reports speak for themselves. The second, on Zimmermann's essay written in March, 1828, reads as follows:

"Der Verfasser glaubte von seiner spekulativen Höhe herab die hier vorkommenden Fragen in Gegensätze in den Systemen leicht abzuthun, und hat daher sich auch nicht die Mühe genommen, die Gegensätze näher zu untersuchen und das philosophisch aufgestellte eygentlich zu begründen. Religion ist das Bewusstsein, dass alles Sinnliche von einem Unsinnlichen abhänge oder = das All für ein göttliches Reich halten. In dem Wesen der Religion hat das Erkennen die Präzetenz, das aber als solches nothwendig auch die übrigen Thätigkeiten bestimmte. Doch soll die Religion zu dem nicht scientia rerum divinarum sein! Die Theorie von Schelling und Hegel Eins sein mit der Theorie des Gefühls. Die Meinungen von Supranaturalismus und Rationalismus wird gar leicht genommen, die Wunder mit ein Paar poetischen Sätzen abgethan. Die Hauptidee der Erlösung ist gut hervorgehoben, aber nicht genauer ausgeführt. Die Leser der Apostel nicht berührt. — Es fehlt an einem consequent durchgeführten Prinzip, und es werden Sätze aus Baader, Hegel und Schleiermacher benutzt."[62]

Several aspects of major importance for Zimmermann's intellectual development stand out in this report. Aside from the reference to religion and the Kingdom of God, the influence of Hegel can be seen especially in his remark that "In dem Wesen der Religion hat das Erkennen die Präzetenz, das aber als solches nothwendig auch die übrigen Thätigkeiten bestimmt." At the same time, however, Zimmermann argues that reason and feeling are essentially the same things and, hence, he can disregard the differences between Hegel and Schelling. Romanticism and Rationalism are merged, for both feeling and reason are considered to be forms of human consciousness through which the eternal spirit works its will on earth. It would appear, therefore, that as far as Zimmermann was concerned one could call this human consciousness by different names yet mean the same thing.

Zimmermann's third and last essay was written during the summer of 1828. The report on it reads as follows:

"Eine fliessende, indess über das Gewöhnliche sich durchaus nicht erhebende Arbeit. Mit Recht darf es dem Ref. zum Vorwurf gemacht werden, dass er nicht auf dem ganzen Umfang der paulinischen Urkunden eine Theorie zu entwickeln suchte, sondern nur nach der Ordnung der Materie, einzelne Stellen meist aus dem Brief an die Römer zusammenträgt, und mit Hilfe der Kommentare länger als nötig bei denselben verweilt. Auf die Frage de conditione origine generis humani lässt er sich gar nicht ein; sondern er beginnt sogleich mit dessen depravation wo er aber mehr beschreibt als entwickelt. Der strengere Begriff von Erbsünde wird hier gefunden aber ihre Zurechnungsfähigkeit geleugnet. Das Verhältnis des

---

[62] Stiftsakten.

Gesetzes zur Moralität ist ziemlich befriedigend dargestellt. Im zweiten Theile vermisst man fasst durchaus eine genaue und sorgfältige Entwicklung der Begriffe. Ganz unzulänglich ist die Definition von Gerechtigkeit: sie sei Justitia hominis legem divinum fideliter executi, probata deo, die erworben werde durch den Glauben, cognitio veri et amor, und wundern muss man sich dass man da doch weiter unten noch den rechten Begriff findet. Über die Frage nach der Vorherbestimmung wird leicht und auf nichtbesagendeweise hinweggegangen und eben so kurz wird über das Pneuma gesprochen. Das Latein ist fliessend."[63]

The content of this essay, as it appears through the report, is so strikingly similar to Zimmermann's enumeration of the essential tenets of the Christian faith as given in his "Vorlesungen über Deutsche Geschichte" of 1838[64] that it seems safe to say that he did not change his views on these matters after his student days, at least not until after the early 1850's. Once he had absorbed Hegel and reconciled him with Baur's interpretation of Christian history, Zimmermann had achieved his world view, a world view with strong pantheistic overtones.[65]

6. THE INFLUENCE OF ROMANTICISM

Although Zimmermann had now found a satisfying philosophical perspective, he does not seem to have intended to pursue a scholarly career of any kind. It is in this context that his association with Waiblinger is important for yet another reason. For it was in this circle of friends that possible literary projects were discussed, particularly dramatic and novelistic treatments of the Swabian Imperial House of Hohenstaufen. Interest in the Hohenstaufen had been sparked by Raumer's thoroughly romantic *Geschichte der Hohenstaufen* which appeared about 1825. Waiblinger and his friends devoured Raumer's study with the greatest of enthusiasm and immediately began laying plans for dramatic treatments of their own. According to his biographer, Mörike and the future Freiburg Catholic historian, Gfrörer, took part in drawing up these plans with Waiblinger.[66] But Zimmermann was almost certainly a party to these plans as well, as we shall see in a moment. At any rate, in the spring of 1826 Waiblinger decided to write a series of Hohenstaufen dramas modelled on Shakespear's Henrician dramas. He was able to persuade the Stuttgart publishing firm of Cotta to finance the project and departed for Italy and Sicily to research his subject. But Waiblinger, who dissipated his energies in Italy even more

---

[63] Ibid.   [64] See Chapter I, p. 8, above.
[65] The report on Zimmermann's trial sermon of February 27, 1828, for example, refers to that sermon as a "poetisch-pantheistische Rede." "Predigtbüchlein angefangen im Winterhalbjahr 1825/26," p. 145. Stiftsakten.   [66] *H. Maync*, Eduard Mörike, p. 147.

than he had at home,[67] died before the project was even decently begun. Nor did any of the others ever complete anything of a similar nature, although Mörike asserted immediately after the 1830 rebellions that he was now going to turn his attention to the Hohenstaufen "im Sturmschritt."[68]

But already on February 28, 1828, Zimmermann had written a letter to Gottfried Basse, bookdealer and publisher in Quedlinburg, stating:

"Habe ich die Ehre den ersten Theil eines aus 3 Theilen bestehenden historischen Romans zuzusenden, mit dem Wunsche, daß Sie Verleger desselben werden möchten."[69]

According to the letter,

"Die Liebe des Königes Enzio, des natürlichen Sohnes Kaisers Friedrich II, zu der schönen Bologneserin Lucia Viadagola, Enzio's Gefangenschaft in Bologna u. Lucia's tragisches Ende ist der Gegenstand des Romans."[70]

Although there are only two letters in existence from Zimmermann to Basse in which this, Zimmermann's first literary enterprise, is discussed — his novel apparently was never published — these letters nevertheless shed considerable light on an important aspect of Zimmermann's intellectual development. To begin with, the fact that he had the first part of an historical novel based on the life of a member of the Hohenstaufen family completed by early 1828 further confirms his association with Waiblinger as well as the fact that he was caught up in the same literary schemes as the rest of the group. Indeed, Zimmermann may well have wished to be the first to publish such an historical novel. It is further evident from the first letter that sometime in 1827 Zimmermann must have decided upon a literary career, for he hoped that this novel would pave the way to such a future.

"Da so viele angehende Novellisten," he wrote, "bey Euer Wohlgeboren ihre literarische Laufbahn begonnen, u. beym Publikum Glück gemacht haben, so wird es Er. W. um so erklärbarer seyn, wie es auch für den Entfernteren einen Reiz haben muß, sein erstes Erzeugnis durch E. W. als Verleger in's Publikum einzuführen."[71]

---

[67] See Ranke's letter to Heinrich Ritter from Rome of Jan. 13, 1830. *W. P. Fuchs*, ed., Leopold von Ranke; das Briefwerk (Hamburg, 1949), pp. 205—206.

[68] *Maync*, Eduard Mörike, p. 147.

[69] Zimmermann to Gottfried Basse, February 28, 1828. In the "Handschriftensammlung" of the Deutsche Bücherei, Leipzig.   [70] Ibid.

[71] Ibid. Although Zimmermann did not receive the doctorate until 1831, he already signed this letter, probably in order to impress the publisher, "Wilhelm Zimmermann, Ph. Doct."

The publisher's response to Zimmermann is not extant. That it must have been cautious, however, is apparent from Zimmermann's second letter to Basse, dated May 10, 1828. Here Zimmermann promised that the second part would be completed in early July and the third part by the end of August. He also assured Basse that

"Wenn auch in keinem andern Blatt, wenigstens im Literaturblatt des Morgen-blattes wird er, wie ich gewiß weiß, einer günstigen Recension sogleich sich zu erfreuen haben."[72]

Not only did he expect a favorable review from the *Morgenblatt*, how-ever, but in an undated letter almost certainly written during this time he asked the editors of the above journal to publish a poem of his

"mit welchem er [Zimmermann] seinen nächstens erscheinenden historischen Ro-man Enzio und Viadagola, oder: der letzte Hohenstaufen ins Publikum einzu-führen wünscht, gefälligst ins Morgenblatt aufzunehmen."[73]

That letter was a little premature, for it was not until 1838—39 that Zimmermann's *Geschichte der Hohenstaufen* appeared, and then in two substantial volumes and not in novel form.[74]

Although Zimmermann's historical novel was never published, it does set the stage for Zimmermann's almost classic development into the ro-mantic historian.[75] Strongly influenced by the early works of Schiller[76] and Byron's romantic heroes, Zimmermann, too, wanted to make a name for himself in the literary world by glorifying the history of his homeland with an historical novel on the tragic fate of the last of the Hohenstaufen. And even though this first literary attempt failed, it was not long after Zim-mermann had left the university that the first edition of his poems, many of which had been written while a student at Tübingen, appeared. This

[72] Ibid. Until Nov. 18, 1827, Zimmermann's friend — at least he claimed him as such — Wilhelm Hauff, had been the editor of the Morgenblatt, a Stuttgart literary journal. But Schwab was also associated with it and so he must have felt certain that at least here his novel would be favorably received.   [73] Zimmermann Nachlass, 36, 997.

[74] In an undated letter to Rudolf Glaser of Prague, probably written in 1839 since it mentions that the second edition of his poems (1839) had just appeared, Zimmermann wrote: "Ein Exemplar meiner Hohenstaufen, eines historischen Werkes, an dem ich gegen dreizehn Jahre sammelte und dachte, werden Sie durch meinen Verleger erhalten." Zim-mermann Nachlass. Thirteen years before 1839 would set the beginning date into 1826, once again into the Waiblinger days in Tübingen.

[75] See especially *D. Levin*, History as Romantic Art (Stanford, 1959).

[76] In his "Lebensgang" Vischer remarked: "Klopstock war unser Mann und Schillers empfindsamste Partien unser Element." Kritische Gänge, VI (1922), 444, edited by *R. Vischer*. We shall see a more direct reference to Schiller from Zimmermann himself later.

was followed in 1833 by a drama dealing with the 17th-century Neapolitan revolutionary, Masaniello, and a number of well-told though largely inconsequential tales.

As a poet, Zimmermann belongs to the younger generation of the Swabian school of Romanticism.[77] Although not a first rate poet like his friend, Eduard Mörike, with whom he edited the *Jahrbuch Schwäbischer Dichter und Novellisten* in 1836, Zimmermann did win enough renown as a poet to have his 1831 collection of poetry enlarged and republished two more times during his lifetime — in 1839 and again in 1854 — and once thereafter, in 1907, edited by Wilhelm Blos. At the same time, he was invited to contribute poems to various literary journals such as the *Deutsche Revue*, (1835),[78] and Christian Schad's *Deutscher Musenalmanach* published in Munich, (1847),[79] to name only a few. He was also asked to participate in the translation of Victor Hugo's writings[80] and became involved in various other literary projects long after he asserted that he had turned entirely to history. Zimmermann's importance as a poet rests not only on his poetry, however, but also on the influence he exercised in this regard on his fellow-students already at Blaubeuren. Of that influence Strauss remarked: "Auch den Sinn für deutsche Dichtung hat er zuerst unter uns geweckt, und unserem Geschmacke die erste Richtung gegeben."[81]

Already in January of 1831, Mörike wrote the following words to Vischer concerning Zimmermann's poems appearing in the *Hochwächter:*

"Das Stuttgarter Blatt der Hochwächter, woran Lohbauer, Mährlen, Rödinger und Zimmermann arbeiten, wird recht gut und enthält zuweilen ein schönes Gedicht von Zimmermann."[82]

And when the first edition of Zimmermann's poems appeared later in the same year, he wrote to his fiance, Luise Rau:

"Der Rike versichere, für die günstige Rezension der Stockmeyerschen Gedichte sei gesorgt. Zwar kommt sie nicht von mir, sondern [Wilhelm] Zimmermann, den ich darum ersucht habe, weil so ein Geschäft weit eher in seiner Art ist, als in der

---

[77] *G. Storz*, Schwäbische Romantik (Stuttgart, 1967), pp. 80—88.

[78] "Um alle diese Bestrebungen werden Heinrich Laube, Heinrich König, der geniale Verfasser der hohen Braut, Wilhelm Zimmermann und Georg Büchner, der Verfasser von Danton's Tod, die Blumenguirlande der Poesie ziehen." Letter of the publisher, C. Löwenthal, from Mannheim in Nov. of 1835. Quoted in *O. Drager*, Theodor Mundt und seine Beziehungen zum Jungen Deutschland (Marburg, 1909), p. 153.

[79] Christian Schad to Zimmermann, Feb. 28, 1847. Zimmermann Nachlass.

[80] J. Bauerlamer to Zimmermann, April 15, 1835. Ibid., Z 1002.

[81] *Strauss*, "Christian Märklin," p. 194.

[82] Mörike to Vischer, Jan. 17, 1831. *R. Vischer*, ed., Briefwechsel zwischen Eduard Mörike und Friedrich Theodor Vischer (München, 1926), p. 27.

meinigen. Wir stehen wirklich besonders gut zusammen: seine Lieder, die eben jetzt im Druck erscheinen, haben mir ihn zum Teil sehr nahe gebracht. Und — Schätzchen! es wurde zwischen uns verabredet, daß er das schöne Exemplar, welches mir zugedacht gewesen, *Dir* eigens zuzuschicken und zu verehren habe."[83]

And in 1832 he again wrote Vischer, comparing Zimmermann's poetry to that of Gustav Pfizer:

"Zimmermann ist, was Behandlung betrifft, und noch mehr, was den süssen sonnerwärmten Kern der Poesie selbst betrifft, mir lieber."[84]

From poetry, Zimmermann turned to tragedy as a form of dramatic expression. As in all his fictional ventures, even to a large extent in his poetry, he chose historical personalities and events for his subjects: in the case of the drama, *Masaniello*, he turned to the Neapolitan fisherman who had led a revolt against the representatives of Spanish rule in Naples in 1647. Unlike Strauss, who turned to biography because he did not consider himself creative enough to write novels,[85] Zimmermann used the historical-biographical details merely as a point of departure for his poetic creativity.

Because Zimmermann had originally intended to devote himself to the literary life, he appears not to have been overly concerned about his expulsion from the *Stift* in February of 1829. From a letter of Julius Krais, Zimmermann's classmate and friend, probably written during the late winter of 1830, it would even appear that Zimmermann wanted to leave. For, apparently together with Krais, Zimmermann intended to spend a year in Munich, there to refine his poetic talents immediately he had served

---

[83] *E. Mörike, Briefe an seine Braut Luise Rau* (München, 1965), p. 181, edited by F. Kemp.

[84] Mörike to Vischer, May 23, 1832. *Vischer, Mörike-Vischer Briefwechsel*, p. 75. In Nov. of 1831, Zimmermann submitted his poems, as partial fulfillment for the degree of doctor of philosophy, to the *philosophische Fakultät* at the University of Tübingen. Since Ludwig Uhland had just begun to teach there, one professor on Zimmermann's doctoral committee, Tafel, requested Uhland's assessment of these poems. In his written *Gutachten*, Tafel stated the following: "Über die hier gleichfalls zurückfolgende poetische Druckschrift, über welche Hn. Prof. Uhland dem Wunsche *amplissimi collegii* zu Folge, von mir eine Äusserung ersucht wurde, erwiederte Hn. Prof. Uhland, dass die Gedichte-Sammlung 'von gebildetem Geiste und schönen poet. Anlagen' zeuge, so wie 'dass mehrere im Einzelnen mit besonderem Lobe zu nennen seyn dürften.'" Zimmermann's Promotionsakten in the University of Tübingen Library archives, 55/7b, Nr. 8.

[85] "Allein das Ueble war: ich konnte keinen schreiben. Hier in der Biographie, war nun der Roman, wie ich ihn schreiben konnte, gefunden. Was ich nicht leisten konnte, die Erfindung, war mir hier gesparrt: die Fabel, die Personen mit ihren Charakteren und Schicksalen, war geschichtlich gegeben." *Strauss*, "Literarische Denkwürdigkeiten," *Kleinere Schriften*, 3rd ed. (Bonn, 1898), p. 35.

his stint as intern in a pastorate.[86] Nevertheless, Zimmermann remained in Tübingen for another six months after his expulsion, preparing himself for the first set of theological examinations administered by the Württemberg Consistory of the Lutheran Church. In his letter of application to that body, asking to be admitted to the examinations slated to be given in early September, 1829, he stated:

"Nach vierjährigem Cursus [at Blaubeuren] kam ich in das theol. Stift zu Tübingen, wo ich 3½ Jahre studierte, und hierauf noch ein halb Jahr meine Studien außer dem Stifte fortsetzte. Von den philosophischen Studien beschäftigte ich mich besonders mit Philologie, Poesie und Geschichte und den neuesten philos. Systemen, was die theol. Studien betrifft, so suchte ich mich außer den Vorlesungen, wovon ich nur die Kirchengeschichte nicht öffentlich hörte, sondern nach einer von Dr. Baur dictirten Hefte privatum studierte, vorzüglich zum Prediger auszubilden, in welcher Beziehung auch die hiesige Fakultät mich im vorigen Jahre des zweyten Predigerpreises würdig erklärte."[87]

As a result of his expulsion, Zimmermann was forced to take his examinations one year before the rest of his colleagues with rather mediocre results. Immediately thereupon he became the assistant to the pastor in the village of Schweinsdorf. From a letter of Zimmermann to the Consistory, requesting admission to the second set of theological examinations, dated February 11, 1831, it is apparent that the pastor was ill the whole time Zimmermann was there; consequently, Zimmermann had to perform all the functions required of a regular pastor.[88] Normally, an assistant had to serve a year's internship, but Zimmermann requested a leave of absence already after nine months, asserting later that he had done as much in those nine months as any other assistant in a year. Unlike classmates such as Strauss, Binder, Märklin and Vischer, however, who all went to Berlin to imbibe Hegelianism at its source, Zimmermann chose to go to Munich. The superintendent of his region wrote the Consistory that Zimmermann had requested the leave of absence in order to go to Munich for half a year to pursue his philosophical, historical, and artistic (probably poetic) studies,[89] but his real interest at this point, as the letter of Julius Krais clearly demonstrates, lay in the realm of poetry and creative writing.

[86] "— Für den Zug nach München, den du mit Anbruch des Frühlings unternehmen wirst, wünsche ich von ganzem Herzen Glück und reichen Gewinn, der dann auf jeden Fall auch mir zugut kommen wird, ob ich gleich nicht unmittelbar daran Teil nehmen kann. Ich habe diesen Plan, wie du vielleicht von Luisen [Zimmermann's fiancé] bereits erfahren hast, wenigstens vor der Hand völlig aufgegeben aus verschiedenen Gründen." Schiller Nationalmuseum, Z 4134.

[87] Landeskirchliches Archiv.   [88] Ibid.

[89] Superintendent Gochs to the Consistory, June 27, 1830. Ibid.

7. JOURNALISTIC AND POLITICAL ACTIVITY

From the same letter, it appears that a publisher in Stuttgart by the name of Frankh had promised to support Zimmermann during his stay in Munich as well as to pay him separately for anything he might write for him.[90] When, therefore, the Minister of Education, on July 12, 1830, granted the request,[91] Zimmermann must immediately have left for Munich. We possess no information whatever regarding the time he spent there, if any, but it is perhaps reasonable to assume that he would have attended Schelling's lectures in philosophy while there. For, as Vischer remarked in his autobiography of his own visit to that city later, it would have been impossible to have been to Munich and not visited Schelling.[92] Whatever the case may be, by late 1830 Zimmermann was back in Stuttgart and by February 11, 1831, was applying for admission to the second set of theological examinations.[93]

In his autobiographical notes written in 1852, Zimmermann remarked that

"zu Ende des Jahres 1830 unternahm ich in Stuttgart mit den Rechtsconsulenten Rödinger u. Tafel, und meinem Freunde Lohbauer ein patriotisches Blatt, das bis zum Ende des Jahres 1832 unter dem Titel 'Der Hochwächter, ein Volksblatt aus Württemberg' erschien, dann vom Bundestag aus unterdrückt wurde, sogleich aber unter dem Namen 'Der Stuttgarter Beobachter' wieder aufstand, und noch zur Stunde in gleicher Richtung besteht."[94]

Since the first edition appeared on December 1, 1830, Zimmermann must have been back in Stuttgart a little prior to that time. The editor-in-chief, Rudolf Lohbauer,[95] had studied in Tübingen as well until the fall of

---

[90] "Dein Vorhaben lässt mich daher auch mit Gewissheit voraussagen, dass Frankh dir einen angemessenen jährlichen Gehalt zugesichert hat, neben welchem jede einzelne Arbeit, die du ihm lieferst, noch besonders honorirt werden muss, da du doch wohl nichts weniger im Sinn hast, als die erhabene Göttin statt einer Magd oder Kuh in die Knechtschaft eines Buchhändlers zu verkaufen." Schiller Nationalmuseum.

[91] Landeskirchliches Archiv.   [92] *Vischer,* "Mein Lebensgang," p. 465.

[93] The only remark Zimmermann makes in his various autobiographical statements on his stay in Munich is the following in his 1854 "Lebensabriss:" "Hier [in Schweinsdorf] versah ich 9 Monate lang das Pfarramt, da der Pfarrer krank war, nahm dann Urlaub, und durfte durch besondere Vergünstigung sofort die zweite Dienstprüfung nehmen." Zimmermann Nachlass, Z 966.

[94] Zimmermann Nachlass, Z 965. In the biography written by his wife, however, the statement is made that "er nahm Teil an der Redaction politischer Blätter in seiner Vaterstadt, wo er im Sommer 1830, kurz nach der Julirevolution, seinen Siz aufschlug." Ibid., Z 1030. Once again, however, the evidence seems to favor Zimmermann's account.

[95] On Lohbauer see *W. Lang,* "Rudolf Lohbauer," Württembergische Vierteljahreshefte für Landesgeschichte, 5 (1896), 149—188.

1827 where Zimmermann had met him. Since that time he had travelled around the country, eventually settling in Stuttgart where he wrote "intertemperate and malicious" theater reviews for the *Stadtpost*, a paper published by the same Frankh[96] who, according to Krais, was to fund Zimmermann's stay in Munich. When this paper went over to another publisher, Frankh must have established the *Hochwächter*.[97] If this assumption is correct, Zimmermann's return to Stuttgart from Munich toward the end of 1830 would seem eminently reasonable since he was being supported by Frankh. At any rate, Frankh, Lohbauer, Rödinger and Tafel were all staunch republicans who had been inspired to establish their paper as a result of the 1830 July Revolution. It was with these men that Zimmermann now associated himself for some time to come, not only as associate editor of the *Hochwächter* but also later as editor of the *Württembergischer Landbote*, also published by Frankh.

Although Zimmermann appears to have been the least politically active of the group — his contributions in the *Hochwächter*, for example, consisted primarily of an occasional poem — his association with this paper marks both the beginning of his growing political involvement as well as the beginning of a growing interest in history. Perhaps it was the 1830 July Revolution which first stimulated this interest in history, for in November of that year he submitted a short history of the Belgian Revolt, which he had apparently written for the *Hochwächter*, to the philosophical faculty at the University of Tübingen in partial fulfillment for the degree of doctor of philosophy.[98] Although a copy of this piece could not be located to date, we do have the Tübingen historian, Haug's, *Gutachten* on it. He described it as follows:

"Sie enthällt eine, für ein größeres Publikum bestimmte im ganzen wohlgeordnete, lebhafte, gut geschriebene Erzählung der belgischen Revolution (bis gegen Ende des J. 1830) mit ihren Ursachen, — soweit sich dieselben aus den Journalen geben ließen. Die widersprechenden Angaben und Urtheile der Letzteren sind auch auf das Urtheil des Verf. nicht ohne Einfluß geblieben, indem öfters ein gewisses Schwanken bemerklich ist; allein theils ist dieses bei einem Gegenstand dieser Art ziemlich verzeihlich, dann ist das Streben nach Unparteylichkeit, das sich selbst in diesem Mangel Kund gibt, an und für sich Lobenswerth."[99]

---

[96] *K. Walter*, "Ernst Friedrich Kauffmann und seine schwäbischen Freunde," Zeitschrift für württembergische Landesgeschichte (1937), 417.

[97] In a letter of Dec. 7, 1830, Vischer wrote Zimmermann: "Steckst du, wie man mich angelegen hat, unter Einer Decke mit dem Hochwächter, so ... Wünsche übrigens gute Evenements, u. dass du bald flott wirst mit Frankh ..." Zimmermann Nachlass, 55, 409.

[98] Promotionsakten, p. 5.   [99] Ibid., p. 25.

It was probably while writing this history of the Belgian Revolt of
1830 that Zimmermann came upon the story of Masaniello as given in
Francois Auber's 1828 opera "La muette de Portici" which had itself been
a significant causative factor in the Brussels uprising. And when the opera
was performed on the Stuttgart stage in May of 1831, Zimmermann must
have decided to write his own version, probably in the hope of achieving
results similar to those achieved by Auber's opera in Brussels.[100] In any case,
it is this fascination with revolution that now becomes characteristic of
Zimmermann's historical writing[101] as well as of his later political activity.

From even a cursory glance at his writings, it becomes immediately apparent that Zimmermann turned from his earlier interest in poetry, drama,
and the writing of short stories to a nearly exclusive preoccupation with
history both sacred and profane in the early 1830's. According to his wife,
this transition began in 1833.[102] Within a short period of time it resulted
in the publication of his *Geschichte Württembergs nach seinen Sagen und
Thaten* in two volumes, 1836—37, *Die Befreiungskämpfe der Deutschen
gegen Napoleon* in 1837, *Prinz Eugen der edle Ritter* also in 1837, and his
two-volume *Geschichte der Hohenstaufen* in 1838—39. This early period
of historical writing culminated in the publication of his massive three-
volume *Geschichte des grossen deutschen Bauernkrieges* in the years 1841—
43, a study he always regarded as his most important work.

8. ZIMMERMANN'S HISTORICAL FRAME OF REFERENCE

Zimmermann's transition from poet, dramatist, and would-be novellist
to historian is of the greatest significance for the creation of his historical
frame of reference. For it is his basically romantic approach to history,
with its classical overtones, which provides him with the grand historical
framework within which the other influences — those emanating from
Baur, Hegel and the revolutionary tradition — became operative. That
this historical perspective should be most clearly delineated — and that in
nearly classic Romantic fashion — in the introduction to his *Geschichte der*

---

[100] See *A. Friesen*, "Zimmermann's Historical Frame of Reference," in *V. G. Doerksen*,
et al., Literary Essays presented to K. W. Maurer (The Hague 1973), for a discussion
of this drama and how it relates to the problem at hand.

[101] This attraction to revolutionary movements was noted even in his Prinz Eugen
by his reviewer in the Hallische Jahrbücher, 270 (Nov. 11, 1838), 2168: "Mit sichtbarer
Vorliebe und unverkennbarem Talente verweilt der Verf. bei dem tyroler Aufstande im
Jahre 1703, und hier, wo es sich um den kleinen Krieg handelt, und von strategischen
Operationen nie die Rede ist, bewegt sich der Verf. auch mehr auf seinem Boden, und
entwirft uns ein lebensvolles Bild dieser denkwürdigen Episode."

[102] *L. Zimmermann*, "Wilhelm Zimmermann," Zimmermann Nachlass, Z 1030.

Hohenstaufen was to be expected, for it was this period of history which had enticed him to try his hand at the historical novel in the first place.

"Die Zeit der Hohenstaufen ist anerkannt an Geist, Leben und Bewegung die reichste in der deutschen Geschichte; ja, sie ist die einzige, deren Charaktere und Kämpfe den Eindruck des Erhabenen im Ganzen machen. Man zeige mir das Werk, in welchem dem großartigen Stoffe die gleich großartige Behandlung geworden! Wo die Kunst der Composition, welche Kämpfer und Kämpfe zum wirklich erhabenen Schauspiel gruppirt? Wo die dramatische Darstellung, welche die todten Skelette des Quellenstudiums über das Meer der gelehrten Untersuchungen nicht nur bloß emporhebt, sondern beseelt, und leibhaftig in schönem, sinnlichem Gewande vor die Augen führt? Wo die Kunst des Kolorits, welche die Zeiten, den Menschen und Thaten die wahre Physiognomie, die wahre Lebensfarbe gegeben? wo die Architektonik, welche dem ganzen Bau und jedem Stockwerk, den ihm eigenthümlichen historischen Charakter und Styl aufgedrückt? Alle Welt sagt, die Geschichte der Hohenstaufen ist die große Tragödie des Mittelalters. Aber wo ist die Bearbeitung, welche dieselbe im tragischen Styl, als Tragödie darböte? Alle dichterischen Versuche sind verfehlt, mißglückt: in Immermanns Friedrich II. allein ist hohenstaufischer Geist. Alle historischen Arbeiten sind weit unter dieser Idee geblieben. Oder wo sind mit kräftiger Hand die zerstreuten Gewitterstoffe der Zeit zusammen gezogen und geladen zum Blitz, zum tragischen Donnerkeil, der einschlägt, einbricht in die Herzen, und erhebt, indem er zermalmt? Hat man nicht vielmehr, statt, wie es die historische Wahrheit verlangt, die Blitze zum tragischen Gewitter zu laden, dadurch, daß man die Schuld der hohenstaufischen Helden nicht nur nicht mit den brennenden Farben der Wirklichkeit zeichnete, sondern sie überall zu entschuldigen suchte und sie ins Schöne malte, gerade das Tragische und die Wirkung vernichtet?"[103]

France, he continued, had its national epic: Segur's history of the great army. Did the Germans really wish to substitute the historical novel in its place? Surely German history had enough great moments which, expressed in the best literary style, could be turned into a national epic. And what material was better suited for this purpose than the history of the Hohenstaufen with its tragically noble struggle of world monarchy against the papacy and republican liberty? He had made the attempt. Let others do so as well! For the time had finally come to demonstrate that history was more than the mere cataloguing of facts; it was an art that demanded the poet's best skills. And those areas of history only dimly lit, who could better illuminate them than the poet with his fertile imagination? This being the case, no other period of German history was better suited for

---

[103] W. *Zimmermann*, Geschichte der Hohenstaufen, vol. I, 2nd ed. (Stuttgart, 1843), p. 5.

the purposes at hand, for the history of the Hohenstaufen was itself the noblest poetry.[104]

History, therefore, to be worthy of the name, should concern itself above all with topics of epic and dramatic proportions — the history of the Hohenstaufen, the German Peasants' War, and the history of the Christian Church. At the same time, these topics should be treated in a manner and a language worthy of the subject matter. The actors must come alive on the printed page, for history was made by living men and should portray them, not deal with musty documents relating to lifeless events only. Thus the tedious burden of archival research could be left largely to others,[105] for Zimmermann intended to portray history in its more literary form as drama and epic.

Nevertheless, within this broader framework, the historian must deal critically and objectively with his material. In this respect, Zimmermann places the same emphasis upon objectivity as his former teacher, Baur. Indeed, when one reads his repeated protestations of objectivity, one might well be led to believe himself in the presence of another Ranke, for Zimmermann can on occasion present a fairly sophisticated view of the historian's craft. In his earliest study, *Die Befreiungskämpfe der Deutschen gegen Napoleon*, for example, he remarked that many previous histories on the same subject, widely disseminated amongst the populace, had deviated from the truth because of their "enthusiasm and partiality" for a given viewpoint. Others had either failed to study the sources in the right light, or altogether. He, in contrast, had attempted to portray those days in their true colors. He had attempted even more: he had sifted the documents and presented his story in a manner designed to afford insight into the motive forces of the period.[106] And in the introduction to his *Geschichte der Hohenstaufen* he stated:

"Ich bin mir bewußt, von keiner politischen, religiösen, poetischen oder sonstigen Illusion auszugehen, wenn es nicht etwa eine Illusion ist, die sittlichen Gesetze als die unverrückbaren Grundpfeiler der Weltgeschichte, als ewig und allgemein gültig zu betrachten."[107]

---

[104] Ibid., pp. 8—10.

[105] Karl Hagen, for example, wrote him on Oct. 22, 1856: "Übrigens ersehe ich dass Du den neuen Schriften, wie z. B. Jörg, denselben Wert beilegst wie ich. In der That, diese Urkundenmenschen thun uns die besten Dienste." Zimmermann Nachlass, Z 1014. He himself acknowledged in the introduction to his Geschichte der Hohenstaufen: "ich gestehe gern, dass ich ohne ihre Arbeiten kaum gewagt hätte, diesen grossen Stoff vorzunehmen," p. 5.

[106] *Zimmermann*, Die Befreiungskämpfe der Deutschen gegen Napoleon (Stuttgart, 1837), pp. 12—13.   [107] *Zimmermann*, Geschichte der Hohenstaufen, I, 6.

Similar statements could be culled from all his other studies. Taken in isolation, however, these remarks give a completely false picture.

Like Baur, Zimmermann, too, assumed that objective historical research could readily be, indeed, must be, combined with the latest philosophical perspective. He appears therefore to have rejected Ranke's position, declaring that the latter's writings lacked character.[108] History had to be more than mere painstaking research.

"Es ist endlich an der Zeit," he wrote in his *Hohenstaufen*, "durch die That zu beweisen, daß man in Deutschland das bloße Aneinanderreihen von aufgethürmten Citaten nicht mehr für Geschichtschreibung hält."[109]

He himself, he continued, had read all the documents these historians had collected on the Hohenstaufen era and had been forced to the conclusion that they had misinterpreted a great many of them because they had not understood what it was that was the motive force of history, or what history's goal. Before one could correctly interpret an age, these things had to be understood.

It is at this juncture that Baur and Hegel become important for Zimmermann's view of history. With Baur, Zimmermann had come to believe that history was moving toward a goal. With Hegel, he had come to recognize that the motive force of history was the rational world spirit which, in cooperation with human reason, was working toward the realization of the Kingdom of God on earth. And like Hegel, he, too, argued that

"Den Inhalt einer Idee erkennt man recht deutlich erst aus ihrer Entfaltung."[110]

The fully developed state of history, however, was the Kingdom of God on earth with its total freedom and brotherhood. That this is so for Zimmermann, the introductory poem to his *Masaniello* demonstrates only too clearly. And this is only confirmed more in his mind as time passes. Thus in his *Lebensgeschichte der Kirche Jesu Christi* he argues with equal if not more conviction that

---

[108] In an essay I have been unable to locate, Zimmermann must have, like Baur, considered the "merely" objective position insufficient, for in his Tagebücher *Varnhagen van Ense*, under the date of January 14, 1848, wrote: "Kleine Schrift gegen Ranke's Geschichtsschreibung, von Zimmermann. Was hier gegen Ranke's 'Preussische Geschichten' gesagt wird, hab' ich längst gesagt, aber auch schon gegen seine 'Geschichte der Reformation.' Es fehlt der Karakter." Aus dem Nachlass Varnhagen's van Ense. Tagebücher von K. A. Varnhagen van Ense, vol. 4 (Leipzig, 1862), p. 234.

[109] *Zimmermann*, Geschichte der Hohenstaufen, I, 9.

[110] *Zimmermann*, Lebensgeschichte der Kirche Jesu Christi, III, 10.

"Eine beschränkte Geschichtsanschauung hat Jahrhunderte lang gehindert, den Plan der göttlichen Vorsehung zu begreifen, welchen sie, Völker erziehend, vorbereitend, und auf dem Wege der menschlichen Freiheit der Reife entgegenführend, in der Weltgeschichte uns vor Augen legt, und es ist ein erfreuliches Zeichen, daß in unsern Tagen Alle darüber einig sind, ohne Unterschied des religiösen Bekenntnisses, Alle, welche den Gang der Weltgeschichte im höheren Lichte betrachten, sey es der philosophirenden Vernunft, oder der Offenbarung."[111]

The idea of the Kingdom of God on earth had been in the process of realization, Zimmermann argued, from the earliest of times, though not too many people had recognized the fact. In order to be fully realized, however, it had to permeate the consciousness of all men and enlist their cooperation. Repeatedly he asserted that the awareness of this idea had been present, however nebulously, already in pre-Christian times.[112] Over the years it had become more and more fully developed, particularly amongst the prophets of the Jewish people, until it culminated in Christ, who gave the most lucid expression to these "Christian" ideas.[113] But the awareness of these ideas amongst the masses and their implementation in society was a much slower and more gradual process.

"Noch heute," he remarked in his *Lebensgeschichte der Kirche*, "nach mehr als achtzehn Jahrhunderten, ist die Fülle der Worte Jesu sich gleich und unversiegbar, ihre Tiefe unerschöpflich, so viel auch von den größten Geistern daraus genommen und verarbeitet worden ist. Ja, daß jetzt erst so Vieles anfängt, in das Leben der Gesellschaft und in die Staatenordnung einzugehen, was schon in den Evangelien enthalten ist und in den Briefen des Johannes und des Paulus; daß jetzt erst die Menschheit zu mancher dieser Ideen heraufgewachsen ist und heranreift, und daß noch viele kommende Jahrhunderte anderer dieser Ideen entgegen zu wachsen und entgegen zu reifen haben werden, ist der augenfällige Beweis für die Fülle und Tiefe der Gedanken, für die Größe der Anschauungen, mit welchen Jesus Christus hineintrat unter sein damaliges Volk."[114]

History, therefore, moved relentlessly forward toward its goal.

But although history moved relentlessly forward, not all of its stages manifested equal progress toward its goal. Some, particularly the revolutionary stages, were marked by a decided accelleration of progress toward freedom. For revolutions were historical moments in which progress took giant strides foward. Hence, Zimmermann's glorification of such revolutionaries as Masaniello and Müntzer as well as the European revolutionary tradition beginning with the German Peasants' War, continuing through the English and American Revolutions, and culminating in the French Re-

---

[111] Ibid., pp. 5—6.   [112] Ibid., I, 13.   [113] Ibid., pp. 73—75.   [114] Ibid., p. 75.

volution. Hence, also, his interest in the July Revolution of 1830 and his personal involvement in the Revolution of 1848. And even after the failure of 1848 he could still write his friend Vischer:

"Sähen wir uns einmal wieder, so würde sich bald heraus stellen, daß wir in den politischen Haupt- und grund-Puncten jezt einander viel näher sind, als früher. Das Ziel liegt für mich, wie für dich, in weiter Ferne. Aber ob auch Welle um Welle sich bricht u. zerschellt, der Strom geht vorwärts."[115]

Prior to 1848, Zimmermann was convinced of the imminent inauguration of the Kingdom of God on earth. We could cite numerous passages to this effect. One, however, should suffice to prove our contentions. In 1847, Zimmermann, who had been a pastor at Hülben and assistant at Dettingen since 1840, was appointed professor of literature, history, and the German language at the *Polytechnischen* and *Oberrealschule* in Stuttgart. But the social ferment of the years 1848—49 was to intrude upon his *vita contemplativa* and draw him into the *vita activa*, as with so many other German professors in those years. Intensely interested in changing the course of German history in a republican direction, Zimmermann ran for and was elected to the national parliament in Frankfurt. Here he joined the radical wing of the Paulskirche known as the "Donnersberg," and, together with Arnold Ruge,[116] became one of its leading spokesmen as well as the eyewitness historian of its proceedings. In 1849 and 1850, he was a representative to the Constitutional Convention assembled in Frankfurt. But because of the failure of the liberal movement and the consequent conservative reaction together with his radical politics and his adherence to the rump parliament of 1851, Zimmermann was dismissed from his teaching post.

It was in a speech delivered in the Paulskirche on Friday, August 25, 1848, that Zimmermann gave classic expression to his belief in the imminent inauguration of the Kingdom of God on earth.

"Wir sind jetzt auf der Schwelle einer neuen Zeit,"[117]

he remarked in a speech on the separation of Church and State. Because this was so, even he was willing to grant to the Church — Protestant and Catholic alike — complete freedom. For not even the Church would be

---

[115] Zimmermann to Vischer, Oct. 30, 1864. Zimmermann Nachlass.

[116] *W. Neher*, Arnold Ruge als Politiker und politischer Schriftsteller (Heidelberg, 1933), p. 174.

[117] Stenographischer Bericht über die Verhandlungen der deutschen constituirenden National-Versammlung zu Frankfurt a. M. (Frankfurt, 1849), III, 1702. The speech begins on p. 1701 and ends on p. 1703.

able to oppose the spirit of the times which was moving so mightily in society at the moment. This spirit of the times was much more powerful than any party or party aims. Thus he remarked:

"Ich will es erleben, meine Herren, daß Viele, ja, daß die Besten, die bisher auf Seite der Kirche, — wieder meine ich, die protestantische, wie die katholische, — die bisher auf Seite der Kirche wider die Freiheit gestanden und gestritten haben, daß Viele zu uns in Bälde herüberkommen werden, und mit uns stehen und gehen. Ich halte auch dafür, insbesondere in dieser Hinsicht, daß gerade die Besten dem Strome des Zeitgeistes nicht werden widerstehen können."[118]

Indeed, he continued, the Church may well have to die before it rises again empowered to perform its true task.

"Der zerrüttende Widerstreit zwischen den Glaubensstücken, welche unhaltbar geworden sind, und zwischen dem Nichtglauben, welcher eines großen Opfers nicht fähig ist, dieser zerrüttende Widerstreit wird sich auflösen in eine hellere Ansicht der ewigen Wahrheiten. Die Religion des Geistes ist im Anzuge, die Zeit des rein innerlichen Gottesreiches ist im Anbruch. Um aber, meine Herren, dahin zu gelangen, daß die Kirche diese glückliche Entwicklung an sich macht, muß sie zuvor frei gemacht werden; nur die freie Kirche wird übergehen in eine Religion des Geistes."[119]

No clearer statement could be given to demonstrate that Zimmermann believed history to be on the threshhold of a new era. That era, indeed, was the consummation of all history. And if one could recognize the content of an idea most plainly in its fully developed state, and if this fully developed state of history was the Kingdom of God on earth whose most prominent characteristic was freedom, then, of course, one could project this idea far back into history and judge all past history in the light of the present. That he himself did this, Zimmermann freely acknowledged to Vischer on one occasion, as Vischer related in a letter to David Friedrich Strauss:

---

[118] Ibid., p. 1703. An interesting confirmation of this, Zimmermann's position, is to be found in a letter from Moriz Carriere to Zimmermann, probably written in Frankfurt in 1848. In it Carriere stated: "Ich schicke dir hier einen Abdruck des früher erwähnten Gedichts; schreibe mir doch mit ein paar Zeilen was du dazu sagst. Manchen wird es nicht gefallen dass hier die religiöse Seite angeschlagen wird, ich erwarte aber von unsrer Politik eher kein Heil als bis das allgemein geschieht. Nur die seltsamliche Verwirrung dass die streng religiöse Leute Legitimisten sind, statt an das Gottesreich der Freien zu denken, dass die Demokraten ihren Humanismus auf den dunklen Grund der Materie statt auf den lichten des göttlichen Selbstbewußtseins pflanzen, und die Rationalisten, nun das sind die constitutionell Liberalen, die Gott erleuchten möchte!" Zimmermann Nachlass.   [119] Stenographischer Bericht, p. 1703.

"Dieser [Zimmermann] badet von Küsterdingen aus hier täglich in Schwefel, hat Gicht, ist aber munter wie immer, und ist gegenwärtig mit einer Bearbeitung deutscher Sagen beschäftigt, worein er, wie er mir heiter sagte, nach Willkür tiefere Ideen hineinträgt."[120]

The same could be said of him, therefore, that he himself said of his hero, Schiller:

"Er [Schiller] liess alle Ideen seiner Zeit, alle grossen menschlichen Interessen in sich einströmen, und strömte sie wieder aus verherrlicht in Ton und Gestalt. Ihm war es unendlich mehr werth, statt der Sitten und Trachten der vergangenen Zeiten seine eigene Zeit kennen zu lernen, ihren Pulsschlag, ihre Wunden und ihre Bedürfnisse, er stattete althistorische Namen als Representanten und Träger modernster Ideen aus, und trug auf sie die Farben der Gegenwart und der Zukunft auf, dessen, was ist, und dessen, was sein soll. Oder that er nicht so im Don Carlos, im Wallenstein, im Tell, im Demetrius? Deutsche Freunde, das habt ihr ihm noch nicht abgelernt."[121]

9. ZIMMERMANN'S CHANGED HISTORICAL PERSPECTIVE

It is within this frame of reference that Zimmermann wrote his *Bauernkrieg*. But events intervened to change his views in significant ways between 1848 and the 1856 revised second edition of the same work. First came the failure of the revolution, and closely on its heels followed Zimmermann's dismissal from his teaching post. Left without a source of income except for his royalties, which, although substantial, were not enough to support his family, Zimmermann was forced to accept aid from Maria Bruinningk, a lady of nobility who had been drawn to him at Frankfurt. Finally, in 1854, the Lutheran Consistory of Württemberg, against the advice of the king, was persuaded to reappoint Zimmermann to a pastorate. He was thereupon given the pastorate at Leonbronn, with the lowest income and farthest removed from Stuttgart, on the promise of his total withdrawal from politics.

Writing in the preface to the 1856 revised edition of his *Bauernkrieg* he himself remarked:

"Ich selbst bin inzwischen nicht nur durch Jahre und Erfahrung überhaupt reifer, kühler und maßvoller geworden, sondern auch mitten in einer ähnlichen Volksbewegung gestanden und habe zum Teil darin mitgehandelt; ich habe an der lebendigen Gegenwart Beobachtungen und Vergleichungen anstellen können, und ich

---

[120] *Rapp*, Strauss-Vischer Briefwechsel, I, 143.
[121] *Zimmermann*, "Der Roman der Gegenwart und Eugen Sue's Geheimnisse," Jahrbücher der Gegenwart, II (1844), 218.

habe auch daraus manches gelernt. Das konnte auf die Auffassungen und Darstellung der Menschen und Dinge in meinem Buche nicht ohne tieferen Einfluss bleiben; es mußte dadurch vieles in Form und Inhalt richtiger, wirklicher, wahrer werden. Alles, was mir jugendlich und idealisierend an der früheren Gestalt des Buches schien, alles Parteifarbige und Tendenziöse habe ich ausgeschnitten, ganz Neues eingefügt, nicht nur sehr vieles, sondern das Ganze in Form umgestaltet. So ist das Buch in Form und Inhalt großenteils ein ganz neues geworden."[122]

From the above, it would appear that the change in Zimmermann was mostly political. It was more than this, however, as a number of factors indicate. Prior to the change, Zimmermann belonged to the Young Hegelians as his poem on Christ, quoted as the introduction to the first chapter, his delineation of the chief tenets of Christianity contained in his lectures on history, and the passage, also quoted in the first chapter, from his review of Eugen Sue's *Mysteres de Paris*, clearly demonstrate. As late as 1847, in his letter of application to the Minister of Education, Schlayer, for the position of professor at the *Polytechnischen* and *Oberrealschule* in Stuttgart, he stated:

"Ich gelte für freisinnig. Ich bin es im edeln und reinen Sinne des Wortes, nicht destruktiv, sondern konservativ. Wo ich einzeln geirrt habe und durch Tatsachen eines Besseren überzeugt worden bin, da änderte ich meine einzelne Ansicht: andere Änderung als die, welche von innen heraus unabweislich sich aufdringt, werden die Grundsätze meines Handelns und Redens nicht erleiden ... Meine religiöse Weltanschauung endlich ist die christliche."[123]

Perhaps the first indication of change comes in a letter of application, one of many, to the Consistory of September 4, 1854, in which Zimmermann remarked:

"Wie sehr meine Ansichten ganz der christlichen Anschauung unserer heiligen Urkunden entsprechen, das glaube ich in meinem neuesten Buche 'Weltgeschichte für gebildete Frauen' durchgängig bewiesen zu haben."[124]

This in itself would not be enough to convince us of any major change. But sometime during late 1854 or early 1855, Zimmermann must have sent a copy of the third edition of his poems to Moriz Carriere in Munich. On February 25, 1855, Carriere responded, thanking for the gift. A certain Geibel, he remarked, had read some of the best poems at a recent gathering with considerable success. But, Carriere continued,

[122] *Zimmermann*, Bauernkrieg, Barge edition, I, XXXV-XXXVI.
[123] Quoted in ibid., p. VIII. The term "Christian" as used here must be understood in the light of Zimmermann's delineation of the tenets of the Christian faith as given in his "Vorlesungen über Geschichte."   [124] Landeskirchliches Archiv.

"Er vermißt ein Gedicht an Christus, warum hast du das nicht aufgenommen?"[125]

It is not evident what Zimmermann's response was, or if he responded at all. Yet it could well be that he had in the meantime changed his mind on the question of the deity of Christ and excluded the poem precisely for that reason. This supposition would seem to be confirmed by a manuscript until recently a part of the "Zimmermann Nachlass" housed in the Schiller Nationalmuseum in Marbach, entitled "Warnung vor der Philosophie." The manuscript is no longer there,[126] however, having been removed at some point after 1921, for in a doctoral dissertation of that year on Zimmermann's poetry, Eugen Stemmer incorporated some of its best parts. In it Zimmermann wrote:

"Seid mir Zeuge, ihr Nächte, da ich an den zerrüttenden Wirkungen dieses Studiums schlaflos zu meinem Gott um Wahrheit flehte, da ich die Hände hilflos zu meinem Heiland erhob; seid mir Zeuge ihr Stunden, da ich durch Todesnacht wandelte, bis die Eindrücke des Hegel'schen Systems, wie ein wüster Traum aus meinem Gehirn entrückt waren."[127]

At the same time, Stemmer continues, Zimmermann turned against all those theologians who (and he quotes from the manuscript once again),

"in ihren Heften einen vernünftig abgeleiteten Glauben fertigliegen haben."[128]

His hero, Stemmer goes on, now became the Romantic philosopher, Friedrich Heinrich Jakobi, to whom he addressed the following words:

"Dein verklärtes Antlitz, Du edler Geist, sehe ich aus reinen Höhen auf mich u. meinen Kampf für die gute Sache herniederlächeln."[129]

Zimmermann praised Jakobi, Stemmer says, because he, Jakobi, had not disdained

"auf den Ruhm der Philosophie zu verzichten, um den unsterblichen Kranz des Christen zu erlangen."[130]

At this point, as Stemmer remarkes, Zimmermann turned not only against Hegel, but also against his former teacher, more than likely Baur, and friends such as Strauss.

---

[125] Zimmermann Nachlass.

[126] Werner Volke, the curator of the manuscript collection at the Schiller Nationalmuseum, wrote me on Oct. 5, 1971: "Zimmermanns 'Warnung vor der Philosophie' wird von Otto von Güntter [who collected the original material] als im Nachlass befindlich angeführt. Tatsächlich aber befindet sich das Manuskript nicht unter den bei uns vorhandenen Beständen. Ich nehme an, dass es bei irgendeiner Gelegenheit dem Nachlass entfremdet worden ist."   [127] *Stemmer*, "Wilhelm Zimmermann," p. 52.

[128] Ibid.   [129] Ibid., p. 53.   [130] Ibid.

"Ihr seid nicht meine Brüder, wenn ihr euch des einfachen durch seine [Jakobi's]
philosophische Wehrlosigkeit allein siegreichen Christentums schämt. Wenn ich je
in Gefahr war, ein Unchrist zu werden, so war es eure Methode, welche, zu-
schwach, die Skepsis, die sie in mir heraufbeschworen, zu bezwingen, mich in die
Versuchung führte. Ihr seid Halbchristen, u. wenn ihr euch abkreuzigt, für eure
Überzeugungen von den Gedanken Wissen zu leihen, so schlägt diese lächerliche
Not eurem Christentum tiefere Wunden, als es eure Gegner tun; lieber wollte ich
mit diesen ein Heide, als mit euch ein Christ sein."[131]

This changed perspective is amply apparent in Zimmermann's four-
volume history of the Christian Church written in 1857—59; but it would
take us too far afield were we to attempt to trace this change here. Suffice
it to say that although the change is there, it is not as profound a change
as Zimmermann seems to imply in his "Warnung vor der Philosophie."
It may well be for this reason that that document was removed from the
rest of his papers. The broad historical framework is still there, only the
motive force has once more become more overtly Christian. It may be for
this reason that Zimmermann turned to the Heidelberg theologian, K. B.
Hundeshagen, a colleague of Richard Rothe, to write the preface to his
history of the Church rather than to his old teacher, Baur.

At the same time, this more Christian content of his thought turned him
away from politics. Writing in his 1854 "Lebensabriss," a document that
no longer contains any proud references to his association with Waiblinger
or his role in establishing the Hegelian philosophy in Tübingen, Zimmermann remarked:

"In dieser meiner öfftl. Laufbahn hatte ich kein anderes Ziel, als diejenigen Rechte,
welche das Evangelium allen Menschen als Kindern Gottes zuerkennt, zur Anerkennung im Staate zu bringen. Aus politischen Rücksichten im Jahre 1851 meiner 'Dienstverrichtungen an der polyt. Schule enthoben', wurde ich, da ich nach
langem Kampfe eine stille Stätte des Friedens suchte, in den letzten Wochen auf
meine Bitte zum Pfarrer allhier [Leonbronn] ernannt, u. trete diesem Beruf an
in der Hoffnung, mehr Früchte meines Wirkens zu erleben, als ich von meinem
früheren öfftl. Wirken erlebte. Gott gebe seinen Segen zu diesem meinem neuen
Amte."[132]

And, as a certain Mehl from the Stuttgart *Staatsdekanatsamt* reported
to the Consistory regarding a conversation he had had with Zimmermann,
the latter

"sprach ... auch gegen mich den dringenden Wunsch aus, 1.) allem politischen
Treiben, das seine Zeit und Kraft früher zu viel in Anspruch genommen habe,

---

[131] Ibid.   [132] Zimmermann Nachlass, Z 966.

ferne zu bleiben, und insbesondere seine Stelle als Abgeordneter der zweiten Kammer in Bälde, noch vor dem Beginn des nächsten Landtags niederlegen zu können, und 2.) in stiller Zurückgezogenheit als Pfarrer sich einer Gemeinde in allen Beziehungen widmen zu können."[133]

But Zimmermann had not given up all hope in the establishment of basic "Christian" tenets as the guiding principles of the State. Writing to Emil Adolf Rossmässler on July 21, 1856, he said:

"Hier siz ich an der Quelle der Zaber in einem wald- u. rebengrünen engen Thal, wie unter den Bäumen einer Insel, seitab von Allem, was die Welt bewegt, u. lebe der Wissenschaft u. dem Glauben an die Zukunft; an das jezt lebende Geschlecht habe ich keinen mehr. Sonst der Alte."[134]

And to his old friend, Vischer, as we have seen, he wrote in 1864:

"Das Ziel liegt für mich, wie für dich, in weiter Ferne. Aber ob auch Welle um Welle sich bricht u. zerschellt, der Strom geht vorwärts."

It is these words that are engraved on his tombstone.

---

[133] Mehl to the Consistory, Sept. 5, 1854. Landeskirchliches Archiv.
[134] Württembergische Landesbibliothek, Stuttgart, Cod. hist. 8° 146, 9.

Chapter VI

ZIMMERMANN'S BAUERNKRIEG

1. THE SETTING OF ZIMMERMANN'S *BAUERNKRIEG*

Immediately after the last volume of his *Bauernkrieg* appeared in print, Zimmermann wrote a letter to the Heidelberg historian, Georg Gottfried Gervinus, requesting a favorable review of that study from him. He dared to do this, he remarked in his opening paragraph, because the latter was in every respect an independent man of noble mind and character. In fact, Zimmermann continued, Gervinus had been his model. Then in words reminiscent of the eloquent description of the historical tradition he had described in the introduction to his *Hohenstaufen*, he wrote:

"Sie werden es gewiß nur natürlich finden, daß ein Schriftsteller, dem historische Kunst und gründliche Quellenforschung in einem Geschichtswerke zu verbinden unerläßlich dünkt, u. der beides bei dieser Arbeit nie aus dem Auge zu lassen sich sorgfältig angelegen sein ließ, an Sie sich wendet, der Sie durch Thaten bewährt haben, wie sehr Sie Geschichtsschreibung und Geschichtsforschung, den Muth, die Ausdauer und das Auge, womit man sich allein mit Glück in die Quellen versenken kann, mit der darstellenden Kunst verbinden. Möchten Eu. Hochw. mir auch das Zeugnis geben können, daß Sie mich auf Ihrer Bahn finden."

At the same time, Zimmermann emphasized the importance he had placed upon archival research and drew attention to the new insights he had brought to bear upon the Reformation era as a whole, not merely upon the Peasants' War, as a result.

"Ein Auge, wie das Ihrige," he remarked, "das die große Epoche der Reformation im rechten, im wahren Lichte zu sehen vermag, wird auch den Gegenstand meiner Arbeit in seiner wahren Bedeutung zu würdigen wissen. Vielleicht finden Sie, daß mein Buch die Reformation selbst von dieser und jener Seite, wo man schon die Acten geschlossen glaubte, auf eine entscheidende Weise neu zu beleuchten beiträgt, indem es seinen Gegenstand unmittelbar aus den Urkunden und unbefangen von jedem hergebrachten Vorurtheil behandelt. Der erste Theil, in Heften ausgegeben, unterlag jedoch der Zensur, und zwar einer sehr verstümmelnden."

Zimmermann's purpose in writing his *Bauernkrieg* was not merely to shed new light on the history of the Reformation era, however.

"Ich wollte," he stated, "meinem Volke ein Buch in die Hand geben, das eine seiner denkwürdigsten Begebenheiten der Wahrheit getreu und würdig erzählen, und das von interessantem Bezug auf seine Gegenwart wäre: hängt doch die grosse Bewegung von 1525 mit der neusten Strebung und Gährung innig zusammen, wenn auch nicht das Gestern, doch wie das Vorgestern mit dem Heute. Die bedeutungsvollsten Klänge, so manichfaltig sie durch die Gegenwart sich ziehen, sind sie nicht dieselben, welche durch das erste Jahrzehnt der Reformation rauschten? Es sind dieselben Saiten, die angeschlagen werden, und der sie spielt, ist ein und derselbe Geist."[1]

And this spirit, of course, was about to inaugurate the Kingdom of God on earth, as Zimmermann asserted in his famous speech to the assembled delegates in the Paulskirche. He it was who had been at work in the first decades of the Reformation era and who now appeared in much more distinct form in the current turmoil.

In his "Lebensabriss" of 1854, Zimmermann had remarked that

"In dieser meiner öfftl. Laufbahn hatte ich kein anderes Ziel, als diejenigen Rechte, welche das Evangelium allen Menschen als Kindern Gottes zuerkennt, zur Anerkennung im Staate zu bringen."

In striving toward this goal, Zimmermann believed himself to be working hand in hand with the spirit of the times whose goal was the establishment of the Kingdom of God on earth. Politics and theology, therefore, must be brought together; there could be no separation of these "two realms." Germany, however, he argued in his "Vorlesungen über Deutsche Geschichte," although richest in intellectual giants, had failed miserably in the realm of politics because of her inability to bring ideas to bear upon political reality.

"Wenn man die deutsche Gesch. in ihrem ganzen Verlaufe übersieht," he remarked, "erblickt man in derselben fast überall die Anfänge der politischen Gestaltungen, die dann in der europäischen Geschichte Epoche machten. Aber auch bei keiner einzigen politischen Schöpfung oder Erneuerung in menschl. u. göttlichen Dingen sind die Deutschen diejenigen gewesen, welche diese neue Gestaltung in ihren rein-

---

[1] Zimmermann to Gervinus, Jan. 12, 1844. Universitätsbibliothek Heidelberg, Heid. Hs. 2529 Nr. 450. Zimmermann concluded the letter with the following paragraph: "Den Regierungen von Baiern u. Baden war es mißfällig, mein Buch den Weg seiner Bestimmung gehen zu lassen: schuldlos wurde es von beiden verboten, geächtet. Nehmen Ew. Hochw. es mit Wohlwollen auf! Beurtheilen Sie seine Unvollkommenheit mit Nachsicht und mit Rücksicht darauf, daß es unter mancherlei Beschränkungen, fern von Bibliotheken und Archiven, fern vom Druckort, unter vielfachen Amtsgeschäften auf einer Pfarrei, einsam u. abgelegen am Fuße der schwäbischen Alp, geschrieben wurde. Sprechen Sie, wenn Sie das Buch dessen Werth finden, ein freundliches Wort für dasselbe, wo Sie können und wollen."

sten u. vollendetsten Umriß darzustellen vermocht hätten. Das Lehenwesen hat seine Anfänge in Deutschland — seine strengsten Formen aber hat es durch Franzosen erhalten in England u. im Königreich Jerusalem."[2]

The same was true, he continued, of the development of the free cities which, although beginning in Germany as well, achieved their greatest independence in Italy and the Netherlands, whereupon the latter soon broke away from Germany. This, Zimmermann continued, was also true of the Reformation.

"In Deutschland war es zuerst, wo die Reformation alle, auch die geringeren Gemeindeglieder, aufrief, selbständig über kirchlich-gesellschaftliche Verhältnisse zu urtheilen u. im Leben die Aussprüche der Vernunft u. der Bibel geltend zu machen; aber nicht in Deutschland, sondern in dem germanischen England, unter Cromwell, und dann jenseits des Ozeans durch die Auswanderungen in Amerika, gab diese freie religiöse Richtung eigenthümlichen politischen Formen im großen Styl eigenthümlichen Staatenbildungen ihr Daseyn."[3]

2. LUTHER'S ROLE IN THE PEASANTS' WAR

The Reformation, Zimmermann asserted, demonstrated only too vividly how brilliantly the Germans could think, invent, speak, debate, and write; but it showed, too, that they were incapable of execution, of carrying through; they could not act.

"Immer war das deutsche Volk der Jüngling mit schönen Gedanken," he lamented, "mit kühnen Entwürfen, mit großen Träumen; aber wie ein solcher Jüngling im Leben, so brachte das deutsche Volk in der Geschichte es nicht zum Handeln, vor laut. Denken u. Träumen nicht zum Handeln, u. darum brachten beide es zu Nichts. Unpraktisch ist das deutsche Volk."[4]

It is at this juncture that Zimmermann sets the stage for his broader interpretation of the Reformation and Luther's role in it.

"Luther," he chided, "konnte mit etwas weniger Theologie, aber mehr Politik, mit etwas mehr Verstand und weniger Glaubenseifer etwas ganz Anderes für Deutschland werden. Aber er verlor über theolog. Sätzen den großen Gedanken des Vaterlandes aus den Augen, und band die eben gelöste, losgerissene Kirche sogleich wieder fest, u. woran? an die Besonderinteressen derj. Fürsten, die seinen Katechismus annahmen."[5]

Luther had indeed preached against the Turks, but not against those internal enemies who were undermining Germany's greatness and hap-

---

[2] Zimmermann Nachlass (no number or pagination).   [3] Ibid.   [4] Ibid.   [5] Ibid.

piness; he had failed to take advantage of the emerging national sentiment, as manifested in 1517, 1523, and 1525, all of which left him cold. He could have prevented the Thirty Years' War had he wished to do so; indeed, he could have prevented many-a-storm yet to come, storms whose forerunners could already be seen on the horizon.

"Aber Luther," Zimmermann complained, "war Theol. etc. es fehlte ihm der großartige, die Geschichte beherrschende Ueberblick, es fehlte ihm der öffentliche polit. Geist, er war nicht praktisch auf dem Markt, auf dem Boden des öffentl. staatlichen Lebens. Es blieb beim Glauben, es kam nicht zum Handeln durch ihn bei dem größ. Theile der Deutschen: über dem Jenseits wurde das Diesseits vergessen u. verachtet, statt daß das Diesseits gerade aus dem Jenseits die Rechte des Volkes auf Erden, vom Himmel herabgeholt u. an den Himmel geknüpft hätten werden sollen."[6]

This criticism of Luther strikes at one of Luther's fundamental concepts: the separation of the two realms. Zimmermann's argument is not so much that Luther did not know what he was doing, or that he had been badly interpreted; it was rather that Luther's position on the separation of the two realms was fundamentally wrong. This is a philosophical judgment. But Zimmermann believed that it was also a historical judgment, for in those countries where such a separation had not been made, the Reformation had helped to establish new forms of government which had brought greater freedom in their train. Stated in its most naked form, Luther's theory of the separation of the two realms militated against the spirit of the times whose aim was to bring the two realms together by implementing the Christian ideals in temporal society. Fundamentally, therefore, Luther must have been a reactionary.

In his *Bauernkrieg*, Zimmermann combined this view, which saw history as moving relentlessly forward and culminating in the establishment of the society of the free in the Kingdom of God on earth, with the belief that revolutions were accelerations of this forward movement of history, a belief influenced by the French Revolution in particular and the revolutionary tradition deriving from it in general. It is through these eyes that he saw the 16th century, but he extended his revolutionary frame of reference farther than anyone before him by placing the Peasants' War into a specific revolutionary context. He saw the era from the Peasants' War to the French Revolution as the life-span of the bourgeois or democratic revolution which had brought the form of government, which he desired for Germany, to England, the United States of America, and France. Ger-

[6] Ibid.

many, where the earliest of such revolutions had taken place, would hopefully achieve the same results by means of revolution in 1848.

Because he believed that revolution, if successful, could prove to be a
giant stride in the forward march of progress toward history's ultimate
goal, Zimmermann saw the peasants and their leaders as the party of progress, and the princes, together with the Luther after 1522, as forces of
reaction trying to retain the *status quo,* at least in the temporal realm.

However, Zimmermann did not simply divide the forces involved in
the struggle into progressive and reactionary forces along class lines: it
was not simply a matter of dividing the participants into oppressors and
oppressed, for there had been those in the ruling class who had taken the
side of the peasants on the basis of principle. Yet he was quite aware that,
had the revolution been successful, a new form of government would in
all probability have been established which would have taken the power,
and possibly the possessions, away from the ruling princes. At the very
least, the abuses would have been abolished. He pointed out with approval
that even Müntzer had been willing to allow the princes a place in his
Bund.[7] They were not to be ostracized from the new social order; rather,
they were to be integrated into it and made an equal part of it in very
much the same way that Zimmermann hoped the Church in his day would
be made, or become, a part of the new society. Thus it was a principle to
which the forces of progress gave assent, a principle to which all enlightened persons must give assent, for the principle of greater freedom and
more rational government was a principle which lay in the very nature
of things.

It was for this reason that Zimmermann took the side of all those who
seemed to be working toward a rule of greater freedom and rationality. It
was for this reason that he found glowing words with which to praise the
deeds of Franz von Sickingen and Ulrich von Hutten who, according to
him, had attempted to reform the German constitution in the direction
of greater freedom.[8] Not only among the lower classes who were oppressed
and abused could one find adherents of this principle of freedom, but
everywhere where rational and enlightened men met.

Yet, if the leaders of the Peasants' War and the peasants had allied
themselves with the forces of progress, Müntzer and his party formed the
shock troops of this progressive movement; it was in the thought of the
latter that Zimmermann espied the 19th century in embryo. But not everyone had belonged to Müntzer's party, although Zimmermann tried to ex-

[7] *Zimmermann,* Bauernkrieg (1841), II, 72—73.   [8] Ibid., I, 355.

tend the former's influence and his Anabaptist disciples to all parts of the Empire. He conceded that the revolt in the south had been motivated by more conservative objectives than the revolt in the north led by Thomas Müntzer, but this did not mean that the movement in the south was any less progressive; both the less radical and the more radical groups had been for progress as understood by Zimmermann.

Viewed from this perspective, all the peasant groups appeared progressive and therefore Zimmermann did not need to stop to ask whether the basic demands the peasants and their leaders put forward were truly progressive or not, whether they indeed went beyond that which they had once possessed or whether they merely demanded the abolition of abuses which had become attached to the freedoms they had once enjoyed. In the early part of his study, he stated that the peasants had risen in sporadic revolts ever since the early Middle Ages, on the one hand to protect existing freedoms and on the other to ward off new and more onerous burdens.[9] But the abuses had crept in nonetheless because the struggle had been an unequal one. Now, however, he stated that their struggle was a struggle for freedom and therefore also for progress, for freedom was the goal of history. Müntzer and his party had demonstrated these progressive ideas in a very striking way. This would lead one to conclude that had Zimmermann been pressed on the question whether the goals of the peasants in the south, which he admitted were directed more toward the abolition of existing abuses than toward radical revolution,[10] were progressive, he would have been forced to admit that they were not, for they looked backwards to ideal conditions in the past. On the other hand, however, he saw in Müntzer and his Anabaptist emissaries the radical wing of the movement which was progressive indeed, containing in embryo many of the ideas which the Enlightenment was later to accept as fundamental.

It was Zimmermann's desire to integrate the two realms and his consequent political orientation combined with his revolutionary frame of reference which also determined his delineation of Luther's role in the Peasants' War. Like other historians of the Peasants' War mentioned earlier in this study, Zimmermann was concerned with the life of Luther only insofar as it impinged upon the course and outcome of the Peasants' War. Consequently he divided Luther's life into three main periods: that before 1517, that from 1517 to 1521, and the period from 1521 to 1525.[11] In the period before 1517 Luther had not been a public figure, therefore this period held little interest for Zimmermann. It lay far outside the sphere

[9] Ibid., I, 49—50.   [10] Ibid., II, 606.   [11] Ibid., I, 347.

of his interests to enquire into the roots of Luther's thought, into his theological development, for Zimmermann was primarily interested only in the political consequences of these teachings.[12] The second period as well as the third, however, were of vital interest to him because these were the years of Luther's involvement in, and rejection of, the revolutionary peasant movement.

Zimmermann, together with others of his time, agreed that the essence of Luther's teachings had been freedom, and particularly freedom from an oppressive ecclesiastical structure. In order to obtain this freedom, the young Luther, especially in the second period, had manifested very definite revolutionary tendencies. Ostensibly quoting Luther from the year 1517, Zimmermann pointed to a passage in which Luther spoke of washing his hands in the blood of the papists.[13] Similar utterances were to be found scattered throughout most of the young Luther's other writings.[14] And as late as 1520, in his "An den christlichen Adel deutscher Nation," this revolutionary spirit was still very much in evidence, for in that address Luther had called for the subordination of all clerical orders, even of the papacy itself, to the secular government, for the eradication of all papal tithes, and for the termination of the system of papal legates.[15]

By 1521, however, Zimmermann noted a change coming over Luther, the beginning of which could be traced to his "An den christlichen Adel" where he had admonished the nobles to let God destroy the power of the papacy and not to attempt the same by their own power.[16] When enlisted by Hutten for the latter's revolutionary cause in 1521, therefore, Luther responded with a similar answer. Any change would have to be brought about by the Word of God and not by the hand of man; the Gospels did not need to be defended by the sword.

According to Zimmermann, this change in Luther was a direct result of the latter's growing awareness that his religiously oriented pronouncements

---

[12] The historiographical problem of Luther's involvement in the Peasants' War has remained essentially the same since Zimmermann's time: those who view this involvement from a political point of view usually condemn him, while those who view it from a theological point of view (not a theologically polemical point of view) tend to justify him.

[13] *Zimmermann,* Bauernkrieg (1841), I, 364, does not give the source of this quotation. It is, however, to be found in the 1520, not the 1517, "Epitoma responsionis ad Martinum Luther per Fratrem Silvestrum de Prierio," WA, VI, 347. The misdating is not Zimmermann's fault, but that of the editors of the Jena edition of Luther's work which he used. The misdating and the fact that it was written in Latin throws a somewhat different light at least on the period from 1517 to 1520 of Luther's life.

[14] Zimmermann, however, fails to provide specific references. Ibid., p. 365.

[15] Ibid.   [16] Ibid.

could have tremendous political repercussions. Consequently, Luther began to try to extricate himself from his predicament. This was a mistake as far as Zimmermann was concerned. Had Luther accepted the political conse-- quences of his actions, he could have become a powerful factor in the peas-- ants' struggle for freedom.[17] He refused to do this, however, and instead tried to rationalize the contradiction inherent in his advocacy of revolution in the religious realm while at the same time trying to retain the *status quo* in the political realm.

Rumors at once began to circulate that he had forsaken the cause of the common man and had gone over to the side of the princes, yet for some time Luther tried to remain impartial in an increasingly polarized society.[18] When the peasants named him to be one of the judges of their cause, Luther had occasion to admonish both prince and peasant to keep the peace and resolve their differences amicably.[19] He did not remain impartial very long, however; events soon led him to the right in strong support of the princes.

When the peasants disregarded his admonition to keep the peace, Luther became somewhat vexed; he was further irritated when his enemies, Carl- stadt and Müntzer, placed themselves at the head of the revolutionary movement. But when Duke George of Saxony blamed the revolution, which had just broken out in Weinsberg, on him and his reformation, Luther opened the locks on his pent up ire and broke into wild hysteria. The pro- nouncements he now made smacked more of despotism than those of the despots; and, without considering that he had just sanctioned many of the demands of the peasants, Luther turned against them in all his fury with his "Wider die räuberischen und mörderischen Rotten der Bauern," calling on the princes to "zerschmeissen, würgen und stechen heimlich und öffent- lich, wer da kann, wie man einen tollen Hund todtschlagen muss." Princes who hesitated to use force in subduing the revolting peasants were not worthy of their office and were guilty of sinning before God; but those who might die in this cause could wish for no more blessed death.[20]

With friend and foe alike attacking him for being overly severe on the poor peasants, Luther only became more stubborn in the defence of his own position. Normally an obstinate man who could tolerate no contradiction, Luther became much more stubborn when he found himself with his back to the wall and bereft of his supporters. Thus, in the face of this massive opposition, he just held all the more tenaciously to his support of the prin- ces and his condemnation of the peasants.[21] Writing to Dr. Rühl at the

---

[17] Ibid., III, 712.   [18] Ibid.   [19] Ibid.
[20] Ibid., p. 713.   [21] Ibid., p. 714.

height of the storm, Luther turned aside the accusations directed against him that there might be innocent peasants among the slaughtered. God would save the truly innocent, he said. Did He not de so, the dying peasants must at the very least have been guilty of sympathizing with the revolutionary cause, if not guilty of secret complicity. Just let the canons roar, Luther concluded, lest the peasants commit crimes a thousand times worse.[22]

Zimmermann saw Luther's predicament as one of his own devising: he had advocated the overthrow of the temporal power of the ecclesiastical princes because he found no sanction for such power in the Bible. But the pedigree of these very princes was older and their right to rule more sanctified by time. Although the right to rule of the secular princes was likewise not sanctioned in the Bible, Luther failed to attack their prerogatives. Why, then, asked the peasants and their leaders, should Luther halt halfway? Why advocate the overthrow of one and not the other when the Bible, which Luther held to be authoritative in these matters, sanctioned the right to rule of neither? Luther himself refused obedience to both pope and emperor; why then should he try to bind the peasants all the more securely to the princely power?

Zimmermann explained Luther's actions by pointing out that Luther had grown up in a *Fürstenstaat* and that this same *Fürstenstaat* had protected him and his reformation while he had been under attack by both pope and emperor. The more Luther feared that his reformation might be destroyed by revolution, the more adamantly he clung to the protection of the princes and the more he justified their right to rule. He went so far in this direction as to say that those who advocated abolishing the servile status of the peasants were rebelling against the Word of God, for Abraham and the Patriarchs had owned slaves and Paul had admonished the servants to obey their masters.[23]

This unpopular stand with regard to the Peasants' War cost Luther the support of the masses. These turned to Thomas Müntzer, to the Anabaptists, and away from Luther. The worst of the consequences, as far as Zimmermann was concerned, however, was that the princes now called upon the authoritative pronouncements of Luther to justify their despotic acts. They pursued their destructive policies, and the Germany that might have

[22] Ibid.
[23] Ibid., pp. 714—717. Zimmermann does not give a reference, but it would seem that he is alluding to a passage in "Wider die räuberischen und mörderischen Rotten der Bauern," WA, 18, 365.

been, the Germany united politically and religiously, was not to be because Luther had refused to accept the political consequences of his religious teachings. As a result, Germany was condemned to languish under
a despotic rule and to remain disunited for centuries to come.[24]

Zimmermann based his picture of Luther on the latter's own writings,
but only on a select few. In the first place, he did not concern himself with
Luther's intellectual development before 1517 at all and, therefore, could
not really appreciate Luther's reasoning during the years of crisis, especially 1525.[25] Secondly, his concept of the revolutionary young Luther
rested essentially on one passage — although he claimed to have found
similar ones elsewhere — a passage attributed to the Luther of 1517 when
it really belonged to the Luther of 1520. Furthermore, the passage was
contained in a Latin tract and could have had little or no effect upon the
German peasants. This passage, together with others Zimmermann utilized,
he misinterpreted because he could see Luther's actions only in relation to
his own philosophy of history, a philosophy which viewed society as moving ever nearer to its goal: the establishment of freedom in the Kingdom
of God on earth. Since, according to Zimmermann, the Peasants' War was
a notable effort to accelerate this progress toward freedom, Luther's condemnation of the revolutionary movement, which he himself had fostered
earlier, made him into a reactionary. Therefore, although Zimmermann
selected his facts, these facts were not the most important factors determining his interpretation of Luther's role in the Peasants' War. That factor
was Zimmermann's philosophy of history which he imposed upon the facts
he had selected.

3. ZIMMERMANN'S GLORIFICATION OF MÜNTZER

In many respects, the study Zimmermann produced was sound, and we
have no desire to deny him due respect. Much of his *Bauernkrieg* rests
squarely on archival research and is sound even today if one divests his
story of its interpretive superstructure. Zimmermann's sections dealing with
the war in southern Germany, where the revolt began and where it was
largely fought, is relatively sound because he was able to consult the ar-

---

[24] *Zimmermann*, Bauernkrieg (1841), III, 719.
[25] The staggering amount of Luther-research done since Karl Holl and the beginnings
of the so-called "Luther Renaissance" should make it only too obvious that Zimmermann was a complete novice in the field of Luther-studies. Yet at the same time, his
preference for the Joachite-Hegelian historical paradigm sharpened his eyes for Luther's
theory of the two realms which he rejected as wrong, however.

chives in Stuttgart[26] and the valuable collection of documents Prälat von Schmidt had painstakingly gathered. This allowed him to draw a fairly accurate picture of the progress of events in Swabia, Franconia, Alsace-Lorraine, Switzerland, and Austria.[27] Nor did Zimmermann deal uncritically with these sources. Before even Ranke pointed an accusing finger at the generally highly esteemed chronicler of the Peasants' War, Gnodalius, in the appendix of his *Reformationsgeschichte* of 1847, Zimmermann had noted, already in 1843, that the story Gnodalius told could not be reconciled with what the documents had to say.[28] In marked contrast to the soundness of the history of the Peasants' War in southern Germany, however, stands his story of the revolution in the north. Here he had no access to the archives and had to make do with meager sources. Particularly weak are his passages dealing with Thomas Müntzer.[29] Although he omitted certain passages in the second edition, was given valuable material on Müntzer and Pfeiffer, collected by the Mühlhausen archivist, Stephan,[30]

---

[26] In the biography of her husband, Zimmermann's wife wrote: "Hier, [Dettingen] in der grossartig schönen Natur des Uracher Thales, in sehr freier Musse, entstand seine 'Allgemeine Geschichte des grossen Bauernkrieges' Stuttgart, 3 Theile, 1841 bis 1844, ganz aus Archivalquellen gearbeitet, die Direktion des königlichen Staatsarchivs zu Stuttgart stellte ihm mit der edelsten Liberalität die Aktenstücke aus Schwaben zur jahrelangen Benützung in sein Haus frei." Zimmermann Nachlass, Z 1030.

[27] *Hausherr*, "Zimmermann als Geschichtsschreiber," p. 180.

[28] Ibid., p. 178. Strobel had already discredited Gnodalius on Thomas Müntzer and Zimmermann was to make extensive use of Strobel's study.

[29] *Hausherr* states: "Anders stehen die Dinge mit dem nördlichen für uns so wichtigen Schwerpunkt der Bewegung, mit dem Sachsen-Thüringen Thomas Müntzers. Hier hat sich Zimmermann in der ersten Auflage mit kümmerlichen Quellen begnügen müssen, Quellen, die noch dazu durch den heftigen Streit zwischen der Partei Luthers und den 'Schwärmern,' zu denen sie Müntzer rechneten, gefärbt waren. So wie die ganze Bauernkriegsdarstellung Zimmermanns eine energische Umwertung der geltenden Urteile, eine mutige Rettung der besiegten Partei darstellt, so gilt dies im besonderen Masse von Müntzer und seinem Kreise, wo der Historiker dann mangels ausreichenden Quellen mehr als anderswo aus seiner wissenschaftlich geschulten Einbildungskraft zu ergänzen hatte. Sein zweifellos sehr revisionsbedürftiges Müntzerbild ..." Ibid., p. 180. Even the Marxist, *Schilfert*, stated: "Daraus ergibt sich, dass Zimmermanns Forschungsergebnis auch nach den damaligen Möglichkeiten nur für Thüringen und vor allem für die Gestalt Müntzers weniger zutrifft. Dennoch ..." Review of the 1952 edition of Zimmermann's Bauernkrieg, Zeitschrift für Geschichtswissenschaft, I (1953), 1, 153. (Hereafter this journal will be cited as ZfG.) Exactly how trustworthy Zimmermann's sources were and how he used them will come to light shortly.

[30] He gratefully acknowledged Stephan's generosity in the introduction to his second edition. *Zimmermann*, Bauernkrieg (1856), I, XXXVI. O. *Merx*, however, did not approve of the way Zimmermann had used the material: "Das Material, welches er [Stephan] gesammelt hatte, bekam und verwerthete W. Zimmermann in der zweiten Auflage seiner Geschichte des grossen Bauernkrieges 2. Bd. Stuttgart 1856. Vor dem Gebrauch der betr. Abschnitte in diesem Werke ist jedoch sehr zu warnen. Denn das von Stephan

and read the biography of Thomas Müntzer by J. K. Seidemann, which appeared in 1842,[31] Zimmermann could not bring himself to change, in any really essential aspects, the unified whole he had made of Müntzer's thought and actions. Nevertheless, this section does show the greatest differences from the 1841—43 edition.

As noted earlier, the foundations for a reinterpretation of Müntzer had already been laid by the time Zimmermann came to write his *Bauernkrieg*. Under the influence of the Enlightenment and the French Revolution, a new appreciation of Müntzer's life and thought had been kindled. Hammerdörfer had already stated that, had Müntzer been victorious, his would have been history's adulation. Strobel had been more cautious, but he had nevertheless produced the first study of Müntzer which did not simply reiterate what others had repeated since Melanchthon's *Die Historia Thomä Müntzers, des Anfängers der Thüringischen Aufruhr, sehr nützlich zu lesen*.[32] Nowhere, he complained, could one find even a list of Müntzer's writings, much less the writings themselves. Therefore he had tried to gather everything relating to Müntzer that had appeared in the writings of the latter's contemporaries, had added a complete list of Müntzer's own writings which he had used for his study, and had appended excerpts from the letters and most important writings of Müntzer.[33] Nor did Strobel merely paraphrase what he found; he exercised discretion and judgment, allowing his readers to follow his reasoning as he proceeded to tell his tale.[34] Zimmermann made extensive use of this study.

Leo von Baczko followed upon the heels of Strobel with another biography, but the tale he told was less critical. He did not discuss the nature nor the trustworthiness of the sources he used, although he made use of most of the material available at the time, including Strobel. It was Georg

gesammelte Material ist darin in sehr oberflächlicher Weise verarbeitet; ja, Zimmermann scheut sich an einzelnen Stellen nicht, die Erzählung auszuschmücken oder gar Begebenheiten und Thatsachen zu erdichten. In welch' unwissenschaftlicher Weise er gearbeitet, geht schon daraus hervor, dass er das in Förstmanns 'Neuem Urkundenbuch' abgedruckte Material nicht zur Benutzung herangezogen hat." Thomas Münzer und Heinrich Pfeiffer 1523—1525 (Göttingen, 1889), p. 5.

[31] *J. K. Seidemann*, Thomas Müntzer, Eine Biographie (Dresden und Leipzig, 1842).

[32] In his introduction, *Strobel* stated: "Bis jetzt haben fast alle die von Müntzern geschrieben, blos der einzigen unvollständigen Nachricht sich bedient, die uns Melanchthon ertheilt hat. Sleidan und Gnodalius haben solche ohne die geringsten Zusätze von Wort zu Wort ins lateinische übersetzt ihrer Geschichte einverleibt, und diese haben nachher fast alle übrigen, die von der Reformationshistorie geschrieben haben, benutzt." Thomas Müntzer, pp. IV & V.

[33] Ibid., pp. V & VI.

[34] For an excellent example of this, see ibid., p. 4.

Carl Treitschke's short study of Thomas Müntzer, however, which seems to have influenced Zimmermann's interpretation of Müntzer by far the most.[35] Of all the studies to appear on Müntzer between that of Strobel and Zimmermann, Treitschke's was undoubtedly the poorest and the most biased in favor of Müntzer. Nor did Treitschke cite any sources upon which he had based his picture of Müntzer.

For his own portrait of Müntzer, Zimmermann drew on the facts according to Strobel and the interpretation according to Treitschke. The progression of events is that of Strobel and at times whole passages not only sound similar but are identical to the punctuation mark![36] Nor is Zimmermann always careful to give Strobel the credit; in the entire study he mentions him only twice![37] Upon these facts he then imposed the interpretation of Treitschke which fitted nicely into his own concept of the meaning of history.

Zimmermann introduced Müntzer to his readers as the precocious young man well ahead of his time. Placing his birth in the year 1498,[38] he argued that Müntzer had been teaching school at Aschersleben, probably at age thirteen, for at fifteen he had been teaching at Halle where he also, for the first time, attempted to set up his secret *Bund* which was destined to reform Christendom.[39] This not sufficing, Zimmermann had Müntzer obtain a doctor's degree, he was not quite sure when, between his revolutionary activity and his teaching duties.[40]

It was also early in his life that Müntzer turned away from Catholicism to the mystics of the Middle Ages where he was particularly impressed by tales of men and women having heavenly visions and communing

---

[35] See Zimmermann's laudatory remarks in the introduction to his 1856 edition. *Zimmermann*, Bauernkrieg (1856), I, XLII. Compare especially *Treitschke*, Thomas Münzer, pp. 205—206, and 255.

[36] These passages will be pointed out in the course of this chapter.

[37] In the 2nd edition he is mentioned a few more times, but here the documents he collected are referred to.

[38] *Zimmermann*, Bauernkrieg (1841), II, 54. Between Zimmermann's first and second edition, Seidemann's biography of Müntzer appeared which placed the latter's birthdate in the year 1490, eight years earlier. See *Seidemann*, Müntzer, p. 1. In his second edition, Zimmermann quoted Seidemann on the date (the only time he referred to the latter's study), but went on to state, rather pathetically, that he had earlier found a reference to the year 1493, but could not remember where. *Zimmermann*, Bauernkrieg (1856), I, 128.

[39] Zimmermann claims to rely on Müntzer's own "Bekenntnis," but the passage shows identical phrases and names to Strobel. Compare, *Zimmermann*, Bauernkrieg (1841), II, 54—55, and *Strobel*, Müntzer, pp. 5—6.

[40] *Zimmermann*, Bauernkrieg (1841), II, 54, does not cite a source. None of his predecessors knew anything of it.

directly with God.[41] Of all the mystics, however, Joachim of Fiore exercised the greatest influence on Müntzer's development with his profound
teachings concerning the coming age of the Spirit in which men would
become true brothers, in which the institutional church with its priestly hierarchy would become superfluous, and in which outside authority would be
superseded by an inner authority. Such ideas, Zimmermann believed, could
not but help spark the already volatile imagination of Müntzer.[42]

In spite of this mystical influence, which Zimmermann stressed because
it could be manipulated at will, Zimmermann was intent upon drawing a
portrait of Müntzer which would emphasize the latter's essentially independent development. Therefore the influence of Luther and the Zwickau
Prophets upon Müntzer had to be played down, if not denied outright.
Zimmermann did admit that Müntzer had at first become Luther's ardent
disciple, but as soon as he discovered that Luther's goal was not his goal,
he parted company with him.[43] He also admitted that it seemed as though
the Zwickau Prophets had influenced Müntzer, especially in regard to their
prophecy concerning God's imminent judgment of the godless and the
consequent erection of the Kingdom of God on earth. But the historians
who had argued for such an influence had really been in error, for Müntzer had not believed in the prophetic calling of these prophets, nor had
he considered Luther's exposure of their errors any great feat.[44] He himself had spoken derogatorilly of them since he had adhered to a prophecy
totally different from theirs.[45] Although he had used the same terms, such
as "spirit" and "revelation," he had really been referring to man's reason.
Nevertheless, he had associated himself with the Prophets because he saw
that he could make use of them and their teachings to further his own
plans.[46]

---

[41] Zimmermann quotes Luther, "Von der Winkelmesse und Pfaffenweihe," WA, 38,
213: "... er liess, unwillig über seine Aufgabe, die Worte der Wandlung aus, und
behielt eitel Brod und Wein, und ass die Herrgötter, wie er die Oblaten nannte,
ungeweiht." This is not cited by Strobel. Luther undoubtedly meant it as a criticism of
Müntzer, but Zimmermann, from his perspective, found it praiseworthy.

[42] Zimmermann, Bauernkrieg (1841), II, 55—57.

[43] Here follows a lengthy passage in which Zimmermann copies Strobel word for
word, ibid., pp. 57—58. For a comparison, see Appendix A.

[44] The passage Zimmermann, Bauernkrieg (1841), II, 60, bases this argument on is
taken from Müntzer's own "Schutzrede," Schriften und Briefe, p. 341. The passage, however, suggests precisely the opposite of what Zimmermann was trying to prove.

[45] In other words, Müntzer had understood these terms as Zimmermann did!

[46] Zimmermann, Bauernkrieg (1841), II, 61. Both Strobel and von Baczko, however,
had stressed the influence of the Prophets on Müntzer. See: Strobel, Müntzer, p. 13, and
von Baczko, Müntzer, pp. 22 & 30.

Zimmermann believed that these plans concerned the future of what he termed "Müntzer's people," the common man. Müntzer felt called of God to free these from their burdens and servile status, and to revenge the injustices done them.[47] He hated the oppressors of the people, both temporal and spiritual, in whom he saw the perverters of a godly order. He hated the entire priesthood because it tyrannized the people in the name of religion,[48] and he hated the temporal rulers because they hindered the establishment of the Kingdom of God on earth.[49] And the more he studied the Old Testament and the mystics, the more he realized that all was not as it should be. It seemed to him the goal of Christianity to make all of life Christian, the State and the social institutions as well as the morals of the people. The ideals of Christianity were to be realized in this world, even in the laws of the State, and thus the equality which existed before God would also come to exist between men on earth. The more his "inner voice" came into agreement on this point with the Old Testament and the mystics, the more Müntzer became convinced of his mission.[50]

At first Müntzer believed that this Kingdom of God could be established through the power of the spoken word, and, as a result, he turned in verbal violence against all those who opposed him. At this point he had even been prepared to use the princes to ensure the spread of his teachings, and *that* by force if necessary, for he believed that if his teachings could only reach the populace, social changes would follow automatically.[51]

But when the princes paid him no heed, Müntzer turned directly to the people. In Allstedt he again erected a secret society, his *Bund*, whose members were sworn to establish the Kingdom of God on earth and to destroy everything that might hinder its realization. No one was excluded from this secret society, not even the princes, but if the latter refused to join they were to be executed or expelled from the land. Once the *Bund* would be in control of the situation, a form of communism would be introduced through which work as well as property would be shared equally. Nor was there to be any tyrant or feudal dues in the new kingdom; no religion bound by a servitude to the letter of Scripture, no priesthood, and no class distinctions were to be tolerated. Even Church and State would eventually be dissolved since everyone would be his own priest and his own ruler.[52]

---

[47] *Zimmermann*, Bauernkrieg (1841), II, 61.
[48] Zimmermann imputes Enlightenment motives to Müntzer here. Ibid., p. 62.   [49] Ibid.
[50] Ibid., p. 63. This last part is deleted from the 1856 edition. Compare (1856), I, 136.
[51] Ibid., p. 68. The whole above paragraph is deleted from the 1856 edition. Compare, (1856), I, 138.
[52] Ibid., pp. 72—73.

Müntzer failed to recognize, however, that this social program could not immediately be realized, argued Zimmermann. Nor, he continued, was absolute equality a desireable goal since it was incapable of realization. Even to achieve the possible, the abolition of the unnatural abuses and inequities, would have taken a thousand years rather than a mere battle.[53] In his youthful enthusiasm, Müntzer had overlooked these factors. The high hopes he nurtured for his people, his overly active imagination, and his ambition to become the liberator of the downtrodden masses had driven Müntzer to the point where he himself no longer knew whether he was being motivated by forces inherent in him or whether some other power had not come over him.[54]

Once he believed himself driven by an external power, however, Müntzer could not but move forward relentlessly. Unlike the Old Testament prophets who had contented themselves with pointing forward to a better world, Müntzer felt compelled to establish this world here and now, and that by revolutionary means if necessary.[55] The more he read his Moses, his Elijah, and his Jeremiah, and the more he took to heart the commands of the Hebrew Jehovah to destroy the godless and avenge an angry God, the more fanatically revolutionary he became. This fanaticism, however, was directed toward bringing happiness to mankind,[56] and the scheme he developed to achieve this end was not politically naive. As a matter of fact, his plan demonstrated a keen and adventurous political mind.[57]

4. THE SOURCE OF ZIMMERMANN'S INTERPRETATION OF MÜNTZER

Zimmermann does not indicate from what sources he developed his thesis of Müntzer as the social revolutionary, but the assumption is certainly not without foundation that he read his own desires, ambitions, and social aims into Müntzer's thought and actions because he saw himself as standing in the same intellectual tradition. In many ways this was correct, as we have seen. Yet in order to make a social revolutionary of Müntzer, Zimmermann had somehow to deny the former's essentially religious motivation. He did this by using the word "spirit," or "inner voice" Müntzer

---

[53] Ibid., p. 63. Deleted from the 1856 edition. Compare (1856), I, 36.   [54] Ibid.
[55] Ibid. Deleted from the 1856 edition. Compare (1856), I, 36.   [56] Ibid., p. 64.
[57] *Hammerdörfer* had already stated in 1793: "Noch gefährlicher für die Idee, eine neue Kirche zu stiften, waren die Lehrsätze des schon genannten Thomas Münzers: Lehrsätze, welche nothwendig Geist- und Weltliche wider den Urheber aufbringen mussten, in denen aber, abgerechnet von der damit vermischten Schwärmerey, sehr viel gesunde Vernunft liegt." Geschichte der Reformation, p. 53.

spoke of, in the sense that Hegel had used the term with reference to a
rational world spirit which was realizing itself in history through human
reason. Zimmermann could the more readily do this because he had come
to believe, as we saw in the last chapter, that these different terms referred
to essentially the same human phenomenon. Different eras had simply referred to this phenomenon with different terms. And for this interpretation Treitschke had prepared the way.

Treitschke began the discussion of the problem of the "inner voice" in
the thought of Thomas Müntzer by saying,

"Man hat Münzern Schuld gegeben, er habe seinen sogenannten Auserwählten ein
Wunderzeichen von Gott versprochen und durch solchen ungestümen Eifer ertrot-
zen gelehrt; aber, wie wir glauben, mit Unrecht."[58]

Treitschke argued he had found no evidence of this in Müntzer's letters.
All he had found was that Müntzer had demanded that God speak to him
and the other elect. The problem was to determine precisely what Müntzer
had meant by this. On occasion Müntzer had stated that God the Father
spoke to the Son in the heart of man or wrote in the hearts of His elect.
Now this could only mean that Müntzer was referring to that "inner
voice" in every man which could be heard by closing out the noise of the
world and relying upon one's emotions. Nor had Müntzer really believed
that God manifested Himself to His elect in dreams, as Melanchthon would
have it, for had not Müntzer refused to follow Pfeiffer into battle despite
the fact that the latter had dreamt they would be victorious? Müntzer had
relied more upon his feelings than his rational faculties — which he possessed only to a lesser degree — but in most instances his emotions had led
him in the right direction.[59]

Thus Treitschke tried, in somewhat romantic fashion, to minimize the
religious moment in Müntzer's thought by emphasizing the emotional element. However, he still argued that Müntzer had not really used his
rational faculties which he had, in fact, possessed only in a limited capacity. Proceeding from Treitschke's portrait of Müntzer, Zimmermann went
on to add shadings of his own. True, Müntzer had been an emotional person, said Zimmermann, but the "inner voice" he had referred to had not
been his emotions; it was, much rather, man's rational faculty. Were one
to look at the broad outlines of the plan Müntzer had created for the
future of his people, one could not but help admit the political genius of
the man.[60]

[58] *Treitschke*, Münzer, p. 207.   [59] Ibid., pp. 207—208.
[60] *Zimmermann*, Bauernkrieg (1841), II, 64.

Müntzer, Zimmermann continued, had fought for a spiritual conception and interpretation of the Bible; indeed, he had placed the Holy Spirit working through man's consciousness, man's rational power itself, above biblical authority. Müntzer had designated this rational faculty in man the purest wellspring of truth. Precisely this rational, perhaps even speculative element, came to play an ever greater role in his teachings.[61]

In light of the above, Zimmermann was of the opinion that he could give the following description of Müntzer's beliefs. Müntzer, he said, rejected as illogical and unchristian the teaching of justification by faith alone without works; he rejected as a flagrant lie the teaching that Christ had died for the sins of the world and had thus satisfied the demands of a righteous God. He taught that one had to find God in oneself, not somewhere afar off in the heavens. The living Word of God was not to be found in the dead letter of a book, but in the enlightened mind, and through this enlightened mind God still revealed Himself today as He had four thousand years ago. Other revelation there was one. Nor was there a devil except the wicked desires of man.

What then was faith? Well, faith was nothing more than the actualization in man of the word of mind and Scripture, and an obedience toward God who renewed and empowered man, who planted love in the heart of man and imparted the Holy Spirit to him. Every man, even the heathen without the Bible, could possess this faith. Nature taught that one should do unto others as one would have others do unto us; to desire this was faith. By putting this faith into action on earth, man created heaven here and now and became like unto God in the process. Everyone possessed the Holy Spirit, for by the Holy Spirit Müntzer had in mind nothing less than our rational powers.[62]

---

[61] Ibid., p. 70. This and the following four paragraphs are deleted from the 1856 edition. Compare (1856), I, 138—139. In another rather lengthy passage, also deleted from the 1856 edition, where Zimmermann discussed Müntzer's *Auseinandersetzung* with Luther, he came back to the same idea: "Müntzer, der auf die allgemeine Vernunft und den gesunden Menschenverstand, der auch dem gemeinen Manne zukam, sich berief, wollte 'das Zeugniss des Geistes nicht ausschliesslich auf die hohe Schule bringen' und nach der hergebrachten Theologie der Gelehrten beurtheilen lassen." (1841), II, 76—77. Compare (1856), I, 141.

[62] A careful study of these articles of faith that Zimmermann lists here show that they are taken from those of Sebastian Franck listed in his Chronica. Strobel had appended these, in modernized German, to his study, Müntzer, pp. 188—194. Zimmermann again took what he wanted, changed, and that sometimes drastically, the meaning, added, deleted, as it pleased him. For a comparison of the passages in question, see Appendix B. In this connection, it is interesting to note that the Marxist, Steinmetz, in his criticism of an article by Hermann Goebke, stated: "Abwegig und irreführend ist es, wenn Herr Goebke versucht ... die 44 Artikel, die Sebastian Franck als exakten

What was more, insisted Zimmermann, to this confession of faith one could add the following statements of Müntzer's followers without any qualms of conscience.[63] There was no hell. Christ was not God but merely a prophet and teacher, and, like the rest of us, had been conceived in sin. The communion service was only an act of remembrance of this Christ, and the bread and wine nothing more than bread and wine.

The reason why others had not seen these outlines of Müntzer's thought clearly before was that Müntzer had not always been able to speak his mind openly; he had had to play the role of the prophet in order to impress the people, for in the 16th century, said Zimmermann, a word spoken as though it came directly from heaven had quite a different effect upon a crowd than a word spoken by a mere man. Müntzer, therefore, believed that he had need of heavenly revelations in order to make the masses believe in his calling. Consequently, he often clothed his ideas in mystical terminology no matter how rationally he really thought.[64]

Thus Müntzer appeared not only far in advance of his contemporaries in political matters, but also far in advance of his contemporaries in religious thought. He had been a man of reason, a fighter for the use of man's rational powers which he wanted to see applied without discrimination to every aspect of life and thought. He had overcome and far surpassed the limited intellectual horizons of the Middle Ages, and therefore had been far ahead of Luther to whom the above articles remained works of the devil.[65]

Through this transformation, Müntzer became a person who, in the words of Treitschke, had anticipated the ideas of William Penn, Philip Jakob Spener, the Graf von Zinzendorf, Jean Jacques Rousseau, the French demagogues of the Revolution, and the philosophers of natural science.[66] The voice of God, that "inner voice" which revealed the will of God to man, had become man's emotions in the hands of Treitschke and man's rational faculty in the hands of Zimmermann.[67] Thus the process by which

---

und gültigen Ausdruck der Lehren Müntzers nimmt und seiner Darstellung zugrunde legt." "Nachwort," G. *Brendler*, ed., Die frühbürgerliche Revolution in Deutschland (Berlin, 1961), p. 302. (Hereafter cited as Frühbürgerliche Revolution.)

[63] Zimmermann based these concluding remarks on such a reliable witness as Luther, whom, on other occasions, he considered most untrustworthy. Bauernkrieg (1841), II, 71. The similarity to Zimmermann's own beliefs is most remarkable!

[64] Ibid., p. 85. Once again, Luther's argument turned on its head.   [65] Ibid., pp. 71—72.

[66] *Treitschke*, Münzer, p. 255. It was precisely this passage that Zimmermann quoted with approbation.

[67] Zimmermann, however, was still torn between what he recognized to be the *Schwärmer* in Müntzer and what he thought was the rationalist. "Man sieht, Müntzer ist ein Fanatiker, aber kein von hohler und überschwänglicher Mystik gefüllter Schwärmer: frisch

God revealed Himself to man had become a secularized one; no longer did He reveal Himself to man in a supernatural way. God revealed only His general laws to mankind through man's rational faculties, but even these laws man had to discover for himself. In order to secularize this process by which God revealed His will to man, however, Zimmermann had to distort his evidence.

5. MÜNTZER'S ROLE IN THE PEASANTS' WAR

Through the imposition of his philosophy of history and the manipulation of his evidence, Zimmermann forced Müntzer into the revolutionary Young Hegelian tradition of his own 19th century. Yet all this would have done him little good unless he could convince his readers that Müntzer had also been the actual leader of the Peasants' War. And this was by no means a small task, for none of Zimmermann's predecessors had seen Müntzer in this capacity.[68]

Zimmermann, therefore, built his case carefully by tracing and emphasizing the successive stages of Müntzer's revolutionary career. Having already asserted that Müntzer had established a secret organization for the radical reformation of Christendom in Halle at fifteen, Zimmermann proceeded to argue that Müntzer had intended to use the Zwickau Prophets for his own revolutionary purposes. The same argument was used to explain Müntzer's wooing of the Hussites after he had been forced to flee Zwickau. But unlike the Prophets, the Hussite ground proved barren of revolutionary fruit and Müntzer was forced to turn elsewhere.

His first real success came in Allstedt toward the end of 1522 where the people flocked to hear Müntzer preach his revolutionary message of social equality.[69] Here he once again established his secret society which was to become the center of his revolutionary conspiracy. From this center he sent his messengers into every part of the Empire to promulgate his revolutionary doctrines.[70]

---

und grün wachsen in ihm die hellsten Gedanken, praktische Wahrheiten und gesundesten Vernunft zwischen vielerlei verworrenen Ranken einer ringenden, des Ausdrucks nicht ganz mächtigen Sprache empor und über seine Zeit hinaus." Bauernkrieg (1841), II, 67. Deleted from the 1856 edition. Compare (1856), I, 137.

[68] For the various appraisals by Zimmermann's predecessors, see Appendix C.

[69] *Zimmermann* is once again following Strobel. Bauernkrieg (1841), II, 68 ff., and *Strobel*, Müntzer, p. 41 ff.

[70] *Zimmermann*, Bauernkrieg (1841), II, 72, bases this statement on Luther's letter to the city council of Mühlhausen of August 21, 1524. Here Luther had stated: "Auch sendt er landlauffer, die Gott nicht gesandt hat (dann sie kunnens nicht beweysen) noch

The continuity of Müntzer's revolutionary activity was difficult to maintain, however, for Müntzer had been expelled from Allstedt late in 1523 for having burned, together with some radical followers, the defenceless chapel at Mallerbach. Once again, therefore, he appeared to be merely another revolutionary without an army. Zimmermann, however, had prepared his readers for just such an eventuality by pointing out that Müntzer had sent his messengers out from Allstedt to prepare the countryside for his teachings. Thus, when he was turned out of Allstedt and went to Nuremberg, Müntzer's followers there welcomed him with open arms. These even pressed him to preach to the populace, but Müntzer declined, stating in a letter to a friend that he had not come to Nuremberg to cause revolution.[71] Nevertheless, the city fathers, being convinced to the contrary, confiscated his books and expelled him from their city.

From Nuremberg Müntzer went to Swabia where he found conditions similar to those he had just left. This being the case, Zimmermann could magnanimously argue that those historians, who had blamed the unrest in upper Germany on Müntzer's presence there, were wrong, only to assert that his followers — the Anabaptists[72] — had preceded him even to this region and kindled the flames of revolt. Müntzer's purpose, therefore, had not been to stir up revolt, but merely to make sure that the revolution was already well underway and to co-ordinate the efforts of his Anabaptist followers.[73]

Through these same followers Zimmermann extended Müntzer's influence to Basel and Zurich in Switzerland, to all of southern Germany and especially into the Allgäu, down the Donau, and into Württemberg. Men of the caliber of a Franz Rabmann of Griessen, a Schappeler of Memmingen, a Heuglin von Lindau of Sernatingen, a Florian of Eichstettin, a Jakob Wehe of Leipheim, a Doctor Mantel of Stuttgart and other leaders of the revolt all worked toward the same goal with Müntzer.[74] As a matter of fact, Zimmermann concluded emphatically, the whole movement with its

---

durch menschen geruffen sind, sondern kumen von in selbst, und gehen nicht zu der thur hineyn ..." WA, 14, 239. Luther does not say how many messengers there were nor whether they were sent to all parts of Germany; Zimmermann assumed this because it suited the role he had mapped out for Müntzer in the Peasants' War.

[71] *Zimmermann*, Bauernkrieg (1841), II, 80—81. It is interesting to note that Zimmermann tries to demonstrate that Müntzer went to Nuremberg precisely because it was a center of unrest. Yet he had no intention of creating unrest; the letter, however, is quoted without comment. Compare with the much more considered report by *Strobel*, Müntzer, pp. 64—68.

[72] *Zimmermann*, Bauernkrieg (1841), II, 83—84.   [73] Ibid., pp. 86—87.

[74] Ibid., p. 96. Deleted from the 1856 edition. Compare (1856), I, 184.

hundreds of itinerant preachers had found the core of its teaching in the ideas of Müntzer. And these preachers were to be found in Franconia, especially in the environs of Rottenburg, toward the end of 1524[75] as well as in the Tyrol.[76] But the real center of Müntzer's revolutionary activity was to be Mühlhausen, for it was from here that he threw his firebrands into Hesse, Saxony, and farther afield into the Netherlands, which set Germany aflame.[77] Thus were Müntzer's revolutionary teachings spread abroad, not only in Germany, partly by himself and his Anabaptist disciples and partly by those who were of a mind with him and stood under his influence.

However, Zimmermann was not content with having established the fact of Müntzer's overriding influence in the uprising of 1525, for he proceeded to argue that the former had also been the moving force behind the formulation of the famous peasant articles. He did this by attempting to demonstrate that Münzer had authored the most radical of these, those first found in Alsace and Austria,[78] and by showing how the famous Twelve Articles had derived from these. He readily admitted that Müntzer could not have formulated the final draft of the Twelve Articles for their tone had been far too mild.[79] Nevertheless, the best informed contemporaries of Müntzer had persisted in fixing the final blame on Müntzer even after the war, and a comparison of the Twelve Articles with Müntzer's ideas demonstrated that the first, second, third, fourth, fifth, and eighth articles contained ideas fundamental to Müntzer's thought.[80] Therefore, it may well have been possible, argued Zimmermann, that Müntzer, when he realized that the peasants in southern Germany did not desire outright revolution but only greater freedom and the abolition of abuses, drew up a set of articles less radical than he might otherwise have done in order to keep the peasants in a belligerent mood at all. From these less radical articles the more moderate Twelve Articles might well have been drawn.[81] But even if this were not the case, the much more radical *Artikelbrief* had most certainly come from Müntzer's pen.[82]

Having established his ultimate leadership in all regions of peasant unrest, Zimmermann brought his hero back to Saxony where he established

[75] Ibid., p. 228.   [76] Ibid., p. 423.
[77] Ibid., p. 606. Deleted from the 1856 edition. Compare (1856), II, 82.
[78] Ibid.   [79] Ibid., p. 108.
[80] Ibid., p. 109. The last sentence is deleted from the 1856 edition. Compare (1856), I, 320.
[81] Ibid., p. 110. This whole section is deleted from the 1856 edition. Compare (1856), I, 320—331.   [82] Ibid., p. 115. Deleted from the 1856 edition. Compare (1856), I, 323.

him in the city of Mühlhausen, to which his supporters had long begged him to come.[83] These used his entry into that city, early in 1525, as the occasion to wrest power from the city council and transfer it to Müntzer and his cohorts. With Müntzer at its head, an "eternal council" was set up and Mühlhausen became the proving ground in miniature for radical ideas of social change. Prominent among these was a primitive kind of communism, similar to that practised by the early Church, and a radical justice which treated all men alike.

It did not take long for Müntzer's presence in Mühlhausen to arouse unrest in the surrounding countryside and further afield. Already in April, Luther set out to try to quiet some of this turmoil through the power of his personality. But lo, the mighty Luther's voice turned out to be but the twitting of a bird in the rumble of an oncoming storm. And while he was yet underway, the storm broke in his very birthplace.

Müntzer now began to work like a man possessed. He turned the *Johanniterkloser* into a veritable munitions factory, organized forays into the surrounding countryside, and sent his emissaries to all parts of the surrounding territories and cities to win the populace to his cause. At the same time, he was also in touch with the leaders of revolt in southern Germany, gageing their progress and trying to coordinate all revolutionary efforts.[84]

But Zimmermann, with the hindsight given most historians, knew that he must prepare his readers for the decline and fall of his hero. He began by informing them that the Thuringians were not Swabians who had grown up gun in hand, or, for that matter, Franconians led by a Florian Geyer, or even sharpshooters from the rugged Alps. They were Thuringians accustomed to little else than hoe and spade. Yet in spite of the fact that Müntzer knew all this, he did not despair of victory.[85] What he had not anticipated was that his friend and most trusted confidant, Heinrich Pfeiffer, was to become his evil genius at the most crucial moment. Müntzer had been waiting for just the right moment to attack, but Pfeiffer forced him

---

[83] Ibid., p. 606. Deleted from the 1856 edition. Compare (1856), II, 211.

[84] Ibid., pp. 630—633. Zimmermann bases his statement concerning Müntzer's contact with the southern revolution on *Bullinger's* statement in his Der Widertoufferen Ursprung: "... / sunder sich widerum herab in Thüringen gethon / und zu Mühlhusen wonet / schrieb er doch brieff sinen vertrutwen haruf / mit denen er ymerder unreuwige lut anzundt unnd hatzt wider jre herren und oberen. Und nit unlang vor dem ufbruch der pürischen ufrur / der in der Landgraffschaft und darumb sich erhub / schickt er einen Botten heruf mit brieffen / unnd ouch mit zadlen / in welche er hatt lassen verzeichnen die kreiss und grosse der kuglen des geschützes / das zu Mühlhusen zu der ufrur schon gegossen was: starckt damit unnd trost die unruwigen ...," p. 2.

[85] *Zimmermann*, Bauernkrieg (1841), II, 766—767.

into playing his hand far too early, before they were strong enough and before the peasants had been roused to revolt. Thus, in order not to lose his influence, Müntzer was forced to move into the field of battle with inadequate forces.[86]

What more needs to be said? Only that when it came to the decisive battles in Saxony, the north Franconians, who had allied themselves with Müntzer's party, failed to keep faith. It was the old problem of German disunity, sighed Zimmermann.[87] But what was still worse was that when the surrounding regions called for help, Müntzer and Pfeiffer could raise only three hundred men in Mühlhausen and its environs to go to their rescue.

Yet in spite of these handicaps, Müntzer somehow managed to gather enough of a motley crew to meet the forces of the princes gathering at Frankenhausen. The story is too well known to be repeated here. Müntzer held his encouraging speech, but not in the words Melanchthon had couched it.[88] It had its usual effect nonetheless. In due course the rainbow appeared, and since the peasants carried the rainbow as a symbol in their flags, they were heartened and began singing, "Komm heiliger Geist, Herre Gott." While they sang and the truce was not yet ended, the treacherous princely canons began to join in the chorus. Surrounded by princely treachery on the one hand and peasant incompetence on the other, Müntzer and his men were doomed to defeat.

Somehow Müntzer managed to escape the melée that ensued only to be discovered in Frankenhausen playing the role of a sick man in bed. Alas for Müntzer, he acted well but left some identifiable artifacts lying about. These were discovered, his true identity revealed, and he himself led captive to his enemies.

What about his end? Had he died well as befitted a hero? Indeed he had! When led to his captors, he had staunchly defended his actions and criticized the princes to their very faces. Faced by the sanctimonious Philip of Hesse, who, Bible in hand, tried to convince him of his errors, Müntzer had disdained to answer. Under cruel torture his tormentors had forced a confession from his lips, but this confession was in reality no confession at all.[89] His last letter to the city of Mühlhausen showed him resigned to his fate as only a great man could be, content with the knowledge that

---

[86] Ibid., p. 767.   [87] Ibid., pp. 770—771.

[88] Already *Strobel* had said: "Sie [the speech] in Melanchthons Hist. Th. Müntzers, und nicht dieser, sondern Melanchthon ist ganz sicher der Verfasser, wie von der folgenden Anrede des Landgrafen Philipps." *Müntzer*, p. 88.

[89] *Zimmermann*, Bauernkrieg (1841), II, 782.

he had done his best. And yet the lie had been promulgated that Müntzer had recanted and returned to the bosom of Mother Church.[90]

Müntzer's real tragedy, however, lay in the fact that the common man, whose welfare he had at heart and for whom all his plans had been laid, betrayed him. Just as he had been ahead of his time in religious and political ideas, so had he also outstripped by far the populace in his audacity and revolutionary courage. He had thought that the same revolutionary courage would be manifested by the oppressed people, but this was not to be. The selfishness and provincial-mindedness which these had demonstrated during the revolt revealed to him that he had misplaced his confidence. Neither the time nor the people had been ripe for his advanced ideas of social equality.

Zimmermann was very much aware that he had given a revolutionary revaluation of Thomas Müntzer despite the beginnings toward a more positive assessment begun by Hammerdörfer and continued by Strobel and von Baczko.[91] But the question which faces us at this juncture is not whether Zimmermann was aware that he had given a revolutionary reappraisal of Müntzer, but whether this reappraisal was firmly founded on the facts.

The revolutionary nature of Zimmermann's reappraisal is shown by the fact that not one of the former's predecessors, from Hammerdörfer to Bensen — not even Treitschke, saw Müntzer playing the role of leader in the entire Peasants' War.[92] At the most, Müntzer had been the leader of the revolt in Thuringia, and the revolt in Thuringia had differed from the revolt in the rest of Germany precisely because Müntzer had been its leader; it had demonstrated greater fanaticism and poorer organization.

In the beginning of this section on Müntzer we noted that Zimmermann was in all probability nearly solely dependent upon Strobel for his factual evidence concerning Müntzer's life. This is proven by the rather lengthy passage we quoted from Zimmermann which was taken word for word directly from Strobel. Not only this very obvious passage, but other expressions, quotations Strobel had used, and other information was taken from

---

[90] Ibid., p. 783.

[91] *Zimmermann* stated: "Noch muss der Geschichtsschreiber einen heftigen Widerspruch von Vielen fürchten, wenn er auf Thomas Münzers Grab die Krone des Märtyrers heftet. Und doch, wie nach der Christuslehre das Weltgericht Gottes, wiegt die Geschichte nicht bloss das Gewordene und Vollbrachte, sondern auch das Denken und Gedachte, das Wollen und Gewollte. Und es ist ein eigenes Geschick: unter den Disteln und Dornen, womit die Verläumdung sein Grab überflocht, sind derselben auch grosse frische Lorbeerblätter entfallen, diese sammelt die Geschichte und flicht sie zum Kranz." Ibid., p. 791.

[92] See Appendix C.

Strobel. This would not have aroused our mistrust so much had Zimmermann openly acknowledged from which source he drew his information. This he failed to do, however. Yet this is not the greatest crime he committed against Strobel. The latter had taken great pains to collect all the material available on Müntzer, be this conflicting or not. Once he had collected the material, he tried to reason, in the presence of his readers, towards a solution. It is here that Zimmermann abused the material collected by Strobel, for he took what he wanted, what suited his purpose, and left the rest. To what lengths he would go in order to make it appear that the facts fitted his philosophical scheme was seen when we compared the former's interpretation of Müntzer's beliefs with the Franck original printed in the appendix to Strobel's Müntzer biography. Words and phrases were left out which significantly changed the meaning Franck had intended, and in other instances whole passages were changed into something drastically different from the original.[93]

In the second place, we noted that Zimmermann read his own political and religious ideas into those of his hero, Thomas Müntzer. Now, there was some excuse for this since they both stood in the same intellectual tradition. But that tradition had also undergone some important changes. Thus Zimmermann could only accomplish his goal by equating Müntzer's religious "inner voice" with the 18th- and 19th-century "rational faculty" of man. In so doing, Zimmermann made of Müntzer a social revolutionary and a man far in advance of his time and contemporaries.

But Zimmermann the historian must have had an uneasy conscience, for the experiences of the 1840's and early 1850's led him to make substantial revisions in the 1856 edition of his *Bauernkrieg*.[94] And these revisions focus on Müntzer. In the second edition those very parts are omitted which tended to remake Müntzer into a 19th-century social revolutionary. A careful study of the passages omitted shows that these refer precisely to the rational and social revolutionary aspects of Müntzer's teachings. The disillusioned revolutionary of 1848 realized he had gone too far and had read too many of his own aims and ambitions into those of his hero, Thomas Müntzer. On the other hand, he was not willing to give up the basic outline he had established in the first edition.

---

[93] See Appendix B.

[94] In his letter to Gervinus requesting a review of the second edition of his Bauernkrieg, dated July 21, 1856, Zimmermann wrote: "Sie nahmen meine Geschichte des Bauernkrieges in ihrer unvollkommeneren Gestalt überaus gütig auf; ich bitte nun das Gleiche auch für das Buch in dieser Gestalt." Universitäts Bibliothek Heidelberg, Heid. Hs. 2529 Nr. 450.

Thirdly, Zimmermann made of Müntzer the great revolutionary hero of the whole Peasants' War on the weakest of evidence and in the face of a host of opinions to the contrary. From Luther's letter to the city council of Mühlhausen he had gleaned the vital information that Müntzer had sent his emmissaries into all parts of Germany even though Luther had not said that much and was evidently trying to place the blame for the entire revolt on Müntzer's shoulders. Whereas Zimmermann would not believe Luther with regard to Müntzer on other occasions, yet here he made more of it than Luther had himself intended. By making the Anabaptists Müntzer's disciples, Zimmermann discovered the emmissaries Luther had referred to, and by discovering Anabaptists in all parts of Germany before, as well as during the revolt, Zimmermann saw these agitators spread Müntzer's teachings far and wide, even to those regions to which Müntzer himself never came. And, finally, by quoting Bullinger, who had stated that Müntzer had sent messengers to southern Germany with letters, he surmised that the latter had been in continual contact with the leaders of the revolt in that region in order to coordinate the revolutionary efforts. It was a magnificent picture, but it hung on thin strands of evidence.

But Müntzer had been even more: he had been the framer of the original peasant articles which had later been developed into the famous Twelve Articles. He was the leader of the Thuringian revolt and the tragic hero of a misguided trust in a selfish people. Indeed, Müntzer had been a man born out of due season and under an unpropitious constellation of the stars. Born into a world not yet ripe for his ideas, Müntzer had been doomed to failure, but failure in a grand manner and in a great cause.[95]

6. THE ANABAPTISTS

In order to build this grand design, Zimmermann had made the Anabaptists into Müntzer's secret agents, spreading his incendiary teachings throughout the length and breadth of Germany and Switzerland. But where had the Anabaptists originated, what were their teachings, and in what relationship did they stand to Müntzer?

Zimmermann accepted the time-worn theory that Anabaptism had originated in Zwickau,[96] but he did not care to admit that Müntzer had been

---

[95] For a discussion of the similarities between the characters portrayed in Zimmermann's drama Masaniello, and Thomas Müntzer as portrayed in his Bauernkrieg, see A. Friesen, "Wilhelm Zimmermann's Historical Frame of Reference."

[96] Zimmermann, Bauernkrieg (1841), II, 83. Zimmermann does not cite a source for his assumption that Anabaptism originated in Zwickau. It is very likely that he simply took it for granted, for the theory was paraded as an established fact in nearly every book

a follower of the Zwickau Prophets and a member of their sect. He tried rather to establish that Müntzer had not been influenced by the Prophets at all but had made use of them to further his designs.[97] He did this in spite of the fact that two of the secondary sources he relied on most for his information about Müntzer stressed the ties between Müntzer and the Prophets rather strongly.[98] From one of these, Strobel, Zimmermann also knew that Müntzer had rejected infant baptism and had blamed the corruption of the Apostolic Church on precisely this practice.[99] On what evidence, then, did Zimmermann hold that Müntzer was not a disciple of the Zwickau Prophets?

To extricate Müntzer from an intimate relationship with the Anabaptists, Zimmermann asserted that historians had mistakenly regarded Müntzer as an Anabaptist, to say nothing of his being taken as their originator. According to the express declaration of Sebastian Franck, one of the most trustworthy and best informed witnesses of the time, Müntzer had not been an Anabaptist, for neither had he ever rebaptized anyone nor had his most intimate disciples, his secret followers, been Anabaptists.[100] Yet Zimmermann accepted the Anabaptists as Müntzer's messengers on Bullinger's evidence. But Bullinger had also very explicitly stated that Müntzer had been the father of Anabaptism.[101] Thus Zimmermann was torn between the evidence of two witnesses both of whom he on occasion accepted as reliable.

It is typical of Zimmermann's study that he does not allow his readers to face these problems. Rather that reason from the evidence, conflicting though it was, Zimmermann chose to take from Bullinger as well as from Franck that which suited his purpose. However, he failed to state that the two were in outright contradiction to one another on the decisive issue.

Zimmermann solved the problem in the following manner. He had already established to his own satisfaction that Müntzer had made use of the Zwickau Prophets for his own revolutionary purposes. He now proceeded to argue that Müntzer had united the vast majority of the Anabap-

---

on Anabaptism until *Heberle's* "Die Anfänge des Anabaptismus in der Schweiz," Jahrbuch für deutsche Theologie (1858), some two years after Zimmermann's revised second edition of 1856 appeared. It is very possible, however, that he took it from Bullinger whom he cited on occasion and whom *Strobel*, Müntzer, p. 70, quoted as authoritative on Müntzer's stay in southern Germany.   [97] *Zimmermann*, Bauernkrieg (1841), II, 61.

[98] *Strobel*, Müntzer, p. 13, and *von Baczko*, "Thomas Müntzer," p. 23.

[99] *Strobel*, Müntzer, p. 198.   [100] *Franck*, Chronica, p. CLX, and p. CLXIIII.

[101] *Bullinger*, Der Widertoufferen Ursprung, p. 2. The same thing was stated more explicitly, as we noted in Chapter III, in *Bullinger's* Reformationsgeschichte, which Zimmermann also cited on occasion.

tists under his leadership (despite the fact that the various groups of Anabaptists had manifested the greatest divergencies in matters of faith). In
the "innocent" religious symbol of adult baptism he created an invisible
sign by which members of his *Bund* recognized one another and were
united for the purposes of revolution. Soon the Anabaptist messengers
were in all parts of Germany, while the strands of this net remained in
his hands.[102] As a result, concluded Zimmermann, about mid-1524 Müntzer had begun to advocate rebaptism for its utilitarian value; he, himself,
however, never rebaptized. In this manner Zimmermann harmonized the
conflicting evidence and at the same time fitted it neatly into the image
of Müntzer as the rational revolutionary which he had created.

If Müntzer was not an Anabaptist, who was? Zimmermann noted that
the Anabaptists did not have a common confession of faith; nevertheless,
he named some specific individuals as Anabaptists. The Zwickau Prophets
were the originators of the sect;[103] they were the first to be called *Täufer*,
for they denied the validity of infant baptism and baptized only those
already instructed in the faith. Conrad Grebel, Balthasar Hubmaier, and
Wilhelm Reublin were others.[104] A third group of Anabaptists was the
Münster contingent, a species of Anabaptism Zimmermann emphatically
condemned.[105] Otherwise Zimmermann used the term very loosely to include all the itinerant *Predikanten* who wandered from one end of Germany to the other ostensibly preaching Müntzer's doctrine of social revolution.[106]

Wherever they went, the Anabaptists stiffened the determination of the
peasants to revolt against their rulers, and where the peasants had not yet
risen, the Anabaptists incited them to revolt. Their outreach into all parts
of Germany was phenomenal, as was their increase in number. Nor did
they shy away from using every possible means of extending their influence; even the belief in signs and wonders was used.[107] And the apocalyptical message they preached forecast doom to the ungodly and the
Kingdom of God to the elect. This Kingdom of God was at hand and
would be inaugurated shortly by the elect of God, sword in hand.[108]

Zimmermann cannot be blamed overly much for falling heir to the
theory of the connection between the Zwickau Prophets and the Swiss

---

[102] *Zimmermann,* Bauernkrieg (1841), II, 83—84.
[103] Ibid., p. 83.   [104] Ibid., pp. 87 & 96.   [105] Ibid., p. 52.
[106] In the 1856 edition, Zimmermann added other specific names to his list of Anabaptists: Jakon Gross of Waldshut, Peter Wagner, Kunz Ziegler, and the brothers Mayr
from the Ansbach region, but especially Hans Hut of Bibra. See (1856), I, 180—182.
[107] *Zimmermann,* Bauernkrieg (1841), II, 546.   [108] Ibid., p. 85.

Anabaptists, for this was the generally accepted interpretation until Heberle propounded the contrary thesis of the autochthonous origin of Swiss Anabaptism in 1858. Nevertheless, there are indications that Zimmermann once more misused his information, or, at the very least, did not lay all his cards on the table, in his analysis of the origins of Anabaptism. He called Sebastian Franck one of the best informed men of his time when he relied upon him to prove that Thomas Müntzer had not been an Anabaptist, but failed to indicate that Franck had also stated that the Anabaptists had arisen only toward the end of the Peasants' War. Nor did he point out that Franck also remarked that many of the Anabaptists later tried to excuse Müntzer's participation in the Peasants' War, or that the vast majority of the Anabaptists had been pacifists. Had he noted this, it might well have appeared to his readers that the Anabaptists had not been revolutionaries like Müntzer, and Müntzer's vast network of conspiratorial followers would have evaporated before his very eyes.[109]

Not only did Zimmermann have a number of his facts wrong, but he also failed to state precisely which the tenets of faith were shared by the Anabaptists and which divided them. The more nebulous he left the realm of their thought the more easily he could fit them into Müntzer's scheme and into their combined role as precursors of Enlightenment ideas. Thus, in the introduction to his second edition of 1856, Zimmermann pointed out that the Anabaptists attempted to establish the Kingdom of God on earth in which both Church and State would become superfluous since man would be ruled directly by God. This idea, said Zimmermann, was very much akin to the idea of the waning away of the State to which Johann Gottlieb Fichte had given such eloquent expression. The Anabaptists, however, overlooked the fact that the abolition of the State would take time, that it was a natural process and would have to run its natural course, instead they demanded the immediate abolition of all government. Nevertheless, this was a seminal idea which bore a somewhat secularized fruit in the Enlightenment.[110]

---

[109] In one instance, where he was speaking about the oath every member had to take to enter Müntzer's Bund, *Zimmermann* stated: "Ochs V, 497, will daraus folgern, dass die Wiedertäufer dabei keine Hauptrolle [as followers of Müntzer] gespielt haben. Ohne Grund: nicht zu schwören, war ein Artikel nur einer Fraktion von Wiedertäufern, bei weitem nicht aller; die Wiedertäufer der That, die Predikanten Vorwärts, die münzerischen Sendboten alle hielten sehr auf Bundeseide und Zusammenverpflichtungen." Bauernkrieg (1856), II, 549.

[110] The preceding passage dealing with Zimmermann's interpretation of Anabaptism was published in *C. S. Meyer*, ed., Sixteenth Century Essays and Studies, vol. I (St. Louis, 1970), *A. Friesen*, "The Marxist Interpretation of Anabaptism," pp. 19—22.

It is obvious from the foregoing that Zimmermann viewed the Peasants' War in terms of a tragedy with Müntzer cast in the role of the tragic hero and Luther in the role of the villain. The similarities between his historical tragic hero, Thomas Müntzer, and his dramatic tragic hero, Masaniello, should already give us cause to question the historical accuracy of Zimmermann's delineation of Müntzer. For the similarities are more than mere coincidence; they are artistically contrived.[111] Whereas Masaniello lacked a real antagonist in the drama,[112] Müntzer, in Zimmermann's *Bauernkrieg*, found such an antagonist in the person of Martin Luther, the erstwhile hero of the Reformation. Here were the protagonists he needed for his fatal confrontation.[113] But these protagonists also stood in a much broader context than merely that of the 16th century: Luther represented the tradition of the separation of the two realms which had been given classic expression by St. Augustine, while Müntzer represented the opposite tradition emanating from Joachim of Fiore and culminating in Hegel's philosophy. It is this setting that gives Zimmermann's *Bauernkrieg* its grandiose scope and universal validity, or so at least Zimmermann thought. Although those who stood in the tradition of Joachim of Fiore had been continually vanquished by the followers of St. Augustine and Luther in the past, the Joachite tradition, culminating in the Hegelianism of his own day, was being proven the only correct point of view. Thus, although Luther and the forces of reaction had been victorious in the 16th century, the ideas of Müntzer and the Anabaptists had gone on to victory in Zimmermann's own day. Luther, therefore, may have won the battle in the 16th century, but Müntzer and the Anabaptists were about to win the ultimate battle and with it the whole war. Though they had lost in the 16th century, they were now the real heroes; and it must have gratified Zimmermann's sense of poetic justice that he had been chosen to rehabilitate them in his *Bauernkrieg*.

Down with Luther and up with Müntzer, that was the rallying cry Zimmermann's message sent out to all who cared to listen. And that rallying

---

[111] See *A. Friesen*, "Wilhelm Zimmermann's Historical Frame of Reference."

[112] See also *Storz*, Schwäbische Romantik, p. 87.

[113] *J. Hillebrand*, Die deutsche Nationalliteratur seit dem Anfange des achtzehnten Jahrhunderts, 2nd ed., III (Hamburg & Gotha, 1851), p. 441, for example, remarked: "Einen wichtigen Beitrag zu der Literatur unserer Volksgeschichte hat W. Zimmermann in seiner 'Geschichte des Bauernkrieges' geliefert. Ihm gebührt der Verdienst, dieses bedeutsame *historische Nationaldrama* zuerst in seiner thatsächlichen und persönlichen Beziehung aus den Quellen gründlich dargestellt und es so auf seinen wahren Standpunkt zurückgeführt zu haben, wobei freilich die urkundliche Schwere den freien Gang der Ausführung nicht immer gestattet." The italics are mine.

cry was based essentially on a value judgment one-hundred-and-eighty degrees opposed to Luther's own value judgments. Thus, Zimmermann agreed with Luther that Müntzer and the peasants had been hiding the real reasons for their revolt behind Scripture. He used this argument especially with regard to Müntzer. Yet in Zimmermann's hands this was a laudable action, especially on Müntzer's part, since otherwise no one would have understood his advanced ideas. The same is true of Luther's heaping the blame for the entire revolt on Müntzer's shoulders in order to turn the Catholic accusations away from himself. Whereas revolution was an evil for Luther, this was no longer the case for Zimmermann. He therefore accepted all of Luther's remarks concerning Müntzer's causative role in the revolution, but once again turned Luther's value judgment on its head. Zimmermann the poet must have felt a sense of pride at this outcome; Zimmermann the historian, however, was to have second thoughts about it, as we have seen.

Chapter VII

ENGELS AND HIS EARLY FOLLOWERS

1. THE RECEPTION OF ZIMMERMANN'S *BAUERNKRIEG*

Zimmermann's history of the Peasants' War was rapturously received not only by important contemporary historians such as Gervinus and Friedrich Cristoph Schlosser;[1] it was also immediately acclaimed by various members of the pre-1848 radical Left. Even before Engels decided to utilize it for his Marxist reinterpretation, others had lauded its revolutionary tenor and its unabashed partisanship for the revolutionary cause of 1525. Wilhelm Weitling, a close friend and associate of Moses Hess, as well as Marx and Engels until their Brussels quarrel of 1846,[2] praised Zimmermann in his "Das Evangelium eines armen Sünders," (1843) for having finally rolled back the veil of abuse that had covered the Anabaptists of the Reformation era. As a result of the revision brought about by Zimmermann's "epoch-making, dispassionate study," the courageous radicals of the Reformation appeared in an altogether different light, while the glory which had thus far surrounded others, especially Luther, had been decidedly diminished.[3] Alexander Weill, an Alsatian living in Paris and a close friend of Heinrich Heine, at that time in Paris as well, also praised Zimmermann's study and used it as the basis for his own interpretation of the Peasants' War.[4] Weill first wrote his book in French in order, as he said,

[1] Zimmermann apparently also sent a copy of his Bauernkrieg to the older Heidelberg historian, Friedrich Christoph Schlosser, for the latter wrote him on February 11, 1844: "Ich kannte Ihr historisches Werk schon aus dem Lobe eines jungen Königsburger Doctors, war daher doppelt erfreut, es von Ihnen zu erhalten. Sie können gewiss darauf rechnen, dass ich Ihnen noch in diesem Jahr in den Heidelberger Jahrbüchern zeige wie wichtig mir die Erscheinung desselben ist." Zimmermann Nachlass.

[2] See Weitling's letter to Moses Hess, *E. Silberer*, ed., Moses Hess Briefwechsel (The Hague, 1959), pp. 151—152.

[3] In *T. Ramm*, ed., Der Frühsozialismus (Stuttgart, 1956), p. 340.

[4] See the introduction by *J. Nohl* to the 1956 East German edition of *Weill's* Der Bauernkrieg (Weimar, 1947), pp. VII—VIII. Weill's Bauernkrieg was first published in French in 1847, under the title, "La guerre des paysans," in Fourier's Democratie pacifique, but shortly thereafter appeared in book form. Weill himself later translated it into German and had it published by C. W. Leske in Darmstadt. See the introduction above, p. VII.

to fill his countrymen, who had forgotten the German past, with a red-hot German fire; in order to show them that their great revolution was not unique in history, that the German people, whom they supposed dreaming and unrealistic, had not always been so. On the contrary, already three hundred years ago Germany had produced men who were more audacious in their thoughts than the French revolutionaries.[5] For both Weitling and Weill, therefore, the main attraction of Zimmermann's *Bauernkrieg* was twofold: its radical reorientation and its consequent glorification of the revolutionaries of 1525, and at the same time its utility in rousing to revolt the oppressed of 1848. It was Zimmermann's interpretation that attracted them, yet both were equally aware that an interpretation had to rest on reliable evidence. It was for this reason that both asserted, as Engels was to do later, that Zimmermann had the best collection of the facts available.[6]

Whereas these pre-1848 radicals were particularly attracted to Zimmermann's delineation of Thomas Müntzer and the Anabaptists, German dramatists, from the relatively obscure, such as Robert Heller in 1848, to the relatively great, such as Gerhart Hauptmann in 1896, were all attracted to his delineation of Florian Geyer and used it as the basis for their dramatic treatments of the latter.[7] Max Lenz, who investigated the historical accuracy of Zimmermann's portrait of Florian Geyer in 1896, remarked:

"Ich beabsichtige nichts weiter als festzustellen, was in den Quellen, soweit sie gedruckt sind, über den fränkischen Ritter überliefert ist, der seit Generationen ein Liebling unserer romantischen Poeten war. Bisher haben über ihn nur diese das Wort gehabt. Denn auch der Historiker des Bauernkrieges, Zimmermann, der in Ritter Florian und seiner schwarzen Schar seiner kranken Zeit Idealbilder eines demokratischen Deutschlands vorhalten wollte, ist ihnen zuzurechnen, und wahrlich nicht an letzter Stelle. Er hat, kann man sagen, die Gestalt des ritterlichen Volksfreundes erst geschaffen und ihr mit der Leuchtkraft seiner farbenreichen Kunst den Hauch revolutionärer Romantik verliehen, der wie über seinem Buch, so über dem Sturm und Drang seines eigenen, an Kampf und Hoffen reichen Zeitalters ruht und die Gestalt des fränkischen Edelmannes den Poeten wert gemacht hat."[8]

But Florian Geyer did not fit into the intellectual tradition begun by Joachim of Fiore and therefore held little interest for the radicals. Thus,

---

[5] Quoted in ibid., p. IX.

[6] See Der Frühsozialismus, p. 340, and *Weill*, Bauernkrieg, p. VIII.

[7] See especially *E. Guggenheim*, Der Florian Geyer-Stoff, pp. 4 ff.

[8] *M. Lenz*, "Florian Geyer," Vom Werden der Nation, p. 161. The essay was first published in the Preussische Jahrbücher, I (1896), 95—127. For Lenz's criticisms of Zimmermann's portrayal of Florian Geyer, see the rest of the essay.

in subsequent historiography on the Peasants' War, at least insofar as it was dependent upon Zimmermann's study, the latter's poetic revolutionary Romanticism came to be separated from his revolutionary Hegelianism.

Whereas the Young Hegelians and other political radicals were attracted to Zimmermann's history of the Peasants' War — Zimmermann himself was called "der Bauernkriegs Zimmermann" while at Frankfurt[9] — his political enemies, aside from seeing to it that his book was banned in Baden and Bavaria, were repulsed by the very characters in the book that so attracted the radicals. Dr. Wolfgang Menzel, the editor of the Stuttgart *Morgenblatt,* who probably wrote the review of Zimmermann's *Bauernkrieg* which appeared in that paper, was no friend of Zimmermann's. Yet he too saw clearly the similarities between Zimmermann's delineation of the radicals of 1525 and those of his own day, without, however, being aware of the fact that Zimmermann had imposed his own ideas upon his heroes of the Peasants' War. Thus, in his review, he made the following seemingly very naive, though in view of the last two chapters, very enlightening remarks:

"Der Bauernkrieg bleibt insofern immer eine höchst auffallende Erscheinung, als er mit andern Ereignissen, denen ein ähnliches Motiv zu Grunde lag, doch so wenig in der Durchführung übereinstimmt. Die Hussiten, die Schweizer, die Friesen und Dithmarschen, die Geuesen, die Tiroler führten auch Volkskriege, als rohe Bauern gegen Ritter und kriegsgeübte Soldheere, aber sie handelten nicht so blödsinnig, unterlagen nicht so schmählich; sondern siegten ruhmvoll oder unterlagen ruhmvoll. Der Unterschied bestand bloß darin, daß die leztern sich discipliniren ließen, während die Bauern von 1525 keinen Befehl annahmen und wie eine tolle Viehheerde durch einander liefen. Aber diese Tollheit muß ihren besonderen Grund haben; im Wesen der Nationalität oder des Bauernstandes liegt er nicht unbedingt. Wie es scheint wurde der Bauer durch die zahlreichen Emissäre des damaligen Communismus irre geleitet. Die Häupter dieser Partei, denen weder die kirchliche, noch die politische Reform genügte, sondern die eine sociale Umwälzung wollten, Thomas Münzer, Karlstadt und Hubmayer, waren mitten unter den Bauern und predigten ihnen (ganz so wie heut zu Tage Bruno Bauer und die Communisten) die Lehre des freien Geistes, allgemeine Gleichheit, Güter- und Weibergemeinschaft, erfüllten sie mit Stolz und Hoffahrt gegen jeden, der an Ansehen und Bildung über ihnen stand, brachten ihnen die Eitelkeit bei, daß sie jezt die Herren seyen (eine Phrase, die durch den ganzen Bauernkrieg wie ein rother Faden läuft), lenkten ihren Sinn auf das Prassen und Schwelgen und den

---

[9] On May 20, 1848, Zimmermann wrote his wife from Frankfurt: "'Der Bauernkriegs-Zimmermann' — so heiss ich zum Unterschied von dem Dr. Eduard Zimmermann, Bürgermeister u. Abg. v. Spandau — ist in Mittel- und Norddeutschland, wie sich zeigt, bekannter als in Schwaben." Zimmermann Nachlass, Z 958.

Genuß der vorher entbehrten Güter hin, machten sie dadurch faul und unthätig, und flößten ihnen endlich noch zum Ueberfluß gegen jeden Anführer Mißtrauen und Verdächtigungen ein, so daß kein Gehorsam in den kriegerischen Bewegungen möglich war. *Ohne diese communistischen Zuträger und Prediger des damaligen Hegelthums* wäre das nüchterne, treuherzige und tapfere Volk der Schwaben nicht in die wunderliche und schimpfliche Situation gekommen, in der es seine eigene Karikatur wurde."[10]

If Menzel, who opposed the Young Hegelians, saw the similarities between Zimmermann's 16th-century heroes and the Young Hegelian radicals of his own day, how much more should those Young Hegelians themselves see the similarities! Even Zimmermann was impressed by these similarities during the 1848 Revolution, for in the second edition of his *Bauernkrieg* he remarked:

"Diese deutschen Revolutionäre des Thomas Münzer glichen in vielem späteren deutschen Revolutionären; sie verloren sich in Träume von der Zukunft und erwarteten die glückliche Erfüllung derselben nicht von sich selbst, von der eigenen Kraft und Tat, sondern von außen her, von günstigen Ereignissen und Wendungen. Besonders glichen die Münzerschen den neuzeitlichen Kommunisten und Sozialisten mit ihrer leicht entzündlichen Einbildungskraft und ihrem Nichtstun."[11]

The popularity of Zimmermann's *Bauernkrieg*, therefore, especially in the more democratic and radical circles of his day, rested on his hegelianized 16th-century radicals in their revolutionary setting; and it was this that made his study so useful for subsequent Marxist historiography of the Reformation as well. Both Weill's and Zimmermann's studies were published anew in the Russian occupied zone of Germany after World War II, Weill's in 1947 and Zimmermann's in 1952. In both instances, the revolutionary aspects were emphasized. Engels himself singled Zimmermann's revolutionary ardor out for special praise; it was this and the latter's portrayal of Müntzer and the radicals that really attracted him to the study. In the introduction to his own reinterpretation he stated:

"Auch das deutsche Volk hat seine revolutionäre Tradition. Es gab eine Zeit, wo Deutschland Charaktere hervorbrachte, die sich den besten Leuten der Revolutionen anderer Länder an die Seite stellen können, wo das deutsche Volk eine

[10] Morgenblatt für gebildete Leser, Nr. 120 (Stuttgart & Tübingen, Nov. 25, 1844), 479. I owe this reference to my good friend, Dr. Victor G. Doerksen, Professor of German literature at the University of Manitoba.

[11] *Zimmermann*, Bauernkrieg (1856), II, 350. It would be of interest to know whether Zimmermann ever became aware of the fact that Engels based his reinterpretation exclusively upon his study, but nothing that I have come across, either in his papers or other writings, suggests that he knew about it.

Ausdauer und Energie entwickelte, die bei einer zentralisierten Nation die groß-
artigsten Resultate erzeugt hätte, wo deutsche Bauern und Plebejer mit Ideen
schwanger gingen, vor denen ihre Nachkommen oft genug zurückschaudern."[12]

Engels' purpose, to rouse the lower classes to such revolutionary fervor
once again two years after the events of 1848, is made only too evident in
the lines following those just quoted:

"Es ist an der Zeit, gegenüber der augenblicklichen Erschlaffung, die sich nach
zwei Jahren des Kampfes fast überall zeigt, die ungefügen, aber kräftigen und
zähen Gestalten des großen Bauernkrieges dem deutschen Volke wieder vorzu-
führen."[13]

Engels had hoped in vain for the proletarian revolution in 1848. He
did not give up, however,[14] for he knew from his and Marx's analysis of
history that the proletarian revolution would come just as surely as the
first phase of the bourgeois revolution had come in 1525. It was therefore
necessary only to rouse the German proletariat to an awareness of this
inevitable revolution and incite it to revolutionary action to produce the
desired result. This is precisely what Marx pointed out in his only reference
to Engels' reinterpretation of the Peasants' War. Writing to Engels in a
letter of 1856, he expressed the opinion that everything would proceed
famously in Germany (the reference is to the Proletarian revolution) if
one could back the Proletarian revolution by some second edition of Engels'
Bauernkrieg.[15] Revolution, therefore, was the theme and revolution the
goal of all Marxist agitation, for through revolution the oppression of the
proletariat would be turned into the dictatorship of the proletariat. And
the dictatorship of the proletariat would lead directly to the classless communistic society, the secularized kingdom of God on earth.

Zimmermann's history of the Peasants' War did not fall into oblivion
after Engels' reinterpretation appeared; it continued to play an important
role in the leftist literature on the social upheaval of 1525. The first to
bring out a new edition of Zimmermann's *Bauernkrieg* after his death was

---

[12] *F. Engels*, "Der deutsche Bauernkrieg," *Marx/Engels*, Werke, vol. VII (Berlin,
1960), 329. (Hereafter cited as M/E, Werke.)

[13] Ibid.

[14] Even as late as 1892 he could still write to Marx's daughter, Laura Lafargue, on
Dec. 5, 1892: "Our revolution of 48/49 was too short and too incomplete to wipe that
[impression of the philistines ... on the working class] out altogether. Of course, the
next revolution which is preparing in Germany with a consistency and steadiness un-
equalled anywhere else, would come of itself in time, say 1889—1904." Friedrich Engels,
Paul et Laura Lafargue, Correspondance, vol. III (Paris, 1959), 238.

[15] Marx to Engels, April 16, 1856. M/E, Werke, XXIX, 47.

Wilhelm Blos[16] for the Dietz Verlag of Stuttgart in 1891. Blos cannot be called an orthodox Marxist,[17] nevertheless, his edition was the edition published by the East Germans in 1952.

Blos had high praise for Zimmermann's history. In his introduction he stated:

"Wer da weiß, wie viel persönliche Liebhaberei und Parteistandpunkt, gepaart mit parteilicher Absicht, in der Geschichtsschreibung von jeher ihr Wesen trieb, der versagt seine vollkommenste Hochachtung einem Manne nicht, der die Quellen der Geschichte unter der rücksichtslosen Aufsicht des Gewissens durchforscht und darnach allein das Urtheil der Geschichte spricht. Nicht mit Unrecht hat ihn darum Fr. Chr. Schlosser den 'Geschichtsschreiber der Wahrheit' genannt."[18]

But in spite of the fact that Blos praised this "truth," he nevertheless felt compelled to prune it considerably in order to produce his *Volksausgabe*. Yet he considered the parts he deleted unimportant for they dealt merely with discourses of a religious nature which the common man would not understand in any case. He averred, however, that he had produced no essential change in Zimmermann's study![19]

Others were also to turn to Zimmermann's study time and again. Kautsky referred to it repeatedly in volume II of his *Vorläufer des neueren Sozialismus*.[20] Belfort Bax, an English socialist, sometime friend and frequent visitor of Engels, praised Zimmermann's work highly.[21] Even Rosa Luxemburg wrote to a friend:

[16] W. Blos, 1849—1927, was a member of the German Social Democratic Party, a historian of sorts, and a journalist who wrote for the Volksstaat as well as Die Zeit, both organs of the above political party. He was also repeatedly a representative of the SPD in the Reichstag and in 1918 became president of Württemberg.

[17] See Bebel's letter to Engels of May 2, 1883, in W. *Blumenberg*, ed., August Bebels Briefwechsel mit Friedrich Engels (The Hague, 1965), pp. 154—155.

[18] W. *Blos*, ed., Dr. W. Zimmermann's Grosser Deutscher Bauernkrieg (Stuttgart, 1891), p. XI.

[19] Ibid., pp. 1—2. Hermann Barge, in the introduction to his 1939 edition of Zimmermann's Bauernkrieg, quotes *Dahlmann-Waitz*, Quellenkunde zur deutschen Geschichte, 1912 edition, which stated: "Die dritte Auflage [Blos's] ist verstümmelt und wissenschaftlich wertlos." I, XXIII.

[20] "Wir kennen unter den selbständigen Darstellungen Münzers nur eine, die der historischen Bedeutung des Mannes und seiner Persönlichkeit gerecht geworden ist: diejenige, die uns W. Zimmermann in seiner 'Geschichte des grossen Bauernkrieges' gibt." K. *Kautsky*, Die Vorläufer des neueren Sozialismus, vol. II (Stuttgart, 1894), p. 41.

[21] "Of all the works on the Peasants' War that of Zimmermann still holds first place alike for comprehensiveness of view and accuracy. Many details, it is true, have been corrected and expanded by later research, but for sympathetic understanding of the movement, combined with historical insight Zimmermann has yet hardly been equalled and certainly not surpassed." E. B. *Bax*, The Peasant War in Germany (London, 1899), p. xi.

"Fein, dass Sie Engels Bauernkrieg lesen. Haben Sie den Zimmermannschen schon durch? Engels gibt eigentlich keine Geschichte, sondern bloss eine kritische Philosophie des Bauernkrieges; das nahrhafte Fleisch der Tatsachen gibt Zimmermann."[22]

The more recent and more dogmatic Marxist literature from Russia and East Germany, especially since 1952, however, obediently repeats Engels' reservation: Zimmermann had the best collection of the facts but failed to see the inner relationship between the material base, class structure, and ideological superstructure. His revolutionary élan, on the other hand, has merited repeated praise from the Marxists.

2. ENGELS' REINTERPRETATION

We noted earlier that the French Revolution had kindled a renewed interest in the history of the German Peasants' War of 1525; the Revolution of 1848 had the same effect. However, there was one salient difference between the people and parties of the 1790's and the 1840's in whom this interest was kindled: those from 1790 to Zimmermann feared the negative effects revolution might have on the progress of civilization, whereas those from the 1840's on, including Zimmermann, believed revolution necessary to progress. But the problem of revolution and its effects on the progress of society was the central issue which attracted the one group as well as the other to the history of the German Peasants' War. Yet it was Zimmermann who first pointed to the revolutionary stages in the history of Western Civilization from the Peasants' War to the French Revolution of 1789, with intermediate stages in England and the United States of America. He saw this era as the era of the bourgeois revolution. Engels viewed these revolutions in much the same light as Zimmermann, the only difference being that whereas Zimmermann believed the democratic revolution to be the last revolutionary stage in history, Engels saw it merely as the last stage on the road to the proletarian revolution[23] and the establishment of communism with its classless society. For both Zimmermann and Engels, however, the period from 1525 to 1789 in France, and, hopefully, 1848 in Germany, began with the Peasants' War of 1525

---

[22] Rosa Luxemburg an einen Unbekannten, April 9, 1915, in *B. Kautsky*, ed., Rosa Luxemburg, Briefe an Freunde (Zurich, 1950), p. 195.

[23] Even before the 1848 Revolution, Engels and Marx believed that the "bourgeois" revolution had to take place in Germany before the proletarian revolution could become a reality. See the letter of Wilhelm Weitling to Moses Hess of March 31, 1846, concerning this problem. Moses Hess Briefwechsel, pp. 150—151.

as the first stage of this revolutionary period. In his *Bauernkrieg* of 1850 Engels had, however, not yet fitted the Reformation era into this larger Marxist frame of reference. Although he spoke of the Reformation as a bourgeois movement,[24] and of Luther as the representative of the bourgeois party,[25] he failed to make clear how every aspect of the Peasants' War related to the concept of the *frühbürgerliche Revolution.*

To call Engels' study of the Peasants' War a "materialistic" or strictly economic study would be to oversimplify his analysis; it was far more a sociological analysis made by means of the sociological categories drawn from the Marxist critique of 19th-century capitalistic society. Because this was so, Engels' sociological analysis was based on certain assumptions. The first and primary assumption was that a given mode of production brought a specific social class to power. A second assumption was that this class would espouse or produce a specific ideology which would express its "class" characteristics. The third assumption was that the ruling class was constantly involved in a continuing, more or less severe, class conflict not only with the class being removed from power but also with the new, emerging class. These assumptions have been built into the Marxist sociological categories, and it is these categories they use to analyze history.

According to these sociological categories, then, the "ultimately" motivating force in history was the mode of production. It was therefore of the first importance that Marx and Engels determine when and where the feudal mode of production, which had been agrarian, had changed to that of capitalism. In "Die deutsche Ideologie," (1845—46), they stated that the first flowering of capitalistic production [26] had taken place in Italy and then in Flanders.[27] Neither here nor later in *Das Kapital* did Marx state exactly when the capitalistic mode of production had begun; it is evident, however, that both Marx and Engels, as well as subsequent Marxist historians, have equated the beginnings of Renaissance culture in Italy with the birth of capitalism and the rise of the bourgeoisie as a

---

[24] M/E, Werke, VII, 347.

[25] Ibid.

[26] According to Marx, the heart of capitalism lay in its mode of production. Therefore, such appearances as the exchange and circulation of goods, money and banking, were secondary manifestations of the basic modes of production. The importation of goods from the Orient and the resulting profits reaped by the merchants, the growth of money and banking, and the formation of companies of merchant adventurers, did not noticeably change the feudal mode of production in Italy. Not until industrial firms appeared which manufactured goods in which laborers worked for hire and the owner reaped the profits, could one, according to Marx, speak of early capitalism.

[27] M/E, Werke, III, 54—55. In Das Kapital, Marx again pointed to Italy as the country in which capitalism originated. Ibid., XXIII, 744, note 189.

class.[28] As a result, 14th-century Florence has been singled out as the birth-place of the capitalistic mode of production where the emerging cloth industry first showed signs of developing such a mode of production.[29] It was the cloth industries of other countries that manifested these same first signs of a capitalistic mode of production as well, utilizing the capital which had been accumulated through trade with the Orient.[30] This trade, the appearance of American gold and silver imports on the European market, the gradual growth and development of the manufacturing indu-stries with the subsequent rapid rise in the volume of trade, all of these called for the existence of a new class, the bourgeoisie, by the 16th cen-tury.[31]

In "Die deutsche Ideologie," Marx and Engels gave only a very general outline of the rise of capitalism; in his *Bauernkrieg* Engels tried to be more specific as to the material basis of the German bourgeoisie of the 16th cen-tury.[32] German industry, Engels began, had experienced a decisive expan-sion in the 14th and 15th centuries. Guild manufacturing in the cities began to replace the more local feudal industries of the countryside, producing goods for an ever increasing local and foreign market. Two industries especially experienced an expanding production and market: the cloth industry, and gold and silver mining which produced the raw materials for the luxury articles demanded more and more by the nobility and the rising bourgeoisie. A number of more or less important scientific dis-coveries, such as the invention of gunpowder and the printing press, had also decisively aided in the upsurge of industry.[33]

With the rise of industrial production, albeit only of a guild nature, came the concomitant rise of trade. Augsburg, long the center of trade for goods coming from the Levant, continued in this role for some time and was joined by Nuremberg to form an axis in the predominantly south-to-north land trade. In northern Germany, the Hansa cities controlled the trade routes as well as the trade centers. At the same time, mining became an important industry and the German miners the most skillful at their trade. And an increasing agricultural production supplied an expanding

---

[28] See *A. Friesen*, "Renaissance" in The Soviet System and Democratic Society, vol. V (Freiburg i. B., 1971). In Das Kapital, Marx was somewhat more specific, stating: "Al-though we come across the first beginnings of capitalistic production as early as the fourteenth or fifteenth century, sporadically, in certain towns of the Mediterranean [not in Florence, as later Marxists have determined], the capitalistic era dates from the six-teenth century." *T. B. Bottomore* and *M. Rubel*, eds., Karl Marx, Selected Writings in Sociology and Social Philosophy (New York, 1956), p. 134.   [29] See *Friesen*, "Renaissance."
[30] "Die deutsche Ideologie," M/E, Werke, III, 55.   [31] Ibid., p. 57.
[32] Engels worked only with the material Zimmermann had collected, and Zimmermann had not been interested in a sociological analysis.   [33] M/E, Werke, VII, 330.

economy with an increasing food supply.[34] But even at this, the German national production had lagged behind that of other countries; its industry had not been able to match the production of the Italian, Flemish, or English industries; its agriculture had produced less than the Dutch and English; and its sea power, and consequently its trading potential, had been overshadowed and then displayed by the Dutch and English sea power, while the center of trade had moved from the Mediterranean to the Atlantic, all but stopping Germany's overland trade.[35]

Engels saw the major reason for Germany's failure to create a centralized government, such as France and England had established, in this very fact that Germany had lagged behind the other countries in industrial production and trading ability. The rise of industrial production and trade in those two countries had made it necessary for them to become a political unity in order to utilize to the fullest their industrial and trading potential. Germany's industrial and trading interests had never become powerful enough for this, and, with Germany's exclusion from the world market by the Dutch and the English sea powers, the political divisions of Germany, stemming from the feudal system, could not be overcome. Instead, the great princes of Germany were able to establish themselves all the more securely in their local territories and conclude pacts with one another to foil the attempts of the Emperor to unify Germany.[36]

Against this background, Engels saw the following changes taking place in the German social structure. The great nobles of Medieval Germany became the nearly autonomous princes of the Reformation. In their rise to power they subjugated a number of free cities and many lesser nobles. But their hunger for power was in no wise satiated, for they still desired to conquer new territories in order further to strengthen their position.[37] As a direct result of this rise to nearly absolute power on the part of the princes, the lower nobility and the knights lost what status they had, thus creating tension between the two estates. The rising cost of living the life of a noble, coupled with the threat of extinction from the more powerful princes, forced them either into the army of the princes or into bourgeois occupations. An important factor in this demotion of the lower nobility was the rise of new methods of warfare and the weapons employed in it.[38]

Opposite, and to a degree on the same social level with the secular noble, stood the prelates of the ecclesiastical establishment. These, according to Engels, were the true exponents of the ideology of medieval feudalism.[39] Like their secular counterparts, they were great lords in their own rights or

[34] Ibid., p. 331.   [35] Ibid.   [36] Ibid., pp. 331—332.
[37] Ibid., p. 332.   [38] Ibid., p. 333.   [39] Ibid., p. 334.

else held sway over vast domains as the vassals of great secular lords. They exercised the same rights over their vassals as the secular lords, but added to these all the chicanery of a religious tyranny which made use of religious threats to keep its subordinates tractable. Thus they garnered in not only great wealth, which, however, never seemed to satisfy their greed, but also the ever-mounting hatred of an oppressed populace, which saw clearly enough the discrepancy between their teaching and their action, and the jealousy of the secular princes who could not harvest as much money as their ecclesiastical counterparts.[40]

A third center of major power in 16th-century Germany had been the cities. At the top of their social hierarchy in rank and power stood the patrician families. They were the richest, exercised the greatest, if not exclusive political power, and, according to Engels, exploited the city's surrounding territory. By the 16th century, however, an opposition, consisting of the rising bourgeoisie and those within the city excluded from the rights of citizenship, began to challenge the patricians' claim to the exclusive right to rule. Especially the bourgeoisie demanded a voice in the political decisions of the city commensurate with its growing financial power. In some instances, it made common cause with the "plebian opposition," but in any case it constituted the great majority of the city's population.[41]

The peasants and the pre-proletariat, forced to bear all the financial burdens and social stigma in order to make life pleasant and leisurely for the rest, took up the bottom rung of the social ladder. In the final analysis, said Engels, this peasantry bore the brunt of the fiscal exploitation, and yet it had been difficult to bring it to revolt. Nor had it been able to rise in revolt successfully until other estates had joined it, as happened in the first years of the Reformation.[42] And this temporary union of the various estates of 16th-century Germany in open revolt against the papacy had only been brought about by the rapid dispersal of the revolutionary religious and political ideas of the Reformation. But, Engels was quick to add, the wars that resulted from the clash of these ideas were in reality motivated by material causes.[43]

[40] Ibid., p. 336.
[41] Ibid., p. 337. Although Engels does not speak out openly and accuse the 16th-century German bourgeoisie of being less revolutionary than it should have been according to the theory of the class war, yet he does say the following: "Wir werden sehen, wie während der Bewegung des sechszehnten Jahrhunderts diese 'gemässigte,' 'gesetzliche,' 'wohlhabende' und 'intelligente' Opposition genau dieselbe Rolle spielt, und genau mit demselben Erfolg, wie ihre Erbin, die konstitutionelle Partei, in der Bewegung von 1848 und 1849."   [42] Ibid., pp. 338—341.   [43] Ibid., pp. 342—343.

3. PROBLEMS IN ENGELS' INTERPRETATION

After having outlined Engels' ideas concerning the material basis for the first bourgeois revolution and the class conflicts resulting from the new mode of production, the question must be asked, exactly what was Engels attempting to prove? The historical fact of the Peasants' War of 1525 lay before him. However, at the same time another historical fact, the Reformation, confronted him from the opposite side. Now, according to Marxist theory, the capitalistic mode of production had begun in the 16th century,[44] and, consequently, if any revolution should have taken place, it should have been the revolution of the bourgeoisie.[45] The bourgeoisie, however, did not revolt.[46] Thus Engels was faced with a Peasants' War he wanted to call a bourgeois revolution; yet the bourgeoisie he needed to satisfy his theoretical requirements did not even have a sufficiently strong capitalistic mode of production upon which to rise to power, for Engels could find only guild production in 16th-century Germany. All he was able to do was to point to a lagging economy and a sagging trade upon which a not very revolutionary bourgeoisie carried out a revolution in religious guise. He emphasized the bitterness of the class conflicts, yet had to admit that a successful revolution could have been brought about only by a closing of the class ranks. Then, when he thought that the bourgeoisie had betrayed the peasant cause, he had bitter words of condemnation for it. According to his theory, the German bourgeoisie should have gained immeasurably in revolutionary ardor between 1525 and 1848, but he was constantly finding the same philistine qualities in the "petite bourgeoisie" of 1525 that so irritated him in the bourgeoisie of 1848.[47]

But in order even to be able to speak of a bourgeois revolution in religious guise, Engels was forced to portray the Roman Catholic Church as the spokesman for feudalism, and nascent Protestantism as the spokesman for the capitalistic bourgeoisie. How could this now be reconciled with Zimmermann's delineation of Luther, Müntzer, and the radicals? Engels accepted Zimmermann's basic description of Luther as a revolutionary-turned-reactionary, yet he modified this image somewhat in his *Bauernkrieg*. He argued here that when Luther had first decided to oppose the

[44] See note 28, above.

[45] It is for this reason, of course, that Marx and Engels could argue that the Peasants' War, especially under the leadership of Thomas Müntzer, could not win; their time in the historical dialectic had not yet come! See *A. Friesen*, "Thomas Müntzer in Marxist Thought," p. 310.

[46] Engels, however, had not yet defined the term with any precision or proven, by concrete examples, that such a class existed in 16th-century Germany, or, if it existed, how large it was.   [47] M/E, Werke, VII, 413.

official teachings of the Church, his teachings had not yet contained any definite characteristics of their own. These had, in fact, not gone beyond any of the previous bourgeois heresies, thus leaving the door open for development in any number of directions. It could not have been otherwise, rationalized Engels, for, in order to overthrow the power of the Church, all opposition had to be united; any merely sectarian movement must of necessity have failed to achieve this goal.[48] Thus peasants, pre-proletarians, the bourgeoisie, the lesser nobility, and even some of the princes had at first joined in the general opposition to the Church, since each had been able to read his own opposition into that of Luther. Eventually, however, this united front had broken into a moderate Lutheran and radical Müntzerian group. The first had sought only to break the power of the established Church and enrich itself at the latter's expense, while the latter had desired to free itself from a more general feudal as well as religious oppression.

Since Engels did not credit Luther's teachings with any inherent attractive powers, he could argue that Luther had really been playing the opportunist, waiting in the wings to see which faction would be victorious before giving content to his teachings. With the emergence of two parties, Luther was forced to make a choice, however. He did not hesitate long, stated Engels, for he turned his back on the popular movement and joined the princes, nobles, and bourgeoisie who constituted the more conservative element. Immediately Luther had made this decision, his demands for a radical war of destruction against Rome ceased and he began to preach change by peaceful evolution rather than by violent revolution.[49]

Luther made this choice, Engels continued, because most of the cities, the lesser nobility, and a fair number of the princes had begun to demand a more conservative reform movement. It had become apparent that the forces of conservatism would be victorious, at least in the greater part of Germany, only as long as a course of peaceful evolution could be pursued. Open conflict with the Church could only lead to war with the peasants and to the alienation of the more conservative reform groups. Had the bourgeoisie allowed itself to have been caught in the press between a radical left and a resurgent Catholic right, it would undoubtedly have been strangled.[50]

---

[48] Ibid., p. 347.   [49] Ibid., p. 348.

[50] Ibid., p. 349. Engels obviously reads the predicament of the 1848 Liberals into Luther's position in the Peasants' War. He himself remarked, in the 1870 introduction to his Bauernkrieg: "Die Parallele zwischen der deutschen Revolution von 1525 und der von 1848/49 lag zu nahe, um damals von der Hand gewiesen zu werden." Ibid., p. 532.

It is this role of the moderate attempting to avoid being destroyed by radical forces on either side that Engels assigns to Luther in the latter's first attempt to mediate between the peasants and the princes. Since the Peasants' War began in southern Germany where the princes belonged nearly exclusively to the Catholic Church, Luther's attempt to mediate was in reality an attempt to keep the moderate party from being crushed in the ensuing struggle.[51]

The attempts at mediation failed, however, and soon the peasants were at war not only with the Catholic princes, but with the Lutheran princes as well. This was no time for continued mediation, but, rather, a time for action. Luther, therefore, forgot his old enmity with the Catholics, joined hands with them, and turned against the peasants with inhuman fury and savagery.[52]

In dependence upon Zimmermann, Engels asserted that Luther had given the popular movement a powerful weapon in his translation of the Bible. From it, he had himself drawn the picture of a primitive, non-hierarchical Christianity which he had used to criticize the feudal and hierarchical Christianity of his own day.[53] It was only natural, then, that the peasants should pick up the weapon and use it for their own ends. With the coming of the Peasants' War, however, Luther turned the Bible against the peasants and demonstrated from it that one must obey the temporal powers without qualification. The validity of princely power by divine right, passive obedience to princely tyranny, yes, even the justification of slavery were now all proven from the same Bible. In doing so, however, Luther not only betrayed his own earlier position as well as that of the peasants, but also the position of the bourgeoisie whose spokesman he was.[54]

Engels' delineation of Luther's role in the Peasants' War was not simply a replica of Zimmermann's; certain aspects had been added. Like Zimmermann, he saw Luther's actions from Müntzer's perspective and therefore condemned the latter's support of the princes in the war.[55] It was this perspective, together with their common theory of historical progress, that determined the picture of Luther as the revolutionary-turned-reactionary. Engels went beyond Zimmermann's analysis, however, and, by means of his sociological categories, he was able, so he thought, to place Luther and his ideas into their social context. Thus Luther became the representative

---

[51] Ibid., p. 349.   [52] Ibid., p. 350.

[53] If Luther had simply revived the picture of a non-feudal early Christianity, how did this fit the ideology of the 16th-century bourgeoisie? Certainly social conditions were no longer the same. Engels himself had stated in another context that early Christianity had been the religion of the slaves.   [54] M/E, Werke, VII, 351.   [55] Ibid., p. 349.

of the bourgeoisie and Protestantism its ideology. And because his historical eyes were so dimmed by the events of 1848 and the failure of the radical cause, he saw all other events only through his own 1848 experiences.[56]

It is higly probable that Engels could the more easily do this since he had very little knowledge of Luther's thought to encumber him. Like Zimmermann, he was concerned primarily with Luther's actions and the reactions to these in society, but he did not really understand why Luther had acted as he had. He saw, as had Zimmermann, that Luther had criticized the Church — sometimes vehemently — but he interpreted this as a criticism of feudalism. He realized that Luther had been critical of the peasants and had turned against them, yet he did not really understand why Luther had done so. Engels saw fairly clearly what Luther had done, and from his perspective of *Parteilichkeit* for Müntzer and the peasants, he reacted in characteristic fashion to this action,[57] but he did not understand why Luther had acted as he had. Yet he saw action as the result of "ultimate" economic motivation, and thought, or ideas, as farthest removed from this social and economic base but nevertheless the result of it. Thus Engels could read Luther's thoughts without having read the thought of Luther and discover motives in him which not even Luther had recognized to be present.

If, as Engels remarked elsewere:

"Luther und Münzer repräsentieren nach ihrer Doktrin wie nach ihrem Charakter und ihrem Auftreten jeder seine Partei vollständig,"[58]

then Müntzer must have represented the radical wing of the revolutionary movement. As late as November of 1843, however, Engels was not yet aware of the extent to which Müntzer had been a proto-communist,[59] for in a short essay of that year he still noted that,

"Der Prediger Thomas Münzer, den sie [the peasants] an ihre Spitze stellten, erließ einen Aufruf, der natürlich voll des religiösen u. abergläubischen Unsinns seiner Zeit war, der aber unter anderem auch Grundsätze wie diese enthielt: Nach der Bibel habe kein Christ das Recht, irgendwelches Eigentum ausschliesslich für

---

[56] Engels was constantly making references to his own 1848 experiences. See ibid., pp. 347, 350, and especially 351.

[57] For a Marxist discussion of *Parteilichkeit* and its role in Marxist historiography, see *J. Kuczynski,* "Parteilichkeit und Objektivität in Geschichte und Geschichtsschreibung," in *F. Klein* und *J. Streisand,* eds., Beiträge zum neuen Geschichtsbild. Alfred Meusel zum 60. Geburtstag (Berlin, 1956), pp. 9—26.   [58] M/E, Werke, VII, 347.

[59] Apparently Engels had not yet read Zimmermann's Bauernkrieg where he was to meet a rationally motivated Müntzer. Zimmermann's portrayal of Müntzer must, therefore, have come as a welcome revelation to him.

sich zu behalten; Eigentumsgemeinschaft sei der einzige geeignete Zustand für eine Gesellschaft von Christen; keinem guten Christen sei erlaubt, irgendeine Herrschaft oder Befehlsgewalt über andere Christen auszuüben, auch nicht irgendein Regierungsamt oder erbliche Macht innezuhaben, sondern im Gegenteil, so, wie vor Gott alle Menschen gleich sind, sollten sie es auch auf Erden sein. Diese Lehren waren nichts weiter als logische Schlüsse aus der Bibel und aus Luthers eigenen Schriften."[60]

Engels, who had just become a communist himself,[61] realized that Müntzer had demanded a communist society, that he had believed such a society would cure the social ills of his time, but Engels was still equally aware that Müntzer had been religiously motivated to make these demands. Obviously, he had not yet discovered that Müntzer had secretly been a rationalist.

A year or so later Engels was still speaking in very much the same terms: Thomas Müntzer, the famous leader of the Peasants' War, he said, had been a real democrat as far as it had been possible at that time.[62] But when he came to write his *Bauernkrieg* in 1850, he was able to omit the conditional clause at the end of this statement, and, on the basis of the latest research, assert that Müntzer had been the famous leader of the Peasants' War who had been a real democrat and had fought for real demands, not illusions,[63] for meanwhile he had discovered from Zimmermann that Müntzer had not been motivated by religious ardor but had cleverly used religion to promote his political aspirations. In these political aspirations he had anticipated the future course of historical events,[64] and, although the historical dialectic had not yet progressed to the stage where the egalitarian society could have been established, the very fact that Müntzer had tried to establish such a society made him a great revolutionary.[65]

If his theology was a mere screen, what then had been Müntzer's true ideology? Engels now discovered this in Zimmermann's study; but he also went a little beyond him. He found the real Müntzer preaching a kind of pantheism under the cloak of Christian forms, for at heart Müntzer had been an atheist whose ideas curiously resembled the modern speculative mode of contemplation.[66] He had been a rationalist who had claimed that faith was nothing but reason come alive in man.[67] Heaven and hell were non-existant and Christ had been but an ordinary man such as you and I.[68]

---

[60] *Engels*, "Fortschritte der Sozialreform auf dem Kontinent," M/E, Werke, I, 489.
[61] See the letter of Moses Hess to Berthold Auerbach of June 19, 1843. Moses Hess Briefwechsel, p. 103.   [62] *Engels*, "Deutsche Zustände II," M/E, Werke, II, 577.
[63] M/E, Werke, VII, 346.   [64] Ibid.   [65] Ibid., p. 353.
[66] Ibid. Zimmermann had not gone so far as to call Müntzer an atheist. [67] Ibid. [68] Ibid.

Müntzer indeed aspired to establish the Kingdom of God on earth, but he had conceived this as

"einen Gesellschaftszustand, in dem keine Klassenunterschiede, kein Privateigentum und keine den Gesellschaftsmitgliedern gegenüber selbständige, fremde Staatsgewalt mehr bestehen."[69]

Not only had Müntzer been the ideological harbinger of modern communism, however, he had also been the revolutionary *par excellence*. As the real leader of the Peasants' War, he had guided and directed its various phases by means of a vast conspiracy of Anabaptists recruited largely from the itinerant journeyman class of the towns.[70] Centered at Mühlhausen, where Müntzer had presided over his underground cell,[71] the conspiracy had drawn into its orbit such men as Balthasar Hubmaier of Waldshut, Conrad Grebel of Zurich, Franz Rabmann of Griessen, and Schappelar of Memmingen, to name only some of the more important.[72] This, of course, had been no mean accomplishment at a time when transportation had been poor, particularism rampant among the peasants, and Müntzer beset by enemies on every hand.[73]

Even this, however, had not been Müntzer's greatest achievement according to Engels. In their discussion of Ferdinand Lasalle's drama, *Franz von Sickingen,* Marx and Engels told Lassalle that revolution in and of itself had no merit; this was the more so since Sickingen the revolutionary had been trying to restore the knights to their old position in the realm. There was nothing really tragic about Lassalle's hero, for, as Marx put it, Sickingen

"ging unter, weil er als *Ritter* und als *Repraesentant einer untergehenden Klasse* gegen das Bestehende sich auflehnte oder vielmehr gegen die neue Form des Bestehenden."[74]

Müntzer, on the other hand, had been the leader of a new movement which one day would be victorious but which could only fail in the 16th century.[75] Therefore, besides being a proto-communist, Müntzer also became a tragic hero caught in the grips of Marxist logic. The time for the communist revolution had not yet arrived, for the bourgeois revolt was just beginning. Müntzer's ideas, therefore, had been far in advance of his

---

[69] Ibid.   [70] Ibid., pp. 355—356.   [71] Ibid., p. 400.   [72] Ibid., pp. 357—358.
[73] Engels himself admitted that the Peasants' War had failed because of what he called *Lokalborniertheit*. Ibid., p. 412.
[74] Quoted in *G. Lukacz*, Karl Marx und Friedrich Engels als Literaturkritiker (Berlin, 1952), p. 19.   [75] Ibid., p. 23.

time, and failure had been inevitable.[76] His failure did not detract from his greatness, however, for this greatness lay in the fact that he had seen the ultimate goal of history and had tried to propel society in that direction.

If this was in fact the first stage of the bourgeois revolution, what kind of role had the peasants played in it? After all, Engels had himself entitled his study the Peasants' War. The question seems to have impinged itself only dimly upon Engels' consciousness in his *Bauernkrieg*. Since this was a peasants' revolt, one would expect to find that Engels and his Marxist followers should have concerned themselves first and foremost with the material causes of the Peasants' War. Such is not the case, however. The answer to this somewhat curious phenomenon lies hidden in the fact that the Marxists have, from the beginning, attempted to place the Reformation and the Peasants' War into its Marxist frame of reference: the *frühbürgerliche Revolution*. In this setting, of course, the peasants could not play the crucial role. Thus Engels could dismiss the causes of the peasant uprising with a few paragraphs in which he painted the plight of the peasants in the darkest of colors. Yet although the peasant estate had been lowly and his burden an onerous one, it had been difficult to induce him to revolt.[77]

As time went on, however, Engels realized that such a general summation needed supplementation. Particularly in an article entitled "Die Mark,"[78] written in 1882, he began to revise and clarify this picture. Here he argued that the 12th century had brought improvements with it for the peasant class which had later been reversed in the 14th century. Yet really unbearable conditions had been imposed upon the peasants only after the Thirty Years' War. The picture he had painted in his *Bauernkrieg*, therefore, needed revision, especially after his reading of Maurer.[79] But Engels was still uncertain as to what extent the peasant conditions had worsened and precisely how bad they had actually been at the time of the Peasants' War. Nor did he commit himself any more fully in a letter on the subject

---

[76] The "telescoping of the revolution" has caused quite a problem in Marxist thought, especially since many revolutionaries could not wait until the historical dialectic had fulfilled the rigid demands of Marxist logic. The classic example of such a "telescoped" revolution, of course, is the Russian Revolution of 1917. See G. *Lichtheim*, Marxism, an Historical and Critical Study (New York, 1960), p. 16.   [77] M/E, Werke, VII, 339—340.

[78] *Engels*, "Die Mark," Marx, Engels, Lenin, Stalin, Zur deutschen Geschichte, vol. I (Berlin, 1953), 142—156.

[79] Engels based his analysis primarily on G. L. *von Maurer's* books: Geschichte der Marken-Verfassung in Deutschland (Erlangen, 1856), and Geschichte der Fronhöfe, der Bauernhöfe und der Hofverfassung in Deutschland, 4 vols. (Erlangen, 1862—1863).

written to Marx on December 16, 1882.[80] In a note to the third edition of Marx's *Das Kapital,* however, he made the following comment:

"Im 15. Jahrhundert war der deutsche Bauer fast überall ein in gewissen Leistungen in Produkt und Arbeit unterworfener, aber sonst wenigstens faktisch freier Mann. Die deutschen Kolonisten in Brandenburg, Pommern, Schlesien und Ostpreußen waren sogar rechtlich als Freie anerkannt. Der Sieg des Adels im Bauernkrieg machte dem ein Ende. Nicht nur die besiegten süddeutschen Bauern wurden wieder leibeigen. Schon seit Mitte des 16. Jahrhunderts werden die ostpreußischen, brandenburgischen, pommerschen und schlesischen, und bald darauf auch die schleswig-holsteinischen freien Bauern zu Leibeigenen erniedrigt."[81]

Thus Engels had come to the conclusion that the Peasants' War had not so much been caused by the oppression of the peasants; rather, the defeat of the peasants had itself been a major cause of this oppression. The peasants' burdens had been only relatively heavier before the Peasants' War when compared with the peasant of the 12th and 13th centuries.

What became of this bourgeois revolution in religious guise in which the peasants were robbed of their important role? In his *Bauernkrieg,* Engels stated that Luther had sold out the revolution of the peasants as well as that of the bourgeoisie to the princes during the Peasants' War.[82] Yet the Reformation had continued on apace as a princely movement. Thus it would seem Engels believed the bourgeois ideology to have undergone a change, making it more acceptable to the princes.[83] This explanation raises a number of problems, however. If Luther could betray the peasant and bourgeois causes to the princes, then he played a far greater role in the history of the Reformation than he should have according to the Marxist theory regarding the role of the individual in history. On the other hand, if Luther's actions were merely the result of a sagging material base on which the bourgeois class of the Reformation rested, then why blame him? If Luther, as Engels asserted elsewhere, was the exponent of the bourgeois ideology,[84] then he could not really be blamed for expressing ideologically what Engels had to admit economically: namely, that the bourgeoisie was losing what little economic base it had. Engels admitted as much later on, in 1884, when he stated:

"Der Welthandelsweg wird Deutschland entzogen und Deutschland in einen isolierten Winkel gedrängt, dadurch die Macht der Bürger gebrochen, der Reformation dito."[85]

---

[80] *Marx-Engels,* Selected Correspondence (New York, 1934), p. 409.
[81] Zur deutschen Geschichte, I, 157.   [82] M/E, Werke, VII, 351.
[83] Again, Engels fails to tell us why and how.   [84] M/E, Werke, VII, 347.
[85] Zur deutschen Geschichte, I, 563.

Engels was wrestling with a major problem here, but a problem of his own making. If, as he was forced to concede in his *Bauernkrieg*, there had only been guild manufacturing in 16th-century Germany, and even this had been lagging behind that of other countries, what could it have been that made a bourgeois revolution possible at all, even if only in religious guise? The problem became even more acute when Engels was forced to admit further that the Hanseatic League had lost its power and prestige and that the center of trade had been diverted from Germany. Either Engels would have to find another definition for the Reformation period or he would have to find more material support for his bourgeoisie, and, hence, for his bourgeois revolution.

In the following years, especially after 1884, Engels came back to the problem posed here time and again, for this was the period in which he began to rethink and plan to rework the whole of his *Bauernkrieg*.[86] To Eduard Bernstein he wrote on November 11, 1884, that the Peasants' War would become the turning point (Wendepunkt) of all German history,[87] and to Sorge he wrote on December 31, 1884, that it would become the pivotal point (Angelpunkt) of German history.[88] In other letters of the same year he remarked that he had been doing a considerable amount of reading and had drawn up some preliminary outlines.[89] In one of these, found in his papers, he wrote:

"Reformation — Lutheranische und Kalvinistische — Revolution Nr. 1 der Bourgeoisie, worin Bauernkrieg die kritische Episode."[90]

Two years later, in his *Ludwig Feuerbach und der Ausgang der klassischen deutschen Philosophie*, he continued:

"als dies Bürgertum hinreichend erstarkt war, begann sein bisher vorwiegend lokaler Kampf mit dem Feudaladel nationale Dimensionen anzunehmen. Die erste große Aktion fand in Deutschland statt — die sogenannte Reformation."[91]

---

[86] On April 18, 1884, Engels wrote to Paul Lafargue: "... et la 4e édition de La Guerre des Paysans — nouvelles révisions et nouvelles préfaces à faire!" Correspondance, I, 197. On April 26, 1884, he wrote Kautsky: "Der Bauernkrieg wird ganz umgearbeitet." B. Kautsky, ed., Friedrich Engels' Briefwechsel mit Karl Kautsky (Wien, 1955), p. 112. (Hereafter cited as E/K, Briefwechsel.) To Bernstein he wrote on May 23, 1884: "Bauernkrieg wird ganz neu, mit Ausnahme der militärischen Geschichtserzählung." E. Bernstein, ed., Die Briefe von Friedrich Engels an Eduard Bernstein (Berlin, 1925), p. 148. (Hereafter cited as Briefe an Bernstein), and again on Nov. 11, 1884, on the same topic, ibid., p. 160.   [87] Briefe an Bernstein, p. 160.

[88] Quoted in Engels, Der deutsche Bauernkrieg (Berlin, 1965), p. 147, note 21.

[89] Engels to Bernstein, May 23, 1884. Briefe an Bernstein, p. 148.

[90] M/E, Werke, XXI, 402.   [91] Ibid., p. 304.

Thus, by 1886, it had become very apparent to Engels that the Reformation was the first stage of the bourgeois revolution in which the Peasants' War was the decisive event. He repeated this in a letter to Kautsky of September 15, 1889, calling the Reformation "die erste buergerliche Revolution in religioeser Verkleidung."[92] And in his last letter to Kautsky of May 21, 1895, he again referred to the Reformation in the same terms.[93]

In another preliminary outline, also dated 1884, Engels delved a little into Germany's pre-Reformation history and pointed to the causes for Germany's ever-increasing political fragmentation.[94] Yet, in spite of these divisive tendencies, he asserted that Germany could have been united politically if only her trade and commerce had developed naturally. This natural development was hindered by two decisive factors, however. In the first place, the German bourgeoisie, instead of consummating a political revolution, had made its revolution in the ideological realm — the Reformation — because of the custom of the time to express everything in religious terminology.[95] But not even this revolution in religious guise could be carried off without the help of the knights and the peasants.[96] In the second place, Germany had lost her position as a world trading center and was forced off the main trading routes; this, according to Engels, broke the power of the bourgeoisie and also, consequently, of the Reformation.

Thus far, Engels remained with his contradiction between a lagging economy and a sagging trade, and the revolution of the bourgeoisie. In 1889, however, Karl Kautsky published a series of articles in *Die Neue Zeit* on "Die Bergarbeiter und der Bauernkrieg," in which he tried to point out that no matter how highly one regarded Müntzer's personal importance for the revolt in Thuringia, the most important question was whether or not Müntzer had come to power here because the miners stood behind him.[97] In these articles, Kautsky drew attention to the fact that the Saxon gold and silver mines were the most important ones in Europe at the time of the Reformation; the only other mines that could come into consideration were those of Hungary. The other European countries produced relatively little gold and silver, and, until after the Peasants' War, imports of precious metals from America had not essentially affected the European

---

[92] E/K, Briefwechsel, p. 247.   [93] Ibid., p. 435.
[94] Another reason why the bourgeois revolution failed in Germany!
[95] Zur deutschen Geschichte, I, 563.
[96] Engels called this revolution, ". . . aber wie lausig!" Quite clearly, Engels was angry with the bourgeoisie of 16th-century Germany because it did not have the revolutionary power and enthusiasm it should have had. Ibid.
[97] K. Kautsky, "Die Bergarbeiter und der Bauernkrieg," Die Neue Zeit, VII (1889), 288—297, 337—350, 410—417, 443—453, and 507—515.

market.[98] Engels immediately grasped the significance of this fact for his interpretation of the Reformation. Writing to Kautsky on September 15, 1889, he stated:

"Die Arbeit klaert ein wesentliches Stueck der deutschen Geschichte auf, es sind einige kleine Luecken hie und da in der Entwicklungskette, aber das ist nicht wesentlich. Mir ist dabei erst recht klar geworden (was ich aus Soetbeer nur undeutlich und unbestimmt erfasst) wie sehr die Gold- und Silberproduktion Deutschlands (und Ungarns, dessen Edelmetal dem ganzen Westen via Deutschland vermittelt wurde) das letzte treibende Moment war das Deutschland 1470— 1530 oekonomisch an die Spitze Europas stellte und damit zum Mittelpunkt der ersten buergerlichen Revolution in religioser Verkleidung, der sogenannten Reformation machte. Das *letzte* Moment in dem Sinn dass es zu der relativ hohen Zunfthandwerks- und Zwischenhandels-Entwicklung kam und damit fuer Deutschland gegenueber Italien, Frankreich, England, den Ausschlag gab."[99]

At last Engels had found the "ultimately motivating factor" that had made Germany the center of the first bourgeois revolution.

It was this same major issue Engels returned to in his last letter to Kautsky, after reading the latter's *Vorläufer des neueren Sozialismus.* Kautsky, apparently, had not learned from Engels' letter of 1889 that it had been Germany's total economic position which made it possible for the Reformation to take place in Germany, for, Engels chided:

"2) hast Du die Weltmarktstellung — soweit davon die Rede sein kann, die internationale oekonomische Stellung Deutschlands Ende des XV. Jahrhunderts nicht voll erfasst. Diese Stellung erklaert *allein* wesshalb die buergerlich-plebejische Bewegung in religioeser Form, die in England, den Niederlanden, Boehmen erlag, im 16. Jahrhundert in Deutschland einen *gewissen* Erfolg haben konnte: den Erfolg ihrer *religioesen Verkleidung,* waehrend der Erfolg des buergerlichen *Inhalts* dem folgenden Jahrhundert und den Laendern der inzwischen entstandnen neuen Weltmarkterichtung vorbehalten blieb: Holland und England. Das ist ein langes Thema, das ich beim Bauernkrieg in extenso darzustellen hoffe — waer ich erst dabei!"[100]

Thus Engels' thesis can be reduced to the following proposition: Although Germany may have been less unified politically and may have possessed less productive industries than other European countries, and although she had begun to lose her trading strength, yet the gold and silver mining industry had kept Germany at the peak of the European trading market, at least until 1530, and had thus made possible the bourgeois revolution in religious guise. Engels conceded that it had not even been the

---

[98] Ibid., p. 292.   [99] E/K, Briefwechsel, p. 247.
[100] Engels to Kautsky, May 21, 1895. Ibid., p. 435.

guild manufacturing centers which had empowered the bourgeoisie, for
Germany's international economic position *alone* explained the limited success of this revolution, a success which lay in its religious victory. However, Engels did not live to deal with this vast topic in extenso or in any
other form, for within a very short time he was dead and the planned revision of his *Bauernkrieg* never realized. The legacy he left behind with
regard to the interpretation of the Peasants' War, however, was filled with
problems of a very thorny nature.

Marx also gathered material for a history of Germany in which the
16th century was to loom large. He never progressed beyond the stage of
setting up a chronological table of events and dates, however.[101] Since these
excerpts contain little, if anything, of interpretive value, they have, as a
result, had very little influence on subsequent Marxist historiography of
the Reformation. Nevertheless, Marx did add a new dimension to the
Marxist interpretation of Luther. In his major work, *Das Kapital*, he
quoted, on four different occasions, from Luther's "An die Pfarrherren,
wider den Wucher zu predigen," of 1540, to support his own moral indignation at the exploitation of man by man.[102] In one instance he remarked:

"In der altmodischen, wenn auch stets erneuten, Form des Kapitalisten, im Wucherer, veranschaulicht Luther sehr gut die Herrschsucht als Element des Berei-
cherungstrieb."[103]

Furthermore, Marx was in complete agreement with Luther, whom he
quoted as saying:

"Die Heiden haben können aus der Vernunft rechnen, dass ein Wucherer, sey ein
vierfältiger Dieb und Mörder. Wir Christen aber halten sie in solchen ehren, das
wir sie schier anbeten umb ihres Geldes willen ... Wer einem andern seine Nahrung aussauget, raubet und stilet, der thut eben so grossen Mord (so viel an jm
ligt) als der einen Hungers sterbet und zu Grunde verterbet. Solches thut aber
ein Wucherer, und sitzet die weil auf seinem Stuel sicher, so er billicher hangen
solt am Galgen, und von soviel Raben gefressen werden, als er gulden gestolen
hatte, wo anders so viel fleisches an jm were, das so viel Raben sich drein stücken
und teilen kundten."[104]

Thus Luther takes on the appearance of a critic of capitalism in Marx's
Das Kapital.[105]

---

[101] *Marx*, "Chronologische Auszüge," Zur deutschen Geschichte, I, 305—313.
[102] M/E, Werke, XXIII, 149, 207, 328, and 619.
[103] M/E, Werke, XXIII, 619.   [104] Ibid.
[105] It is interesting to note in this regard that Marx did not see the Roman Catholic
Church as such a strong bastion of feudalism either. See his "Grundriss der Kritik der
politischen Ökonomie," Zur deutschen Geschichte, I, 169—170, written in 1857/58.

If Luther was a critic of capitalistic fiscal policies, how then could he also have been the representative of the bourgeoisie? The apparent contradiction does not seem to have occured to Engels' or to Marx's mind, for Marx also asserted, in another context, that Protestantism was the bourgeois form of the Christian ideology.[106] Since Luther had been the father of Protestantism, Marx would also have been forced to argue that Luther had represented the bourgeoisie.

4. SIMILARITIES TO THE OLDER CATHOLIC INTERPRETATION

Engels' view of the Reformation has much in common with the older Catholic interpretation. We already noted the similarities between Müntzer's and the peasants' intellectual paradigms of the ideal Christian society and the Catholic concept of the Corpus Christianum in the second chapter of this study. When, therefore, Zimmermann emptied Müntzer's ideology of its religious overtones, Engels recognized the affinity of Müntzer's position to his and Marx's readily enough. Yet the judgments that resulted from the imposition of this paradigm, whether secularized or not, upon the history of the 16th century remained fundamentally the same. It is for this reason that many Marxist Reformation scholars have relied heavily upon the older Catholic interpretations of the Reformation to substantiate their own assertions. The similarities between the two interpretations became apparent as early as 1856. In that year, Heinrich Leo, a historian at the University of Halle as well as an adamant opponent of the Young Hegelians, wrote a short essay on Thomas Müntzer[107] in which he attempted to free Luther and the Reformation from the charges of revolution. In the process, Luther appeared as a person who, although he had sympathized with Sickingen's and Hutten's plan for a secularization of Church property, had been hindered from embarking on the road to revolution because of extreme radicals like Carlstadt and Müntzer.[108] Leo therefore emphasized Luther's break with his youthful, more radical days and proceeded to make him over into a loyal servant of the princes[109] who had hurried back from the Wartburg in order to stem the tide of revolution[110] and halt the radical innovations initiated in Wittenberg by Carlstadt.[111]

It is instructive to note that although Leo directed his thrust against the current Catholic interpretation of Luther and the Reformation as the

---

[106] M/E, Werke, XXII, 93.
[108] Ibid., p. 4.
[110] Ibid., p. 10.

[107] *H. Leo,* Thomas Münzer (Berlin, 1856).
[109] Ibid., p. 11.
[111] Ibid., p. 11.

source of all revolutions,[112] Marx interpreted the essay, which he read only in part, as an attack on Engels' portrait of Müntzer and the Reformation.

"Vater Leo hat vor dem Koenige eine Vorlesung ueber *Muenzer* gehalten (abgedruckt zum Teil in der 'N(euen) Pr(eussischen) Z(eitung)'. Man moechte sagen, dass sie direkt gegen Deinen Aufsatz in der 'Revue der N(euen) Rh(einischen) Z(eitung)' gerichtet ist. Die Reformation muss natuerlich von dem Vorwurf befreit werden, die Mutter der Revolution zu sein. M(uenzer) war ein 'Schwarmgeist', der sagte: 'intelligo ut credam'. Luther sagte: 'credo ut intelligam'. Die 'Spenersche'[113] hat geantwortet: Luther habe in spaetern Jahren die elende Rolle, die er politisch gespielt, bereut etc. Du siehst, dass die Gaerung selbst in der offiziellen Schicht durchbricht."[114]

It is quite possible that the introduction to the essay was omitted in the *Neue Preussische Zeitung*, otherwise Marx would have realized that the essay had not been directed against Engels' reinterpretation. Marx's error is significant, however, for the Catholic interpretation of Luther and the Reformation as the source of revolution in 16th-century Germany fitted nicely into the Marxist scheme of the Reformation as an early phase of the bourgeois revolution. It then also becomes apparent why Marxist historians like Hanna Köditz can rely so heavily on Janssen's *Geschichte des deutschen Volkes*[115] despite the fact that Engels, in a letter to Kautsky, referred to Janssen's interpretation as "der bornirten katholischen Bekaempfung"[116] of the Protestant Luther-legend.

5. KAUTSKY'S REVISIONS

Engels must not have been fully satisfied with his own delineation of Luther's life and thought, or convinced of its persuasiveness, however, for in 1892 he wrote Kautsky:

"Es ist mir dieser Tage eingefallen, dass eine Darstellung *Luthers* aus seinen Thaten und Schriften eine sehr noetige Arbeit waere."[117]

---

[112] Leo stated very explicitly: "Der von Katholiken so oft wiederholte Vorwurf, die Deutsche Reformation sey nicht blos ein revolutionärer Vorgang gewesen, sondern auch die Wurzeln aller späteren revolutionären Bewegungen, welche das Leben der Europäischen Völker erschüttert haben, ist eben so oft dadurch zurückgewiesen worden, dass die Deutsche Reformation nur auf die ursprünglichen Aufgaben das Leben gemessen, also überall keine sittlichen Grundlagen zerstört, sondern nur die vorhandenen von darüber gestürzten Schutte gereinigt, dass sie also in der That nur reformirt nicht revolutionirt habe." Ibid., p. 1.   [113] This is likely a reference to Leo.

[114] Marx to Engels, March 5, 1856. M/E, Werke, XXIX, 24—25.

[115] See *H. Köditz*, "Die gesellschaftlichen Ursachen des Scheiterns des Marburger Religionsgesprächs vom 1. bis 4. Oktober 1529." ZfG, 2 (1954), I, 37—70.

[116] Engels to Kautsky, Feb. 1, 1892. E/K, Briefwechsel, p. 328.   [117] Ibid.

Interested primarily in producing a convincing account of Luther's life from the Marxist point of view, Engels wanted also to combat the "Protestant legend" on the one hand and the "narrow-minded" Catholic polemic on the other.[118] He had no intention, however, of attempting to give an objective account, for he wanted Kautsky to prove

"von *unserm* Standpunkt, wiesehr die Reformation eine *buergerliche* Bewegung, direkt nothwendig [gewesen]."[119]

He even told Kautsky how to go about his task: he was to demonstrate the parallel development between the Luther during the period from 1520 to 1526, on the one hand, and the bourgeoisie from before to after 1848 on the other. The change in Luther was to be brought out very clearly. Here, concluded Engels, was an important task still to be undertaken. Nor would it be overly much work! And Kautsky was the man for the job.[120]

But even though, or precisely because, Kautsky proceeded from the frame of reference set him by Engels, and although he laid claim to having read all of Luther's writings pertaining to the Peasants' War,[121] he could come to no deeper appreciation of Luther's thought than had Engels before him. Thus he asserted that Luther had not demonstrated any originality of thought, and had been overshadowed by many of his contemporaries.[122] Events and people had forced Luther to break with the pope, not any initiative of his own. If Luther condemned the papacy in 1519, to which he had still clung in 1518, this was not due to any new or more profound insights into the nature of the papacy he had gained in the meantime; it was much rather the result of outward influences which had impinged upon him.[123] Even Luther's courageous "Here I stand, I can do no other, so help me God!" had been forced from his lips because Kautsky believed Luther had been cunning enough to realize that he had burned his bridges behind him; hence, since a recantation would not have won over his enemies and only alienated his supporters, Luther had had no choice but to stand firm. At the same time, he knew that if he did stand firm the princes and the knights would not desert him.[124]

The only ability Kautsky was willing to concede to Luther was the ability of the agitator. Luther, although an academician, had understood

---

[118] Ibid. Engels refers specifically to Janssen's Geschichte des deutschen Volkes (Freiburg i. B., 1876).   [119] Ibid.   [120] Ibid.

[121] Kautsky to Engels, Feb. 19, 1892. Ibid., p. 329.   [122] *Kautsky*, Vorläufer, p. 14.

[123] Ibid., p. 17.

[124] Ibid., pp. 17—18. Kautsky's point of view becomes very obvious when he quotes Müntzer's comment on Luther's stand at Worms with full approval. See Müntzer's "Hochverursachte Schutzrede," Schriften und Briefe, p. 341.

the needs, feelings, and the thoughts of the common man and had known
how to use his language as no other. A master of polemical debate, Luther
had been able to unite the classes in this manner against the pope; all his
forerunners had been able to reach only one class at a time.[125]

Like Engels before him, Kautsky argued that the causes for the unrest
in Germany were not to be found in men like Luther, but primarily in
the economic realm. Here he pointed to an apparent contradiction: that
Germany was rich and yet complained more than any other country
about the money drained by Rome. The contradiction was only apparent,
however, for the richer a country, the more it hurt to pay. Thus Kautsky
saw Luther's attack on the indulgence traffic as assaulting the heart of the
Church's fiscal system, and, therefore, attracting those who were hardest
hit by this system because they hoped to free themselves from it.[126]

Yet Kautsky sought the particular reason for the beginning of the Reformation in the rise of the mining industry in Saxony, which, together
with the increasing exchange of products, had brought wealth to that
region. With this wealth, however, had come increased friction between the
classes since only the merchants, landlords, and nobles had benefitted from
the profits. Increased production had brought higher prices, but not
financial gain to the peasants; and in the cities it had brought only more
severe wage battles. Class antagonisms, therefore, had become especially
acute in Saxony.[127]

The Dukes of Saxony, owners of these mines, reaped the lion's share
of the profits. Coming as they did at the beginning of this economic
boom, the profits gave the dukes, particularly Frederick the Wise, tremendous power at a time when the German Electors were selling their
electoral votes to the highest royal bidder. Because of this wealth, Frederick
became the "king maker" as well as the rallying point in Germany for the
forces of princely absolutism. When, therefore, Luther turned against the
Church, Frederick the Wise was able to protect him.

Despite the fact that Kautsky was more specific as to the material base
of the region in which the Reformation ideas had originated,[128] he nevertheless failed to answer the essential question concerning the relationship

---

[125] *Kautsky*, Vorläufer, p. 18.   [126] Ibid., pp. 7—9.   [127] Ibid., pp. 23—27.
[128] It is quite clear that Engels and Kautsky did not see the Reformation (and the
Peasants' War) on the same levels. Engels was trying to grasp it in its totality as an
historical epoch, whereas Kautsky was content to look at it more locally and as cause
and effect. Thus Engels' criticism of his book, that Kautsky had not grasped the total
picture which alone explained the partial success of the German bourgeois revolution
of the 16th century, was quite justified from Engels' point of view.

of Luther's ideas with the local social and economic conditions. There may
be some truth in the supposition that the Duke of Saxony's financial
power and consequent relative independence made it possible for him to
protect Luther when the latter came into conflict with the pope and
emperor, but it in no way answered the far more important question concerning the relationship between the origin of Luther's thought and the
rise of the bourgeoisie and of trade and commerce in Saxony.

In his first publications on the Peasants' War, Kautsky turned his attention in characteristic Marxist fashion to the working classes rather than
to the peasants. All he had to say about the peasants was that they had
been the vanguard of the dissatisfied lower classes.[129] In his *Vorläufer des
neueren Sozialismus*, he directed a little more attention to the peasant
plight but took much the same position on the problem as Engels had
taken in his "Die Mark." There had been some oppression before the
Peasants' War, but the real oppression came later.[130] It was his portrayal
of Müntzer and the Anabaptists, however, which deviated most from
Engels' assessment.

It is doubtful whether Engels had read any of Müntzer's writings when
he prepared his interpretation of the latter's role in the Peasants' War;[131]
this is not true of Kautsky. The latter first turned his attention to Müntzer in 1889 when he wrote a series of articles on the role of the miners
in the Peasants' War. In one of these,[132] he attempted to trace Müntzer's
influence on the miners in Thuringia. He was convinced it had been great.
Yet in the decisive moments of the war, none of the miners had followed
Müntzer into battle.[133]

---

[129] *Kautsky*, "Die Bergarbeiter und der Bauernkrieg," p. 289.

[130] *Kautsky*, Vorläufer, pp. 59—64. Even in this study, Kautsky was primarily concerned with the working classes of the time and not with the peasants. In a letter of
Feb. 19, 1892, he wrote Engels: "Ich liess daher die Münzergeschichte stehn und wen-
dete mich den ökonomischen Wurzeln der damaligen Arbeiter-Bewegung zu; die erste
Frucht war eine Arbeit über die Bergarbeiter. Eine andere habe ich, soweit es auf Material ankommt, fast vollendet; über die Wollenweber, die m. E. die Träger des damaligen primitiven Kommunismus waren; auch darüber habe ich schon ziemliches Material.
Eine vierte Arbeit endlich sollte einen Abriss der kommunistischen Bewegung von den
Hussiten bis Münster geben. Das Ganze wollte ich dann in einem Band, 'Die Arbeiter-
bewegung im Zeitalter der Reformation' vereinigen." E/K, Briefwechsel, p. 329.

[131] Engels stated explicitly that "All the material relating to the peasants' revolts
and to Thomas Münzer has been taken from Zimmermann." M/E, Werke, VII, 531.

[132] *Kautsky*, "Thomas Münzer und die Bergarbeiter," Die Neue Zeit, 7 (1889), 443
—453.

[133] He tried to explain this fact in the following way: "Im Laufe der Bewegung hört
man nichts mehr von den Bergarbeitern, es ist nur noch von den Bauern die Rede. Dies
ist wohl nicht einem wirklichen Zurücktreten der ersteren, sondern der kurzen und

Although Kautsky noted in a footnote that Seidemann's Müntzer biography was the best for facts and chronology concerning the latter's life,[134] he nevertheless preferred Zimmermann's interpretation. In a letter to Engels of 1892, he wrote:

"Ich habe ja s. Z., wie Du Dich vielleicht noch erinnerst, den ganzen Muenzer durchgearbeitet, ebenso die Schriften Luthers u. Melanchthons, soweit sie den Bauernkrieg behandeln, dann die ganze Literatur ueber Muenzer, die ich im br(itischen) Museum fand. Ich gab die projektirte Arbeit ueber Muenzer auf, da ich fand, nichts Neues sagen zu koennen. Zimmermann hat in allem Wesentlichen das Richtige getroffen, ich haette nur in Kleinigkeiten ueber ihn hinaus gehen koennen, soweit es die *Ereignisse* anbelangt."[135]

Two years later Kautsky was studying Müntzer's writings again, this time in preparation for his *Vorläufer des neueren Sozialismus*.[136] Despite the fact that Kautsky had asserted that Zimmermann had hit the nail on the head in all essential points, he now proceeded to make substantial revisions in both Zimmermann's and Engels' portrait of Müntzer.

Because he had meanwhile studied the medieval antecedents of movements like Müntzer's, Kautsky was not at all convinced that Müntzer had been as far ahead of his time as Zimmermann had averred. He asserted, rather, that he could find "[keinen] neuen Gedanken bei Müntzer."[137] Nor was Kautsky willing to concede that Müntzer's communism had been new, or even that Müntzer had been a great revolutionary.[138] Müntzer had been great nevertheless, for although he had not surpassed his contemporaries in philosophic conceptions and in organizational talent, it was "seine revolutionäre Tatkraft und vor allem sein staatsmännischer Blick" which had raised him above his contemporaries.[139] Müntzer's true greatness, therefore, had consisted in his revolutionary ardor and breadth of vision, for

"weit entfernt, seine Wirksamkeit auf eine kleine Gemeinde Rechtgläubiger zu beschränken, appellierte er an alle revolutionären Elemente jener Zeit, suchte er sie alle seiner Sache dienstbar zu machen."[140]

---

ungenauen Ausdrucksweise des Berichterstatters zuzuschreiben, der, wie die Schriftsteller über den Bauernkrieg in der Regel, die Aufständischen einfach als Bauern bezeichnet, aus welchen Klassen immer sie rekrutiert sein mochten." Ibid., p. 453.   [134] Ibid., p. 451.

[135] Kautsky to Engels, Feb. 19, 1892. E/K, Briefwechsel, p. 329.

[136] Kautsky to Engels, July 23, 1894. Ibid., p. 406.

[137] *Kautsky*, Vorläufer, p. 42. Of Zimmermann's study he now stated: "Erscheint uns die Auffassung Zimmermanns im allgemeinen wohl begründet, so können wir ihm doch in einem sehr wesentlichen Punkte nicht zustimmen: er fasst Münzer auf als ausserhalb seiner Zeit und über ihr stehend ..."   [138] Ibid.   [139] Ibid.   [140] Ibid.

Although Kautsky asserted that Müntzer's failure had been inevitable, he admitted that Müntzer had been, as a rule, unsuccessful in his efforts to bring about a cooperation of the revolutionary movements in the various districts of Saxony.[141] Even with these concessions, however, he still ran into a problem when he attempted to reconcile his portrayal of Müntzer with the latter's confession and ostensible recantation. In his letter to the council of Mühlhausen, Müntzer had exhorted his friends not to exasperate the higher authorities since the death penalty, which hung over his head, was deserved and well calculated to open the eyes of the foolish.[142] Unlike Zimmermann who had attempted to put a more favorable construction on it, Kautsky admitted that the letter did betray faintheartedness.[143] But all was not lost! By impugning the genuineness of the letter, Kautsky arrived at the conclusion that it had been a forgery of the princes calculated to produce despondency among the besieged.[144] Since it had not been in Müntzer's own hand, Kautsky believed this to be a justifiable conclusion. But no matter what the actual facts of the case, in the eyes of the German working-classes Müntzer was and is the most brilliant embodiment of heretical communism.[145]

Nor did Kautsky see the Anabaptists in the same light as Zimmermann and Engels, or, for that matter, rely upon Zimmermann for his material;

---

[141] Ibid., p. 43.   [142] Ibid., p. 101.   [143] Ibid., p. 102.   [144] Ibid.
[145] Ibid., p. 103. Kautsky wrote Engels again on March 5, 1895: "Schwer wars, in Bezug auf Muenzer zu wesentlich neuen Gesichtspunkten zu kommen. Das entscheidende Material hat Zimmermann bereits beigebracht — gerade ueber die Muenzersche Bewegung sind alle bedeutenden Monographien vor Zimmermann erschienen und von ihm benutzt worden. Und die materialistische Beleuchtung hast Du bereits gegeben. Da war fuer mich nicht viel zu machen." E/K, Briefwechsel, p. 423. Nevertheless, Kautsky had, through his broader study of late medieval heretical movements, noted nothing new in Müntzer in contrast to Zimmermann. And Engels had the following words of praise for this part of Kautsky's book: "Von Deinem Buch kann ich sagen dass es sich bessert je weiter man darin kommt. Plato und das Urchristentum sind noch zu ungenuegend nach dem urspruenglichen Plan behandelt. Die mittelalterlichen Sekten schon viel besser und zwar crescendo. Am besten die Taboriten, Muenzer, die Wiedertaeufer ..." Ibid., pp. 434—435. In the 1908 edition of Engels' Bauernkrieg, F. Mehring, the editor, commented on this aspect as follows: "Wichtiger ist der Widerspruch, den Kautsky dagegen erhebt, dass Zimmermann in Münzer einen ausserhalb seiner Zeit und über ihr stehenden Denker erblickt. Zimmermann, dessen Darstellung Kautsky sonst übrigens in vollem Masse anerkennt, komme zu dieser Auffassung, indem er Münzer mit späteren Denkern wie Penn, Zinsendorf, Rousseau u. a. vergleiche. Hätte er ihn dagegen mit früheren kommunistischen Sekten verglichen, so würde er gefunden haben, dass Münzer sich ganz in deren Gedankenkreis bewegt habe. Kautsky gesteht, keine neuen Gedanken bei Münzer gefunden zu haben, und meint auch dass Münzers organisatorische und propogandistische Bedeutung überschätzt worden sei ... Hiernach wäre denn auch zu berichtigen oder einzuschränken, was Engels über ... Münzer sagt," p. 123.

particularly for this part of his book he did extensive research.[146] He began his analysis of Anabaptism with the statement that there had been two centers of Anabaptism: one in Saxony, the other in Switzerland.[147] The Anabaptists in Saxony had indeed originated with the Zwickau Prophets, but their most important disciple had been Thomas Müntzer.[148] Zwickau, therefore, had been the center of revolutionary Anabaptism. The other center, Zurich, had been the source of pacifistic Anabaptism.

Nor had the Zurich Anabaptists sprung from the same source. Kautsky did not develop this theory himself; he found it newly formulated by the Leipzig church historian, Ludwig Keller.[149] Keller saw the origins of Anabaptism in the continued existence of medieval heretical sects, particularly the Waldensians, in areas where the printing trade was carried on. Basel was one of the chief centers of heretical ideas precisely for this reason. With the coming of the Reformation and the destruction of the absolute rule of the Catholic Church by Luther, these heretical groups began to emerge from the twilight realm of secrecy into the light of day.[150] Kautsky accepted this theory, as well as the fact that the Swiss Anabaptists had been pacifistic.

However, Keller not only separated the Zurich Anabaptists from the Zwickau Prophets and Thomas Müntzer,[151] he also argued that the latter had not really been Anabaptists.[152] Kautsky, on the other hand, knew of the letter the Swiss Anabaptists had written to Müntzer, which he found printed in Cornelius.[153] Therefore, despite the fact that he noted that the Swiss Anabaptists had taken exception to Müntzer's warlike rhetoric, Kautsky stressed that they had also written,

---

[146] He wrote to Engels on March 5, 1895: "Hast Du nicht Zeit oder Lust, das Ganze zu lesen, dann bitte ich Dich, wenigstens das Kapitel über die Wiedertaeufer zu lesen, das mich besonders interessiert hat. In den frueheren Kapiteln wirst Du theils schon Bekanntes finden, theils sind sie, als Einleitung, nur kursorisch gehalten . . .

"Dagegen bei den Wiedertaeufern fand ich jungfraeulichen Boden. Hier konnte ich auch, im Gegensatz zu den Taboriten, auf die Quellen zurueckgehen. Wenigstens so weit sie gedruckt vorliegen, habe ich sie entweder an der hiesigen Bibliothek oder im Buchhandel gefunden. Der westphalische Dialekt machte mir allerdings einige Schwierigkeiten. Aber ich habe mich hineingelesen. Vom holländischen Material musste ich leider absehen. Aber ich denke, ich habe genug gefunden, um die charakteristischen Merkmale der Bewegung festzustellen und sie begreiflich zu machen. Und soviel ich weiss, bin ich darin der erste. In diesem Kapitel hoffe ich, etwas geleistet zu haben." E/K, Briefwechsel, p. 423.   [147] *Kautsky*, Vorläufer, p. 107.   [148] Ibid., p. 37.

[149] *L. Keller*, Die Reformation und die älteren Reformparteien (Leipzig, 1885).

[150] Ibid., pp. 365—395.   [151] Ibid., p. 371.   [152] Ibid.

[153] *C. A. Cornelius*, Berichte der Augenzeugen über das Münsterische Wiedertäuferreich (Münster, 1853), II, 240.

"und daß Du mitsamt Karlstadt bei uns für die reinsten Verkünder und Prediger des reinsten göttlichen Wortes geachtet sind."[154]

He also cited the passage in Sebastian Franck's *Chronica* which stated that Müntzer's disciples in Thuringia were not Anabaptists and that Müntzer himself never rebaptized, as well as the fact that the various groups of Anabaptists unanimously and consistently protested that Müntzer had never been one of them.[155] In spite of all this, Kautsky held fast to the theory he probably found in Bullinger (whom he quoted at length in other contexts) that Müntzer had met with the Zurich Anabaptists on the Swiss border while in southern Germany.[156] His evidence was the passage in Müntzer's "Protestation" in which the latter traced the corruption of the Apostolic Church to the practice of infant baptism. He admitted, however, that the actual practice of adult baptism was begun in Zurich early in 1525. Indeed, he remarked that by the time the Zurich Anabaptists began to practise adult baptism, Müntzer had become so involved in his great revolutionary drama that such sectarian *Kleinkram* must have appeared totally meaningless to him.[157]

6. THE CONTRIBUTION OF BELFORT BAX AND ERNST BLOCH

Neither Kautsky, nor August Bebel[158] before him or Franz Mehring after him, saw the Reformation in the context Engels had placed it. Unlike Kautsky, however, neither Bebel nor Mehring added any substantially new aspects to the Marxist interpretation of the Reformation. This is particularly true of Mehring who was in all probability very deeply indebted to Kautsky for his own insights into the period.[159] Nevertheless, these men were not bound by any rigid rules of Marxist orthodoxy, and especially Kautsky's revisions seem to have impressed Engels. But perhaps the person who deviated farthest from Engels' position was E. Belfort Bax. Bax, writing his history of the Peasants' War four years after Kautsky, in 1899, portrayed Luther in much the same way as Zimmermann had, for, since he was no dogmatic Marxist follower, the class approach was lacking.[160] For the same reason, he went on to modify Zimmermann's and Engels' picture of Müntzer even more than had Kautsky.

Although Bax praised Zimmermann's sympathetic treatment of the Peasants' War, he proceeded to attack two basic theories Zimmermann

---

[154] *Kautsky*, Vorläufer, p. 128.   [155] Ibid., p. 129.   [156] Ibid., p. 128.
[157] Ibid., p. 129.   [158] *A. Bebel*, Der deutsche Bauernkrieg (Braunschweig, 1876).
[159] *F. Mehring*, Deutsche Geschichte vom Ausgang des Mittelalters (Berlin, 1946).
[160] *Bax*, The Peasant War. See Engels' evaluation of Bax in a letter to Sorge of Dec. 7, 1889. Selected Correspondence, p. 460.

had propounded: the theory of Müntzer's influence in the southern theater of the Peasants' War,[161] and the theory which had it that Müntzer was a social revolutionary.[162] Nor did Bax believe that Müntzer's communism had had any similarities to the 19th century variety, or even anticipated it. On the contrary, it had been quite medieval.[163] As far as Bax was concerned, Müntzer remained

"as before everything a theologian. This is noticeable in his pamphlets down to the very eve of the Peasants' War."[164]

And even though Müntzer had attacked the princes spiritual and temporal, Bax could find

"no evidence of any constructive theory in him beyond the most casual expressions."[165]

There had been a political aspect to Müntzer's activity, however; this had made its appearance after 1525 and was directed toward the establishment

"of the new kingdom of God on earth, a kingdom based on the model of the primitive Christian Church as he supposed it to have been. Freedom and equality must reign here. The princes and the great ones of the earth refused to espouse the new Gospel. Hence, they must be overthrown, and the 'common man,' who was prepared to embrace the Gospel, must be raised up in their place. He who would not become a citizen of the kingdom of God must be banished or killed. The great barrier to the awakening of the inward light was the riches of this world. Hence, in the kingdom of God, private wealth should cease to be, and all things should be in common."[166]

Despite the fact, however, that Bax saw nothing new in Müntzer's theories, and agreed with Lassalle that

"although on the positive side the movements were reactionary, [yet] on the negative side [they were] sufficiently in accord with the contemporary trend of social evolution."[167]

Therefore he was able to see some progressive tendencies in Müntzer's thought, or at least in the effects of that thought, as well.

"Münzer's communism was still-born, but his antagonism to feudal and ecclesiastical privileges became commonplaces of the democratic thought of a later age. Again, his insistence on the paramount nature of the 'inner light' was simply

---

[161] *Bax*, The Peasant War, p. 34.   [162] Ibid., p. 86.   [163] Ibid., p. 87.
[164] Ibid., p. 234.   [165] Ibid.   [166] Ibid., p. 240.   [167] Ibid., p. 256.

a mystical way of asserting the rights of the individual within his own sphere against external authority — ideas that have likewise become the theoretical cornerstones of post-medieval movements."[168]

But if Müntzer did retain some progressive tendencies, it was more in spite of himself than otherwise.

It was Ernst Bloch, however, who stressed an aspect of Müntzer's thought which had been noticed by Engels, Bebel, Kautsky, and Bax, but which, with the exception of Bax, had not played a significant role in their assessment of the man. This was Müntzer's chiliasm. Bloch asserted that from July 1523 onward, after his open breach with Luther, Müntzer became a "klassenbewußter, revolutionärer, chiliastischer Kommunist."[169] As far as Bloch was concerned, Müntzer's essential importance lay precisely in his ability to inspire the peasants and the city proletariat with this chiliastic vision — the Kingdom of God on earth where equality would reign.[170]

The impact of this vision, according to Bloch, had been particularly great because the material conditions of the peasants and city workers had been getting worse. This had increased their desire for justice, which, in many instances, had taken the form of a longing for the return of a just ruler, such as Barbarossa. Time, however, changed this longing into a desire for a simpler, more primitive form of Christianity.[171] Prophets, such as Joachim of Fiore, had appeared from time to time to play upon and strengthen the desire for the Kingdom of God. It had imbued the Hussite movement and the peasants' revolt of 1525.[172] Even astrologers had believed that the year 1524 would bring some apocalyptical event. All these things had made people, especially the oppressed classes, accept the ideas of Müntzer who had promised them the Kingdom of God here on earth. This apocalyptical vision had, according to Bloch, answered the needs of the time and spurred the peasants on to revolution. It was the "myth" they needed to propel them into action.[173]

With Bloch's study, Marxist historiography of the Reformation had, in many ways, come full circle. Many of the typically Marxist features re-

---

[168] Ibid., pp. 256—257.

[169] E. Bloch, Thomas Münzer als Theologe der Revolution (Berlin, 1960), p. 26. The first edition was published in Munich, 1921.

[170] Concerning the use of "myths" to inspire revolutions, see the study by G. Sorel, Reflections on Violence (New York, 1961).   [171] Bloch, Münzer, p. 46.   [172] Ibid., p. 51.

[173] Bloch's emphasis on Müntzer's chiliasm, of course, stands in close connection with his own Prinzip der Hoffnung philosophy. See his Das Prinzip Hoffnung, 3 vols. (Berlin, 1954—1959).

mained — such as the emphasis upon the class structure of society and revolution — but the hope for and anticipation of the utopian society on earth once more became much more important than the historical dialectic or materialistic determinism. Yet the flexibility in the interpretation of the Reformation manifested in the above pages was not to last very long, for the rise of "Marxist" countries was to dampen the Marxist historians' enthusiams for innovation.

CHAPTER VIII

THE DILEMMA OF MARXIST NEO-ORTHODOXY

1. THE MARXIST CALL TO REWRITE REFORMATION HISTORY

It was not until after World War II that the Marxists came back to the problem of the relationship of the Reformation to the Peasants' War; then, however, new dimensions were added. Those who wrote "Marxist" histories of the Reformation before this time had been in direct contact with Engels, and from numerous letters between the various personalities involved, it is clear that Engels learned as much from the others as they from him. This free exchange of opinion led to certain changes in interpretation, but with the beginning of Russian and East German historiography of the Reformation definite guidelines were laid down by party leaders which were then discussed at historical congresses and implemented by writers and teachers alike.[1] In an address to an assembly of archivists, for example, Leo Stern, one of the foremost East German historians involved in the rewriting of German history after the war, laid down guidelines for the new interpretation. Stern demanded that the East German historians shake off the disastrous ballast of traditional German historicism and pick up, once again, the strands of "progressive" historical writing which the Renaissance Humanists had initiated and which had found its greatest exponents in Marx and Engels.[2] At the same time, the reactionary ideological rubble of 19th-century idealistic philosophy, as well as the Romantic-Catholic Restoration ideology, must be swept aside. In accordance with the "progressive" nature of the historian's task, the German revolutionary tradition, begun in the Middle Ages, which found its finest expression in the great Peasants' War of 1525, was to be glorified. Furthermore, the East German historian was to emphasize Germany's great cultural heritage — the ideas of progress, democracy, freedom, and

---

[1] See, for example, the discussion by *J. von Hehn*, "Die Sowjetisierung des Geschichtsbildes in Mitteldeutschland," Europa Archiv, 9 (1954), 2929—2938, and 2973—2977.

[2] Thus the Marxists see themselves as the last in the great progressive tradition — a tradition which points to Marx and Engels from its earliest beginnings.

humanism — and bring this heritage into organic connection with the progressive aims of the German Democratic Republic. He was to glorify the examples of courage, heroism, patriotism, and dedication to the cause of the German people in German history, and he was to fight against the nihilistic tendencies aimed at dissolving the German nation which had produced such great men as Walther von der Vogelweide, Hans Sachs, Albrecht Dürer, Thomas Müntzer, as well as Martin Luther and others. Thus it was the duty of the teachers of history to free the schools and universities of the German Democratic Republic from all reactionary ballast and mobilize Germany's past history in the fight for peace, democracy, progress, and a united Germany. By doing this, the historian would fill the citizen of the German Democratic Republic with a *sanctus amor patriae* which would sweep aside their inferiority complex and the idea that Germany's history had been "eine Misere in Permanenz,"[3] and, instead, awaken in them a proud self-confidence.[4]

2. THE WORK OF M. M. SMIRIN

Before this call already, the new orthodoxy had been brilliantly illustrated in the eminent Russian historian's study on *Die Volksreformation des Thomas Münzer und der grosse Bauernkrieg*, written in 1947.[5] All the ideas of Engels were faithfully accepted and defended in chapters filled with lengthy, involved, though for the most part unconvincing argumentation. A typical mode of reasoning is the following:

"Engels schätzt die Ansichten Münzers vollkommen anders ein. Zwar ist Münzer nicht frei von chiliastischen Schwärmereien des Urchristentums; allein Engels findet bei ihm die ersten 'Antizipationen der folgenden Geschichte' und eine neue Begründung der in seiner Lehre enthaltenen kommunistischen Anklänge. 'Erst bei Münzer', schreibt Engels, 'sind diese kommunistischen Anklänge Ausdruck der Bestrebungen einer wirklichen Gesellschaftsfraktion, erst bei ihm sind sie mit einer gewissen Bestimmtheit formuliert, und seit ihm finden wir sie in jeder großen Volkserschütterung wieder, bis sie allmählich mit der modernen proletarischen Bewegung zusammenfließen."[6]

---

[3] Engels, however, had called Germany's history exactly this. In a letter to Mehring of Sept. 28, 1892, he wrote: "In studying German history — the story of a continuous state of wretchedness — I have always found that only a comparison with the corresponding French periods produces a correct idea of proportions." Selected Correspondence, p. 543.

[4] Given in an appendix to *Hehn's* article, Europa Archiv, 9 (1954), 6936—6937.

[5] German translation (Berlin, 1952). This is the edition that will be cited here.

[6] Ibid., p. 59. Other instances can be found on pages 87, 99, 278, 302, 445, 565, and others too numerous to mention.

After this *ex cathedra* judgment of the "Marxist Father" has been quoted, Smirin marshalls the facts to substantiate it. In this context, it is interesting to note that Kautsky is discounted as a reactionary and a revisionist, and his differences with Engels regarded as rank heresy.[7] Engels had himself written Kautsky, as we noted, and commended the latter on his book, particularly on the section dealing with Müntzer. Thus Smirin, in his zeal for orthodoxy, went some seven hundred pages out of his way to prove what Engels had tacitly admitted as being wrong.

As the title indicates, the stress throughout is on the *Volkstümlichkeit* of Müntzer. He is seen as the great leader of the downtrodden masses,[8] whose religion stressed man's participation in society.[9] Even his concept of the Kingdom of God had in reality been devoid of any religious connotations, for religion had served him only as a means of communication with the people, this being the only language they understood. Therefore Smirin was once again in complete agreement with Engels whom he quoted:

"Unter dem Reich Gottes verstand Münzer aber nichts anderes als einen Gesellschaftszustand, in dem keine Klassenunterschiede, kein Privateigentum und keine den Gesellschaftsmitgliedern gegenüber selbständige, fremde Staatsgewalt mehr bestehen ... alle Arbeiten und alle Güter sollten 'gemeinsam' sein, und es sollte 'die vollständigste Gleichheit durchgeführt werden.'"[10]

Nor had Müntzer's ideas remained sectarian. Rather, they had given expression to the peoples' conception of what the Reformation should be.[11] And although the people had talked in biblical terms, Müntzer had really reached beneath this outer shell and penetrated to the heart of the matter.[12]

---

[7] Ibid., p. 276. Kautsky, by asserting that he could find no new ideas in Müntzer, really negated Zimmermann's and Engels' concept of a Müntzer as the rational social revolutionary, of the man far in advance of his time. It is no wonder, therefore, that Smirin, in strict dependence upon Engels, should attack Kautsky. In her review of Smirin's book, Hanna Köditz remarked: "In diesem ersten Teil seines Werkes gelingt es Smirin, die These Kautsky's, Müntzer sei in seiner theoretischen Grundlage nicht über die mittelalterlichen Sekten hinausgelangt, überzeugend zu widerlegen. Er bringt den eindeutigen Beweis, dass die Lehre Müntzers auf völlig neuen Voraussetzungen beruhte." ZfG, 1 (1953), 3, 508.   [8] *Smirin*, Volksreformation, p. 59.

[9] Ibid., p. 83.   [10] Ibid., p. 87.   [11] Ibid., p. 279.

[12] One could also, depending upon one's ideological position, characterize Smirin's dependence upon Engels as Hanna Köditz did in her review: "Es ist ein Beweis für die Genialität Engels', wenn der sowjetische Forscher fast hundert Jahre später nach gründlicher Untersuchung der nunmehr erheblich umfangreicheren Quellenmaterials in seinem Werk, das, wie Umfang, Fülle der verarbeiteten Literatur und Sorgfalt der Quellen-

Although Engels had stressed the communistic tendencies in Müntzer's thought and although Smirin affirmed that these were undoubtedly there, yet he argued that to empasize them unduly as goals Müntzer had tried to realize in the Peasants' War would never do. To do so would only make these aims appear contradictory to the desires of the peasants who had been fighting for their property rights unencumbered by the rights of the overlords, and make it impossible to fit Müntzer meaningfully into the context of the *frühbürgerliche Revolution:* he must ever appear as someone who had anticipated a future society but had not had his feet on solid bourgeois ground. Engels had not faced this problem because he had not formulated his theory of the early bourgeois nature of the Reformation period until sometime after he had written his *Bauernkrieg.* Smirin, however, came face to face with it and was therefore forced to tone down Müntzer's communistic tendencies in order to allow the latter to play an important role in the *frühbürgerliche Revolution.* Therefore Smirin argued that Müntzer had seen the Peasants' War as a period of transition to the classless society, but had not really hoped to realize such a society in his day. His program, therefore, had been reduced essentially to confiscating the nobles' lands in order to redistribute them among the poor, and to destroying the power of the princes and transferring control of the government to the common man. Despite the fact that Smirin was constrained to tone down Müntzer's communistic tendencies, he allowed the latter to remain the representative of the peasant-plebian wing of the movement as well as the exponent of a *Volksreformation* which had shown the bourgeoisie the way it could have inaugurated the bourgeois era but which had not really been bourgeois itself.[13]

Smirin's study appeared in 1947 and was translated into the German in 1952. In that same year, Alfred Meusel also brought out a book, *Thomas Müntzer und seine Zeit,* but this was little more than a repetition of the insights arrived at by earlier Marxists.[14] Although Max Steinmetz praised it for its *Parteilichkeit* for Müntzer and the peasants,[15] he still had to criticize more than he could praise.[16] In the following year, Heinz Kamnitzer, who had assembled the documents appended to Meusel's study, turned

---

analyse zeigen, ein Ergebnis jahrelanger Studien ist, die grundsätzlichen Schlussfolgerungen Engels' aufs neue bestätigt, erläutert und vertieft. Smirin beweist gleichzeitig die Überlegenheit der sowjetischen Geschichtswissenschaft, die sich die Methode des historischen Materialismus zu eigen gemacht hat, gegenüber der bürgerlichen Geschichtsschreibung." ZfG, 1 (1953), 3, 506.   [13] *Smirin*, Volksreformation, pp. 296—324.

[14] *A. Meusel*, Thomas Müntzer und seine Zeit (Berlin, 1952).

[15] Review of Meusel's book in ZfG, 1 (1953), 6, 971.   [16] Ibid.

to the same subject with equally disasterous results.[17] In one instance he even asserted that,

"Müntzers Lehre wurde im Laufe der Jahre eine lückenlose Weltanschauung, ein geschlossenes System, [like Marxism] dem sich niemand entziehen dürfte; während bei den Taboriten, beim Bundschuh und beim Pfeiffer von Niklashausen genossenschaftliche Ansichten vorkamen, entwickelte Müntzer eine solidarische Gesellschaftsordnung, ohne jedoch die Anforderungen seiner Zeit je aus den Augen zu verlieren. Er wußte in Allstedt genau, daß er in einer Zeit der revolutionären Vorbereitung und nicht in einer Zeit des revolutionären Kampfes lebte."[18]

It was noted in the chapter on Zimmermann that an integral aspect of the social revolutionary Müntzer image was the assumption that Müntzer had been the originator of the Twelve Articles, or, at the very least, had exercised a decisive influence on the initial stages of the revolution in the south. Smirin had argued for such an influence despite the fact that there was no evidence for it in the documents.[19] It was no wonder, then, that a student of his should try to prove that Müntzer, or at least a member of his entourage, had been the author of a pamphlet entitled: "An die Versammlung gemeiner Bauernschaft ..."[20] Hesselbarth found that the content of this document came closest to the teachings of Müntzer, but he had difficulty finding certain typically Müntzerian concepts in it. Hence he was forced to argue, as had Smirin before him, that Müntzer had himself begun to give up trying to implement his communistic ideas.[21] Thus, in order to make Müntzer's influence extend into the southern part of Germany and have him play an integral role in the bourgeois revolution, Hesselbarth had to play down those ideas of Müntzer which had made him most attractive to the Marxists in the first place. Hesselbarth concluded his article by arguing that even if Müntzer had not written the tract, Hans Hut, the faithful follower of Müntzer, could well have done so and spread Müntzer's teachings throughout Franconia.[22]

Although Smirin and Hesselbarth were beginning to see the implications of Engels' theory of the early bourgeois nature of the Reformation era for the role Müntzer was to play in this setting, those writing on Luther failed to see the implications for their own hero. In his *Vorge-*

---

[17] *H. Kamnitzer*, Zur Vorgeschichte des deutschen Bauernkrieges (Berlin, 1953), p. 120.
[18] Ibid., p. 123. *R. Müller* remarked in her review: "Aber die Behauptung, 'Müntzer's Lehre wurde im Laufe der Jahre eine lückenlose Weltanschauung, ein geschlossenes System, dem sich niemand entziehen dürfte,' dürfte übertrieben sein." ZfG, 2 (1954), 4, 134—135.
[19] *Smirin*, Volksreformation, p. 445.
[20] *H. Hesselbarth*, "Eine Flugschrift aus dem Grossen Deutschen Bauernkrieg," ZfG, 1 (1953), 4, 527—551.   [21] Ibid., p. 538.   [22] Ibid., p. 550.

schichte des Bauernkrieges, for example, Kamnitzer not only failed to add any new insights to the Marxist interpretation of Luther,[23] he also failed to see the basic irreconcilability of Engel's delineation of Luther with his concept of the *frühbürgerliche Revolution*. For, according to Engels' portrayal, Luther went through three phases, beginning as a man of the people, progressing to the representative of the bourgeoisie, and ending as a hireling of the princes. In the same way, Luther's teachings — the ideology of the bourgeoisie — also passed through three stages: in the first stage it was an undogmatic opposition toward feudal Catholicism; in the second, it became the ideological expression of the bourgeoisie; and, in the third, it expressed the ideas of princely absolutism. How could this be if Luther was to be the ideolog of the bourgeoisie? Kamnitzer did not answer. Nor did he even bring an elementary knowledge of basic Christian concepts to his subject. Hence, remarks like the following:

"Man glaubte an das Ende der Welt ebenso wie an die Wiederkehr Christi — oft zu gleicher Zeit und oft die gleichen Menschen."[24]

In spite of this lack of basic knowledge, Kamnitzer still asserted that Luther had given a mighty weapon to the people in his German translation of the Bible, for he rested on the authority of Engels. But if the Bible had been the weapon, what happened to the economic causes? Kamnitzer conveniently forgot about these to the extent that he made Luther responsible for the future course of German history.[25] All in all, Kamnitzer's study was obviously a somewhat hurried and not very consistent answer to the call Stern had issued for Marxist histories of Germany.

3. THE BEGINNING OF THE EAST GERMAN CONTRIBUTION

Zimmermann and Engels had come to the conclusion that Luther had begun his career as a revolutionary and ended it as a reactionary without having studied much of Luther's thought. If Luther's actions had been

---

[23] Even his Marxist reviewer remarked: "Kamnitzer hat in seiner vorliegenden Schrift darauf verzichtet, diese und andere noch grundsätzlich zu klärenden Fragen zu erörtern ... Das sich bei einer solchen Beschränkung notwendig weithin nur eine zusammenfassende Wiederholung bereits vorliegender Ergebnisse marxistischer Forschung ergeben, dass eine Antwort auf die oben umrissenen Fragen dabei nicht erstrebt werden konnte, war so nicht zu vermeiden." *Müller*, ZfG, 2 (1954), 4, 134.

[24] Vorgeschichte des Bauernkrieges, p. 89. See the further criticisms of his Marxist reviewer, ZfG, 2 (1954), 4, 134.

[25] Vorgeschichte des Bauernkrieges, p. 90. Once again Rosemarie Müller took him to task, this time for overemphasizing Luther's personal role in the outcome of the Peasants' War! ZfG, 2 (1954), 4, 134.

determined by Germany's political situation and his class position, then, from the Marxist point of view, Luther's thought should reflect or rationalize his actions. But, until 1953, no one had attempted an analysis of Luther's thought from the Marxist perspective.

Karl Kleinschmidt's book on Martin Luther[26] was a first attempt to relate Luther's ideas to the role the Marxists had assigned him in the Peasants' War. In it, Kleinschmidt portrayed Luther as a man who had worked himself into a state of acute mental anguish because of his attempt to identify with a Roman Catholic ideology which the new capitalistic mode of production had made anachronistic. Since the Catholic ideology no longer reflected the material base, a new ideology had become necessary. Luther's attempt to identify with a superseded ideology therefore led only to frustration and failure; nor did he recognize the true nature of the struggle going on in his soul.[27]

As a result of his mental anguish, Luther turned to the Bible. In it he discovered that God's righteousness condemned man only as long as he did not believe in Christ. Once there was faith in the sacrifice of Christ, God's righteousness was imputed to man whereby he was saved. Through this theory, asserted Kleinschmidt, Luther not only supplanted the Catholic concept of God with another, but also undermined an ideology that had given a religious sanction to the feudal system. Thus the transition from the feudalism of the Middle Ages to the period of royal and princely absolutism had been ideologically prepared. From this new position, Luther could then change his mental anguish into a revolutionary criticism of the Church.[28]

But others had criticized the Church before, why then should Luther's criticism have been so much more effective? Unlike previous criticisms, Luther's had struck at the very heart of the Church, touching not only isolated aspects of its teachings and practice. For this reason, Luther's criticism had also led to a real *Volksbewegung,* while that of his predecessors had led only to sectarian responses. But this central criticism had remained on paper only for the time being, according to Kleinschmidt, since Luther had not intended to make it public.[29]

Not even in his Ninety-five Thesis had Luther overtly expounded his new theory; yet, in spite of this, the reaction of the masses had been immediate, for they stopped buying indulgences and rallied to Luther's support. Thus the *Volksbewegung* was underway before Luther had ver-

---

[26] *K. Kleinschmidt,* Martin Luther (Berlin, 1953).
[27] Ibid., pp. 1—31, but especially 31—32.   [28] Ibid., p. 43.   [29] Ibid., p. 45.

balized his new theory of grace, which, according to Kleinschmidt, had been responsible for the *Volksbewegung* in the first place! Nor did Kleinschmidt come back to the problem, being happy to be well rid of it.

He had not forgotten, however, that Stern had set him the task of making a national hero of Luther. In order to do this, Kleinschmidt emphasized Luther's heroic first period; yet he had to contend with the reactionary second period as well, which, in the eyes of the Marxist historians, had always overshadowed the first. Kleinschmidt therefore tried to lessen this emphasis by concluding:

"Doch Luther ist nicht tot. Tot ist der Luther, der widerrief, nicht der Luther der 'Thesen', des 'Sendschreibens an den Adel', der 'Babylonischen Gefangenschaft', der seine lieben Deutschen einen wollte im Kampf gegen ihre Verderber. Und lebendig wie je ist der Luther, der uns das Band der Einheit schenkte, das keine Macht der Erde zu zerreißen vermag: die Einheit unserer Sprache. Aus Luthers Liebe zu seinen lieben Deutschen ist sie geboren und so groß und kräftig geworden, daß sie kein 'Widerruf', selbst der ihres Vaters nicht, mehr aufhalten konnte, ihr Wort zu Fleisch und Blut zu machen in einem einigen unabhängigen Deutschland, in dem jeder Fürst und Herr ist, der die deutsche Sprache spricht."[30]

Thus Kleinschmidt attempted to salvage some pieces of the Luther wrecked on the Marxist rock of offence, the Peasants' War.

Leo Stern, who had called the East German historians to arms, himself showed the way in the same year with a brief study on the early years of the Reformation. It was more ambitious than Kleinschmidt's, for it attempted to place into Marxist perspective the role of Humanism and the Reformation in 16th-century Germany. Stern believed that humanistic and reformed thought were both intellectual traditions which had a long history and were the ideological expressions of a revolution in the socio-economic realm.[31] In this way he tried to diminish Luther's role in the genesis of Reformation thought.[32] But Stern was also aware that the content of humanistic and reformed ideas had not been the same, despite

---

[30] Ibid., p. 50. The Marxists, however, did not have to look far for these noble characteristics of Luther; they had already been emphasized by Engels, though not to the extent they now were. Engels had stated: "Luther not only cleaned the Augean stable of the Church but also that of the German language; he created modern German prose and composed the text and melody of that triumphal hymn which became the Marseillaise of the sixteenth century." 1892 introduction to "Socialism: Utopian and Scientific," On Religion, p. 154.

[31] *L. Stern*, Martin Luther und Philipp Melanchthon (Berlin, 1953), pp. 15—16.

[32] This stands in direct contradiction to Kleinschmidt who had emphasized Luther's discovery of the new bourgeois ideology, only to forget about it later on.

the fact that he asserted both were bourgeois ideologies. He explained the differences by pointing to analagous contradictions in the economic realm inherent in a period of economic transition.[33] Although these contradictory conditions existed in the economic and intellectual realms, Luther had nevertheless been able to unite all Germany against Rome. Stern saw the reason for this in a quotation from Engels, not in any factual evidence.[34]

Stern was concerned to demonstrate further that Luther's religious discovery had been eminently political in its effects.[35] He was able to stress this aspect of Luther's thought since he had already proven that ideas were the outgrowth of socio-economic conditions. By proclaiming justification by faith alone, Luther had made superfluous all the good works and other obligations laid on the Christians by the Roman Catholic Church, and had made possible the realization of a "cheap" bourgeois church.[36]

Along with nearly everyone else, the younger Humanists had also joined Luther during the first years. Rather than espouse his cause, however, they had used Luther's religious attack to achieve their own political ends.[37] Consequently, after Luther betrayed Hutten, Humanism and the Reformation began to drift apart.[38]

4. GROWING AWARENESS OF THE PROBLEMS INHERENT IN THE CONCEPT OF THE FRÜHBÜRGERLICHE REVOLUTION

Having arrived at 1521, Stern could turn his undivided attention to the Marxists' favorite topic: Luther's reactionary stand during the Peasants' War. The old clichés, the numerous quotations from Engels, and, of course, Luther's dastardly attack on the peasants at the height of the Peasants' War were all reiterated in correct Marxist fashion.

In an earlier chapter we noted how Engels had come to revise his view of the peasant conditions pertaining in the Reformation era. He did not, however, go as far as Ernst Bloch who denied the "ultimate" motive force of economics in history completely.[39] Thus, Marxist historiography of the Reformation continued to stress the material conditions of the peasants as causes of the revolution. In his *Volksreformation*, Smirin indicated what his position on this question would be,[40] but it was only in his *Deutschland vor der Reformation* that he dealt with the problem at length.

---

[33] *Stern*, Luther und Melanchthon, p. 17.   [34] Ibid., p. 61.
[35] Ibid., p. 62.   [36] Ibid., p. 63.   [37] Ibid.   [38] Ibid., p. 73.
[39] *E. Bloch*, "Blick in den Chiliasmus des Bauernkrieges und Wiedertäufertums," Genius, Zeitschrift für werdende und alte Kunst, vol. I (München, 1920), 310—313.
[40] *Smirin*, Volksreformation, p. 19.

Meanwhile, however, his East German colleagues expressed their views. Meusel, for example, did not find it necessary to delve into the problem of causes very seriously. It was enough to state that exploited and oppressed classes were not in the habit of revolting when their condition was bad, but only then when these conditions got radically worse quickly.[41] Nor did Kamnitzer go beyond Engels in his *Vorgeschichte des Bauernkrieges*. Although he painted the oppression of the peasants in the darkest of colors, in the final analysis he argued only for a relative worsening of peasant conditions in the 15th and 16th centuries as causes of the Peasants' War.[42] Others, however, like Kleinschmidt and Stern, portrayed the peasant conditions in the worst possible light.[43]

Smirin's study on Germany before the Reformation went into greater detail than these. Characteristically, he began his chapter on the lot of the peasantry with the remark that Engels had written, concerning the development of agricultural conditions in Germany, that the period in which the peasants had occupied a relatively favorable position had not lasted very long. Already in the 14th, and especially in the 15th century, a renewed pressure had been exerted on the peasants.[44] With this introductory sentence, Smirin opened his defence of Engels' analysis in "Die Mark." Like Engels, Smirin therefore also saw the peasant in the eastern regions as freer and less burdened than his counterpart in the rest of Germany,[45] and the center of feudal reaction, after the relative leniency of the lords in the 13th century, as well as the early part of the 14th century, in southern Germany, especially in upper Swabia and the region of the Black Forest in which a system of mixed landholding was practised by the lords. These attempted to raise the peasants' rents and services and to weaken his rights of ownership in order not to be dependent upon a fixed money rent which meant static income in a period of inflation.[46] Even the attempt by the lords to consolidate their scattered territories into political entities, argued Smirin, had been ultimately motivated by their desire to tighten their grip over the economic resources of the land.

The lords achieved their goals through the reintroduction of serfdom. It was from the claim to ultimate control over their vassals that they justified their generally increased demands upon free and unfree peasants alike. This "feudal reaction," Smirin asserted, had led directly to

---

[41] *Meusel,* Müntzer und seine Zeit, p. 11.
[42] *Kamnitzer,* Vorgeschichte des Bauernkrieges, p. 24.
[43] *Kleinschmidt,* Luther, p. 63; and *Stern,* Luther und Melanchthon, p. 24.
[44] *M. M. Smirin,* Deutschland vor der Reformation (Berlin, 1955), p. 47.
[45] Ibid., p. 50.   [46] Ibid., pp. 73—74.

the ever-increasing number of peasant revolts beginning in the 14th century. But the crowning glory of this reactionary policy came only after the Peasants' War of 1525 with the introduction of the so-called "second serfdom."[47]

The problem of causation, however, was of secondary importance when compared with the problem of determining the role of the peasant in this early bourgeois revolution. Engels, as we noted, reached the conclusion that 15th-century Germany had witnessed the first stage of the bourgeois revolution only some time after he had written his *Bauernkrieg*. Consequently, the role which the peasants were to play in this perspective had not been delineated. But he did note in his study that the peasants alone had been unable to create a national uprising in Germany before 1525, for they had been opposed by the united forces of the princes, nobles, and cities. Only in conjunction with another class could the peasants have succeeded, but with whom should they have allied themselves?[48] A little farther on he pointed to the fact that, as the Reformation progressed, two major parties had emerged out of the national opposition to the Roman Catholic Church: the moderate bourgeois Lutheran party, and the revolutionary peasant and pre-proletariat party, which had been pitted against the conservative Catholic or reactionary feudal party.[49] The pre-proletariat party, however, had been merely an appendage of the peasant party except where, as in Mühlhausen, Thomas Müntzer had momentarily gained control of the revolutionary movement.[50]

In spite of the fact that Engels broke the opposition group into the bourgeois and peasant wings, he nevertheless believed the bourgeoisie to have been the natural allies[51] of the peasants in 1525, for both had been fighting against feudalism. On the other hand, however, he had to admit that their interests had in fact not been the same. The bourgeoisie had wanted reforms of a legal nature; their demands, therefore, were more moderate.[52] The peasants, however, had made more radical demands which the bourgeoisie could not share.[53] Thus, in fact, the two wings had not been allies and the revolutionary peasants had been forced instead to ally themselves with the pre-proletariat who, in some instances, had been even too radical for the peasants.[54]

The precise nature of the role the peasants were to play in the Reformation still remained unclear. Thus he could still remark, in 1873:

---

[47] Ibid., p. 101.
[48] M/E, Werke, VII, 340.
[49] Ibid., p. 347.
[50] Ibid., p. 339.
[51] Ibid., p. 413.
[52] Ibid., p. 337.
[53] Ibid., p. 413.
[54] Ibid.

"Das deutsche Bürgertum machte seine Revolution, die zeitgemäss in religiöser Form erschien, in der [Form der] Reformation. Aber wie lausig! Ohne Reichsritterschaft und Bauernschaft [war es unmöglich, sie] durchzuführen. Aber alle drei Stände [waren] verhindert [zusammenzugehen] durch widersprechende Interessen: [die] Ritter [waren] oft Räuber der Städte (siehe Mangold von Eberstein), und [die] Bedrücker der Bauern und [die] Städte [waren] ebensolche Bauernschinder (Ulmer Rat und Bauern!). [Die] Ritter zuerst erheben sich, werden von [den] Bürgern im Stich gelassen, gehn unter; [die] Bauern erheben sich, werden von [den] Bürgern *direkt bekämpft*."[55]

In the early 1880's, however, he came to the conclusion that the

"Reformation — Lutheranische und Kalvinistische — [war die] Revolution Nr. 1 der Bourgeoisie, worin Bauernkrieg die kritische Episode."[56]

And in 1892 he made explicit the meaning of the above statement in his observation that the peasants in the great Peasants' War of 1525

"wurden erdrückt, hauptsächlich infolge der Unentschlossenheit der meistbeteiligten Partei, der Städtebürger."[57]

It had therefore become obvious to Engels in the meantime that, since the Reformation had in reality been an early stage of the bourgeois revolution, the burghers of the towns should have come to the aid of the peasants, for only together could they have been strong enough to achieve their respective goals. The burghers, however, had failed to recognize with any clarity where their "true" interests lay, and, as a consequence, both parties had been doomed to defeat.

In the process of evolving his theory of the *frühbürgerliche Revolution*, therefore, Engels came into conflict with certain conclusions reached in his *Bauernkrieg*. Here he had remarked that the bourgeoisie had opposed the peasants precisely because their "real" interests had not been those of the peasants. Seen in the larger context of the Marxist theory of history, however, these interests should have been the same. Once again, therefore, the theory did not fit the facts. Rather than sacrifice the theory, however, Engels preferred to blame the bourgeoisie for its indecision and its failure to recognize its "true" interests. And in the process, the peasants were robbed of the individuality of their struggle and forced into playing an assisting role in the bourgeois drama.

[55] *Engels*, "Notizen über Deutschland," Zur deutschen Geschichte, I, 563.
[56] Given in M/E, Werke, XXI, 402.
[57] *Engels*, Introduction to the 1892 English edition of his "Socialism: Utopian and Scientific," M/E, Werke, XXII, 300.

It was only with the beginning of Marxist historiography in Rùssia, as we have seen, that the problem became acute once more. Smirin recognized the problem once again, but his attempt to solve it failed. Although he argued that, in the final analysis, the peasant wars of the 15th and 16th centuries had been directed against the feudal system and that the peasant programs had set goals broad enough to be able to include all the anti-feudal groups, he still had to confess that the Peasants' War of 1525 had been lost because of the unique character of the German bourgeoisie.[58] This bourgeoisie had contained "progressive" elements, but the Peasants' War had demonstrated its weakness as a class, and, therefore, the bourgeoisie as a whole had been in no position to lead the popular movement in a consistent and energetic war against the feudal reaction, and in the final analysis betrayed the interests of the masses.[59] Time and again, particularly in Chapter III, he was driven to concede that the cities, which had housed the bourgeoisie, had feared revolution rather than welcomed it.[60] Nevertheless, he asserted that there had been some revolutionary elements among the German bourgeoisie.[61] The contradiction was becoming all too obvious, however, for how could one have a burgeois revolution with a docile bourgeoisie? Engels' theory had apparently begun to run into factual opposition.

5. THE SLAVIC DEBATE

Shortly after Khruschev's denunciation of the Stalin era with its "personality cult" at the Twentieth Party Congress, February, 1956, the first critical voice was raised in opposition to this thesis. In an article in *Voprosi Istorii*,[62] Madame O. G. Chaikovskaia remarked that the thesis which held that the Reformation was the first stage of the bourgeois revolution not only contradicted a number of very specific, concrete Marxist historical studies, but that it also contained a number of internal contradictions.[63] She herself, however, was caught between the Scylla of Marxist theoretical orthodoxy and the Charybdis of historical evidence.

In order to avoid floundering on the rock of Marxist orthdoxy, Chaikovskaia pointed out that Engels had not distinguished clearly enough between the burghers, the class that rose to power on guild and handi-

---

[58] *Smirin*, Deutschland vor der Reformation, p. 378.

[59] Ibid., pp. 379—380.   [60] Ibid., p. 109, and also pp. 110—111.

[61] Ibid., p. 156, and again in his concluding chapter, pp. 374—380.

[62] *O. G. Chaikovskaia*, "Vopros o kharaktere Reformatsii i Krestianskoi voine v Germanii v sovietskoi istorigrafii poslednich let," Voprosi Istorii, 12 (1956), 129—143. (Hereafter this journal will be cited as VI.)   [63] Ibid., p. 129.

craft production in the cities, and the bourgeoisie, the class that controlled the capitalistic mode of production.[64] By distinguishing between
these two, she attempted to prepare her readers for the conclusion that
the Reformation and Peasants' War were not, as Engels had asserted
toward the end of his life, the "bourgeois revolution no. 1," for these
had taken place at a time when one could not yet speak of a bourgeoisie.

In order to substantiate this argument, she turned to Engels' *Bauernkrieg*. Here Engels had argued that Germany had been economically backward at the time of the Reformation when compared with countries like
France and England. If this were true, then why should the bourgeois
revolution first appear in Germany?[65] Smirin had solved the problem by
relying upon the late Engels who, thanks to Kautsky's researches, had
been able to reverse himself on this issue. But Chaikovskaia, by attacking
Smirin, also indirectly attacked Engels for his inconsistencies. Therefore
she was forced to cover her tracks by attempting to negate the substance
of Engels' last utterances on the subject.[66] Having done this, she returned
to Engels' *Bauernkrieg*, for it was here that he had spoken so clearly of
Germany's lagging behind the other European countries in industrial
production that no one could doubt his meaning, in spite of the fact that
he had also spoken of an economic upsurge due to a growing guild production. Nowhere, however, had he spoken of capitalistic production in
Germany during this period.[67]

Clearly, therefore, Engels had not thought of the events of 1525 as
constituting a bourgeois revolution. With the help of numerous citations
from his writings, she then proceeded to demonstrate what Engels had
really meant. Since he had spoken only of guild production, Engels could
not have had the kind of bourgeois revolution in mind contemporary
Russian Marxists had.[68] This factor, together with the meaning he had
given to the term burghers, made it obvious that one could only speak
of a revolt of the peasants and the pre-proletariat, together with a few
burghers, against feudalism. The Reformation era, therefore, could not
have experienced a bourgeois revolution.[69]

[64] Ibid.
[65] "In a word, the proponents of the above view will have to explain why, and upon
what foundation the first bourgeois revolution took place in one of the backward, still
strongly feudalized countries of Western Europe." Ibid., p. 131.
[66] "This statement, which, incidentally, contradicts the utterances of Marx and Engels
about the economic and political state of Germany quoted by Smirin elsewhere, proves
nothing in this context." Ibid., p. 132.
[67] Ibid., pp. 133—134.
[68] Ibid., p. 137.   [69] Ibid., pp. 142—143.

In coming to the above conclusion, Chaikovskaia made use of many local studies, mostly in the form of dissertations, which attempted to come to grips with the historical evidence. The emphasis she placed on such studies prompted her to say that the problems raised by her could only be solved by means of research dealing with concrete examples.[70] But when she tried to do just that with the concrete studies at her disposal, she was forced to interpret Engels' theory differently from the rest of her colleagues in order to make it fit the facts.

In her article, Chaikovskaia pointed to a number of discrepancies she felt existed in Smirin's studies. It was little wonder, then, that Smirin should be the first to answer the charges.[71] In characteristic Marxist fashion, Smirin began with a documentation of the thesis of the Reformation as the first act of the bourgeois revolution from the writings of Engels.[72] From this he turned to a lengthy discussion of the mining industry in Germany, since Engels had stressed its central importance in his letters of September 15, 1889, and May 21, 1895, to Kautsky. Confining his study to very limited sources, Smirin nevertheless believed he could detect capitalistic elements in the German mining industry of the 16th century.[73] The same, he argued, had been true of the textile industry. Finally, he came to the central issue: the revolutionary or non-revolutionary character of the 16th-century German bourgeoisie. From a few documents and a few isolated cases, he tried to prove that this bourgeoisie had indeed been revolutionary.[74]

Smirin concluded his article with a characteristic Marxist question: how had Engels understood the term "bourgeois revolution?" The question was rhetorical but the answer devious, for Smirin avoided a direct response by explaining what Chaikovskaia had meant by the term! If one followed the author's train of thought, he remarked, one could readily come to the conclusion that Engels had understood the term "bourgeois revolution" as a definition for the reactionary movement which had attempted to retain guild manufacturing. But this would be an utterly unreasonable conclusion.[75] After all was said and done, Smirin had said much but proven little.

---

[70] Ibid., p. 138.

[71] *M. M. Smirin*, "O kharaktere ekonomicheskogo podiema i revolutionnogo dvishenia v Germanii v epochu Reformatsii," VI, 6 (1957), 84—101.   [72] Ibid., pp. 84—86.

[73] He had three primary sources: Peter Albinus' Meissner Berg Chronica, Agricola's De Re Metallica, and the sermons of Johannes Mathesius. It was pointed out in later articles that very little could be proven from such limited sources.

[74] Here again, later Russian articles pointed out that Smirin's evidence was in no way convincing.   [75] Ibid., p. 100.

Smirin was followed by A. D. Epstein.[76] Although Epstein rejected Chaikovskaia's criticisms of Engels' interpretation and declared himself in agreement with Smirin's defence of it, he nevertheless stated that Smirin had not supported his arguments as comprehensively as he might have. Two things were necessary for an understanding of this exceedingly difficult period: first, a sound understanding of the views of the Marxist classics; secondly, lucid generalizations from the historical evidence.[77] Consequently, Epstein also began with a documentation of Engels' utterances concerning the nature of the 16th-century German conflict. Chaikovskaia, said Epstein, had rejected Engels' last statements on this problem; Smirin, however, had countered this position by emphasizing those statements of Engels which tended to deny his earlier conception. But Smirin had not explained the apparent contradictions and thus his reasoning had not been convincing.[78] Chaikovskaia had also remarked that she would admit the possibility of a bourgeois revolution in 16th-century Germany only if a rapid increase in capitalistic manufacture could be proven and the reasons for such an increase clearly delineated. This, asserted Epstein, had already been proven; one had only to read the more than hundred monographs and forty source publications of German bourgeois historians to be convinced of this.[79]

Epstein stressed the fact that Engels had seen the bourgeois revolution in three stages, the first of which had taken place in Germany during the Reformation. Obviously, Engels had been attempting to point out that there were various stages in this revolution. The differences between the three stages were, in fact, so great that, were one to compare them, there would be greater differences than similarities between them. A major difference, for example, between the German bourgeoisie of the 16th century and the bourgeoisie of 17th-century England had been that the former had not played a leading role in the German bourgeois revolution![80] As a matter of fact, according to Engels, it had even actively opposed the popular masses and taken sides with the princes.[81]

Against Smirin and in agreement with Chaikovskaia, Epstein asserted it had been perfectly clear to Marx and Engels that one could not speak of a bourgeois class in 16th-century Germany, for as early as 1847 Engels had spoken of its absence during this period. Nonetheless, he had never wavered in the belief that the Peasants' War and the Reformation had constituted the first act of the bourgeois revolution. Epstein therefore

---

[76] *A. D. Epstein,* "K voprosu o Reformatsii i Krestianskoi voine v Germanii kak piervoi bourgeoisoi revolutsii," VI, 8 (1957), 118—142.   [77] Ibid., p. 119.
[78] Ibid., p. 122.   [79] Ibid.   [80] Ibid., p. 125.   [81] Ibid., pp. 126—127.

concluded that Engels had treated the events of Reformation Germany as a bourgeois revolution without a bourgeoisie![82]

Needless to say, such a statement needed clarification, and Epstein hurried to do just that. Marx and Engels, he maintained, had never called the burgher class of the 14th to 16th centuries a bourgeoisie. The confusion between the two terms had crept in as a result of faulty translations of Marx and Engels' works from the German to the Russian.[83] By means of a number of examples, Epstein demonstrated how the Russian translators had even spoken of a revolutionary city bourgeoisie in the Middle Ages! Marx and Engels, however, had never done so, for in 1847 already Engels had spoken of a petite burgher class as opposed to a bourgeoisie in the late Middle Ages. But the Russian translators, once again, had rendered this with petite bourgeoisie. The burghers, of course, had merely been city dwellers and not a bourgeoisie in possession of a nascent capitalistic industry.

Epstein was forced to concede, however, that at various times in his life Engels had held three different views of Germany's economic position at the time of the Reformation: in 1850 he spoke of Germany's economic backwardness; in 1873 he spoke of an economy as high as any other; and towards the end of his life, he spoke of an economy higher than any other.[84] Epstein then proceeded to demonstrate that Germany's economy had indeed been higher than any other at the time, primarily because of trade and commerce, however, and not because of any beginnings of capitalistic manufacturing industries.[85] Although capitalism had begun at this time, it had been controlled by the great monopolies. It was the owners of these monopolies which had constituted the truly progressive party of the time, but their influence had been offset by the reactionary city burghers whose aim had been to imitate the nobility rather than stir

[82] Ibid., p. 127. Epstein remarked that if one were to give up the term bourgeois revolution for the Reformation, one would also have to give up all the scientific and political conclusions a concept of this nature supplied!   [83] Ibid., pp. 128—130.

[84] Epstein explains Engels' changing view as resulting from the publication of new sources of German bourgeois historians! If this were so, Engels would certainly have pointed these out to Kautsky in his letter of Sept. 15, 1889, and May 21, 1895. He did not do so, however, and it is very doubtful whether he was even aware of these; at least nothing in his letters would lead one to believe so. Quite on the contrary, Engels' study habits were always superficial, as he admitted to Laura Lafargue in a letter of 1891: "I had to read the whole literature on the subject (which entre nous, I had not done when I wrote the book — with a cheek worthy of my younger days), and to my great astonishment I find that I had guessed the contents of all these unread books pretty correctly — a good deal better luck than I had deserved." Correspondance, III, 63.

[85] *Epstein,* op. cit., pp. 139—140.

up revolution.[86] The clash between these two parties, Epstein believed, offered the solution to the problem of a bourgeois revolution without a bourgeoisie.

Epstein was somewhat unclear as to the consequences of all this, however, for he proceeded to argue that the conflict in 16th-century Germany was essentially the tail end of a two-hundred-year-old battle, whose form may have changed somewhat, but whose participants had remained the same.[87] Thus it would seem that he did not really believe the Reformation to have been the first stage of the bourgeois revolution after all, but rather the last act of a medieval struggle.

In a fourth article, J. M. Grugorian set out to prove that a new capitalistic approach to industry had indeed been present in Germany as well as responsible for the progress achieved in mining.[88] But, he added, it would be wrong to assume that the total results achieved in this area had been the result of capitalistic innovations, as Smirin seemed to indicate. This appeared to be true of other industries as well. Nevertheless, side by side with these larger, somewhat more capitalistic industries there existed many smaller ones which had not been run on a capitalistic basis.[89]

Nor was Smirin's contention, that Germany had reached Europe's economic pinnacle because of the distinct capitalistic tendencies in her industries, correct. Other European countries had most assuredly manifested these as well. The reasons for her leading position had much more to be sought in her natural products, her money, and her abundance of labor which had increased the pace of Germany's capitalistic development.[90]

Arriving finally at the crucial issue, Grugorian emphatically denied that one could speak of a bourgeois class in 16th-century Germany. Such a class had first appeared there in the 19th century; the 16th century had merely seen its beginning.[91] It was further obvious that the power behind the popular movement of 1525 had been the peasants and the pre-proletariat.[92] Nevertheless, the bourgeoisie had played the key role in the revolt since it had been its decision that had determined the outcome of the struggle. Had it sided with the peasant cause, the revolt could have

---

[86] Ibid., p. 142.   [87] Ibid.

[88] *J. M. Grugorian*, "K voprosu o wrovne ekonomiki, o kharaktere Reformatsii i Krestianskoi voine v Germanii," VI, 1 (1958), 123—139.

[89] Ibid., pp. 132—133.   [90] Ibid., pp. 133—134.   [91] Ibid., pp. 134—135.

[92] Grugorian bases this argument on Engels' criticism of Lassalle's drama, Franz von Sickingen. See *Friesen*, "Thomas Müntzer in Marxist Thought," p. 310.

succeeded. But because its interests had still been strongly intertwined with those of feudalism, it decided against the peasants.[93]

The argument over the nature of the Reformation period continued on, however, with Joseph Macek, a Czech historian, being the next to take up pen in defence of Engels.[94] Macek asserted that Chaikovskaia's thesis tended to portray the Peasants' War as merely another peasants' war in the period of nascent capitalism. This would never do, for such a thesis stood in direct contradiction to the most recent historical research, created confusion in the Marxist ranks, and, most significantly, stood in blatant contradiction to the Marxist understanding of the historical role of the bourgeois revolution.[95] Yet Macek himself gave the problem an entirely new perspective. Rather than attempt to demonstrate that the bourgeoisie had in fact participated in the struggle on the side of the peasants, or had even led the peasants in the war, Macek saw the Peasants' War as a form of bourgeois revolution quite apart from any bourgeois revolutionary movements in the cities. Chaikovskaia had tried to place the Peasants' War on a par with other peasant wars before it and thus separate it from the *parallel* bourgeois movements in the cities, as well as from the ideologies of Luther, Zwingli, and Calvin. Macek rejected this.

As the point of departure for his argumentation, Macek used Engels remark that everywhere where the personal relationship in feudal society was replaced by a money relationship, the payment in kind replaced by payment in money, there bourgeois relationships arose in place of the older feudal relationships.[96] This process took place on the land as well as in the cities, and, as a result, one could find the repeated demand in peasant articles to abolish serfdom and replace the personal-bond relationship with a money-rent relationship. The battle of the peasants, therefore, had been a battle to establish a new bourgeois economic order.[97] Thus, in all three *parallel* aspects of the early bourgeois revolution — the Peasants' War, the attempts of the bourgeoisie in the cities to gain political power, and in the ideological battle of Luther, Zwingli, and Calvin against the ideology of the feudalized Church — the same bourgeois "revolutionary process" had been at work.[98]

But Macek had not really answered the question of the relationship of the Peasants' War to the bourgeois revolution in Engels' terms, and Stam, the last of the Slavic sextet to enter the argument, recognized this

[93] *Grugorian*, op. cit., pp. 136—137.
[94] *J. Macek*, "K diskuissi o kharaktere Reformatsii i Krestianskoi voine v Germanii," VI, 3 (1958), 114—121.
[95] Ibid., p. 114.   [96] Ibid., p. 118.   [97] Ibid., p. 119.   [98] Ibid., pp. 119—121.

clearly enough.[99] It was not a question of parallel movements; it was a question of a united front of peasants and bourgeoisie.

Stam believed he could point not only to the beginnings of capitalistic development in Germany at this time, but also to the fact that this development had raised a whole host of economic and social frictions which had not been present in the other countries. He saw the reason for the bourgeois revolution, which, he admitted, had really come too soon, precisely in this friction. He agreed that the bourgeoisie had as yet not been "ripe" enough to play the leading role in the revolution; but the great anti-feudal uprising of the peasants in 1525 had given the German bourgeoisie the brilliant opportunity to unite with the peasants and to change Germany into a bourgeois nation.[100] There had been revolutionary groups within the bourgeoisie before the Peasants' War which had made common cause with the insurgent peasants, and even during the great Peasants' War of 1525 the bourgeoisie, in many of the smaller German cities, goaded into action by the pre-proletariat, had joined the peasants in their war. On the whole, however, the bourgeoisie proved incapable of fulfilling its obligation in the *frühbürgerliche Revolution*, demonstrated great vacillations in its attitude toward the peasants, and, in the final analysis, the greater part joined Luther in betraying the peasant cause.[101]

Stam specifically rejected Chaikovskaia's interpretation of 16th-century Germany as that of a Peasants' War in the period of emerging capitalism. He accused her of reviving the outdated liberal conception of the Reformation as a bourgeois-Lutheran movement which had had social and political consequences, but which had not really been a social and political movement. Were this conception correct, he continued, then Müntzer would indeed appear to be the dreamer without any "real" basis for his actions the bourgeois historians had made him out to be. Engels, however, had ranged Müntzer with the heroic fighters for the liberation of the German masses, Smirin had confirmed this view, and this was sufficient for Stam.[102] To deny the Marxist concept of the Reformation era as an early stage of the bourgeois revolution would of necessity lead back to the typical separation of Peasants' War and Reformation in bourgeois

---

[99] The discussion was discontinued by the editor of Voprosi Istorii with the promise of a final summation. This, however, never appeared. See *Max Steinmetz*, "Über den Charakter der Reformation und des Bauernkrieges in Deutschland," Wissenschaftliche Zeitschrift der Karl Marx Universität, 14 (1965), 3, 391. (Hereafter this journal will be cited as WZdKMU.)

[100] *S. M. Stam*, "Chem zhe v Deistvitelnosti bila Reformatsia v Germanii?" VI, 4 (1958), 102.   [101] Ibid., p. 103.   [102] Ibid., p. 106.

historiography; and this, in turn, would lead to the bourgeois interpretation of the Reformation as essentially an intellectual movement.[103]

6. THE EAST GERMAN DEBATE

From Russia, the discussion moved to Germany. But historians in East Germany had been somewhat slow to answer the call of Walter Ulbricht and Leo Stern for a revision of German history as issued in 1952, and, except for a few isolated studies, nothing was really done until Max Steinmetz opened the discussion with thirty-five theses on the nature of the *frühbürgerliche Revolution* in Germany. In these theses, Steinmetz restated the fundamental Marxist position once again: the *frühbürgerliche Revolution* could have achieved its aim — the formation of a unified national state — had it had a leadership conscious of and willing to fulfill its historical duty. History had ordained the bourgeoisie for a particular task at this particular moment; but the city bourgeoisie had failed to heed the call of history.[104] At the congress of East German historians gathered at Wernigerode in 1961 to discuss the nature of and problems surrounding the concept of the *frühbürgerliche Revolution*, Steinmetz pursued the issue. In his introduction to a volume of essays that resulted from the congress,[105] he posed what was now becoming the central question for the Marxist historians on the subject: why did the bourgeoisie not live up to the role it should have played in this earliest of bourgeois revolutions? The great task that had faced all "progressive" forces in 15th-century Germany had been the task of creating a united Germany and of destroying everything that stood in the way of achieving this goal. This meant that the bourgeoisie should have at least helped in destroying an anachronistic feudalism which was standing in the way of a developing capitalism. Since the Roman Catholic Church had been the exponent of the feudal ideology, its power should have been destroyed first.[106] In order to do this, the bourgeoisie should have made common cause against feudalism with all other forces of opposition, but especially with the revolutionary peasants and the pre-proletariat.[107] The destruction of the power of the Roman Catholic Church had indeed been partially achieved by Luther, the ideological representative of the bourgeois class,[108] but the "real" feudalism

---

[103] Ibid., p. 113.

[104] *M. Steinmetz*, "Die frühbürgerliche Revolution in Deutschland (1476—1535), Thesen," ZfG, 8 (1960), 1, 123.

[105] *G. Brendler*, ed., Die frühbürgerliche Revolution in Deutschland (Berlin, 1961).

[106] *Steinmetz*, "Probleme der frühbürgerlichen Revolution," ibid., p. 42.

[107] Ibid., p. 46.   [108] Ibid., p. 44.

had remained undestroyed because the bourgeoisie had failed to join the forces of opposition and lead them on to victory.[109]

Several other essays in the same volume were also dedicated to the problems raised by the concept of the early bourgeois revolution as applied to the Reformation era. In one of these, Karlheinz Blaschke attempted to demonstrate that Germany's political particularism in the 15th and 16th centuries had not led to economic particularism; rather, the economy had been very much intertwined and interdependent. In fact, the tension created by an interdependent economy and political particularism had added to the friction already existing in Germany.[110] In another, Gerhardt Heintz pointed to the disintegration of guild production brought about by a system whereby peasants were used to produce the finished product from raw materials farmed out to them.[111] In still another, Eckhard Müller-Mertens blamed the failure of the German bourgeois revolution on the absence of a king in Germany with whom the bourgeoisie could have made common cause against the powers of feudalism.[112] And in a fourth, Ingrid Mittenzwei remarked that the Soviet discussion on the topic had shown that 16th-century Germany had not had a bourgeois class. If this were true, could a bourgeois revolution have taken place? To answer this question one had first to point out that the absence of a bourgeois class did not preclude the rise of capitalism. To the extent that Germany had developed a capitalistic mode of production, to the same extent the seeds of a bourgeois class had been present. But in spite of this, one had to remember that the bourgeoisie could never achieve as profound an understanding of its historical role as the proletariat because it had not discovered the scientific laws of history![113]

In a commentary on these essays, Smirin returned to the problem. The Marxists, he remarked, would have to free themselves from several traditionally accepted theories: first, that Germany in the 16th century had been an economically backward country; and, secondly, that the whole of

---

[109] Ibid., p. 47.

[110] K. Blaschke, "Deutsche Wirtschaftseinheit oder Wirtschaftspartikularismus?" Frühbürgerliche Revolution, pp. 52—58.

[111] G. Heintz, "Zu einigen wirtschaftlichen Fragen der frühbürgerlichen Revolution in Deutschland und die Rolle des Königtums," ibid., pp. 59—63.

[112] E. Müller-Mertens, "Zu den Aufgaben der frühbürgerlichen Revolution in Deutschland und die Rolle des Königtums," ibid., pp. 81—90.

[113] I. Mittenzwei, "Bemerkungen zum Charakter von Reformation und Bauernkrieg in Deutschland," ibid., pp. 101—107.

the burgher class had been traitors.[114] He had nothing to say about the role of the peasants in the *frühbürgerliche Revolution,* however. Indeed, as the discussion continued in spite of Smirin's summation and attempt to close discussion on the problem, the role of the peasants faded more and more into the background. This role had never really been in doubt once the theory had been formulated; it had been the revolutionary bourgeoisie which the Marxists had sought in vain to lead the peasants. Thus Steinmetz, in his textbook,[115] could put the peasants in their collective places with the following few chosen words: as the "fighting arm" in the hand of the progressive bourgeoisie, he said, the peasants played an important role in all bourgeois revolutions. This was even truer in Germany where the bourgeoisie still lacked, to a great degree, any kind of revolutionary energy.[116]

The discussion of the problem involved in the Marxist concept of the *frühbürgerliche Revolution* would not be stopped, however. In 1952, Joseph Macek published a book on the Hussite Revolution[117] in which he attempted to place this revolution on a par with the German Peasants' War. In 1954, his book was translated into Russian, but in the introduction the Russian editors were careful to note that Macek's view was not the correct one;[118] the Hussite Revolution could not be considered an early form of the bourgeois revolution. In 1961, the same topic was approached from the philosophical perspective by another Czech historian, Robert Kalivoda. In his lengthy introductory background to the movement, Kalivoda traced the economic conditions of the time. More in accordance with the non-Marxist approach to the problem, Kalivoda pointed to the commercial capitalism of the 14th to the 16th centuries as the disintegrating force of the time, not to productive capitalism as the Russian and German Marxists had, for the latter had only been present in isolated instances.[119] Since Kalivoda chose to make commercial capitalism instead of productive capitalism responsible for the disintegration of feudalism, and since commercial capitalism had obviously been present in Czechoslovakia from the 14th to the 16th century, the Hussite Revolution had to be considered the first of the early bourgeois revolutions.

---

[114] *M. M. Smirin*, "Zu einigen Fragen der Geschichte der deutschen Reformation," La Renaissance et la Reformation en Pologne et en Hongrie (Budapest, 1963), eds., Gy. Szekely and E. Fugedi, pp. 211—233.   [115] *M. Steinmetz*, Deutschland von 1476 bis 1648.
[116] Ibid., p. 128.   [117] *J. Macek*, Husitské revolucni hnuti (Praha, 1952).
[118] *B. Töpfer*, "Fragen der hussitischen revolutionären Bewegung," ZfG, 11 (1963), 1, 149.   [119] Ibid., p. 146.

No notice was taken of Kalivoda's book in the discussion until Bernhard Töpfer turned to it in an article entitled, "Fragen der hussitischen revolutionären Bewegung."[120] In a critical comment on Smirin's article in *Voprosi Istorii* regarding the presence of productive capitalism in 16th-century Germany, Töpfer remarked that although it was important to analyse the economic structure of a period in order to place that period into its historical context, yet one could not make the characterization of a given epoch dependent upon the economic factor alone. Important were also the historical events themselves, the conscious or unconscious aims of the movement, and the social classes participating in the events. If one approached the problem from this perspective, then one would have to agree with the Czech historians that the Hussite Revolution was indeed on a par with the German Peasants' War. Therefore, if the latter was to be classified as a *frühbürgerliche Revolution*, then so must the Hussite Revolution.[121]

In spite of the fact that Töpfer admitted the presence in isolated instances of productive capitalism, and, consequently the beginnings of a modern bourgeoisie, he nevertheless argued that this bourgeoisie had not been strong or coherent enough to form a class that could even have played a supporting role in the peasant struggle. He was, therefore, one with Epstein who had called the Peasants' War a *frühbürgerliche Revolution* without a bourgeoisie.[122] The aim of the revolution should have been to form a unified state, as an increasing number of German Marxist historians had been pointing out, and this in itself justified one in speaking of a *frühbürgerliche Revolution*. Therefore, the aim of the Peasants' War had not been the destruction of feudalism as such, much rather it had been the creation within feudalism of a more propitious foundation upon which productive capitalism could arise.[123]

Töpfer's article brought the topic of the nature of the Reformation period up for discussion once more. A year later he was answered by Gerhard Zschäbitz who admitted that the commercial capitalists of the 16th century had only invested their money in productive capitalistic ventures with reluctance and had turned into a true bourgeoisie very slowly. Many ties had still bound them too closely to feudalism.[124] Nevertheless, the lower classes, which had always been the carriers of revolution, had fought against various aspects of feudalism: first had been the struggle against

---

[120] See above, note 118. [121] Ibid., pp. 149—150. [122] Ibid., p. 150. [123] Ibid., p. 151.
[124] G. Zschäbitz, "Über den Charakter und die historischen Aufgaben von Reformation und Bauernkrieg," ZfG, 12 (1964), 2, 177—188.

the reactionary Roman Catholic Church; second had been the city bourgeoisie's battle against feudal bondage; and last had been Müntzer's attempt to destroy the princes.[125] Therefore, in spite of the fact that he
conceded the docile nature of the bourgeoisie, Zschäbitz argued that the
total movement, in its "objective" duty and "subjective" aims, had been
directed toward the destruction of the hindrances feudalism was placing
in the path of the development of early capitalism. Furthermore, the
movement had grown out of a social structure which had contained the
seeds of the later capitalistic society in it and had passed through phases
similar to other bourgeois revolutions. And lastly, continued Zschäbitz,
the Peasants' War had been an early form of the bourgeois revolution because in those regions where the peasants and plebians had gained temporary control of government they had initiated measures which would have
resulted in a more rapid development of capitalism had these measures
not been repealed after the defeat of the peasants.[126] This, together with
the fact that capitalistic production had been present in 16th-century
Germany and absent in Bohemia at the time of the Hussite Revolution,
placed the Peasants' War in the category of the *frühbürgerliche Revolution*
and the Hussite Revolt outside it.[127]

In 1965 Steinmetz came back to the problem as well.[128] Once again he
made the point, in opposition to Töpfer, that the decisive element in the
discussion of the problem was the degree of development capitalistic production had reached in the two countries. Progress in the discussion would
not be achieved by pitting example against example; the problem had
to be seen in its European context and in the context of the transition
from the medieval to the modern era. In medieval times, continued Steinmetz, one could speak only of nascent capitalistic production; with the
15th century, however, one was forced to speak of the presence of capitalistic production on a broad scale and as a European phenomenon. The
appearance of capitalism and of a bourgeoisie was the new, the important,
and in the final analysis, the decisive element at work.

---

[125] Ibid., p. 185.   [126] Ibid., p. 187.   [127] Ibid.
[128] *M. Steinmetz*, "Über den Charakter der Reformation und des Bauernkrieges in
Deutschland," WZdKMU, 14 (1965), 3, 389—396.

CHAPTER IX

RENEWED REVISIONISM

1. THE IMPLICATIONS FOR THE MARXIST INTERPRETATION
OF ANABAPTISM

The implications of the debate delineated in the preceding chapter did not immediately become apparent for all aspects of the Marxist historiography of the Reformation. Nevertheless, the theoretical clarity concerning the nature of the early 16th-century bourgeois revolution which resulted from the prolonged debate over that revolution was the most influential factor in determining the current state of Marxist scholarship in the field. In the area of Anabaptist studies, for example, it was relatively late before this aspect of the Reformation was integrated into the broader Marxist 16th-century frame of reference. Here the tendency to see the Anabaptists as Müntzer's revolutionary agents continued to dominate the scene, although more and more Marxist historians began to differentiate between the Saxon group and that of Zurich as Kautsky had first done.

We need not here go into the details of the Marxist interpretation of Anabaptism;[1] suffice it to say that although Ernst Bloch, Smirin and other Marxist historians did follow Kautsky's lead in differentiating between the two groups, they have nevertheless argued for a decisive influence of Müntzer over all Anabaptists. At the same time, like Kautsky, they have also argued that the Anabaptists were drawn from the proletarian or lower classes during the early years of the Reformation.

Gerhard Zschäbitz disagreed with Kautsky that only the proletariat joined the Anabaptist ranks; its social base was much broader he believed.[2] Anabaptism to him was the

"Sammelbecken der vielgestaltigen revolutionären Impulse der Volksmassen. Obrigkeitsfeindschaft, Vergeltungsgedanken, entsagender Verzicht, Verachtung der

---

[1] See A. Friesen, "The Marxist Interpretation of Anabaptism."
[2] G. Zschäbitz, Zur Mitteldeutschen Wiedertäuferbewegung nach dem grossen Bauernkrieg (Berlin, 1958), p. 160.

Welt und der weltlichen 'Gottesdiener', Verzweiflung, die nach größerer Gottes-nähe drängte, asketischer Stolz — alles dies rankte sich an den Täuferlehren empor."[3]

Those who espoused the teachings of Anabaptism came from the social elements which were experiencing an economic recession due to the price revolution.[4]

Although Zschäbitz knew better, he portrayed the pacifism of the Ana-baptists as the result of the defeat of the Peasants' War[5] and the Münt-zer debacle.[6] He made these social upheavals responsible for the Anabap-tists' pacifism and he also saw lurking behind every Anabaptist theological tenet the hatred of the exploited masses against the government. The separation of Church and State, for example, and the Anabaptist rejection of the temporal governing authorities, according to Zschäbitz, were ex-pressions of hatred toward the governing Church and State authorities.[7] Similarly, adult baptism,[8] the Anabaptist spiritual interpretation of the Eucharist,[9] the implementation of church discipline,[10] and the community of goods[11] were all "objective" manifestations of the suppressed hatred of the lower classes against the existing power structure of Church and State.

Zschäbitz did not concern himself in the least with the genesis of Ana-baptist thought in Zurich as it developed in the *Auseinandersetzung* be-tween the radicals and Zwingli. Even with regard to the Anabaptism of central Germany, he began his sociological analysis with the following remark:

"Die soziale Herkunft der vor Gericht gestellten Täufer läßt sich am besten er-mitteln, wenn wir uns an die Berufsangaben halten. Dabei lassen sich Fehlschlüsse ausschalten, die sich bei einseitiger Betrachtung der Sprecher der Täuferbewegung aufdrängen könnten."[12]

---

[3] Ibid., p. 168. In his "Die Stellung der Täuferbewegung im Spannungsbogen der deut-schen frühbürgerlichen Revolution," Frühbürgerliche Revolution, p. 155, he specified the following as social groups: "Der sozialen Herkunft nach treten uns städtische Plebejer und Vertreter des Vorproletariats, Gesellen, kleine Handwerker bestimmter Berufsgrup-pen, Bauern, aber auch hin und wieder Vertreter aus den Bildungsschichten entgegen, die um eine neue, organisierende Ideologie rangen." He cited P. Peachey, Die soziale Her-kunft der Schweizer Täufer in der Reformationszeit (Karlsruhe, 1954), as his source.

[4] Zschäbitz, Wiedertäuferbewegung, p. 158. Zschäbitz does not prove this, he merely assumes it. In a footnote just prior to this statement he quoted from Peachey, Die soziale Herkunft, p. 86: "Obschon diese Linien später abbrachen und die Täufer sich nur in den entlegenen und ärmeren Orten halten konnten, zeigt es sich doch klar, dass das Täufer-tum sich zunächst in den wirtschaftlich bestgestellten Gebieten der Schweiz verbreitete."

[5] Ibid., p. 158.   [6] Ibid., p. 166.   [7] Ibid., pp. 83—87.   [8] Ibid., pp. 90—94.
[9] Ibid., p. 97.   [10] Ibid., p. 99.   [11] Ibid., p. 106.   [12] Ibid., p. 155.

Zschäbitz apparently did not think it would lead to false conclusions were he to leave the leading Anabaptists completely out of the picture, for he proceeded to do precisely this. Nor did he even enquire into the relative wealth of those he did cite.

To substantiate the conclusions he reached for central Germany, Zschäbitz turned to the sociological study of Swiss Anabaptism by Paul Peachey.[13] However, as Claus-Peter Clasen has correctly pointed out, Peachey, without making this very clear, most assuredly spoke of well-to-do artisans, masters, and peasants, whereas Zschäbitz automatically assumed that Peachey had referred to the poorest elements of these classes.[14] It is no wonder, therefore, that Zschäbitz could assume that Peachey's study in reality supported the Marxist thesis.

In a subsequent article, written in 1960, Zschäbitz proceeded to place the Anabaptist movement into its Marxist frame of reference: the *frühbürgerliche Revolution*.[15] Having demonstrated that Anabaptism had been a movement of those social classes which had manifested an underlying political hatred of the governing authorities because they were destined to economic ruin by the effects of the price revolution, Zschäbitz could argue that Anabaptism was a continuation, in a somewhat changed form, of the revolutionary tendencies of Müntzer's *Volksreformation*.[16] After the Peasants' War the revolutionary tendencies in the masses had gone underground or had hidden themselves behind religious facades only to erupt again in isolated instances such as the revolt of the Münster Anabaptists. It was because Mennonite historians had argued against any influence of Anabaptism's revolutionary wing on the origins of peaceful Anabaptism in Zurich that Zschäbitz felt compelled to turn against Harold S. Bender time and again; for if there was no connection between the two movements, Anabaptism could hardly be portrayed as the expression of a mass movement after the defeat of the peasants.

But this was precisely what Zschäbitz intended to do.[17] He therefore argued that the teachings of Anabaptism had contained the "objective" protests of all those who had been disappointed in the practical results of the bourgeois Lutheran Reformation and the failure of the Peasants' War. Anabaptism, of course, had not been the only response of the masses to these phenomena. Many returned to the bosom of the Catholic

---

[13] See above, note 3.

[14] *C. P. Clasen*, Die Wiedertäufer im Herzogtum Württemberg und in benachbarten Herrschaften (Stuttgart, 1965), p. 118, note 1.

[15] *Zschäbitz*, "Die Stellung der Täuferbewegung im Spannungsbogen der deutschen frühbürgerlichen Revolution," Frühbürgerliche Revolution, pp. 152—162.   [16] *Ibid.*, p. 153.

[17] Ibid., p. 155.

Church, others submitted unwillingly to the *status quo,* but not a few strove to develop new forms of social life and thought and therefore offered a fruitful terrain for teachings which opposed those of the established churches. The emerging Anabaptist movement had supplied precisely such poles around which the elements of discontent could crystallize. These appeared first in the cities and then on the land. In effect, therefore, Anabaptism gave a reorientation to the forces opposed to feudalism, and to a certain degree formed the avant guard of this opposition.[18]

Since Anabaptism was to constitute the tail end of the great *Volksbewegung* of the Reformation era, it was important to stress that the movement had been fluid in its initial stages and had encompassed a large following from the lower classes before it became sectarian in character.[19] With the defeat of the Münster Anabaptists, however, the movement lost the last of its revolutionary tendencies for the following reasons: in the first place because of the increased severity of persecution by the governmental authorities, and secondly because of an inner structural change which resulted in the expulsion of the radicals The cause as well as the effect was that the ideological leadership of the movement was transferred into the hands of the petite bourgeoisie and the preproletariat excluded. Under Menno Simons the movement then became a sectarian one.[20]

2. TOWARD A CONSISTENT VIEW OF MÜNTZER

Although a veritable spate of articles and books appeared from Marxist pens dedicated in whole or in part to Thomas Müntzer in the latter half of the 1950's, it was the study by Zschäbitz on the *Wiedertäuferbewegung nach dem grossen Bauernkrieg* which revised most clearly Engels' portrait of Thomas Müntzer. A few studies preceded that of Zschäbitz, however. In 1956, a German translation of Müntzer's "Prague Manifesto", which had originally been translated into the Czech language, was published by Eberhard Wolfgram.[21] In the introduction, he attempted to place the blame for Müntzer's failure to rouse the citizens of Prague on this poor translation.[22] The following year, Hermann Goebke, on the basis of some new evidence relating to a Thomas Müntzer, asserted that the latter had really been born in 1467 or 1468 and had gained his religious and social views

---

[18] Ibid.   [19] Ibid., p. 160.   [20] Ibid., p. 162.
[21] *E. Wolfgram,* "Der Prager Anschlag des Thomas Müntzer in der Handschrift der Leipziger Universitätsbibliothek," WZdKMU, 6 (1956/57), 1, 295—308.   [22] Ibid., p. 298.

from the Augustinian monastery in Quedlinburg where he had been a monk before matriculating as the University of Leipzig in 1506.[23] But although his article was printed in the collected essays on the *frühbürgerliche Revolution*,[24] Steinmetz, one of the editors, criticized it rather severely in a concluding summation.[25]

In the same year, a Czech study attempted to revaluate the Hussite impact upon Müntzer resulting from the latter's visit to Prague.[26] In order to demonstrate the significance of this impact, and thus bring Müntzer into the orbit of the revolutionary Hussite influence, Husa stressed Müntzer's adherence to Lutheran ideas prior to the visit.[27] Nor did he believe that Müntzer had imbibed his revolutionary chiliastic teachings from the Zwickau Prophets; these teachings, in fact, could be found in Saxony only after Markus Stübner, one of the Prophets, had himself returned from Prague.[28] Therefore, Müntzer's development into the *Volksreformator* and his subsequent break with Luther was the direct result of his Prague visit. And his "Prague Manifesto" marked the beginning of this transition.[29] But the really important reinterpretation came from the pen of Gerhard Zschäbitz.

In an earlier part of this study it was noted that Engels had come to modify his position vis-a-vis Müntzer and the Peasants' War toward the end of his life. Three letters in particular bear testimony to this modification, or, as Engels might have preferred, this clarification.[30] Especially

[23] H. Goebke, "Neue Forschungen über Thomas Müntzer bis zum Jahre 1520," Harz-Zeitschrift, 9 (1957), 3—6.

[24] H. Goebke, "Thomas Müntzer — familiengeschichtlich und zeitgeschichtlich gesehen," Frühbürgerliche Revolution, pp. 91—100.

[25] Ibid., pp. 301—302. The following non-Marxists also took issue with Goebke: A. Zumkeller, "Thomas Müntzer — Augustiner?" Augustiniana, IX (1959), 380—385; G. Franz, "Zeitschriftenschau," ARG, 50 (1959), 258; and, lastly, E. Iserloh, "Zur Gestalt und Biographie Thomas Münzers," Trierer Theologische Zeitschrift, 4 (1962), 248—253.   [26] V. Husa, Thomas Müntzer á Cechy (Praha, 1957).

[27] Ibid., p. 29. In contrast to Smirin, Volksreformation, pp. 88 and 110, who argued for an early break with Luther to demonstrate Müntzer's independent development. See also H. Kirchner, Johannes Sylvius Egranus (Berlin, 1961), who stated: "Smirins massgebliche These ist, das zwischen Luther und Müntzer, und zwar von Anfang an, ein prinzipieller Gegensatz bestand, eindeutig feststellbar seit 1520, dem Auftreten Müntzers in Zwickau," p. 48.

[28] Husa, Thomas Müntzer, p. 35. Husa was also of the opinion that the rejection of infant baptism had been imported from Bohemia.

[29] Ibid., p. 90. Husa was criticized by both J. Macek and B. Töpfer in their reviews for having overemphasized the influence on Müntzer of his Prague visit. See especially Töpfer's review in ZfG, 8 (1960), 7, 1689.

[30] Engels to Bloch, Sept. 21, 1890. Selected Correspondence, p. 475; Engels to Mehring, July 14, 1894, ibid., p. 510; and Engels to Kautsky, May 21, 1895. E/K, Briefwechsel, p. 423.

in his letter to Joseph Bloch, dated September 21, 1890, Engels made some revealing statements. Here he remarked that neither he nor Marx had ever said that the economic element was the only determining one, but only that it was the most important element. Thus he could go on to say:

"Die ökonomische Lage ist die Basis, aber die verschiedenen Momente des Über-baus — politische Formen des Klassenkampfes und seine Resultate — Verfassun-gen, nach gewonnener Schlacht durch die siegende Klasse festgestellt usw. — Rechtsformen, und nun gar die Reflexe aller dieser wirklichen Kämpfe im Ge-hirn der Beteiligten, politische, juristische, philosophische Theorien, religiöse An-schauungen und deren Weiterentwicklung zu Dogmensystemen, üben auch ihre Einwirkung auf den Verlauf der geschichtlichen Kämpfe aus und bestimmen in vielen Fällen vorwiegend deren *Form*."

In the same letter he stated further that he and Marx were, however, responsible in part for the fact that younger writers placed more stress on the economic side that was due it, for he and Marx had been defending the materialistic interpretation of history, and in so doing had overstated their case. Those "Marxist" followers, however, who had later written on the same subject, had become far too narrow-minded and exclusive in their materialistic approach. Therefore Engels concluded the letter with the following words:

"Und diesen Vorwurf kann ich manchem der neueren 'Marxisten' nicht ersparen, und es ist da dann auch wunderbares Zeug geleistet worden."

It was this reflective position of Engels which Gerhard Zschäbitz took as the point of departure for his study of Müntzer and Anabaptism in central Germany. This made historical interpretation more difficult for Zschäbitz[31] since a monistic approach from the materialistic point of view was no longer tenable; he had to take into consideration above all, once again, religion.[32] But although he argued that the importance of religion as an historical phenomenon could hardly be overestimated during this period, he denied that this religious activity had arisen out of an innate human need, for religion had been imposed upon the masses from above by the ruling classes and their minion educators who punished every infraction or deviation from the accepted norm with great severity.[33] Zschäbitz, therefore, still denied man's need for religious expression; religion, however, was no longer a facade behind which one must dis-cover the essential Müntzer, but was recognized as an historical force,

---

[31] *Zschäbitz*, Wiedertäuferbewegung, p. 119.   [32] Ibid.   [33] Ibid., pp. 19—20.

a part of that ideological superstructure which rested on the economic base, but which in turn modified the influence of that base. Once, of course, it was granted that the economic factor was only one of many factors active in the historical process, albeit the most important of these, there was created an opportunity for a divergence of opinion in the Marxist interpretation of history. And Zschäbitz did take issue, however gently, with former Marxist interpretations of this period, not only with those of revisionists like Kautsky, but with the orthodox themselves: Engels and Smirin.[34]

It was Zschäbitz' considered opinion that the crux of the Müntzer problem lay precisely in how to differentiate between the religious and the social-revolutionary elements in Müntzer's thought, for these two strands seemed inextricably intertwined. To try to eliminate the religious element completely, or to view it as a mere facade for his revolutionary plans, as Engels and Smirin had done, and give Müntzer the appearance of a modern Marxist revolutionary, was highly dubious.[35] Müntzer had been a theologian, and, even measured by the standards of his own day, a deeply religious man.[36] At the same time, however, there had been certain progressive aspects to Müntzer's total concept which had been expressed in regard to his social-revolutionary activity. Yet his main idea, that of the union of the elect and their separation from the godless, had had its origin in the chiliastic expectations of the Middle Ages. And it was precisely this chiliastic expectation which held together the two disparate elements in Müntzer's thought — the mystical-religious and the social-revolutionary.[37]

---

[34] See especially ibid., pp. 38—39, and 44—46.   [35] Ibid., pp. 36—37.

[36] This tendency to play down the "modern" aspect of Müntzer's thought was noted and commended by his Marxist reviewer: "Beachtung verdienen hierbei die Ausführungen über Thomas Müntzer, weil Z. den ernsthaften Versuch macht, ein Bild des Sozialrevolutionärs Müntzer zu geben, ohne diese Persönlichkeit in unhistorischer Weise zu modernisieren und die religiösen Grundaspekte seiner Anschauungen zu schmälern. Wenn man sich auch gewünscht hätte, dass Z. hierbei seine vom bürgerlichen Müntzerbild abweichende Auffassung ebenso präzise formuliert hätte wie seine kritischen Bemerkungen zu dem Buch von Smirin (S. 36 f., 44), so wird man diese doch grösstenteils akzeptieren können. Sicher hat Z. auch recht, wenn er Müntzers nach seiner Gefangennahme geschriebene Abmahnung an die Mühlhäuser vom 17. Mai 1525 für echt hält, in der Müntzer die Ursache der Niederlage der Bauern vor allem darin sucht, dass diese zu sehr ihren eigenen Nutzen gesucht hatten. Gerade in diesem Briefe, dessen Verständnis von einem modernisierenden Standpunkt aus kaum möglich ist, deutet sich eine Stimmung an, die im Gefolge der Niederlage der Bauern eine weite Verbreitung findet und die gekennzeichnet ist durch ein Zurücksinken der revolutionären Impulse sowie durch eine Abschwächung der sozialen Komponente im Vergleich zu den religiösen Bewusstseinsinhalten." Bernhard Töpfer, ZfG, 9 (1961), 2, 281—282.

[37] Zschäbitz, Wiedertäuferbewegung, p. 39.

Müntzer's chief objective had been to establish the Kingdom of God on earth; this had entailed a complete social revolution, for the elect were to inherit the earth and destroy the godless opposed to the Kingdom. Although his conception of the new order had not been clear in all its details, it had nevertheless been clear enough to give expression to the somewhat nebulous aspirations of the lower classes of both town and country who had been involved in a class struggle with the feudal nobility. The two groups had nearly been at cross purposes, however, for while Müntzer had aspired to an egalitarian social order for the sake of the Gospel, the mass of his followers had aspired to such an order for material reasons. By quoting from Müntzer's letter to the Mühlhausen council, Zschäbitz showed that Müntzer had blamed the failure of the whole enterprise on precisely these selfish aspirations of his followers. Because of this, God had not been able to prosper their cause and had been forced to punish them through the ruling class.[38]

Despite the fact that Müntzer had been motivated by religion and had not anticipated the Marxist revolutionary theories of the 19th and 20th centuries, Zschäbitz nevertheless asserted that he had still been a great revolutionary. His religious ideas, applied to the social realm, had worked as a catalyst to bring about armed insurrection against oppression, for they had objectified the desires of the downtrodden masses. Nor had his recantation, or his letter to the Mühlhausen city council, both of which Zschäbitz accepted as reliable historical evidence, detracted from his stature as a revolutionary. In fact, in neither of these documents had Müntzer made any retractions, for he had only confessed that his followers had sought selfish ends against which he had warned them time and again. God had to punish such conduct, and Müntzer had no quarrel with God's judgment. Therefore, rather than demonstrating cowardice, these documents really manifested the greatness of a much maligned man.

Bernhard Töpfer, Zschäbitz' Marxist reviewer, however, had the uneasy feeling that Zschäbitz had perhaps not been as specific in his formulation of the Marxist Müntzer-image as he had been in his criticism of Smirin's tendency to modernize Müntzer. The question, what really remained of the Marxist Müntzer if one placed him back into his own century of religious turmoil and social unrest and admitted his primarily religious orientation, seemed to worry Töpfer.[39] It seemed also to worry Steinmetz, for in his Thesis he returned to Engels' assumption that Müntzer had anticipated the future course of historical events, stating that he

[38] Ibid., p. 47.   [39] See note 60, above.

had created an ideology which had anticipated that of Marxism. His ideology, he argued, was not bourgeois but manifested itself as a *Vorform* of the proletarian class ideology. Müntzer went beyond the confines of his own time and pointed the way to a solution as yet unrealizable but which should prove to be the only correct solution for the future.[40]

Steinmetz, therefore, still held to the belief that Müntzer's ideology had anticipated that of the Marxists; but he also added a new dimension to Müntzer's stature, for he portrayed him as the German national hero who had fought for the unity of the torn German fatherland.[41] In order to portray him as such, Steinmetz had once again to stress the fact that Müntzer's teachings had influenced the entire revolutionary movement.[42] Here he encountered some difficulty, however, for in a previous thesis he had accepted Macek's argument for Zwingli's and Gaismaier's influence in the southern theater of the Peasants' War. The ideology of these two, Macek had argued, had been truly progressive and bourgeois, whereas Müntzer's had attracted only the poor peasants and the city paupers. Indeed, Macek continued, in contrast to Luther, Zwingli had created the truly authentic bourgeois ideology of the Reformation, for he had made it into a really revolutionary force which had gripped the peasants of southern Germany as well as a large part of Switzerland. Nor had Zwingli, like Luther, gone over to the side of feudalism, for he had died doing battle for his cause.[43] To counter this, Steinmetz now tried to place Gaismaier and Müntzer on the same plane, stating that the radical wing had stood under the overwhelming influence of Müntzer and Gaismaier, whereby the activity of the latter had extended over the Alpine region, while that of Müntzer had reached into the West, Southwest, and Central Germany.[44] Yet he was forced to concede that Gaismaier had perhaps been more bourgeois than Müntzer.[45]

Steinmetz, however, failed to explain how Müntzer could remain a person motivated by religion and at the same time anticipate the Marxist

---

[40] *Steinmetz*, "Thesen," ZfG, 8 (1960), 1, 123. But Steinmetz had to modify this statement in the following way: "Bei diesem Programm aber handelt es sich zweifellos um eine keimhaft-unreife, für ihre Zeit letztlich utopische, im ganzen aber doch geniale Antizipation der wahrhaft nationalen Politik der deutschen Arbeiterklasse," p. 124.

[41] Ibid., p. 123.   [42] Ibid.

[43] *J. Macek*, "K diskuissi o kharaktere Reformatsii i Krestianskoi voine v Germanii," VI, 3 (1958), 120. See also his "Das revolutionäre Programm des deutschen Bauernkrieges von 1526," Historica II (Prague, 1960), pp. 111—144.

[44] *Steinmetz*, "Thesen," ZfG, 8 (1960), 1, 123.

[45] Ibid.

theory of the coming victory of the proletariat.[46] The answer to this problem was given in 1962 by Ernst Werner[47] who asserted that Müntzer had been the *prophet* of a new class. By stressing this prophetic aspect, Werner was able to keep Müntzer within the context of the religious 16th century, but at the same time make him into the warrior of the downtrodden masses he believed ordained of God to inherit the kingdom.[48] Müntzer, therefore, had anticipated an idea for which neither the masses nor the historical dialectic had been ready, even if the idea itself had still been clothed in religious terminology.[49]

In attempting to realize this classless Christian society on earth, Müntzer also became the *prophet* of revolution. The more the princes opposed him in Thuringia, the more fanatical his denunciations of the ruling classes became. Aware that the power at his disposal could not have sufficed to bring about a radical reorganization of social conditions on earth, Müntzer had been forced to rely upon a power above the human. This, Werner believed, was amply demonstrated by the fact that Müntzer, like Gideon in his day, had departed for Frankenhausen with three hundred men to do battle against the enemies of God.[50]

Werner believed Müntzer had raised himself above other representatives of the Messianic movements precisely because he had recognized that the salvation of mankind would come from a social force, from the poor people, whose prophet and leader he wanted to be.[51] According to Müntzer, therefore, the Kingdom of God was to come into being through the revolutionary initiative of the poor and exist for the poor. His tragedy, however, lay in the fact that he had overrated the power and self-consciousness of that social strata which seemed to him predestined to save mankind.[52]

To a certain extent, Müntzer had anticipated the future course of social development. It was for this reason that his teachings had had to remain confined within the boundaries of religious categories. The catastrophy of Frankenhausen had not, however, discredited the idea of the saving function of the lower classes; it had only demonstrated the fallibi-

---

[46] That Steinmetz was reluctant to admit Müntzer's religious motivation is indicated in his complaint that "die 'Ketzer' wie Müntzer nicht nur in dem bekannten Buch von Nigg, sondern auch bei Hassinger und anderen gleichsam heimgeholt (werden) in die Kirche, um sie den Marxisten zu entreissen." "Probleme der frühbürgerlichen Revolution," Frühbürgerliche Revolution, p. 36.

[47] E. *Werner*, "Messianische Bewegungen im Mittelalter," ZfG, 10 (1962), 2, 370—396, and 10 (1962), 2, 598—622.

[48] Ibid., p. 613.   [49] Ibid., p. 614.   [50] Ibid.   [51] Ibid., p. 615.   [52] Ibid., p. 616.

lity of the religious principle of salvation.[53] This religious principle had
proven to be the Achilles heel in Müntzer's ideological armor. His religious motivation, which could no longer be denied after Zschäbitz' investigation, had demonstrated its inability to initiate social change.[54]

3. TOWARD A CONSISTENT VIEW OF LUTHER

Because Zimmermann had tampered less with the "orthodox" view of
Luther than he had with Müntzer, revision in the Marxist interpretation
of Luther was even slower in coming. Thus, as late as 1964, well after
the debate on the nature of the early bourgeois revolution had run its
course, Rosemarie Müller-Streisand,[55] the Marxist reviewer of Kamnitzer's *Vorgeschichte des Bauernkrieges*,[56] still attempted to portray Luther
by means of the categories Engels had set for Kautsky — to portray the
difference between the Luther before Carlstadt, the Anabaptists, and the
Peasants' War with the Luther after. Her avowed purpose was twofold:
she intended to view Luther's intellectual development from the materialistic point of view[57] and attempt a periodization of Luther's thought.[58]
In order to do this she did not find it necessary to read all of Luther's
writings during the time in question, for she made use only of his Table
Talk and polemical works.[59]

The pattern into which Müller-Streisand's periodization was to fit had
already been established by Zimmermann and Engels. It consisted of two
poles: the early revolutionary, and the more mature reactionary Luther.
That her results should fit into the scheme is therefore not too surprising.[60] She began by trying to determine what was *das Reformatorische*
in Luther's theology, but stated that the change in Luther's thought could

---

[53] Ibid.

[54] It is, however, not too clear exactly why the "religious principle" is made responsible for Müntzer's failure to establish his religious classless society when the historical
dialectic would not have allowed it in any case.

[55] *R. Müller-Streisand*, Luthers Weg von der Reformation zur Restauration (Halle/S.,
1964).

[56] In her criticism of Kamnitzer's book, she complained that no one had as yet attempted a study of Reformation theology from the Marxist point of view. This, she
asserted, was a very necessary undertaking. ZfG, 2 (1954), 4, 134.

[57] *Müller-Streisand*, Luthers Weg, pp. 5—6.   [58] Ibid., p. 71.   [59] Ibid.

[60] "... und es erwies sich, dass die ursprüngliche Arbeitshypothese, dass sich Luthers
Theologie am klarsten von seiner kirchlichen Existenz her periodisieren lassen müsste,
tatächlich nicht nur für die Periodisierung als solche ein günstiger Ausgangspunkt war."
Ibid. However, in order to show this contrast she had had to, "was beiden Perioden
gemeinsam ist, im Interesse einer möglichst klaren und scharfen Fragestellung zurück-
zustellen." Ibid.

best be seen in his *Kirchenkritik*.[61] Proceeding from two different testi-
monies of Luther, an early and a late one,[62] she asked the question whether
or not the mature Luther had given up basic aspects of his Reformation
thought.[63] She came to the conclusion that Luther had indeed retreated
from his early position and manifested a marked tendency to return to
a more Catholic theological position.[64]

Müller-Streisand found the reasons for this change in Luther formulated in the latter's discussion with Agricola of 1538. Quoting Luther, she
remarked:

"Dabei ist Luther bereit, Agricola zuzugeben, daß er sich zu Recht auf Äußerungen aus Luthers Frühzeit berufe. Ungemein aufschlußreich ist nun die Begründung, mit der Luther von seinen früheren Äußerungen abrückt: er erklärt, die
Situation habe sich grundlegend geändert. Früher habe man die unter dem Papst-
tum erschrockenen, ängstlichen und angefochtenen Gewissen trösten müssen, da sei
nicht die Verkündigung des Gesetzes, sondern die des Evangeliums notwendig
gewesen, um sie schnellstmöglich aus der Hölle zu führen. Jetzt aber seien die
Menschen sicher und böse, sie seien Epikuräer und fürchteten weder Gott noch
Menschen. Die Antinomer übersähen, wie völlig verderbt die Gegenwart sei und
machten die ohnehin Sicheren noch sicherer."[65]

Having established the fact that Luther had retreated from his early
position, Müller-Streisand then proceeded to seek the background and the
causes for this retreat.[66] Here she was forced to return to the old thesis
of Engels, so dear to all Marxists, that the economic conditions created
by a nascent capitalism had already begun to crack the ideological unity
wrought by the Catholic Church.[67] These new economic conditions,
which, in the final analysis, had created the social tensions and the resulting social upheaval, had also determined Luther's retreat to a more conservative theology: Luther's conservative reaction to the radical social
demands of his time was therefore reflected in his return to a more Catholic theology.[68] Thus Müller-Streisand had not only proven Engels'
contention that Luther had shifted his position from that of a radical
to that of a conservative, but she had also demonstrated how Luther's
reaction to the social upheaval of his own day had determined his theo-

---

[61] Ibid.   [62] Ibid., p. 20.   [63] Ibid., p. 14.   [64] Ibid., p. 78.   [65] Ibid., pp. 78—79.

[66] It is significant that Müller-Streisand, like all other Marxists dealing with the
intellectual history of a period, can find no real integral connection between Luther's
thought and the material conditions. She can only bring up the old theories and old
clichés without tracing any specific connections.

[67] For an interesting commentary on the relationship between Catholic and Marxist
interpretations of the Reformation as seen by Müller-Streisand, see Appendix D.

[68] *Müller-Streisand*, Luthers Weg, p. 98.

logical development. And, of course, the economic conflicts with their respective class conflicts had brought about the social upheaval.

In his volume in the series *Lehrbücher der deutschen Geschichte*,[69] Steinmetz summarized the results of Marxist Reformation research. With regard to Luther and his religious crisis, he accepted Kleinschmidt's[70] argument that the nascent capitalistic mode of production had made the feudal Catholic ideology anachronistic. Therefore Luther's attempt to identify with it led necessarily to his mental anguish.[71] Out of this mental agonizing had come Luther's discovery that God justified men by imputing His righteousness to them and not by demanding righteous acts from them. This new approach to salvation had consequently made superfluous the saints and a priestly hierarchy which could deny the parishioner salvation by withholding the sacraments from him. Thus, continued Steinmetz, Luther's intellectual achievement appeared as the objective expression of the economic and political struggle of the bourgeoisie and the masses against the Roman Catholic Church. This new theology made the old church superfluous and aimed at a "cheap" bourgeois church.[72]

Despite these progressive tendencies in Luther's thought, however, the latter had not been able to free himself from the otherworldliness of the Christian Middle Ages. Precisely these "medieval" tendencies in his theology were strengthened under the influence of the activity of the revolutionary peasants.[73] But even the progressive tendencies in Luther's thought had not been responsible for his importance to the early phase of the Reformation or for the progressive role he played during this period, for his teachings contained important aspects which attacked precisely the progressive process of secularization. His progressive role had, in fact, really been forced upon him by the dialectic of the class struggle which had pushed him relentlessly forward from position to position until the break with Rome, which he had not wanted, had become inevitable.[74] But when Steinmetz came to portray the course of events which led to this break, he was constrained to come back to the Leipzig disputation and other intellectual milestones in Luther's career which had convinced the latter of the inevitability of the break with Rome.[75]

According to Steinmetz and the other Marxists, Luther had sought to destroy ecclesiastical feudalism. However, the increasing friction between the various classes of the time made it inevitable that the revolt against

---

[69] *Steinmetz*, Deutschland von 1476 bis 1648.
[70] Ibid., pp. 80—88.   [71] Ibid., p. 88.   [72] Ibid., p. 90.
[73] The similarity to Müller-Streisand's thesis of the re-catholicization of Luther's thought is obvious.   [74] Ibid., p. 92.   [75] Ibid., pp. 98—102.

the papacy should lead directly to an attack on secular feudalism, for only the total destruction of feudalism in Germany could have insured the destruction of the Roman influence. Thus, after 1521, Luther himself was forced to decide whether or not he was prepared to draw the "objective" conclusions of his call to destroy ecclesiastical feudalism and support the social revolution initiated from below. Luther's negative response was not merely the result of his intellectual development, stated Steinmetz, for it had been determined much more by those social forces which he began increasingly to represent. His decision, therefore, had not so much determined events as events had determined his decision.[76]

Luther's attitude toward the radical movement became apparent only too quickly upon his return from the Wartburg. Once in Wittenberg, he turned decisively against the disturbers of the peace and stated that reform should be effected only by the princes and the governments of the cities, not by anarchic popular movements.[77] The Wittenberg incident was quickly followed by Luther's pamphlet, "Eine treue Vermahnung," in which he turned against a social reformation and demanded that the ruling powers alone carry out the ecclesiastical reforms. Steinmetz, however, had to admit that these ideas were not new to Luther since they had already been expressed in his pamphlet on the "Freiheit eines Christenmenschen." Now, however, they were used to dampen the initiative of the masses. Thus Luther turned his Reformation over to the princes and the weaker bourgeoisie under the control of the princes. Henceforth, therefore, the Reformation represented only that part of the city bourgeoisie which had become dependent upon the princes and which had failed to play its historical leading role in the *frühbürgerliche Revolution*.[78]

Luther, therefore, had not played such a vacillating role in the history of the Reformation after all, and Bensing could state that,

"Nun ist es nicht zu bestreiten, daß sich Luthers Entscheidung gegen die aufständischen Bauern mit innerer Notwendigkeit aus seiner theologischen Grundkonzeption, insbesondere aus seiner Auffassung von Obrigkeit und Gehorsamspflicht der Untertanen ergab."[79]

Nevertheless, a poorly advised, inhumane and reactionary position should not be sanctioned because it derived from the "inner necessity" of a theological system. Certainly it would be wrong to attempt to im-

---

[76] Ibid., p. 106.   [77] Ibid., pp. 108—109.

[78] Ibid., p. 109. Steinmetz is obviously trying to make Luther appear to be more consistent as a representative of the bourgeoisie than was previously the case.

[79] *Bensing*, Müntzer, p. 198. See also p. 200.

pute superficial political motives to Luther; he was defending his Reformation, and in so doing admonished pope, princes, and Fuggers as well as peasants. He had even been willing to distort the truth in order to do this.[80]

Luther had realized, continued Bensing, that his teachings stood or fell with the established order of his day.[81] Thus his pamphlets against the peasants had not so much been attempts to spur the princes on to suppress the revolt — for this purpose they arrived too late — as they were attempts to justify the bloodbath of Frankenhausen and the bloody suppression of the peasant movement in Thuringia as such.[82]

4. THE INTEGRATION OF THE MARXIST INTERPRETATION OF THE REFORMATION

As the Marxists have arrived at greater clarity with regard to the precise nature of the *frühbürgerliche Revolution,* their delineation of the roles played in this drama by the peasants, Müntzer, Luther and the princes has been modified accordingly. This is particularly true with regard to Thomas Müntzer and first becomes clearly apparent in Steinmetz's *Deutschland von 1476 bis 1648.* Here Steinmetz asserted that Müntzer's most important achievement had been his new conception of history and the role which the masses were to play in realizing history's goal. According to his theory, the time had arrived for the overthrow of the established order on earth by the revolutionary masses. It was their active role in history which was to bring about the classless society characterized by the absence of a coercive government.[83]

At first Müntzer had believed this goal could be achieved by peaceful means; revolution would only be necessary in the event that the princes should decline to aid in spreading his teachings. Steinmetz tried to explain away the fact that Müntzer had attempted to woo the princes into supporting his cause by stating that this attempt had not been a concession to princely rule, for it had arisen out of the insight that the people had not been mature enough for the battle and therefore in danger of doing battle for egotistical reasons. It was true, Steinmetz continued, that Müntzer had been too optimistic about being able to conclude an "honest agreement" with the princes, but political reality had corrected him.[84] Once Müntzer had recognized the immaturity of the masses, he attempt-

---

[80] Ibid., p. 198.   [81] Ibid., p. 200.   [82] Ibid., p. 197.
[83] *Steinmetz,* Deutschland von 1476 bis 1648, p. 120.   [84] Ibid., p. 121.

ed to educate them to see beyond their selfish desires to the needs of Germany as a whole.[85]

Müntzer had been portrayed as a proto-communist by Engels, as the great *Volksreformator* who had allowed his communistic tendencies to fade momentarily into the background by Smirin, but Steinmetz changed the emphasis still more. The Slavic and German discussions concerning the nature of the *frühbürgerliche Revolution* in 16th-century Germany had made in only too painfully obvious that one had to stretch the imagination somewhat to be able to speak of a bourgeois revolution without a bourgeoisie, to use Epstein's terminology. Smirin's attempt to make Müntzer into a *Volksreformator* had not gone far enough because the full extent of the problem only became apparent during the course of the discussion. Without a bourgeois element in his following, Müntzer still had not entered the central historical stream of his time: he still remained outside the realm of the bourgeois revolution even if he had been a great *Volksreformator*. Somehow, therefore, Müntzer had to be portrayed as having won some kind of bourgeois following.

Like Smirin, Steinmetz too asserted that Müntzer had realized that the Reformation era had in reality been only a period of transition to the classless society, not the period of its inauguration. This realization had come to him through his observation of the political events of his day. As a result, Müntzer had allowed his social ideal of a classless society to retreat momentarily into the background so that he might unite the *various oppositional elements*,[86] not *merely* the peasant-plebian wing as Smirin had claimed, in order to achieve at least that for which history had been ripe: the abolition of princely rule and the destruction of feudalism. Consequently, he had also modified his political program in order to give expression to the radical bourgeois-democratic demands of his time. Primitive communistic demands had been totally lacking in these programs.[87]

Another reason for toning down the communistic tendencies in Müntzer's thought was to make it easier for Steinmetz to extend the former's influence into the regions of the Peasants' War outside of Thuringia, for, as Smirin had already realized, the communistic ideas espoused by Müntzer had not found much of an echo amongst the peasants. If this was so, and Müntzer made to espouse radical communistic aims, then the latter's influence in other parts of Germany could obviously not have been very great. But Steinmetz once again chose to propound the Zimmermann-

---

[85] Ibid.   [86] Ibid., p. 122.   [87] Ibid., pp. 123, and also 142.

Engels thesis of Müntzer's influence in all parts of the Peasants' War because he wanted to make Müntzer into the German national hero who had tried to unify a badly splintered fatherland. Consequently, Mühlhausen once again became the center of revolutionary activity in Germany from which Müntzer had tried to stir the whole country to revolt.[88]

Since the revolt had begun in southern Germany near the Swiss border, Steinmetz was concerned to demonstrate that Müntzer had decisively influenced the early stages of the revolution in this region. The latter's brief visit here in the fall of 1524 was therefore portrayed as the decisive event in the initiation of revolution.[89] Müntzer was further pictured as having won many disciples on this visit; even Balthasar Hubmaier and Hans Müller von Bulgenbach, the leader of the Stühlingen peasants, had been persuaded by Müntzer's revolutionary logic.[90] Besides these adherents in the southern theater of the revolt, Müntzer had also won a disciple in Jakob Wehe, the leader of the Leipheimer peasants, and numerous others in the Thuringian theater. But beyond that, Müntzer had maintained contact with the insurgents in Fulda, and, since these had had contacts with Hesse, Würzburg, Bildhausen, and even distant Deiningen, it was apparent that Müntzer's supporters had aimed at a working agreement with the insurgents in the various regions of Germany from the very beginning.[91]

Steinmetz divided the entire peasant movement into two main wings once more: a radical wing and a more moderate one inclined toward compromise with the existing power structure. The radical wing, with the *Artikelbrief* as its declaration of aims, was also brought within the orbit of Müntzer's influence by Steinmetz through his assertion that this same *Artikelbrief* owed its radical nature to the inspiration of Müntzer.[92] Thus, by stating that Müntzer's utopian ideals had faded into the background more and more as the conflict drew nearer and had been replaced by radical bourgeois-democratic demands, and by asserting that the declaration of aims of the radical wing of the movement had been inspired by Müntzer, Steinmetz could move Müntzer's influence into every region where more radical demands had been made by the peasants than were contained in the Twelve Articles.

Even in Thuringia, where Müntzer and his followers had formed the core of the revolutionary conspiracy, the aims had remained those of the *Artikelbrief*. Not only, however, were Müntzer's communistic tendencies

---

[88] Ibid., p. 127.   [89] Ibid., pp. 124 and 130.   [90] Ibid., p. 130.
[91] Ibid., p. 140.   [92] Ibid., p. 134.

toned down to make it possible for Steinmetz to extend Müntzer's influence, his revolutionery élan was also deemphasized and Müntzer made to advocate change by peaceful means. But this was merely another attempt to extend Müntzer's influence into the less radical wing of the peasant movement.[93]

Müntzer's role in the Thuringian theater of the Peasants' War was the central theme of the latest study on Müntzer.[94] Bensing, whose book was preceded by a number of more particular studies on various aspects of Müntzer's life,[95] once more repeated the Marxist commonplaces concerning Engels' interpretation of Müntzer.[96]

In dependence upon Ernst Werner,[97] Bensing saw Müntzer's teachings and activity from two aspects: from the religious frame of reference, but also from the latter's social-revolutionary activity. Thus, Müntzer was portrayed as the messianic prophet of a future class as well as the executor of God's will on earth. Basing his philosophy of history on the Book of Daniel, Müntzer had developed a theory of the imminent transformation of the world. At the same time, Bensing continued, Müntzer had seen

"In der 'jetzigen Christenheit', im auserwählten Volk Gottes, in den 'armen leien vnd bawrn',"[98]

the means by which God would change the existing social order. But Müntzer had been forced to educate the masses for their historical role since these had neither been ready for such a role nor had they even realized what role they were to play. Thus Müntzer spent the summer of 1524 trying to do this.[99]

Müntzer had at first hoped that the new social order would be inaugurated peacefully, and to this end he had wooed the princes into his

[93] "Hervorstechend ist das Bemühen, ein recht umfassendes, bis in die Reihen der städtischen Ehrbarkeit und des Adels reichende Bündnis zu schaffen. Bei freiwilliger Unterwerfung unter den Willen des Volkes billigte Müntzer weitgehende soziale Zugeständnisse. Diese Taktik zeigt, dass er als vordringliche Aufgabe die politische Entmachtung der Fürsten und Herren betrachtete, um — wie er glaubte — den Weg für die weiter friedliche Umgestaltung des gesellschaftlichen Lebens freizulegen. *Dieser Grundsatz macht die grosse Resonanz des Müntzerschen Programms bei den verschiedenen sozialen Schichten verständlich und verlieh dem Wirken Müntzers und seiner Anhänger radikal-demokratische Züge.* Utopisch-kommunistische Forderungen treten während des Aufstandes völlig zurück. Wo sie sich in den Verhören der Müntzeranhänger finden, spiegeln sie allein den ernsthaften Vorsatz wider, nach dem Sieg über die weltliche und geistige Obrigkeit zum antizipierten vollendeten Gesellschaftszustand weiterzuschreiten." Ibid., p. 142.

[94] *Bensing*, Müntzer. The book grew out of Bensing's 1962 dissertation, which, together with Bensing's other articles, was used by Steinmetz and explains the latter's interpretation to a large degree. See Bensing's own statement on p. 1.

[95] For a list of these, see ibid., pp. 271—272.

[96] Ibid., p. 44.   [97] Ibid., p. 45.   [98] Ibid., p. 47.   [99] Ibid., p. 53.

Bund. This had not been a concession to princely absolutism, however, Bensing hastened to add, nor had Müntzer merely wanted to become another Daniel who advised princes. He had only been prepared to tolerate a friendly working partnership between the princes and the people and to allow the princes their privileges until the people had been sufficiently educated for their role and could be entrusted with self-government. At that point the princes would be gently stripped of their power.[100]

The increasing hostility between the various classes forced Müntzer to change his views about the princes and the role they were to play in his future society, however. Because they misused the sword, Müntzer concluded that it was God's will that this sword should be taken from them and given to the lower classes. Concomitant with this changed view of the function of the princes came a change in Müntzer's plans. Previously he had tried to educate the masses for their new role; now, however, he decided that society had first to be changed before the new church could be established which would manifest in its members the human characteristics Müntzer was seeking.[101]

Müntzer was convinced, however, that the coming struggle could only be a prelude to the establishment of the classless society he had vaguely envisioned. Therefore he modified his socio-political objectives, giving them the forms of a radical democratic program which corresponded with the historically possible at the time. Then, in order to realize such a program, Müntzer broadened the social base of his support to include peasants, plebians, and the progressive bourgeoisie.[102]

His calculations proved correct, for precisely this modification of his socio-political aims to meet the needs of the time explained his popular appeal and leadership particularly in the Thuringian revolt. Here, in Mühlhausen, Müntzer tried to achieve his goals by organizing his supporters in the various surrounding districts. These organizations[103] had been made up of members from various social groups, each of whose interests and aims had coincided only partially with those of Müntzer. It was precisely because Müntzer's ideology had not given expression to the desires of any one class that had enabled it to spread so quickly.[104]

Although Bensing tried to portray Müntzer as a man who had read the "signs of the time" aright, and although he paid lip service to the criticism that Engels had unduly modernized Müntzer,[105] he himself

---

[100] Ibid., p. 54.   [101] Ibid., p. 57.   [102] Ibid., p. 61.   [103] Ibid., p. 132.
[104] Ibid., pp. 132—133.   [105] Ibid., p. 132.

proceeded to do the very same. Zschäbitz had asserted that Müntzer had indeed been a religious man and a child of his time, but he had been followed by Ernst Werner who had again pointed the way in which Müntzer could be brought back into the Marxist fold. Therefore, Bensing could once more state that Müntzer's teachings had in fact contained historically new aspects: they had pointed prophetically to nearly all the major issues that were to become acute in the succeeding centuries.[106] But in the 16th century this had been possible only through the association with the ideas of messianic prophecy, Old Testament prophecy, or the chiliastic spiritualism of early Christianity.

Precisely because Müntzer's program had gone beyond the demands of the pre- or early proletarian groups, who, incidentally, had not shared this prophetic outlook into the future and had fought for very real present temporal interests,[107] it had been the only program which could have, and in reality attempted to centralize and coordinate the revolt in Germany.[108] This program contained three main aspects: (1) a kind of maximum program which consisted of the much-debated *omnia sunt communia*, but which played an insignificant role in the actual struggle; (2) a kind of minimum program for the present period of transition which aimed at giving political power to the common people, but which was also open to a compromise agreement with those princes who would join the Bund; and lastly (3) a tactical aspect which envisioned the establishment of the new order without recourse to the sword.[109]

But Bensing faced a problem with regard to Müntzer's involvement in the Thuringian phase of the Peasants' War: if Müntzer's social and political program had indeed been in accord with what was historically possible at the time, how did one explain his defeat? Bensing tried to solve his dilemma by arguing that a strong moderate wing had existed within the Thuringian revolutionary movement. However, as long as the radical wing had made steady progress, the moderate wing had not really been able to assert its power. But as soon as the radical wing suffered the slightest setback, the moderate wing immediately asserted itself.[110] Thus a conflict had arisen in the revolutionary camp which had destroyed its unity.[111] This same conflict was mirrored on a smaller scale in the conflict between Pfeiffer and Müntzer.[112]

---

[106] *Bensing*, Müntzer, p. 133.   [107] Ibid., p. 232.   [108] Ibid., p. 135.

[109] Ibid., pp. 138—139. Bensing turned against the opinion of his Marxist colleagues who had made Müntzer's communistic ideas responsible for the alienation of the bourgeoisie from the revolutionary movement. Ibid., p. 140.

[110] Ibid., p. 164. [111] Ibid. See *Bensing's* summation on p. 173. [112] Ibid., pp. 183—188.

Yet this was not the real cause of failure as far as Bensing was concerned. He tried to soften the impact of this question by arguing further
that one could not judge Müntzer merely by what he had achieved, one
had rather to judge him by what he had aimed at.[113] This argument was
necessary because, although Bensing asserted that Müntzer had adjusted
his teachings to coincide with the historically possible, the historically
possible had not taken place because of the *Lokalborniertheit* of those
involved in the revolt.[114] Müntzer had won a large following, but in the
decisive moments this following had left him in the lurch.[115] He had been
a great man who had expounded an ideology which had mirrored the
social conditions that had fitted into the historical dialectic, but despite
all this he had failed. What, then, was the overriding cause?

Luther had seen Frankenhausen as God's judgment on Müntzer, but
even Müntzer himself had looked upon this defeat as a judgment of God.
Consequently, he had turned his back on revolution in his letter to the
citizens of Mühlhausen. In the same letter, Müntzer had blamed the participants in the struggle for having sought their own interests, thus, in
essence, placing the blame upon those "poor people" whom, according to
Bensing, he had formerly seen as the saviors of mankind. Obviously
Müntzer had become disillusioned in the principle of salvation through
these same "poor people." Yet Bensing chose to reason that the decision
at Frankenhausen had not signified a defeat of the idea of the "saving
function of the masses, of the poor people",[116] rather it had demonstrated
the fallibility of the religious principle of salvation.[117] Müntzer had
expected too much from the common man with his ethical-religious
imperative. In the period of declining feudalism "egoism," not "sacrifice,"
had been the necessary means by which one had to assert oneself. But, of
course, Müntzer had not been able to recognize that this egoism had not
been a consequence of mankind's subjective corruption, for it had arisen
out of the as yet "unripe" social conditions.[118] Thus Müntzer had not

---

[113] Ibid., p. 135.   [114] Ibid., p. 194.   [115] Ibid., p. 136.
[116] Ibid., p. 233.   [117] Ibid., p. 234.

[118] The crucial aspect of the interpretation comes to the fore here: Müntzer had not
been able to recognize what really motivated man's actions. Hence, he had placed the
blame in the wrong place. But Bensing should have reasoned a little farther. If the only
means by which the "historically possible" could have been achieved at the time had
been through egoism, for, according to Bensing this had been the "form" demanded by
the contemporary social conditions, then Müntzer's teachings had not really given expression to these social conditions nor coincided with the "historically possible." What
is more, it would indicate that Müntzer was not really concerned with the class war,
but rather used it to fight his "holy War."

really read his times aright, for he had read it through religious eyes, yet precisely religion had been proven wanting at Frankenhausen. Religion, therefore, became the tragic flaw in Müntzer's ideological coat of armor.

Although Steinmetz and Bensing both initiated a departure from the frame of reference Engels had   set Kautsky for his interpretation of Luther, the most apparent departure from this frame of reference came in the 1967 study of Luther by Gerhard Zschäbitz.[119] No longer is Luther portrayed as the perambulating theologian, moving from one ideological position to another until he ends up in the camp of the princes; rather he is seen as the consistent exponent of the ideology of the moderate 16th-century German bourgeoisie.[120] Naturally, Luther viewed himself as a theologian and his struggle with Rome as a spiritual struggle; nevertheless, argues Zschäbitz, Luther remained the "unconscious" representative of the moderate bourgeoisie.[121] Since Luther's theory and actions are seen as consistent with the wishes of the moderate bourgeoisie, the falling away of the peasants and radicals like Müntzer and Carlstadt must be explained differently than before, as must also Luther's support of the princes. Like Engels and other Marxists, Zschäbitz also begins by remarking that Luther's earliest writings had manifested opposition merely against the papacy.[122] It was for this reason that all the elements of 16th-century German society had been able to unite behind him.[123] Nevertheless, the destruction of the papal power only was the exclusive desire of the moderate bourgeoisie, for the radical elements aimed at social as well as religious innovations.[124] When this became apparent to Luther, he began to warn against such secular revolutionary tendencies. This did not mean, however, that Luther had changed his position; it simply meant that the two parties were beginning to see each other more clearly.[125] Therefore Zschäbitz could argue, toward the end of his study, that Luther had not been a *Bauernverräter*.[126]

The attack from the left, which gained immeasurably in momentum from 1521 to 1524, forced the moderate bourgeoisie, which would not accede to the left's desire to abolish the secular feudal power as well, to seek an accomodation with the feudal princes. It did this because the differences between these two groups were not yet as great as their mutual interest in law and order, and because the bourgeoisie had still not developed enough for it to be fully aware of the innate antagonism that

---

[119] *G. Zschäbitz*, Martin Luther, Grösse und Grenze (Berlin, 1967).
[120] Ibid., p. 63 and numerous other instances.   [121] Ibid., p. 67, and p. 69.
[122] Ibid., p. 72.   [123] Ibid., p. 130.   [124] Ibid., pp. 108—109.
[125] Ibid., pp. 151—153.   [126] Ibid., p. 208.

existed between itself and the feudal princes.[127] Thus Luther's support
of the princes could be explained in terms of the position of strength the
social class he represented had reached by the 1520's. Consequently, he
could no longer be accused of having become a princely hireling.

Thus have all the elements been fitted into the early bourgeois frame
of reference Engels gave to the Reformation era, in spite of the fact that
the dilemma of the "bourgeois revolution without a bourgeoisie," which
Engels bequeathed to his followers, has not really been resolved. In the
process, the peasants have been robbed of their essential role in the
Peasants' War and made to play a supporting role in a bourgeois revolution that did not take place, for it lacked a revolutionary bourgeoisie.
Luther, from the vacillating ideolog of many colors, has been transformed
into the consistent exponent of the ideology of the moderate bourgeoisie,
while Müntzer's communistic tendencies have been toned down and his
religious sincerity restored to allow him to assume the guise of a radical
bourgeois character and play an integral part in the 16th-century stuggle.
And, finally, the Anabaptists, drawn from the revolutionary masses that
supported Müntzer, appear after the revolution as the disillusioned who
exchanged their revolutionary ardor for a sullen pacifism and little by
little excluded all revolutionary elements from their ranks after the last
revolutionary outburst — the Münsterite debacle of 1534/35 — joining
the ranks of the petite bourgeoisie.

[127] Ibid., p. 152.

CHAPTER X

REVOLUTION AND REFORMATION

1. CRITIQUE

The Marxists have attempted to reduce the Peasants' War and the Reformation to a common denominator: the *frühbürgerliche Revolution*. In the process of reduction, however, they have added contradiction to contradiction essentially because of their attempt to analyze the 16th-century by means of a wrong set of categories.[1] They have proceeded from a principle, whereas they should have proceeded from the historical facts: the principle being that modes of production are mutually antago-nistic. To this, the Marxists have superimposed the class conflicts between the owners of the means of production and those exploited by them. The seeming truths these categories revealed when applied to capitalistic society have enticed the Marxists to apply them to other historical con-texts as well. Applied to medieval society, the theory of the class struggle may still seem to have some relevancy, but when the Marxists assert that the capitalistic mode of production was inherently antagonistic to the feudal mode of production, whatever they may mean by the latter, they miss the central issue entirely. Feudalism was based on an agrarian society; industry, of course, is not. Therefore the two could and, in fact, did exist side by side. According to the Marxists, however, these two modes of production should have entered a life-and-death struggle during the period of transition from feudalism to capitalism.

The fallacy of this abstract assumption is proven by the facts of history. Certainly there were frictions between the emerging cities and the nobles or bishops who claimed rights of rule and taxation over the towns. This was not caused by an antagonistic mode of production, however, but

[1] *J. Delumeau*, Naissance et Affirmation de La Réforme (Paris, 1965), p. 267, has also stated: "Ainsi, la conception marxiste de la Réforme a péché par anachronisme, en trans-posant dans le XVIe siècle des realités et des conflits du XIXe. Les rapports entre la foi et la mentalité des foules lui on échappé. Ne voir dans les débats religieux que des epiphénomènes, des 'fioritures,' comme l'a écrit Corr. Bargaballo, c'est se refuser à comprendre pourquoi 15 000 Calvinistes acceptèrent de mourir de faim à La Rochelle durant le siège de 1628."

rather by the desire of the princes to gain political control over a financially lucrative venture and to consolidate their power over a given territorial region. Not only did the nobles attempt to gain political control over the new centers of trade and commerce, many of the landed nobility moved to the cities, donned the robes of a merchant, married a bourgeois girl, and commenced to live the life of the bourgeoisie. Nor did the latter find itself in exclusive antagonism to the nobility either, despite the fact that it frequently tried to free itself from the political control of nobles and bishops alike. Much more, it aspired to noble status and landed property in order to invest the money it had gained in commercial ventures.[2]

Unlike the Marxists, non-Marxists do not speak of a capitalistic mode of production in this period. The attempts, especially of Smirin and Grugorian, to discover the beginnings of a capitalistic mode of production in 16th-century Germany have their value, but they do not explain the nature of the capitalism of the period. Insofar as one can speak of capitalism at all, one must speak of a commercial capitalism.[3] This means, of course, that the theory of antagonistic modes of production becomes applicable only with the beginning of the Industrial Revolution. At any rate, the bourgeoisie which constituted the historical force of the 16th-century was one involved in trade and commerce, not manufacture.

If, then, the conflict between the nobles and the rising bourgeoisie was not severe, as even some Marxists have conceded, and if, further, there was no real conflict between modes of production in the period of transition from feudalism to commercial capitalism, what was the relationship between the bourgeoisie of the time and the Peasants' War? The answer to this crucial question, of course, will determine whether or not Reformation and Peasants' War constituted an early phase of the bourgeois revolution. There were certain instances in which cities did come into contact with the revolutionary peasants, but these are few in number. In Heilbronn, Schweinfurt, Regensburg, Nordhausen, Rothenburg o. d. T., and Mühlhausen under Müntzer,[4] as well as in the larger cities of Prussia,[5]

---

[2] These facts have been pointed out often enough. Even A. D. Epstein drew attention to *A. von Martin's* 1933 Soziologie der Renaissance, pp. 29—30, where the latter had called attention to the nobles that merged into the bourgeoisie. See also: *H. Kellenbenz*, "Die Unternehmerische Betätigung der verschiedenen Stände während des Übergangs zur Neuzeit," Vierteljahrschrift für Sozial- und Wirtschaftsgeschichte, 44 (1957), 6 (hereafter this journal will be cited as VfSW); and *P. Schmidt*, Luther und der Klassenkampf (St. Gallen, 1933), p. 30.

[3] See *F. Mauro*, "Pour une théorie du capitalisme commercial," VfWS, 42 (1955), 117.

[4] *B. Moeller*, Reichsstadt und Reformation (Gütersloh, 1962), p. 21.

[5] *F. L. Carsten*, "Der Bauernkrieg in Ostpreussen 1525," International Review for Social History, III (1938), 406.

such contacts between the insurgent peasants and the cities were established. But only in Mühlhausen did it come to a closer working together of the two. On the whole, the evangelical preachers of the cities turned against the revolt of the peasants, and even where the party of reform was in opposition to the city council, as in Schwäbisch-Gmünd, for example, it consciously dissociated itself from the Peasants' War.[6] Nor were the relationships that did exist brought about because of a similarity of aims, rather the example of the peasants seems to have encouraged the city bourgeoisie to rise in its own cause.[7] At the most, therefore, one can speak in terms of parallel uprisings, as Macek did, and not of any integral relationship between the two movements. The peasant aims remained peasant aims, and the Peasants' War remained a peasants' war.

Because the Marxists postulate an integral relationship between peasant and bourgeois movements, and because they consider the Reformation merely the ideological expression of the bourgeoisie, they were able to assert that the back of the Reformation was broken with the defeat of the peasants. Franz Lau has given the lie to this theory by demonstrating that the Lutheran Reformation continued to capture city after city in northern Germany for some time after the defeat of the peasants.[8] Bernd Moeller has observed that this does not only hold true for northern Germany, but also, and especially, for the free cities of southern Germany.[9] Nor were the transitions from Catholicism to Protestantism in these cities the product of the town councils, but much rather of the citizens themselves, very often in opposition to the town councils.[10] Consequently, not only did the Reformation as a popular movement not cease with the defeat of the peasants, but the outcome of the Peasants' War seems to have had little influence one way or the other on the progress of the Reformation in the cities; only where the princes used the pretext of bourgeois complicity in the Peasants' War to attack the cities, or, on the other hand, where, as in the case of Mühlhausen, the city had become directly involved in the struggle, did the Peasants' War affect the Reformation movement in the cities.[11] These facts would certainly seem to negate the Marxist theory of

[6] *Moeller*, Reichsstadt und Reformation, p. 21.

[7] *Carl Hinrichs,* "Deutschland zwischen Kaisertum und Libertät," Die deutsche Einheit als Problem der europäischen Geschichte, ed. Carl Hinrichs und Wilhelm Berges (Stuttgart, 1960), p. 98. See also *Franz*, Bauernkrieg, p. 296.

[8] *F. Lau,* "Der Bauernkrieg und das angebliche Ende der lutherischen Reformation als spontaner Volksbewegung," Lutherjahrbuch, XXVI (1959), 109—134.

[9] *Moeller*, Reichsstadt und Reformation, pp. 22—23.   [10] Ibid., p. 24.

[11] Ibid., pp. 21—22. Moeller points to the interesting fact that Mühlhausen and Nordhausen, both centers of the Müntzer revolt, returned to Catholicism after the defeat

the common aims as well as the theory of the integral relationship between the two movements.

The Marxist theory of the *frühbürgerliche Revolution* seems, therefore, to have little, if any, relevancy to the historical facts and is more a figment of their imagination than that it rests on any factual evidence. What has happened is that the Marxists have been caught in a web of their own spinning and are now attempting to reconcile the historical evidence with their finely spun theory. We have seen the consequences of this particularly with regard to their portrayal of Thomas Müntzer. From the proto-communist of Engels' writings, the Marxists have gradually transformed Müntzer into the radical bourgeois reformer in order to fit him the more easily into their ever-maturing theory of the *frühbürgerliche Revolution*. At the same time, they still claim to be true to the views of Engels. In fact, however, they are caught between the early and the late Engels and are attempting to reconcile the two without admitting that the Müntzer Engels conceived was not the Müntzer pregnant with bourgeois ideas. Precisely what role the objective facts of history have played in the process, the Marxists conveniently omit to tell us.

The theory that the Reformation was a bourgeois movement is older than the Marxists, however. The latter have taken over the theory from the 19th-century liberals and forced it into their dogmatic mold. The theory obviously developed in the late 18th and early 19th century out of an attempt by the liberals to remake Luther in their own image as the great liberating force at the crossroads of the Middle Ages and Modernity. For Zimmermann and his sympathy for Müntzer and the peasants' cause, however, Luther had stopped half-way while others pursued his revolutionary thought to its logical conclusion. This view was the result of a political orientation and a perspective deriving from Joachim of Fiore which wanted to apply Christian teachings to the temporal realm in order to bring about the Kingdom of God on earth.

This one-sided approach is apparent in the Marxist historiography of the Reformation as well, perhaps even more so since it is dogmatically grounded. Hence, Max Steinmetz can accuse the West German church historians of falsifying Reformation history into a "strictly theological phenomenon."[12] Bernd Moeller has remarked that there is a great deal of

---

of the peasants by the request of the populace. Note 16, p. 21. This would tend to confirm further our contention of the innate similarities between the paradigms of Müntzer and Catholicism.

[12] *Steinmetz*, "Probleme der frühbürgerlichen Revolution," Frühbürgerliche Revolution, p. 32.

truth in this accusation;[13] nevertheless, the accusation, as it stands, stems from a viewpoint much more exclusive than that of the church historians, for, in the final analysis, it denies the ultimate force of ideas in history and attempts to explain the latter through social phenomena, whereas the theologians, dealing with the conflict of ideas, fail to trace their effects on the social realm, or their modifications in that realm. The problem, however, has two aspects, and the Marxists demonstrate their one-sidedness only too openly when they call the Reformation an early phase of the bourgeois revolution and try to explain Luther's thought from this perspective.

2. ALTERNATE INTERPRETATION

But if the Marxist view is one-sided, there must at least be some truth to it. Certainly, as Moeller has pointed out on the basis of a comprehensive survey of the secondary literature on the subject, the cities became the home of the Reformation,[14] and this often in spite of the opposition of the ruling patrician class, which either left after the inauguration of the Reformation or remained behind to constitute the center of the Catholic opposition.[15] Often the demand for a Lutheran minister went hand in hand with demands for social reform, but Moeller indicates that this conjunction of demands sooner hindered than expedited the progress of the Reformation.[16] However, he proceeds to show that most often the bourgeoisie desired the Reformation for purely religious reasons.[17] This, of course, the Marxists cannot understand.

The Reformation did not only conquer the cities of Germany, however, for at least until 1525 the peasants in many regions of the country, if not in all, considered themselves *the* carriers of Luther's teachings and his chief supporters.[18] This would indicate that there was nothing innately antagonistic between the peasantry and Luther's teachings, quite on the contrary.[19] The reasons for the disillusionment of the peasants, to the extent it actually occurred, lies elsewhere, in their defeat and in Luther's denun-

---

[13] B. Moeller, "Probleme der Reformationsgeschichtsforschung," Zeitschrift für Kirchengeschichte, LXXVI (1965), III/IV, 246.

[14] Moeller, Reichsstadt und Reformation, p. 22.

[15] Ibid., p. 27.   [16] Ibid., p. 22.   [17] Ibid., pp. 28—32.

[18] Uhrig, "Der Bauer in der Publizistik." See also Harold J. Grimm, "Social Forces in the German Reformation," CH, XXXI (1962), 8. Even Gerhard Brendler has stated: "Die Reformation — auch die Reformation Luthers! — war Jahrelang vorwiegend eine Sache des Volkes, die vom Volke gegen die Obrigkeit vertreten und zum Siege geführt wurde." Das Täuferreich zu Münster, p. 63.

[19] Grimm, "Social Forces in the German Reformation," p. 6.

ciation of their cause. But not even this denunciation can be termed a bourgeois act.

Not only, however, did Lutheranism find a broad response in the peasantry and the townsfolk; princes and patricians also joined its ranks, and this not merely for selfish, material reasons.[20] Similarly, Anabaptism drew its following from a wide spectrum of the social order.[21] The Marxist argument that one prince remained a Catholic because he hoped to extend his power by so doing, while another turned Protestant for the same reason, is merely an unconvincing attempt to rationalize their way out of a predicament of their own devising. The cardinal point, of course, is that there were men and women in all walks of life who chose to espouse Protestantism, and precisely this phenomenon the class approach to the problem fails to explain. And if this is so, as it manifestly is, then Lutheranism was not the ideology of any one class, otherwise we would have to argue with the Marxists that those of the other classes who espoused Lutheranism did not recognize their true interests, or, on the other hand, that they merely used Lutheranism behind which to hide these class interests. But if we use these arguments, then we will have to agree with Engels that Luther's teachings had not gone beyond any of the previous bourgeois heresies. To do so, however, would only be to demonstrate our ignorance concerning Luther's thought.

One of the problems is that the Marxists do not take individuals seriously enough, if they take them seriously at all. Were they to do so, they would not simply avoid and ignore, or attempt to explain away, individual differences. But the fact remains that these individual differences are present and spoil the Marxist theory of class conduct.[22] Once it is admitted that the theory does not hold true in all instances, then one must begin to seek for the motives in concrete historical situations; and if it is not true that all people are, in the final analysis, motivated by economic and social forces, then perhaps a variety of forces might conceivably be at work. Therefore, rather than argue about how Engels should be interpreted, the Marxists should begin to attempt more ideologically unencumbered studies of specific historical instances. Precisely this, however, they will not do. Therefore they justify their one-sided approach to history with the argument that all history is *parteilich* in any case.[23] Since they believe this to be true, they can proceed to use history for

[20] Ibid., pp. 7 & 10.
[21] *Clasen*, Die Wiedertäufer im Herzogtum Württemberg, pp. 118—142.
[22] *Grimm*, "Social Forces in the German Reformation," p. 8.
[23] *Brendler*, Das Täuferreich zu Münster, p. 9.

propaganda purposes to further the cause of that class their fantasy has ordained shall inherit the earth.

If the Marxists have erred in their analysis of the Reformation era, what, then, was the nature of the relationship between Peasants' War, bourgeois revolts in the cities, and the Reformation as an intellectual movement? Peasant wars and bourgeois revolts in the cities had been going on more or less independently of one another long before Luther appeared on the scene. Hence, according to Marxist theory, these must have been bourgeois and peasant movements without a bourgeois or peasant revolutionary ideology. The weakening of the central monarchy had been proceeding apace, as had the consolidation of territorial power by the princes, before ever Luther turned into a "princely hireling." Conflicts between these territorial powers and the various other estates, or conflicts between the various estates themselves, had been present. The rise of commercial capitalism certainly added its share to the conflicts of the time, but Luther was not a champion of capitalistic fiscal policies as much as the Roman Catholic Church was, despite the fact that she had a heavy stake in the feudal system and condemned the practice of usury. Nor did Luther attack feudalism in the form of its ideological exponent as much as he attacked the Church's involvement in the things that belonged rightly in the realm of the mundane. Into all these tensions and social conflicts, into the sincere desire for religious renewal as well as political and social reform, came Luther's pamphlets with their religious conviction and moral indignation. Obviously, the response had to be varied. Some modified these teachings to suit their needs, others used them to justify selfish ends, but there were those as well who saw in them the answer to their religious needs and who modified their social and economic positions in order to remain true to these teachings. To do so, thousands suffered death, the loss of property, while others fled to safer territories leaving all their earthly goods behind.

Sixteenth-century Germany witnessed an interaction between Reformation theology, be this Lutheran, Zwinglian, Calvinistic, or Anabaptist, and the social aspirations of the people from all the various estates of the realm. How this Reformation theology was received by the individual must be determined on an individual basis, not by means of an abstract theory of class conduct. Much work still remains to be done in this regard, but it is obvious already that the different reactions within the same estate to Luther and his Reformation cannot be explained away, they must much rather be investigated. And if they cannot be explained away, the Marxist theory of the class conflict has little relevancy as a category for investigating history. If these are necessary and logical deductions from an historical observation, then it must follow that the economic factor is not the ultimately motivating force in history.

If, then, the Peasants' War and bourgeois revolts in the cities and towns proceeded independently of one another, and if the bourgeois revolts had their own interaction with Reformation theologies, we are left here with a peasant revolt in the social realm and the Reformation in the intellectual realm. Between the Peasants' War and this Reformation there was a very tangible interaction, not merely because there was a simultaneous crisis in the social and intellectual realms, but much more because, as we saw in Chapter III, men brought these two realms into integral relationship by means of their concepts of the ideal Christian society. This was as true of the Catholic Church and the peasants with their ideal of the *Corpus Christianum* as it was of Müntzer with his ideal of the Kingdom of God on earth. The interaction took place on the part of the peasants and Müntzer because they believed that their view of the Christian teachings should affect their social conditions. The Marxists see the same kind of integral relationship between ideas and social milieu; only for them ideas are the result of the social conditions, although they concede that ideas may in turn modify the social milieu. Luther, however, through his doctrine of the separation of the two realms, viewed the intimate union of these two realms to be an unholy alliance and the greatest bane to the Church. Müntzer and the peasants, on the other hand, believed their society to be a Christian society, and if a Christian society, then nothing was more relevant to that society's reformation than a purified Christian theology. These two positions, as we noted in Chapter II, find their ultimate source in two different world views: that of Joachim of Fiore and that of St. Augustine. They may also be categorized basically as variations of Old and New Testament types. To create the perfect society on earth or to live in tension between the real and the ideal, that was and has remained the problem from St. Augustine to Marx.

3. MARX, MÜNTZER AND JOACHIM

But whereas the Joachite tradition, which hoped for the ultimate resolution of the tension between the real and the ideal in the Kingdom of God on earth, believed God (or, in Hegelian terms, the rational world spirit) to be guiding history to its goal, Marx rejected such an idealistic solution. He still believed in the ultimate resolution of these tensions in a secularized Kingdom of God on earth — the classless communistic society — but, being a materialist, he had to make other forces responsible for the realization of his ideal society. These forces he discovered at work in the laws of historical materialism — the dialectic of history that proved how one economic age superseded another until the classless communistic society would be inaugurated by the downtrodden proletariat.

How similar to Joachim and Müntzer! History's goal, the dedicated nucleus of the elect — all are there. Yet how different the means: God on the one hand, the dialectic of the class struggle on the other. Motivated by the tensions created by the Industrial Revolution, Marx, too, longed for the perfect society. But rather than leave the inauguration of such a society to some extraneous force, he chose to place his hopes in tangible material powers.

The point of departure for all those who stand in the tradition beginning with Joachim of Fiore and ending in Marx is an eschatalogical one: because one cannot live in the tension between the real and the ideal, one must posit a future in which this tension will be resolved. Such a future, however, can only be a matter of hope, not of scientific certainty. To begin, then, at such an eschatalogical position of hope and proceed from there to determine how that hope will be realized in history seems to be presumption on the grandest of scales. Yet Marx did precisely this, as is apparent from a letter of Moses Hess to Marx of July 28, 1846:

"Mit Deinen Ansichten über die kommunistische Schriftstellerei, die Du neuerdings Daniel mitteiltest, bin ich vollkommen einverstanden. So notwendig im Anfange ein Anknüpfen der kommunistischen Bestrebungen an die deutsche Ideologie war, so notwendig ist jetzt die Begründung auf geschichtliche und ökonomische Voraussetzungen, sonst wird man weder mit den 'Sozialisten,' noch mit den Gegnern aller Farben fertig."[24]

But the laws of history and economics devised by Marx and Engels, when applied to the 16th-century, have led to a myriad of problems. And one is therefore tempted to assume that if these laws are not applicable to past history, it is even more doubtful that they will hold true for the future.

The basic difference between the Marxist and the Joachist position on the problem is manifested in the Marxist historiography of Thomas Müntzer. Engels' view that Müntzer had essentially been an atheist rested, as he himself admitted, on the "findings" of Zimmermann. But Zimmermann bent the truth somewhat in order to make a Young Hegelian

---

[24] Moses Hess Briefwechsel, p. 165.

radical of Müntzer. He relied upon Sebastian Franck's account of Müntzer's teachings for his evidence concerning the latter's beliefs. Franck,
however, who had himself been not a little influenced by Thomas Müntzer and the spiritualistic ideas of his day, knew well what he meant when
he spoke of Müntzer's "inner voice." But precisely this "inner voice' became the rational faculty in Zimmermann's historical workshop. Zimmermann's reinterpretation, however, was not merely a misinterpretation;
it rested upon a conscious falsification.

This falsification was welcomed by Engels because it made Müntzer
into a rational social revolutionary, and when this was combined with the
latter's communistic tendencies, Müntzer appeared to be a precursor of
modern atheistic communism. But it was precisely this religious element
in Müntzer's thought which Kautsky and Bax felt constrained to replace
and which Engels tacitly agreed to in his last letter to Kautsky. Smirin,
however, in strict dependence upon Engels, turned against Kautsky and,
by "proving" Engels' theory, also "proved" Zimmermann's consciously
falsified portrait of Müntzer as the rational social revolutionary. Yet
although Smirin was profuse in his argumentation, his Marxist colleagues
have not seen fit to follow him in denying Müntzer's religious sincerity.
Zschäbitz was the first to revise Engels' and Zimmermann's thesis after
the return to Marxist orthodoxy by Smirin, and although he has been
criticized by some of his colleagues, his thesis of the religious sincerity
of Müntzer has not again been denied.

It must be pointed out here, however, that although contemporary
Marxist scholars have conceded Müntzer's religious sincerity, they have
made this sincerity the fatal flaw in his intellectual armor. His religious
perspective kept him, they have argued, from realizing that his ethical-
religious principles required too much of the people: it kept him from
seeing that the social and economic conditions of his day had forced the
people to be egoistic, for egoism was a basic characteristic of capitalistic
society.

It is interesting to note, therefore, that this turnabout in Marxist historiography with regard to Müntzer's religious sincerity has also changed
the Marxist argumentation regarding the causes of his failure. Engels
had placed the blame for failure in the fact that Müntzer had misjudged
the historical dialectic. Once his religious sincerity had been granted,
however, it was argued that the anticipation of the classless society had
been possible in the 16th century only in certain categories of religious
thought. But Müntzer's defeat at Frankenhausen had demonstrated the
fallibility of the religious principle of salvation, for it had shown the

impossibility of achieving a classless society on the basis of religious principles. Müntzer's aim had been correct, but he had not been able to realize that aim because of the religious error of his century.

The ultimate goal of Müntzer and Marx were identical, but the means of arriving at the goal were different. Would God or man overcome the tensions in society and establish the Kingdom of God on earth? That was the major issue that separated Marx from the Joachite tradition which culminated in Hegel. One could quibble over the means, but the goal remained the same. When compared with the position of St. Augustine and Luther, this tradition, and even the position of the materialist, Marx, is much more utopian and idealistic.

APPENDIX A

Here follows a lengthy passage in which Zimmermann copies Strobel word for word. It is given here, together with the equivalent passage in Strobel, as proof of Zimmermann's dependence upon Strobel.

Zimmermann:

Im Jahr 1520 wurde er als erster evangelischer Prediger nach *Zwickau* berufen, er war übrigens, wie manche andere, mit *Luther nicht zufrieden, weil ihm diese* Reformation nicht leistete, was er von ihr erwartete und forderte, nämlich eine Reform des ganzen christlichen Lebens. Und er verhehlte dieses Missvergnügen nicht. *Die Gewalt des Papstes sagte er, den Ablass, das Fegfeuer, die Seelenmessen und andere Missbräuche verwerfen, wäre nur halb reformirt. Man müsse die Sache mit mehr Eifer angreifen, es sei eine völlige Absonderung von andern nöthig, es müsse eine ganz reine Kirche von lauter ächten Kindern Gottes gesammelt werden, die mit dem Geist Gottes begabt und von ihm selbst regiert werde. Luther sei ein Weichling, der dem zarten Fleisch Kissen unterlege, er erhebe den Glauben zu sehr und mache aus den Werken zu wenig, er lasse das Volk in seinen alten Sünden und diese todte Glaubenspredigt sei dem Evangelium schaedlicher, als der Papisten Lehre. Man müsse auf* den inwendigen Christus dringen, *den Gott allen Menschen gebe, man müsse nur oft an Gott den-*

ken, der noch jetzt mit den Menschen ebensowohl durch Offenbarungen handle, als vordem. (1841), II, 57—58.

Strobel:

In *Zwickau* trat er sein Lehramt im *Jahre 1520* an, und hielt seine erste Predigt am Tag Mariä Himmelfahrt. Schon in dieser eiferte er sehr scharf wider das Pabsttum, und zeigte sein Missfallen an verschiedenen Irrlehren desselben. Er war nicht lange hier, so liess er sichs deutlich genug merken, noch mehr aber, als er nach Altstedt kam, dass er mit der von *Luthern* unternommenen Reformation *nicht ganz zufrieden sey, weil sie gröstentheils nur das äusserliche beträfe. Die Gewalt des Pabstes, den Ablass, das Fegfeuer, die Seelenmessen und andere Missbräuche verwerfen, wäre nur halb reformirt. Man müsse diese Sache mit Eifer angreifen, es sey eine völlige Absonderung von andern nöthig, es müsse eine ganz reine Kirche von lauter ächten Kindern Gottes gesammelt werden, die mit dem Geist Gottes begabt, und von ihm selbst regiert werde. Luther sei ein untüchtiger Reformator, ein Weichling, der dem zarten Fleisch Kis-*

sen unterlege, er erhebe den Glauben zu sehr, und mache aus den
Werken zu wenig. *Er lasse das
Volk in seinen alten Sünden, und
diese todte Glaubenspredigt sey
dem Evangelio schädlicher, als der
Papisten Lehre.* Er aber drang auf
den inwendigen Christentum, *den*

*Gott allen Menschen gebe, man
müsse sich nur* recht demüthigen,
sein Fleisch kreuzigen, sich von allem äusserlichen entziehen, *und oft
an Gott denken, der noch jetzt mit
den Menschen eben so wohl durch
Offenbarungen handle, als vor
diesem* u. a. m. pp. 12—13.

APPENDIX B

The following presents a comparison of Müntzer's articles of faith as given by Zimmermann and as given by Sebastian Franck, quoted in the appendix to Strobel's *Müntzer,* pp. 188—194.

Sebastian Franck:

1. Alle Papistische und vermeinte Evangelische Prediger sind Schriftgelehrte, die allein von der Schrift und nicht von Gott weder gelehrt noch gesandt sind. Alle Prediger auf einen Haufen seyen Schriftgelehrte, die ihr Evangelium nicht von Gott, sondern von der Schrift empfangen haben. Dass kein Schriftgelehrter beruffen sey, noch des lebendigen Gottes Wort habe noch predige, sondern den todten Buchstaben der Schrift. Er hält nichts von der Schrift oder dem äusserlichen Wort, dass der Glaub dadurch komme oder gegeben werde, sondern von der himmlischen Stimme und lebendigen Worte Gottes; darum er von vielen ein himmlischer Prophet spottweise, von etlichen seiner Jünger ernstlich ist genennt worden.

2. Man muss nicht durch Bücher oder Predigt, sondern von der Lebendigen Stimme Gottes gelehrt werden, und von dem innern himmlischen Wort. Dass alle Predigt oder Lesen vergebens sey, wo nicht zuvor der Mensch Christum in seinem Herzen hab predigen hören. Dass die unversuchten Prediger nicht Gottes Wort predigen, wo sie nicht von Gott dazu beru-

fen und getrieben sind, und das Wort, so sie predigen, in ihnen lebe, das sie im Grund ihrer Seelen empfunden und erfahren haben.

3. Man soll die schuldige Pflicht der Ehe nicht zahlen, man habe dann eine Stimme vom Himmel gehört, dass aus diesem ehelichen Werk ein gut auserwählt wolgefällig Kind werde, und läst sich merken, als sey der Welt und viel der Geistlichen Ehe nichts dann eine erbare Hurerey.

4. Das lebendig machende Wort sey, das ohne Mittel von dem Mund Gottes ausgehe und nicht, das aus den Büchern gestohlen wird, weil Moses Deuter. 8. spricht, das ausgehet aus dem Mund Gottes, und nicht vom Mund der Menschen oder Büchern.

5. Das äusserliche Wort sey eigentlich nicht das Wort Gottes, sondern allein ein Zeugnis des lebendigen Worts, man müsse die lebendige Stimme Gottes im Abgrund der Seele hören. Gott redet zu unserm Herzen in aller Gelassenheit. Wenns nicht also von Herzen komme und entspringe, sey es ein Menschenwort, das die Schriftgelehrten verdamme, die die heiligen Worte Gottes also von Ihrem Nächsten stehlen, Jer. 23. Darum

sollen sie Fleiss ankehren, dass man von Herzen prophetizire und weissage durch das einleuchtende Wort und lebendige Stimme, aus einem erleuchteten Geist, nicht aus der Charten des gestohlnen todten Buchstabens hersagen, sonst ist die Theologie und das gestohlene Wort Gottes ein Menschentand.

6. Man muss Gott nicht von weitem ausser uns, sondern nahe in uns wahrnehmen. Die Tafeln unsers Herzens sind mit fleischlichen Begierden überzogen, die da hindern den Finger Gottes.

7. Das ehelich Bett der unglaubigen und fleischlichen ist kein rein unbefleckt Bett sondern ein Hurenbett oder Teufels hurenhauss, *Satanae lupanar,* dero Begierden den h. Geist Gottes hindern.

8. Man muss den Mund Gottes fragen, wenn man die schuldige Willfahrt auch in der Ehe zahlen soll, damit die Furcht Gottes und der Geist der Weisheit von der viehischen Lust nicht ersäuft werde.

9. Es ist ein greulich Irrthum, ein Fegfeuer Läugnen, denn die es verläugnen, dass sie nicht verstehen die Schrift, noch die Uebung des Geistes, doch der Papisten Fegfeuer ist nichts.

10. Den Glauben mag man aus keinem Buchlesen oder hören erlangen, auch gebe ihn kein todten Buchstabe, sondern die himmlische Stimme in unsere Herzen, so man den zulasse.

11. Die Ankunft des Glaubens sey, wenn wir im höchsten Unglauben beschlossen, und in Erkenntnis unserer selbst gestellet sind.

12. Man soll nicht leichtsinnig sein, zu glauben, denn wer bald glaube, sey eines leichtfertigen Herzens.

13. Des Glaubens Ankunft sey die Furcht, Trübsal, Zittern und Erbidmen von unsern Sünden und Unglauben. Also sey Abraham und alle Patriarchen glaubig worden. Jer. 36. Jud. 8.

14. Schwerlich komme man zum Glauben. und wer bald dazu komme, der falle bald wiederum davon ab.

15. Wenn einer sein Lebenlang die Bibel weder gelesen noch gehört hätte, könnte er wol einen ungefärbten Glauben haben durch die Lehre des h. Geistes, wie alle die gehabt haben, die ohne alle Bücher der h. Schrift geschrieben, und den Glauben beschrieben haben aus dem Buch ihres Herzens.

16. Die Schrift lehret nichts, sondern bezeugt allein, macht auch kein Wesen im Menschen, ja tödtet nur. 2. Cor. 3.

17. Die Berechnung des Glaubens bey den bewährten im Glauben muss aus der Ankunft, und nicht aus der Schrift gegeben werden.

18. Die Schriftgelehrten wähnen, der Glaube komme aus dem Gehöre, Röm. 10. so doch die ganze

Schrift darauf dringt, dass wir müssen von Gott gelehrt werden, Joh. 6. Jes. 14. Jer. 36. Hiob 35. Ps. 22, 24, 33, 36, 70.

19. Dass der Glaub nichts anders sey, denn so das Wort in uns vermenscht Fleisch und Christus in uns gebohren wird.

20. Dass der Glaub der Gehorsam Gottes sey, derohalben niemand glauben möge, und in der Sünde leben.

21. Dass der Glaube den Menschen versetze von Adam in Christum und verneue, wieder gebähre, mit Kraft anthue aus der Höhe, die Liebe ausgiesse in unser Herz, den H. Geist bringe Joh. 7.

22. Wo diese Stücke nicht sind, sondern noch alles alt wie von Anfang Lust, Wille, Werk, Herz, Fleisch, Gedanken, da glaubt man nicht, denn wo Adam lebt, da sey Christus todt.

23. Die Schrift soll man dazu nutzen, dass man über solche trefliche Werke Zeugnis habe, und die Geister bewehre.

24. Die Schrift sey nicht darum anzunehmen, dass sie von den Alten der Kirche auf uns kommen sey. Denn also bestätigt auch der Heid, Jud, seinen Glauben, sondern dass wir also erfahren haben im Abgrund unsers Herzens, wie die Schrift zeuget, und wissen, dass ihm also sey.

25. Man soll nicht eher glauben, man sey denn des zuvor inwendig vergewissert in der Verwunderung.

26. Die Gewaltigen müssen aus dem Sattel gehoben werden Luc. 1.

27. Es muss ein ieder die Kunst Gottes, den rechten christlichen Glauben nicht von aussen hinein durch den Athem der Schriftgelehrten schöpfen, sondern durch das ewig kräftig Wort des Vaters im Sohn mit Erleuchtung des H. Geistes, und also erfüllet werden mit der lebendigen Stimme in der Seele nach der Länge, Weite, Breite, Tiefe u. Höhe. Ephes. 3.

28. Ob iemand schon die Bibel gefressen hätte, hilft nicht, man muss die scharfe Pflugschar erleiden, und den Schlüssel David, der alle Propheten aufthut, überkommen. Niemand hat einen Glauben, bis dass ihn Gott selber gibt, und lehret in der Erfahrung unter dem H. Creuz in der Schule Christi.

29. Allen Gottlosen und Schriftgelehrten ist die Schrift ein verschlossen Buch.

30. Es ist erlogen, dass Christus für uns hat genug gethan, wie die unversuchten, zarten, wollüstigen Schriftgelehrten davon sagen.

31. Versucht ist, der der Welt einen Honigsüssen Christum predigt, wohlgefällig der Natur, das heist mit den Türken in ein Loch blasen.

32. Alle Dinge muss man im Grund der Seele erfahren, und den inwendigen Schulmeister zum Zeu-

gen nehmen, was er gefragt zu allen Dingen sage wahrnehmen, und nach dieser himmlischen Stimme sich richten.

33. Sagen, der Glaub rechtfertig allein, ohne alle Werke, item Christus hat für uns genug gethan, und alles ausgericht, ist viel zu stumpf und kurz geredet.

34. Die durch den Glauben des Fleisches Lust und Ruhm suchen, dass sie frey vom Gesetz nicht mehr dürfen thun, und nicht so sauer werden lassen, die verstehen nicht, was Glaube ist. Der Glaube muss im Unglauben, der Himmel in der Hölle gefunden werden, es gilt erst Leidens, denn der Glaube wird nicht gelehrt und gegeben, dann unter dem Heil. Creutz, in der höchsten Armuth des müden, abgearbeiteten, erlegenen Geistes, der um gar keinen Glauben mehr weiss, und gar in der Tiefe der Hölle stecket.

35. Nach diesem Kampf Jacobs und Uebergang Gottes kommet erst die Morgenröthe, also dass der Tag anbricht in unserm Herzen.

36. Paulus hat uns gegeben Gewalt und Freiheit zu freyen und heyrathen, aber allein im Herrn 1 Cor. 7.

Zimmermann:

1. Nicht das aus Büchern Gestohlene, sondern das aus einem erleuchteten Geist Ausgehende sei das lebendig machende Wort.

2. Den heiligen Geist habe jeder Mensch. Denn der heilige Geist sei nichts anders, als die Vernunft und unser Verstand.

3. Gott offenbare sich noch heute, wie vor vier Tausend Jahren; es gebe keine andere Offenbarung, als die noch fortdauernde.

4. Er lehrte, man müsse Gott nicht von weitem ausser uns, sondern in uns wahrnehmen.

5. Es sei auch kein anderer Teufel, als die bösen Begierden und Neigungen des Menschen.

6. Es gebe keine jenseitige Hölle oder Verdammniss, und sündigen könne nur, was den heiligen Geist, das heisse, Vernunft habe.

7. Jeglicher Mensch, auch ein Heide, ohne alle Bibel, könne den Glauben haben.

8. Der Glaube sei nichts anderes, als das Wort (der Vernunft und der Schrift) in dem Menschen wirklich werde, ein Gehorsam gegen Gott, der uns erneue, mit Kraft aus der Höhe anthue, die Liebe in unser Herz ausgiesse und den heiligen Geist bringe.

9. Der Mensch werde hier auf Erden dadurch, dass das Wort in ihm lebendig werde, vergöttlicht, und so zu sagen der Himmel, in dem der Mensch versetzt werden soll, sei in diesem Leben noch zu suchen und zu finden.

10. Nur die Natur lehre, dass man dem Nächsten thun soll, was man sich wolle gethan haben. Solches Wollen sei der Glaube.

11. Er verwarf als unverständig und unchristlich die Lehre von der Rechtfertigung durch den Glauben allein ohne die Werke, als eine wollüstige Lüge die Lehre, als hätte Christus für aller Welt Sünde genüge gethan und Alles ausgerichtet.

APPENDIX C

The problem of Müntzer's involvement in the Peasant War had been variously appraised by Zimmermann's predecessors. Hammerdörfer, *Reformationsgeschichte*, p. 57, stated: "Während dies in Franken und Schwaben vorgieng, fieng es auch an in Thüringen ziemlich unruhig zu werden. Man giebt lutherischer Seits die erste Schuld dieser Empörung Münzern, so wie die Ursache der ganzen Unruhe von den Katholiken Luthern beygelegt wird, weil alle Partheyen sich ganz von aller gegebnen Veranlassung frey machen wollten ..." Hammerdörfer, therefore, would at the most, see Müntzer as the leader in Thuringia. Sartorious, *Bauernkrieg*, p. 312, stated: "... Dass Münzer selbst in Schwaben früher gewesen, und an den Gränzen der Schweiz gepredigt habe, ist ausser Zweifel, und er selbst hat es in seinem peinlichen Verhör nachher gestanden; dass er aber der Urheber jener Empörungen im südlichen Deutschland war, dass er besonders dazu mitgewirkt, ist ganz falsch; er scheint nicht einmal in einer genauen Verbindung mit den Anführern gestanden, noch nach einem Plan mit ihnen gehandelt zu haben ..." Strobel, *Müntzer*, pp. 68—72, did not commit himself as to Müntzer's influence, but it seems he believed the former must have had some influence in the south, for he said: "Diese eben ietzt angeführte Worte und sein Aufenthalt in Schwaben, wo der Aufruhr der Bauern zuerst ausbrach, gaben Veranlassung, dass ihm einige die zwölf Artickel der Bauern zuschrieben ...," p. 71. Von Baczko, *Münzer*, p. 40, also felt that despite Müntzer's activity in the south he had not really influenced the revolt there. "Er hatte die Denkungsart des grossen Haufens auf seinen Zügen hinreichend kennen gelernt; schon während seines Aufenthaltes in der Schweiz, waren Empörungen in Schwaben ausgebrochen, und er würde vielleicht jetzt thätigen Antheil daran genommen haben, wenn er nicht den Ruf als Prediger nach Mühlhausen erhalten ..." Even Treitschke, *Münzer*, p. 228, stated: "... Aber obgleich die dortigen Theologen, Ökolampadius und Hugefeld, an seiner Lehre Gefallen fanden, und ihn selbst zum Predigen ermahnten, so ward ihm doch das Geschäft, dem rasenden Pöbel das Evangelium zu predigen, bald verleidet. Diese Menschen hassten ihre Herren nicht, wie Münzer, als Feinde des Glaubens, sondern als Beeinträchtiger ihrer Freyheit und ihres Eigenthums ... Gleichwohl hörten die Bauern Münzers feurige Predigten gern, und lagen ihm an, bey ihnen zu bleiben, aber er verschmähete dieses, und eilte zurück nach Mühlhausen, wo er sein Lehren und sein Werben zu dem Bündniss für das Evangelium eifriger und mit besserm Erfolg als je trieb." Streif, *Münzer*, p. 45, also felt Müntzer had had little, if any, influence in the south. "Nach dem vielbewegten Süd-

Deutschland flüchtete der Vertriebene, dort für seinen unruhigen Geist und seine unglücksschwangern Pläne einen günstigen Boden und grössern Wirkungskreis suchend. Er war in Basel, sprach bei Oekolampadius ein, predigte unter den aufrührerischen Bauern des Clegau's und Schwarzwaldes, als er aber auch dort seine Rechnung nicht stand, begab er sich nach Nürnberg . . ." Streif has the wrong sequence of events here. Of the same opinion was Heinrich Wilhelm Bensen, *Geschichte des Bauernkrieges in Ostfranken aus den Quellen bearbeitet* (Erlangen, 1840), p. 2. "Der Zeit nach hatte der Bauernkrieg früher an der Schweizergränze in Südschwaben begonnen; seine politische Bedeutung gewann er erst in Ostfranken. Die Zertrümmerung des Landes in viele Gebiete, die bäuerlichen Verhältnisse halfen dazu, noch mehr der eigentliche Volkssinn und die Erinnerung an die alte fränkische Freiheit. Die Häupter des Aufstandes sind hier keine Fanatiker, sondern kaltentschlossene Reformer, welche ihre Sache mit dem Schwert durchzuführen gedenken, lieber eine Burg brechen als Psalmen singen und — ganz verschieden von dem thüringischen Münzer — auf gutes Geschütz mehr halten als auf lange Predigten . . ."

APPENDIX D

In an interesting footnote to the problem of the materialistic motivation of Luther's thought, Müller-Streisand compared Marxist and Catholic interpretations. ". . . Wie unabgeschlossen die Diskussion der ideologie-geschichtlichen Bewertung in dem von Engels gespannten Rahmen ist, zeigen so unterschiedliche Arbeiten wie die von Leo *Stern*, Martin Luther und Philipp Melanchthon — ihre ideologische Herkunft und geschichtliche Leistung. Eine Studie der materiellen und geistigen Triebkräfte und Auswirkungen der Reformation, Bln, 1953, und die gediegene Analyse von M. M. *Smirin*, Die Volksreformation des Thomas Müntzer und der große Bauernkrieg. Bln, 1952. Von bürgerlicher Seite sind insbesondere katholische Geschichtsschreiber den historischen Bedingungen der Reformation mit Erfolg nachgegangen; das Interesse, dem protestantischen Gegner materialistische Motive nachzuweisen, führt hier teilweise zu erstaunlichen historischen Erkenntnissen, ist aber natürlich nicht durch die Anerkenntnis einer allgemeinen dialektisch-materialistischen Gesetzlichkeit der Geschichte bestimmt. Vgl. u. a. Johannes *Janssen*, Geschichte des deutschen Volkes seit dem Ausgang des Mittelalters. Freiburg 1807, (sic) Heinrich *Denifle* Alb. M. *Weiss*, Luther und Luthertum. 2. Bd. Mainz 1909, J. Lortz a. a. O. Allerdings ist neuerdings bei Johannes *Hessen* — Luther in katholischer Sicht, Bonn 1947 — bereits kritisch auf die Verwandtschaft dieser Darstellungen zum materialistischen Geschichtsbild hingewiesen worden: offenbar wird heute eine Distanzierung von diesem für notwendiger erachtet als die konfessionelle Polemik. Wiederum im Dienst der Aufhebung dieser Polemik versucht Karl August *Meissinger*, Luther, die deutsche Tragödie 1521, München, 1953, von protestantischer Seite her, katholischer Sicht entgegenkommend, mit explizit konziliarischem Interesse eine Darstellung der historischen Bedingungen der Reformation zu geben, die weithin auf die materiellen Voraussetzungen eingeht." *Luthers Weg von der Reformation zur Restauration*, p. 178, note 633. With the growing influence of ecumenicity manifested in Luther research, the Marxists may well feel that they are losing their one ally in the West. It is from this viewpoint that Steinmetz's complaint becomes significant: "Bemerkenswert ist in diesem Zusammenhang ein Vorgang, der eigentlich bereits nach der Grossen Sozialistischen Oktoberrevolution einsetzte, aber erst nach 1945 seine volle Bedeutung erhielt: Ich meine die Eliminierung der alten konfessionellen Gegensätze, die sich ja immer wieder gerade bei der Behandlung und Darstellung der Reformationszeit neu entzündet hatten, in der heutigen westdeutschen Reformationshistoriographie. J. Lortz ist dafür im katholischen Lager kennzeichnend mit seinem Höchstmass von Annäherung an das protestantische Bild von Luther und der Reformation . . ." "Probleme der frühbürgerlichen Revolution," *Frühbürgerliche Revolution*, pp. 34—35.

LITERATURE

A. PRIMARY SOURCES

Arnold, Gottfried, Unparteyische Kirchen- und Ketzer-Historie, vom Anfang des Neuen Testaments biss auf das Jahr Christi 1688. Schaffhausen, 1748.

Beck, Joseph, Die Geschichtsbücher der Wiedertäufer in Österreich-Ungarn. Wien, 1883.

Böhmer, Heinrich, und *Kirn, Paul*, hrsg., Thomas Müntzer's Briefwechsel. Leipzig und Berlin. 1931.

Bossert, Gustav, hrsg., Quellen zur Geschichte der Wiedertäufer, 1. Band. Herzogtum Württemberg. Leipzig, 1930.

Bracht, Tieleman van, Het Bloedig Toonel of Martelaers Spiegel der Doopsgesinde of Weerloose Christenen. 2nd edition. Amsterdam, 1685.

Brandt, Otto, Thomas Müntzer: Sein Leben und Seine Schriften. Jena, 1938.

de Bres, Guy, De Wortel, den Oorspronck ende het Fondament der wederdooperen, oft Herdooperen van onsen tijde. Amsterdam, 1570. (Translated from the original French edition of 1565.)

Bullinger, Heinrich, Reformationsgeschichte. Frauenfeld, 1838.

— Der Widertöuffern Ursprung / Fürgang / Secten, etc. Zürich, 1561.

Cornelius, C. A., hrsg., Berichte der Augenzeugen über das Münsterische Wiedertäufer-reich. Münster, 1853.

Fast, Heinold, hrsg., Der linke Flügel der Reformation. Glaubenszeugnisse der Täufer, Spiritualisten und Antitrinitarier. Vol. 4, Klassiker des Protestantismus. Bremen, 1962.

Fellmann, Walter, hrsg., Hans Denck Schriften. Gütersloh, 1955—56.

Franck, Sebastian, Chronica, Zeitbuch unnd Geschichtsbibell von anbegyn bis in diss gegenwertig 1536. iar verlengt. Strassburg, 1536.

Franz, Günther, hrsg., Quellen zur Geschichte des Bauernkrieges. München, 1963.

— Thomas Müntzer: Schriften und Briefe. Gütersloh, 1968.

Fuchs, Walter Peter, und *Franz, Günther*, hrsg., Akten zur Geschichte des Bauernkrieges in Mitteldeutschland. Vol. 2. Jena, 1942.

Hillerbrand, Hans J., The Reformation: A Narrative History Related by Contemporary Observers and Participants. New York, 1964.

Hinrichs, Carl, hrsg., Thomas Müntzer, Politische Schriften. Halle/S., 1950.

Kappens, M. Johann Erhard, hrsg., Kleine Nachlese Einiger grossten Theils noch unge-druckter, zur Erläuterung der Reformations-Geschichte nützlicher Urkunden. Leipzig, 1727.

Kessler, Johannes, Sabbata mit kleineren Schriften und Briefen. St. Gallen, 1902.

Köhler, Walter, Sohm, Walter, Sippell, Theodor, und *Franz, Gunther*, hrsg., Urkundliche Quellen zur hessischen Reformationsgeschichte, IV. Band, Wiedertäuferakten 1527—1626. Marburg, 1951.

Koller, Heinrich, hrsg., Reformation Kaiser Siegmunds. Stuttgart, 1964.

Krebs, Manfred, und *Rott, Georg*, hrsg., Quellen zur Geschichte der Täufer, VIII. Band. Elsaß I. und II. Teil. Gütersloh, 1959—1960.

Luther, Martin, D. Martin Luther's Werke. Kritische Gesamtausgabe. Weimar, 1883—1966.

— Sämtliche Schriften. Vol. XVI. St. Louis, Missouri, 1899.

Meshovius, Arnold, Historiae Anabaptistarum. Coloniae, 1617.

Müller, Lydia, hrsg., Glaubenszeugnisse oberdeutscher Taufgesinnten. Leipzig, 1938.

Muralt, Leonhard von, und *Schmidt, Walter*, hrsg., Quellen zur Geschichte der Täufer in der Schweiz. Vol. I. Zürich, 1952.

Ottio, Joh. Henrico, Annales Anabaptistici hoc est, historia universalis de Anabaptistarum origine, progressu, factionibus, etc. Basel, 1672.

Schornbaum, Karl, hrsg., Quellen zur Geschichte der Wiedertäufer, II. Band, Markgraftum Brandenburg, Bayern, I. Abteilung. Leipzig, 1934.

Schornbaum, Karl, hrsg., Quellen zur Geschichte der Täufer, Bayern, II. Abteilung. Gütersloh, 1951.

Stierlin, E., und *Wyss, J. R.,* hrsg., Anselm Valerius: Berner Chronik. Bern, 1831.

Tschackert, Paul, hrsg., Urkundenbuch zur Reformationsgeschichte des Herzogtums Preussen. Publicationes aus den K. Preussischen Staatsarchiven. 3 vols. Leipzig, 1890.

Westin, Gunnar, und *Bergsten, Torsten,* hrsg., Balthasar Hubmaier Schriften. Gütersloh, 1962.

Wigandum, Johannem D., De Anabaptismo Grassante adhuc in Multis Germaniae, etc. Lipsiae, 1582.

Wolkan, Rudolf, hrsg., Geschicht-Buch der Hutterischen Bruder. Wien, 1923.

Ziegelschmidt, A. J. F., hrsg., Das Kleine Geschichtsbuch der Hutterischen Brüder. Philadelphia, Penn., 1943.

— Die Älteste Chronik der Hutterischen Brüder. Philadelphia, Penn., 1943.

B. SECONDARY SOURCES
MARXIST LITERATURE

Adler, Friedrich, hrsg., Victor Adler: Briefwechsel mit August Bebel und Karl Kautsky. Wien, 1954.

Bax, Ernest Belfort, German Society of the Middle Ages. London, 1894.

— The Peasant War in Germany. London, 1899.

— The Religion of Socialism. 3rd edition. London, 1891.

Bebel, August, Aus Meinem Leben. Stuttgart, 1914. (Edited by Karl Kautsky.)

— Der Deutsche Bauerkrieg. Braunschweig, 1876.

Bensing, Manfred, Thomas Müntzer und der Thüringer Aufstand 1525. Berlin, 1966.

— „Thomas Müntzer und Nordhausen (Harz) 1522, Eine Studie über Müntzers Leben und Wirken zwischen Prag und Allstedt," Zeitschrift für Geschichtswissenschaft, 10 (1962), 1095—1123.

Bernstein, Eduard, hrsg., Die Briefe von Friedrich Engels an Eduard Bernstein. Berlin, 1925.

Bloch, Ernst, „Blick in den Chiliasmus des Bauernkrieges und Wiedertäufertums," Genius, Zeitschrift für Werdende und Alte Kunst, 1 (1920), 310—313.

— Das Prinzip Hoffnung. 3 vols. Berlin, 1954—1959.

— Thomas Münzer als Theologe der Revolution. Berlin, 1960. (The first edition appeared in Munich, 1921.)

Blos, Wilhelm, hrsg., Dr. W. Zimmermann's Grosser Deutscher Bauernkrieg. Stuttgart, 1891.

Blumenberg, Werner, hrsg., August Bebels Briefwechsel mit Friedrich Engels. The Hague, 1965.

— Karl Kautskys literarisches Werk. The Hague, 1960.

Bottomore, T. B., and *Rubel, Maximilien,* eds., Karl Marx, Selected Writings in Sociology and Social Philosophy. New York, 1956.

Brendler, Gerhard, hrsg., Die frühbürgerliche Revolution in Deutschland. Berlin, 1961.

— „Die Täuferische Reformationsbewegung in Münster in Westfalen als Teilerscheinung der frühbürgerlichen Revolution in Deutschland," Wissenschaftliche Zeitschrift der Karl-Marx-Universität, 14 (1965), 3, 501—504.

— Das Täuferreich zu Münster. Berlin, 1966.

Chaikovskaia, O. G., „Vopros o kharaktere Reformatsii i Krestianskoi," Voprosi Istorii (1956), 12, 129—143.

Cornu, Auguste, und *Monke, Wolfgang,* hrsg., Moses Hess: Philosophische und Sozialistische Schriften 1837—1850. Berlin, 1961.

Engels, Friedrich, Der deutsche Bauernkrieg. Berlin, 1965.
— The Peasant War in Germany. 2nd edition. New York, 1934.
— Der deutsche Bauernkrieg. Berlin, 1908. (Edited and annotated by *Franz Mehring*.)
Engels, Friedrich, „Der deutsche Bauernkrieg," Neue Rheinische Zeitung. Politisch-ökonomische Revue. Köln, 1850. (Edited by *Karl Marx*.)
— „Der deutsche Bauernkrieg," Karl Marx und Friedrich Engels, Werke. Berlin, 1958—1967.
Engels, Friedrich, et *Lafargue, Paul* et *Laura*, Correspondance. 3 vols. Paris, 1956.
Epstein, A. D., „K voprosu o Reformatsii i Krestianskoi voine v Germanii kak bourgeoisoi revolutsii," Voprosi Istorii (1957), 8, 118—142.
Fabiunke, Gunther. Martin Luther als Nationalökonom. Berlin, 1963.
Fuchs, G., „Karlstadt zwischen Luther und Müntzer," Wissenschaftliche Zeitschrift der Martin-Luther-Universität, 3 (1953/54), 523—552.
Goebke, Hermann, „Neue Forschungen über Thomas Müntzer bis zum Jahre 1520," Harz Zeitschrift, 9 (1957), 1—30.
— „Thomas Müntzer — familiengeschichtlich und zeitgeschichtlich gesehen," Die frühbürgerliche Revolution in Deutschland, 91—100.
Grugorian, U. M., „K voprosu ob wrovne ekonomiki, o kharaktere Reformatsii i Krestianskoi voine v Germanii," Voprosi Istorii (1958), 1, 123—139.
Hesselbarth, Helmut, „Eine Flugschrift aus dem Großen Deutschen Bauernkrieg," Zeitschrift für Geschichtswissenschaft, 1 (1953), 527—551.
Husa, Vaclav, Thomas Müntzer á Cechy. Prague, 1957.
I. L. (?), „Zum Lutherjubiläum," Die Neue Zeit, 1 (1883), 489—496.
Kamnitzer, Heinz, Zur Vorgeschichte des deutschen Bauernkrieges. Berlin, 1953.
Kardos, Tibor, „Entwicklungsgang und osteuropäische Merkmale des ungarischen Humanismus," Renaissance und Humanismus in Mittel- und Osteuropa, *Johannes Irmscher*, hrsg. Vol. 2. Berlin, 1962.
Kautsky, Benedikt, hrsg., Friedrich Engels' Briefwechsel mit Karl Kautsky. Wien, 1955.
— Karl Kautsky, Erinnerungen und Erörterungen. The Hague, 1960.
Kautsky, Karl, „Die Bergarbeiter und der Bauernkrieg," Die Neue Zeit, 7 (1889), 288—297, 337—350, 410—417, 442—453 und 507—515.
— Die historische Leistung von Karl Marx. Berlin, 1908.
— Die Vorläufer des neueren Sozialismus. Vol. 2. Stuttgart, 1894.
— Foundation of Christianity. New York, 1953.
— Materialistische Geschichtsauffassung. 2 vols. 2nd edition. Berlin, 1929.
— Thomas More und seine Utopie. Offenbach/M., 1947.
Klein, Fritz, und *Streisand, Joachim*, hrsg., Beiträge zum neuen Geschichtsbild. Alfred Meusel zum 60. Geburtstag. Berlin, 1956.
Kleinschmidt, Karl, Martin Luther. Berlin, 1953.
Kobuch, Manfred, „Thomas Müntzers Weggang aus Allstedt. Zum Datierungsproblem eines Müntzerbriefes," Zeitschrift für Geschichtswissenschaft, 8 (1960), 1632—1636.
Köditz, Hanna, „Die gesellschaftlichen Ursachen des Scheiterns des Marburger Religionsgesprächs vom 1. bis 4. Oktober 1529," Zeitschrift für Geschichtswissenschaft, 2 (1954), 37—70.
— „Die Volksbewegung in Mühlhausen in Thüringen 1523—1573." Unpublished doctoral dissertation, University of Jena, 1959.
— Review of Smirin's Die Volksreformation des Thomas Müntzers. Zeitschrift für Geschichtswissenschaft, 1 (1953), 505—513.
— „Zur Ideologie der Täuferbewegung in Mühlhausen in Thüringen," Die frühbürgerliche Revolution in Deutschland, 184—207.
Kuczynski, Jürgen, „Parteilichkeit und Objektivität in Geschichte und Geschichtschreibung," Beiträge zum neuen Geschichtsbild. Berlin, 1956.

Liebknecht, Wilhelm, hrsg., Briefwechsel mit Karl Kautsky und Friedrich Engels. The
   Hague, 1963.
Lösche, Dietrich, „,Achtmänner, Ewiger Bund Gottes und Ewiger Rat,' Zur Geschichte der
   revolutionären Bewegung in Mühlhausen i. Th. 1523 bis 1525," Jahrbuch für Wirt-
   schaftsgeschichte, 1 (1960), 135—160.
Lukacz, Georg, Karl Marx und Friedrich Engels als Literaturkritiker. Berlin, 1952.
Luxemburg, Rosa, Briefe an Freunde. Zürich, 1950. (Edited by Benedikt Kautsky.)
Macek, Joseph, „Das revolutionäre Programm des deutschen Bauernkrieges von 1526,"
   Historica, II (Prague, 1960), 111—144.
— Husitske revolucni hnuti. Praha, 1952.
— „K diskuissi o kharaktere Reformatsii i Krestianskoi voine v Germanii," Voprosi
   Istorii (1958), 3, 114—121.
— The Hussite Movement in Bohemia. Prague, 1958.
— „Zu den Anfängen des Tiroler Bauernkrieges," Historica, I (Prague, 1959), 135—195.
Marx, Karl, und *Engels, Friedrich,* Werke. 34 vols. Berlin, 1958—1967.
— Selected Correspondence. Moscow, 1953.
— Selected Correspondence. New York, 1934.
— Ausgewählte Briefe. Zürich, 1934.
— On Religion. New York, 1964. (With an indroduction by Reinhold Niebuhr.)
Marx, Karl, Frühe Schriften. Vol. I. Darmstadt, 1962.
Marx, Engels, Lenin, Stalin. Zur deutschen Geschichte. 3. vols. Berlin, 1953—1954.
Mehring, Franz, Aus dem literarischen Nachlaß von Karl Marx, Friedrich Engels und
   Ferdinand Lassalle. 4 vols. Stuttgart, 1913.
Mehring, Franz, Deutsche Geschichte vom Ausgang des Mittelalters. Berlin, 1946.
— Zur deutschen Geschichte. Berlin, 1946.
Meusel, Alfred, Thomas Müntzer und seine Zeit. Berlin, 1952.
Müller, Rosemarie, Review of Kamnitzer's Vorgeschichte des Bauernkrieges. Zeitschrift
   für Geschichtswissenschaft, 2 (1954), 130 ff.
Müller-Streisand, Rosemarie, Luthers Weg von der Reformation zur Restauration.
   Halle/S., 1964.
Pianzola, Maurice, Thomas Munzer ou la Guerre des Paysans. Paris, 1958.
Plekhanov, George V., In Defence of Materialism. London, 1947.
— Essays in Historical Materialism. New York, 1940.
— The Role of the Individual in History. New York, 1940.
Ramm, Thilo, hrsg., Der Frühsozialismus, Ausgewählte Quellentexte. Stuttgart, 1956.
Ryazanoff, D., ed., The Communist Manifesto of Karl Marx and Friedrich Engels. New
   York, 1930.
Schildhauer, Johannes, Soziale, politische und religiöse Auseinandersetzungen in den
   Hansestädten Stralsund, Rostock und Wismar im ersten Drittel des 16. Jahrhunderts.
   Weimar, 1959.
Schilfert, Gerhard, „Engels' Schrift vom Bauernkrieg und die Quellen seiner Geschichts-
   auffassung." Unpublished doctoral dissertation, University of Halle/S., 1948.
— Review of the East German Blos edition of Zimmermann's Bauernkrieg, Zeitschrift
   für Geschichtswissenschaft 1 (1953), 152—157.
Schilfert, Gerhard, „Zum Erscheinen des ersten Bandes des Sammelwerkes ‚Marx, Engels,
   Lenin, Stalin. Zur deutschen Geschichte,'" Zeitschrift für Geschichtswissenschaft, 1
   (1953), 367—376.
Selektor, M. S., „Das Prinzip der kommunistischen Parteilichkeit in der Ideologie,"
   Sowjetwissenschaft — Gesellschaftswissenschaftliche Beiträge, 3 (1958), 275—276.
Sieber, Siegfried, „Die Teilnahme erzgebirgischer Bergleute am Bauernkrieg 1525," Berg-
   bau und Bergleute. Neue Beiträge zur Geschichte des Bergbaus und der Geologie,
   (1955), 83—106.
Silberer, Edmund, hrsg., Moses Hess Briefwechsel. The Hague, 1959.

Smirin, M. M., Die Volksreformation des Thomas Müntzer und der große Bauernkrieg. Berlin, 1952.

— Deutschland vor der Reformation. Berlin, 1955.

— „Eine Anonyme Politische Flugschrift aus der Zeit des Grossen Bauernkrieges," Beiträge zum neuen Geschichtsbild, 72—87.

— „O kharaktere ekonomicheskogo podiema i revolutionnogo dvishenia v Germanii v epochu Reformatsii," Voprosi Istorii (1957), 8, 82—101.

— „Zu einigen Fragen der Geschichte der deutschen Reformation," La Renaissance et la Réformation en Pologne et en Hongrie, 211—233.

Sorel, George, Reflections on Violence. New York, 1961.

Stam, S. M., „Chem zhe v deistvitelnosti bila Reformatsia v Germanii," Voprosi Istorii (1958), 4, 100—113.

Steinmetz, Max, „Die frühbürgerliche Revolution in Deutschland (1476—1535), Thesen," Zeitschrift für Geschichtswissenschaft, 8 (1960), 113—124.

— Deutschland von 1476 bis 1648. Berlin, 1965.

— „Reformation und Bauernkrieg in der Historiographie der DDR," Zeitschrift für Geschichtswissenschaft, 8 (1960), 160 ff.

— „Über den Charakter der Reformation und des Bauernkrieges in Deutschland," Wissenschaftliche Zeitschrift der Karl Marx Universität, 14 (1965), 3, 389—396.

— „Zur Entstehung der Müntzer-Legende," Beiträge zum neuen Geschichtsbild, 35—70.

Stern, Leo, Karl Marx. Berlin, 1954.

— Martin Luther und Philipp Melanchthon. Berlin, 1953.

— „Zur geistigen Situation der bürgerlichen Geschichtswissenschaft der Gegenwart," Zeitschrift für Geschichtswissenschaft, 1 (1953), 836—849.

Streisand, Joachim, „Progressive Traditionen und reaktionäre Anachronismen in der deutschen Geschichtswissenschaft," Zeitschrift für Geschichtswissenschaft, 9 (1961), 1775—1788.

Szekely, Gy., and *Fugedi, E.*, eds., La Renaissance et la Réformation en Pologne et en Hongrie. Budapest, 1963.

Töpfer, Bernhard, Review of Zschäbitz' Zur Mitteldeutschen Wiedertäuferbewegung nach dem grossen Bauernkrieg, Zeitschrift für Geschichtswissenschaft, 9 (1961), 681—687.

— Review of Vaclav Husa's Thomas Müntzer á Cechy, Zeitschrift für Geschichtswissenschaft, 8 (1960), 1685—1691.

Tschistoswonow, A. N., „Die soziale Basis und der historische Ort des revolutionären Täufertums," Wissenschaftliche Zeitschrift der Karl Marx Universität, 14 (1965), 3, 407—418.

Vogler, Günter, „Gab es eine radikale Reformation," Wissenschaftliche Zeitschrift der Karl Marx Universität, 14 (1965), 3, 495—500.

Weill, Alexander, Der Bauernkrieg. Weimar, 1947.

Werner, Ernst, „Der Florentiner Frühkapitalismus in marxistischer Sicht", Studi Medievali, 1 (1960), 661—686.

— „Messianische Bewegungen im Mittelalter," Zeitschrift für Geschichtswissenschaft, 10 (1962), 370—396, und 598—622.

— Review of G. Brucker's Florentine Politics and Society 1343—1376, Zeitschrift für Geschichtswissenschaft, 11 (1963), 998 ff.

— Review of Enrico Fiumi's Storia economica e sociale di San Gimignano, Zeitschrift für Geschichtswissenschaft, 10 (1962), 1721 ff.

Wolfgramm, Eberhard, „Der Prager Anschlag des Thomas Müntzer in der Leipziger Universitätsbibliothek," Wissenschaftliche Zeitschrift der Karl Marx Universität, 6 (1956/57), 295—308.

Zschäbitz, Gerhard, Martin Luther, Größe und Grenze. Berlin, 1967.

— „Über den Charakter und die historischen Aufgaben von Reformation und Bauernkrieg," Zeitschrift für Geschichtswissenschaft, 12 (1964), 277—288.

— „Von der newen wandlung eynes Christlichen Lebens' — eine oft missdeutete Schrift
    aus der Zeit nach dem Grossen Deutschen Bauernkrieg," Zeitschrift für Geschichts-
    wissenschaft, 8 (1960), 908—918.
— Zur Mitteldeutschen Wiedertäuferbewegung nach dem grossen Bauernkrieg. Berlin,
    1958.
Zschäbitz, Gerhard, und Brendler, Gerhard, „Geschichtswissenschaft und sozialistische
    Erziehung," Leipziger Volkszeitung, 22. Oktober (1966), 5.

                          NON-MARXIST LITERATURE

Althaus, Paul, Luthers Haltung im Bauernkrieg. Basle, 1953.
Andrea, Johann Valentin, Christianapolis. New York, 1916. Edited by Felix Emil Held.
Ammer, Felix, „Ein wirtschaftsgeschichtlicher Beitrag zur Sonderstellung Bayerns im deut-
    schen Bauernkrieg." Unpublished doctoral dissertation, University of Munich, 1943.
Andreas, Willy, Deutschland vor der Reformation. 6th edition. Stuttgart, 1959.
Baczko, Leo von, Thomas Münzer, dessen Charakter und Schicksale. Halle und Leipzig,
    1812.
Bainton, Roland, The Reformation of the Sixteenth Century. London, 1953.
Barge, Hermann, Luther und der Frühkapitalismus. Gütersloh, 1951.
Bäring, Georg, „Hans Denck und Thomas Müntzer in Nürnberg, 1524," Archiv für
    Reformationsgeschichte, 50 (1959), 2, 145—181.
Barnikol, Ernst, „Der Briefwechsel zwischen Strauss und Baur," Zeitschrift für Kir-
    chengeschichte, 73 (1962).
Barth, Karl, From Rousseau to Ritschl. New York, 1959.
Becker, Carl, The Heavenly City of the 18th Century Philosophers. New Haven, Conn.,
    1932.
Bender, Harold S., Conrad Grebel 1489—1526, Founder of the Swiss Brethren. Goshen,
    Ind., 1950.
— „The Zwickau Prophets, Thomas Müntzer and the Anabaptists," The Mennonite
    Quaterly Review, XVII (January, 1953), 3—16.
Bengel, Johann Albrecht, Exposition of the Apocalypse. London, 1758.
Bensen, Wilhelm, Geschichte des Bauernkrieges in Ostfranken aus den Quellen bearbeitet.
    Erlangen, 1840.
Benz, Ernst, „Die Kategorien des eschatalogischen Zeitbewusstseins," Deutsche Viertel-
    jahrsschrift für Literaturwissenschaft und Geistesgeschichte, 11 (1933).
— Ecclesia Spiritualis, Kirchenidee und Geschichtstheologie der Franziskanischen Refor-
    mation. Stuttgart, 1934.
Benz, Ernst, „Johann Albrecht Bengel und die Philosophie des deutschen Idealismus,"
    Deutsche Vierteljahrsschrift für Literaturwissenschaft und Geistesgeschichte, 27 (1953), 4.
— Schellings theologische Geistesahnen. Wiesbaden, 1955.
Bergmann, Wilhelm, Die Täuferbewegung im Kanton Zürich bis 1660. Leipzig, 1916.
Bergsten, Torsten, Balthasar Hubmaier, Seine Stellung zu Reformation und Täufertum
    1521—1528. Kassel, 1961.
Bernhöfer, Elsa, „Täuferische Denkweisen und Lebensformen im Spiegel ober- und mittel-
    deutscher Täuferverhöre." Unpublished doctoral dissertation, University of Freiburg
    i. B., 1955.
Blanke, Fritz, „Das Reich der Wiedertäufer zu Münster," Archiv für Reformations-
    geschichte, XXXVII (1940), 13—37.
— Brüder in Christo. Zürich, 1955.
Bober, M. M., Karl Marx's Interpretation of History. 2nd edition. Cambridge, Mass.,
    1948.

Bofinger, Wilhelm F., „Zur Rolle des Luthertums in der Geschichte des deutschen Stände-Parlamentarismus," *Heinz Liebing* und *Klaus Scholder,* hrsg., Geist und Geschichte der Reformation (Berlin, 1966), 397—417.

Böhmer, Heinrich, „Thomas Müntzer und das jüngste Deutschland," Gesammelte Aufsätze (Gotha, 1927), 190—222.

Bohnenblust, Ernst, Kampf und Gewissen, Luthers Haltung im Bauernkrieg. Bern und Leipzig, 1929.

Bornkamm, Heinrich, Luther im Spiegel der deutschen Geistesgeschichte. Heidelberg, 1955.

Brazill, Wm. J., The Young Hegelians. New Haven, Conn., 1970.

Brecht, Martin, „Johann Albrecht Bengels Theologie der Schrift," Zeitschrift für Theologie und Kirche, 64 (1967).

Bruck, Moeller van den, Das dritte Reich. München, 1923.

Brunner, Otto, „Feudalismus" — Ein Beitrag zur Begriffsgeschichte. Akademie der Wissenschaften und der Literatur, Abhandlungen der Geistes- und Sozialwissenschaftlichen Klasse, Nr. 10. Wiesbaden, 1958.

Butterfield, Herbert, Man on his Past. Boston, 1960.

— The Whig Interpretation of History, London, 1930.

Calvey, Jean-Yves, Karl Marx, Darstellung und Kritik seines Denkens. Freiburg i. B., 1964.

Carriere, Moriz, Die philosophische Weltanschauung der Reformationszeit. Leipzig, 1887.

Carsten, Francis L., „Der Bauernkrieg in Ostpreussen 1525," International Review for Social History, III (1938), 398—410.

Cellarius, Helmut, Die Reichsstadt Frankfurt und die Gravamina der deutschen Nation. Leipzig, 1938.

Clasen, Claus-Peter, Die Wiedertäufer im Herzogtum Württemberg und in benachbarten Herrschaften. Stuttgart, 1965.

Clough, Shepard B., and *Cole, Charles W.,* Economic History of Europe. Boston, 1952.

Cohn, Norman, In Pursuit of the Millenium. New Jersey, 1957.

Cranz, Edward F., An Essay on the Development of Luther's Thought on Justice, Law, and Society. Cambridge. Mass., 1964.

Crossley, Robert Nelson, „Martin Luther and the Great Peasants War: A Study of Luther's Economic and Political Theories in Relation to his Stand during the Peasant Revolt." Unpublished doctoral dissertation, University of Michigan, 1960.

Cullmann, Oscar, Der Staat im Neuen Testament, Tübingen, 1956.

Daniels, Robert Vincent, „Fate and Will in the Marxian Philosophy of History," Journal of the History of Ideas, XXI (1960), 538—552.

Deane, Herbert A., The Political and Social Ideas of St. Augustine. New York and London, 1963.

Delumeau, Jean, Naissance et Affirmation de La Reforme. Paris, 1965.

Deppermann, Klaus, Der hallische Pietismus und der preussische Staat unter Friedrich III. Göttingen, 1961.

Dohna, L. Graf zu, Reformatio Sigismundi. Göttingen, 1960.

Elliger, Walter, Thomas Müntzer. Schriften der evangelischen Forschungsakademie, Band 6. Berlin, 1960.

— „Zum Thema Luther und Thomas Müntzer," Lutherjahrbuch, XXXIV (1967), 90—116.

Esch, Margarete, „Thomas Münzer und Lenin. Ein Beitrag zum vergleichenden Studium der Geschichte des Kommunismus." Unpublished doctoral dissertation, University of Köln, 1920.

Fast, Heinold, „Pilgrim Marbeck und das oberdeutsche Täufertum. Ein neuer Handschriftenfund," Archiv für Reformationsgeschichte, XLVII (1956), 212—242.

— Bullinger und die Täufer. Weierhof/Pfalz, 1959.

Federn, Karl, The Materialistic Conception of History. London, 1939.

Fetscher, Iring, „Die bolschewistische Religionskritik und die Wissenschaft," Zeitwende, 32 (1961), 798—808.

Fischer, Karl, und *Kraus, Rudolf,* hrsg., Eduard Mörikes Briefwechsel. 2 vols. Berlin, 1903.

Footman, David, Ferdinand Lassalle, Romantic Revolutionary. New Haven, Conn., 1947.

Forell, George W., „Thomas Müntzer; Symbol and Reality," Dialog, II (Winter, 1960), 1—12.

Forster, Karl, hrsg., Wandlungen des Lutherbildes. Würzburg, 1966.

Franz, Günther, Der deutsche Bauernkrieg. 4th edition. Darmstadt, 1956.

— „Die Entstehung der ‚Zwölf Artikel' der deutschen Bauernschaft," Archiv für Reformationsgeschichte, XXXVI (1939), 193—213.

— „Zeitschriftenschau," Archiv für Reformationsgeschichte, L (1959), 258 ff.

Friedmann, Robert, „The Christian Communism of the Hutterite Brethren," Archiv für Reformationsgeschichte, XLVI (1955), 196—209.

— „The Essence of Anabaptist Faith," The Mennonite Quarterly Review, XLI (1967), I, 5—24.

Friedmann, Robert, „The Nicolsburg Articles, a Problem of Eearly Anabaptist History," Church History, XXXVI (1967), 4, 392—409.

— „Thomas Müntzer's Relation to Anabaptism," The Mennonite Quarterly Review, XXXI (1957), 75—88.

Friesen, Abraham, „Renaissance," The Soviet System and Democratic Society. Vol. V. Freiburg i. B., 1972.

— „Reformation," The Soviet System and Democratic Society. Vol. V. Freiburg i. B., 1972.

— „The Marxist Interpretation of Anabaptism," Carl S. Meyer, ed., Sixteenth Century Essays and Studies, vol. I (St. Louis, 1970), 17—34.

— „Thomas Müntzer in Marxist Thought," Church History, XXXIV (1965), 306—327.

— „Wilhelm Zimmermann's Historical Frame of Reference," V. G. Doerksen, et. al., Deutung und Bedeutung. Literary Essays presented to K. W. Maurer. Leiden, 1972.

Goeters, J. F. Gerhard, „Die Rolle des Täufertums in der Reformationsgeschichte des Niederrheins," Rheinische Vierteljahrsblätter, 24 (1959), 3/4, 217—236.

— Ludwig Hätzer, Spiritualist und Antitrinitarier. Eine Randfigur der frühen Täuferbewegung. Gütersloh, 1957.

Goetze, A., und *Schmitt, L. E.,* Aus dem Sozialen und Politischen Kampf. Flugschriften aus der Reformationszeit. Vol. 20. Halle/S., 1953.

Goertz, Hans-Jürgen, Innere und Äußere Ordnung in der Theologie Thomas Müntzers. Leiden, 1967.

Gollwitzer, Helmut, „Die marxistische Religionskritik und der christliche Glaube," Marxismusstudien (1962), 1—143.

Greschat, Martin, „Luthers Haltung im Bauernkrieg," Archiv für Reformationsgeschichte, LVI (1965), 31—47.

Grimm, Harold, The Reformation Era. New York, 1954.

— „Social Factors in the German Reformation," Church History, XXXI (1962), 3—13.

Gritsch, Eric W., „Thomas Müntzer and the Origins of Protestant Spiritualism," The Mennonite Quarterly Review, XXXVII (1963), 172—194.

— Thomas Müntzer, Reformer without a Church. Philadelphia, Penn., 1967.

Grundmann, Herbert, Neue Forschungen über Joachim von Fiore. Marburg, 1950.

— Studien über Joachim von Fiore. 2nd edition. Darmstadt, 1966.

— „Kirchenfreiheit und Kaisermacht um 1190 in der Sicht Joachims von Fiore," Deutsches Archiv für Erforschung des Mittelalters, XIX (1963), 353—396.

Guggenheim, Ernst, Der Florian Geyer-Stoff in der deutschen Dichtung. Berlin, 1908.

Hacker, Paul, Das Ich im Glauben bei Martin Luther. Graz, 1966.

Hammerdörfer, Karl, Geschichte der Lutherischen Reformation. Leipzig, 1793.

Hast, Johannes, Geschichte der Wiedertäufer. Münster, 1836.

Hausherr, Hans, „Wilhelm Zimmermann als Geschichtsschreiber des Bauernkrieges," Zeitschrift für Württembergische Landesgeschichte, X (1951), 166—181.

Hausrath, A., David Friedrich Strauss und die Theologie seiner Zeit. 2 vols. Heidelberg, 1876.

Haym, Rudolf, Hegel und seine Zeit. Berlin, 1857.

Headely, John, Luther's View of Church History. New Haven, Conn., 1963.

Heberle, S., „Die Anfänge des Anabaptismus in der Schweiz," Jahrbuch für deutsche Theologie (1858), 258 ff.

Hegel, G. W. F., Phenomenology of Mind. 7th edition. London and New York, 1966.

Hehn, Jürgen von, „Die Sowjetisierung des Geschichtsbildes in Mitteldeutschland," Europa Archiv, 19/20 (1954), 6929—6976.

Heine, Heinrich, „Französische Zustände," Werke und Briefe. Vol. 4. (Berlin, 1960), 514 ff.

Hermelink, Heinrich, Geschichte der Evangelischen Kirche in Württemberg von der Reformation bis zur Gegenwart. Stuttgart, 1949.

Herte, Adolf, Die Lutherkommentare des Johannes Cochläus. Münster, 1935.

— Das katholische Lutherbild im Bann der Lutherkommentare des Cochläus. 3 vols. Münster, 1943.

Hertz-Eichenrode, Dieter, „Karl Marx über das Bauerntum und die Bündnisfrage," International Review for Social History, XI (1966), 3, 382—402.

Hillerbrand, Hans J., Die politische Ethik des oberdeutschen Täufertums. Leiden, 1962.

— „The Origins of Sixteenth-Century Anabaptism: Another Look," Archiv für Reformationsgeschichte, LIII (1962), 152—180.

— „Thomas Müntzer's Last Tract against Luther," The Mennonite Quarterly Review, XXXVIII (1964), 20—36.

Hinrichs, Carl, „Deutschland zwischen Kaisertum und Libertät," *Hinrichs, Carl,* und *Berges, Wilhelm,* hrsg., Die deutsche Einheit als Problem der europäischen Geschichte (Stuttgart, 1960), 97—124.

— Luther und Müntzer. Berlin, 1962.

Hodgson, Peter C., The Formation of Historical Theology. A Study of Ferdinand Christian Baur. New York, 1966.

Hoffmeister, Johannes, hrsg., Briefe von und an Hegel, Vol. I. Hamburg, 1952.

Holborn, Hajo, A History of Modern Germany, vol. I, the Reformation, New York, 1959.

Holl, Karl, „Luther und die Schwärmer," Gesammelte Schriften, Vol. I. (Tübingen, 1932), 420—467.

Houben, Heinrich, hrsg., Aus dem Nachlaß Varnhagen's van Ense. Tagebücher von K. A. Varnhagen van Ense. Vol. IV. Leipzig, 1862.

Hruby, Fr., Die Wiedertäufer in Mähren. Leipzig, 1935.

Huegli, Albert E., ed., Church and State under God. St. Louis, 1964.

Iserloh, Erwin, „Zur Gestalt und Biographie Thomas Müntzers," Trierer Theologische Zeitschrift, 71 (1962), 1, 248—253.

Janssen, Johannes, History of the German People at the close of the Middle Ages. Vol. IV. New York, 1966.

Jenny, Beatrice, „Das Schleitheimer Täuferbekenntnis 1527," Beiträge zur vaterländischen Geschichte, 28 (1951), 5—81.

Kaminsky, Howard, „Chiliasm and the Hussite Revolution," Church History, XXVI (1957), 43—71.

Kantzenbach, Friedrich Wilhelm, Orthodoxie und Pietismus. Gütersloh, 1966.

Kawerau, Peter, Melchior Hoffman als Religiöser Denker. Haarlem, 1954.

Kellenbenz, Hermann, „Die unternehmerische Betätigung der verschiedenen Stände während des Übergangs zur Neuzeit," Vierteljahrsschrift für Sozial- und Wirtschaftsgeschichte, 44 (1957), 1—25.
Keller, Ludwig, Die Anfänge der Reformation und die Ketzerschulen. Berlin, 1897.
— Ein Apostel der Wiedertäufer, Hans Denck. Leipzig, 1882.
— Die Reformation und die älteren Reformparteien. Leipzig, 1885.
Kemp, Friedhelm, hrsg., Eduard Mörike, Briefe an seine Braut Luise Rau. München, 1965.
Kestenberg-Gladstein, Ruth, „The 'Third Reich.' A Fifteenth-Century Polemic against Joachim, and its Background," Journal of the Wartburg and Courtauld Institutes, 18 (1955), 245—267.
Kirchner, Hübert, Johannes Sylvius Egranus. Berlin, 1961.
— „Neue Müntzeriana," Zeitschrift für Kirchengeschichte, LXXII (1961), 113—116.
Kirchhoff, Albrecht, „Johann Herrgott, Buchführer von Nürnberg und sein tragisches Ende," Archiv für Geschichte des deutschen Buchhandels, I (1878), 15—55.
Kiwiet, Jan J., Pilgram Marbeck. 2nd edition. Kassel, 1958.
Klassen, Herbert, „The Life and Teachings of Hans Hut," The Mennonite Quarterly Review, 33 (1959), 3, 171—205, and 4, 267—305.
Klassen, Peter J., The Economics of Anabaptism 1525—1560. The Hague, 1964.
Klassen, Walter, „Spiritualism in the Reformation," The Mennonite Quarterly Review, XXXVII (1963), 67—77.
Klemperer, Klemens von, Germany's New Conservatism. Princeton, 1957.
Klempt, Adalbert, Die Säkularisierung der Universalhistorischen Auffassung. Göttingen, 1960.
Kolb, Franz, Die Wiedertäufer im Wipptal. Innsbruck, 1951.
Krahn, Cornelius, Dutch Anabaptism. The Hague, 1968.
Krajewski, Ekkehard, Leben und Sterben des Zürcher Täuferführers Felix Mantz. Kassel, 1958.
Künzli, Arnold, Karl Marx, Eine Psychographie. Wien, 1966.
Kupisch, Karl, Vom Pietismus zum Kommunismus. Berlin, 1953.
Lackner, Martin, „Von Thomas Müntzer zum Münsterschen Aufstand," Jahrbuch des Vereins für Westfälische Kirchengeschichte, 53/54 (1960—1961), 9—24.
Lang, Wilhelm, „Rudolf Lohbauer," Württembergische Vierteljahreshefte für Landesgeschichte, 5 (1896), 149—188.
La Piana, George, „Joachim of Flora: A Critical Survey," Speculum, VII (1932).
Lau, Franz, „Der Bauernkrieg und das angebliche Ende der lutherischen Reformation als spontaner Volksbewegung," Lutherjahrbuch, XXVI (1959), 109—134.
— „Die prophetische Apokalyptik Thomas Müntzers und Luthers Absage an die Bauernrevolution," Beiträge zur historischen und systematischen Theologie. Gedenkschrift für Werner Elert. Berlin, 1955.
— „Luther — Reaktionär oder Revolutionär?" Luther — Mitteilungen der Luthergesellschaft, 3 (1957), 109—133.
— Luthers Lehre von den beiden Reichen. Berlin, 1952.
Lehmann, Hartmut, Pietismus und weltliche Ordnung in Württemberg vom 17. bis zum 20. Jahrhundert. Stuttgart, 1969.
Lenz, Max, Vom Werden der Nation. München und Berlin, 1922.
Leo, Heinrich, Thomas Müntzer — Ein Vortrag. Berlin, 1856.
Leonhard, Wolfgang, Die Revolution entläßt ihre Kinder. Köln, 1955.
Leube, Martin, Die Geschichte des Tübinger Stifts. Stuttgart, 1954.
Levin, David, History as Romantic Art. Stanford, 1959.
Lichtheim, George, Marxism, a Historical and Critical Study. New York, 1961.
Lidtke, Vernon L., „Bebel and German Social Democracy's Relation to Christian Churches," Journal of the History of Ideas, XXVII (1966), 2, 245—264.

Liebel, Helen P., „The Bourgeoisie in Southwestern Germany, 1500—1789: A rising Class?" International Review for Social History, X (1965), 2, 283—307.

Liber, Hans-Joachim, Philosophie und Geschichte im Marxismus-Leninismus. Berlin, 1965.

Link, Wilhelm, Das Ringen Luthers um die Freiheit der Theologie von der Philosophie. 2nd edition. Darmstadt, 1969.

Locher, Gottfried, „Die Wandlungen des Zwinglibildes in der neueren Forschung," Zwingliana, XI (1963), 9, 560—585.

Loetscher, Valentin, Der deutsche Bauernkrieg in der Darstellung und im Urteil der Zeitgenössischen Schweizer. Basler Beiträge zur Geschichte. Vol. 43. Basel, 1948.

Loewenich, Walter von, „Reformation oder Revolution?" Iserloh, Erwin, und Manns, Peter, hrsg., Festgabe Lortz I Reformation, Schicksal und Aufgabe. Baden-Baden, 1958.

Loewith, Karl, Meaning in History. Chicago, 1949.

Lohmann, Annemarie, Zur geistigen Entwicklung Thomas Müntzers. Leipzig, 1931.

Lortz, Joseph, Die Reformation in Deutschland. 2 vols., 4th edition. Freiburg i. B., 1962.

Lütge, Friedrich, „Luthers Eingreifen in den Bauernkrieg," Jahrbuch für Nationalökonomie und Statistik, 158—160 (1943—1944), 370—401.

Mälzer, Gottfried, Johann Albrecht Bengel. Stuttgart, 1970.

Manuel, Frank, The Prophets of Paris. Cambridge, Mass., 1962.

Martin, Alfred von, Soziologie der Renaissance. Frankfurt/M., 1949.

Maync, Harry, Eduard Mörike. Sein Leben und Dichten. 5th edition. Stuttgart, 1944.

Meyer, Gustav, Friedrich Engels. New York, 1936.

Mecenseffy, Grete, „Die Herkunft des oberösterreichischen Täufertums", Archiv für Reformationsgeschichte, XLVII (1956), 252—259.

Meinhold, Peter, Werner, Robert, und Kernig, Claus D. „Christentum," Sowjetsystem und Demokratische Gesellschaft, vol. I, 984—1011. Freiburg i. B., 1966.

Mellink, A. F., „The Mutual Relations between the Münster Anabaptists and the Netherlands," Archiv für Reformationsgeschichte, L (1959), 1, 16—33.

— De Wederdopers in de Noordlijke Nederlanden, 1531—1544. Groningen, 1954.

Mendel, Arthur P., „Current Soviet Theory of History: New Trends or Old?" The American Historical Review, LXXII (October, 1966), 1, 50—73.

Merx, Otto, Thomas Münzer und Heinrich Pfeiffer 1523—1525. Göttingen, 1889.

Moeller, Bernd, Reichsstadt und Reformation. Gütersloh, 1962.

— „Probleme der Reformationsforschung," Zeitschrift für Kirchengeschichte, LXXVI (1965), III/IV, 246—257.

Mohl, Robert von, Lebenserinnerungen. Stuttgart und Leipzig, 1902.

Moltmann, Jürgen, „Jacob Brocard als Vorläufer der Reichs-Gottes-Theologie und der symbolisch-prophetischen Schriftauslegung des Johannes Coccejus," Zeitschrift für Kirchengeschichte, LXXI (1960), 110—129.

Müller, Gotthold, Identität und Immanenz. Zur Genese der Theologie von D. F. Strauss. Zürich, 1968.

Müller, Lydia, Der Kommunismus der Mährischen Wiedertäufer. Leipzig, 1927.

Näf, Werner. Vadian. 2 vols. St. Gallen, 1957.

Naujoks, Eberhard, Obrigkeitsgedanke, Zunftverfassung und Reformation. Stuttgart, 1958.

Neher, Walter, Arnold Ruge als Politiker und politischer Schriftsteller. Heidelberg, 1933.

Nigg, Walter, Das Buch der Ketzer. Zürich, 1949.

Nipperdey, Thomas, „Theologie und Revolution bei Thomas Müntzer," Archiv für Reformationsgeschichte, LIV (1963), 145—181.

Oechsle, Ferdinand Friedrich, Beiträge zur Geschichte des Bauernkrieges in den schwäbisch-fränkischen Grenzlanden. Heilbronn, 1830.

Oyer, John S., Lutheran Reformers against Anabaptists. The Hague, 1964.

Parsons, Howard L., „The Prophetic Mission of Karl Marx,“ The Journal of Religion, XLIX (1964), 1, 52—71.

Peachey, Paul, Die soziale Herkunft der Schweizer Täufer in der Reformationszeit. Karlsruhe, 1954.

Rapp, Adolf, hrsg., Briefwechsel zwischen Strauss und Vischer. 2 vols. Stuttgart, 1953.

— „Wilhelm Zimmermann,“ Schwäbische Lebensbilder, vol. VI, (Stuttgart, 1957), 266 bis 285.

Riggenbach, Bernhard, „Martin Borrhaus (Cellarius) ein Sonderling aus der Reformationszeit,“ Basler Jahrbuch (1900), 47—81.

Ritter, Gerhard, Luther, Gestalt und Tat. Gütersloh, 1962.

Ritter, Joachim, Hegel und die französische Revolution. Köln, 1956.

Rupp, E. Gordon, „Andrew Karlstadt and Reformation Puritanism“, Journal of Theological Studies, X (1959), 208—225.

— „Luther and Thomas Müntzer,“ Luther Today. Vol. I. Iowa City, 1957.

— „Thomas Müntzer, Hans Huth and the ‚Gospel of all Creatures,‘“ Bulletin of the John Rylands Library, 43 (1960—1961), 492—519.

— „Word and Spirit in the first years of the Reformation,“ Archiv für Reformationsgeschichte, XLIX (1958), 13—26.

Sachse, Carl, „Die politische und soziale Einstellung der Täufer in der Reformationszeit,“ Zeitschrift für Kirchengeschichte, LXXIV (1963), III/IV, 282—315.

Sartorius, Georg, Versuch einer Geschichte des deutschen Bauernkrieges. Frankenthal, 1795.

Schäufele, Wolfgang, Das Missionarische Bewußtsein und Wirken der Täufer. Neukirchen Vluyn, 1966.

Schiff, Otto, „Thomas Müntzer und die Bauernbewegung am Oberrhein,“ Historische Zeitschrift, 14 (1913), 67—90.

Schmidt, Martin, „Das Selbstbewußtsein Thomas Müntzers und sein Verhältnis zu Luther,“ Theologia Viatorum, VI (1954—1958), 25—41.

Schmidt, Martin, Wiedergeburt und neuer Mensch. Witten, 1969.

— „Luther und Spener,“ Lutherjahrbuch, XXIV (1957), 102—129.

Schmidt, Peter Heinrich, Luther und der Klassenkampf. St. Gallen, 1923.

Schonbaum, Herbert, Kommunismus im Reformationszeitalter. Bonn und Leipzig, 1919.

Schubert, Hans von, Revolution und Reformation im XVI. Jahrhundert. Tübingen, 1927.

Schulz, Harold, Evangelischer Utopismus bei Johann Valentin Andrea. Stuttgart, 1957.

Seibt, Ferdinand, „Probleme des böhmischen ‚Feudalismus‘ in der marxistischen Mediaevistik,“ Vierteljahrsschrift für Sozial- und Wirtschaftsgeschichte, 55 (1964), 289—301.

— „Utopie im Mittelalter,“ Historische Zeitschrift, 208 (1969), 555—594.

Seidemann, J. K., Thomas Münzer. Dresden und Leipzig, 1842.

Schrey, Heinz-Horst, hrsg., Reich Gottes und Welt: die Lehre Luthers von den zwei Reichen. Darmstadt, 1969.

Sommerland, Theo, Martin Luther und der deutsche Sozialismus. Halle/S., 1934.

Spitz, Lewis W., The Religious Renaissance of the German Humanists. Cambridge, Mass., 1963.

Stadler, Peter, „Wirtschaftskrise und Revolution bei Marx und Engels: Zur Entwicklung ihres Denkens in den 1850er Jahren,“ Historische Zeitschrift, 199 (1964), 113—144.

Stauffer, Ethelbert, „Märtyrertheologie und Täuferbewegung,“ Zeitschrift für Kirchengeschichte, 52 (1933), 545—598.

Stauffer, Richard, Luther as seen by Catholics. Richmond, 1967.

Stayer, James M., „Hans Hut's Doctrine of the Sword: an attempted Solution,“ The Mennonite Quarterly Review, XXXIX (1965), 3, 181—191.

Stern, Alfred, Über die Zwölf Artikel der Bauern. Leipzig, 1868.

Stolzenau, Karl-Ferdinand, Die Frage des Widerstandes gegen die Obrigkeit bei Luther zugleich in ihrer Bedeutung für die Gegenwart. Münster, 1962.

Stolze, Wilhelm, Bauernkrieg und Reformation. Leipzig, 1926.

Storz, Gerhard, Schwäbische Romantik. Stuttgart, 1967.

Strauss, D. F., Kleinere Schriften. 3rd edition. Bonn, 1898.

— „Justinus Kerner," Hallische Jahrbücher, 2 (Jan. 2, 1838), 8—27.

— Gesammelte Schriften. Bonn, 1876.

Strauss, Gerald, Historian in an Age of Crisis. The Life and Work of Johannes Aventinus. Cambridge, Mass., 1963.

Streif, Paul, Thomas Münzer oder der Thüringische Bauernkrieg. Leipzig, 1836.

Strobel, G. Th., Leben, Schriften und Lehren Thomae Müntzers. Nürnberg und Altdorf, 1795.

Taubes, Jakob, Abendländische Eschatologie. Bern, 1947.

Teufel, Eberhard, Luther und Luthertum im Urteil Sebastian Francks. Tübingen, 1922.

Thier, Erich, Das Menschenbild des jungen Marx. Göttingen, 1959.

Toffanin, Giovanni, Geschichte des Humanismus. Pantheon, 1941.

Treitschke, Georg Carl, „Thomas Münzer," Archiv für Geographie, Historie, Staats- und Kriegskunst (April-Mai, 1811), 205—255.

Uhrig, Kurt, „Der Bauer in der Publizistik der Reformation bis zum Ausgang des Bauernkrieges," Archiv für Reformationsgeschichte, XXXIII (1936), 70—125, und 165—225.

Unruh, Benjamin, „Die Revolution und das Täufertum," Gedenkschrift zum 400jährigen Jubiläum der Mennoniten oder Taufgesinnten (Ludwigshafen, 1925), 19—47.

Vischer, Friedrich Theodor, Kritische Gänge. 6 vols. Stuttgart, 1922. Hrsg. von Robert Vischer.

Vischer, Robert, hrsg., Briefwechsel zwischen Eduard Mörike und Friedrich Theodor Vischer. München, 1926.

Waas, Adolf, „Die große Wendung im deutschen Bauernkrieg," Historische Zeitschrift, 158 (1938), 457—491, und 159 (1939), 23—53.

— Die Bauern im Kampf um Gerechtigkeit, 1300—1525. München, 1964.

— Die alte deutsche Freiheit. München und Berlin, 1939.

Waiblinger, Wilhelm, Die Tagebücher 1821—1826. Stuttgart, 1956.

Walter, Karl, „Ernst Friedrich Kauffmann und seine schwäbischen Freunde," Zeitschrift für württembergische Landesgeschichte (1937).

Walter, L. G., Thomas Munzer et Les Luttes Sociales a L'Epoque de la Réforme. Paris, 1927.

Wappler, Paul, Die Täuferbewegung in Thüringen von 1526—1584. Jena, 1913.

— Thomas Müntzer in Zwickau und die „Zwickau Propheten." 2nd edition. Gütersloh, 1966.

Weiss, Ruth, „Die Herkunft der osthessischen Täufer," Archiv für Reformationsgeschichte, L (1959), 1—16, und 182—198.

— „Herkunft und Sozialanschauungen der Täufergemeinden im westlichen Hessen," Archiv für Reformationsgeschichte, LII (1961), 162—188.

Wenger, John C., Die dritte Reformation. Kassel, 1963.

Wetter, Gustav A., Sowjetideologie Heute. Dialektischer und historischer Materialismus. Frankfurt/M., 1962.

Wichelhaus, Manfred, Kirchengeschichtsschreibung und Soziologie im neunzehnten Jahrhundert und bei Ernst Troeltsch. Heidelberg, 1965.

Widmoser, Eduard, „Das Täufertum im Tiroler Unterland." Unpublished doctoral dissertation, University of Innsbruck, 1948.

Williams, George Hunston, The Radical Reformation. Philadelphia, Penn., 1962.

Wiswedel, Wilhelm, „Zum Problem inneres und äußeres Wort bei den Täufern des 16. Jahrhunderts," Archiv für Reformationsgeschichte, XLVI (1955), 1—19.

Wopfner, H., „Die Forschung nach den Ursachen des Bauernkrieges und ihre Förderung durch die Geschichtliche Volkskunde," Historische Zeitschrift, 153 (1936), 88—106.

Yoder, John H., Täufertum und Reformation in der Schweiz. Die Gespräche zwischen Täufern und Reformatoren 1523—1538. Weierhof/Pfalz, 1962.
— „The Turning Point of the Zwinglian Reformation,“ The Mennonite Quarterly Review, XXXII (1958), 128—140.
Zahn, Peter von, „Studien zur Entstehung der Sozialen Ideen des Täufertums in den ersten Jahren der Reformation.“ Unpublished doctoral dissertation, University of Freiburg i. B., 1942.
Zeller, Eduard, hrsg., Ausgewählte Briefe von David Friedrich Strauss. Bonn, 1895.
Zimmermann, Wilhelm, Geschichte des großen deutschen Bauernkrieges. Stuttgart, 1841— 1843. 3 vols.
— Geschichte des großen Bauernkrieges. 2 vols. Naunhof und Leipzig, 1939. Hrsg. von Hermann Barge.
— Der große deutsche Bauernkrieg. Berlin, 1952. (East German edition of the revised version edited by Wilhelm Blos in 1891.)
— Dr. W. Zimmermann's Großer Deutscher Bauernkrieg. Stuttgart, 1891. (Edited and drastically revised by Wilhelm Blos.)
— Geschichte des großen Bauernkrieges. Stuttgart, 1856. 2nd edition.
— Die Deutsche Revolution. Karlsruhe, 1848.
— „Der Roman der Gegenwart und Eugen Sue's Geheimnisse,“ Jahrbücher der Gegenwart. II (Tübingen, 1844).
— Geschichte der Hohenstaufen. 2 vols., 2nd edition. Stuttgart, 1843.
— Die Befreiungskämpfe der Deutschen gegen Napoleon. Stuttgart, 1837.
— Geschichte der prosaischen und poetischen deutschen Nationalliteratur. Stuttgart, 1846.
— Lebensgeschichte der Kirche Jesu Christi. 4 vols. Stuttgart, 1857—1859.
— Das Modell. Stuttgart, 1834.
— Gedichte. Stuttgart, 1831.
Zuck, Lowell H., „Anabaptism, Abortive Counter-Revolt within the Reformation,“ Church History, XXVI (1957), 212—226.
— „Fecund Problems of Eschatological Hope, Election Proof and Social Revolt in Thomas Müntzer,“ Franklin H. Littell, ed., Reformation Studies (Richmond, 1962), 239—250.
Zumkeller, A., „Thomas Müntzer — Augustiner?“ Augustiniana, 9 (1959), 380 ff.

INDEX

Band 39 LÉOPOLD SCHUMMER, **Le Ministère Pastoral dans l'Institution Chré-tienne de Calvin à la Lumière du Troisième Sacrement.** *1965. VIII, 108 S., brosch. DM 16,80, Ln. DM 20,—*

Band 40 ALEXANDRE GANOCZY, **Le jeune Calvin.** Genèse et Evolution de sa Vocation Réformatrice. Einleitung von J. Lortz. *1966. XXXII, 382 S., brosch. DM 58,— Ln. DM 64,—*

Band 42 **Die Texte des Normannischen Anonymus.** Unter Konsultation der Teilausgaben von H. Böhmer, H. Scherrinsky und G. H. Williams neu aus der Handschrift 415 des Corpus Christi College Cambridge heraus-gegeben von KARL PELLENS. *1966. XLII, 262 S., Ln. DM 60,—*

Band 43 HANSGEORG MOLITOR, **Kirchliche Reformversuche der Kurfürsten und Erzbischöfe von Trier im Zeitalter der Gegenreformation.** *1967. XVI, 213 S., 1 Karte, Ln. DM 42,—*

Band 44 ARNO SCHIRMER, **Das Paulusverständnis Melanchthons 1518—1522.** *1967. XII, 104 S., Ln. DM 24,—*

Band 46 PETER MANNS, **Lutherforschung heute.** Krise und Aufbruch. *1967. XVI, 75 S., brosch. DM 14,—*

Band 48 JOSEPH VERCRUYSSE, **Fidelis Populus.** Eine Untersuchung über die Eccle-siologie in M. Luthers Dictata super psalterium. *1968. VIII, 222 S., Ln. DM 38,—*

Band 51 GABRIEL LLOMPART, **Gaetano da Thiene 1480—1547.** Estudios sobre un reformador religioso. *1969. IV, 324 S., 8 Taf., brosch. DM 20,—. Vgr.*

Band 53 ROBERT STALDER, **Grundlinien der Theologie Schleiermachers.** I. Zur Fundamentaltheologie. *1969. XXIV, 401 S., Ln. DM 48,—*

Band 54 GEORGETTE EPINEY-BURGARD, **Gérard Grote (1340—1384) et les Débuts de la Dévotion moderne.** *1970. XVI, 335 S., Ln. DM 52,—*

Band 56 JARED WICKS, **Man Yearning for Grace.** Luther's early spiritual teach-ing. Nachdruck d. amerikan. Originalausgabe, erweitert um ein Vor-wort, eine deutsche Zusammenfassung und Luthers Ablaßtraktat in dt. Übersetzung. *1969. XX, 438 S., Ln. DM 50,—*

Band 57 FRIEDHELM KRÜGER, **Bucer und Erasmus.** Eine Untersuchung zum Einfluß des Erasmus auf die Theologie Martin Bucers. *1970. X, 233 S., Ln. DM 40,—*

Veröffentlichungen des Instituts für Europäische Geschichte Mainz
Abteilung für Abendl. Religionsgeschichte — Herausgegeben von Joseph Lortz

Band 1 EMIL MÖLLER, **Das Abendmahl des Leonardo da Vinci.** *1952. 195 S. mit 115 Abb., Ln. DM 84,— (Verlag für Kunst und Wissenschaft, Baden-Baden)*

Band 6 **Bernhard von Clairvaux – Mönch und Mystiker.** Internationaler Bernhardkongreß Mainz 1953. Hrsg. und eingeleitet von Joseph Lortz. *1955. LVI, 245 S., Ln. DM 20,80*

Band 7 HANS WOLTER, **Ordericus Vitalis.** Ein Beitrag zur kluniazensischen Geschichtsschreibung. *1955. VIII, 252 S., 1 Stammtafel, Ln. DM 18,—*

Band 8 ERWIN ISERLOH, **Gnade und Eucharistie in der philosophischen Theologie des Wilhelm von Ockham.** Ihre Bedeutung für die Ursachen der Reformation. Mit einer Einleitung von Joseph Lortz. *1956. XL, 286 S., Ln. DM 28,—*

Band 12 VICTOR CONZEMIUS, **Jacob III. von Eltz.** Erzbischof von Trier (1567 bis 1581). Ein Kurfürst im Zeitalter der Gegenreformation. *1956. XII, 272 S., Ln. DM 19,80*

Band 18 **Europa und das Christentum.** Drei Vorträge von Walther von Loewenich, Fedor Stepun, Joseph Lortz. Hrsg. J. Lortz. *1959. VIII, 204 S., Ln. DM 18,—*

Band 20 ENGELBERT MONNERJAHN, **Giovanni Pico della Mirandola.** Ein Beitrag zur philosoph. Theologie des italien. Humanismus. *1960. XII, 236 S., Ln. DM 21,—*

Band 24 GERHARD KAISER, **Pietismus und Patriotismus im literarischen Deutschland.** Ein Beitrag zum Problem der Säkularisation. *1961. VIII, 302 S., Ln. DM 32,—*

Band 25 HERMANN SCHÜSSLER, **Georg Calixt – Theologie und Kirchenpolitik.** *1961. XII, 245 S., Ln. DM 28,—*

Band 26 **Paolo Sarpi – Lettere ai Gallicani.** Edizione critica, saggio introduttivo e note a cura di BORIS ULIANICH. *1961. CCVII, 308 S., Ln. DM 56,—*

Band 31 **Gabrielis Biel Canonis Misse Expositio.** Ediderunt HEIKO A. OBER-
bis 34 MAN et WILLIAM J. COURTENAY. *Pars Prima (Bd. 31) 1963. XXVI, 363 S., Ln. DM 50,—. Pars Secunda (Bd. 32) 1965. XIII, 462 S., Ln. DM 60,—. Pars Tertia (Bd. 33) 1966. XII, 333 S., Ln. DM 50,— Pars Quarta (Bd. 34) 1967. XII, 246 S., Ln. DM 50,—*

Band 58 ENRIQUE DUSSEL, **Les Evêques Hispano-Américains.** Défenseurs et Evangélisateurs de L'Indien 1504–1620. *1970. LXI, 286 S., Ln. DM 56,—*

Band 60 VINZENZ PFNÜR, **Einig in der Rechtfertigungslehre?** Die Rechtfertigungslehre der Confessio Augustana und die Stellungnahme der katholischen Kontroverstheologie zwischen 1530 und 1535. *1970. XIII, 432 S., Ln. DM 56,—*

Band 61 HEIDE STRATENWERTH, **Die Reformation in der Stadt Osnabrück.** *1971. VIII, 185 S., brosch. DM 28,—*

Band 62 HELMUT FELD, **Martin Luthers und Wendelin Steinbachs Vorlesungen über den Hebräerbrief.** Eine Studie zur Geschichte der Neutestamentlichen Exegese und Theologie. *1971. VIII, 277 S., Ln. DM 48,—*

Band 64 HANS JÖRG URBAN, **Bekenntnis, Dogma, kirchliches Lehramt.** Die Lehrautorität der Kirche in heutiger evangelischer Theologie. *1972. X, 401 S., Ln. DM 58,—*

Band 66 JÜRGEN BÜCKING, **Frühabsolutismus und Kirchenreform in Tirol (1565—1665).** Ein Beitrag zum Ringen zwischen „Staat" und „Kirche" in der frühen Neuzeit. *1972. XIV, 306 S., 2 Kt., Ln. DM 64,—*

Band 67 DAVID FLOOD, **Peter Olivi's Rule Commentary.** Edition and Presentation. *1972. XVI, 200 S., Ln. DM 44,—*

Band 68 WALTHER VON LOEWENICH, **Duplex Iustitia.** Luthers Stellung zu einer Unionsformel des 16. Jh. *1972. VIII, 84 S., brosch. DM 18,—*

Band 69 KARL PELLENS, **Das Kirchendenken des Normannischen Anonymus.** *1973. IXX, 333 S., Ln. DM 50,—*

Band 71 ABRAHAM FRIESEN, **Reformation and Utopia.** The Marxist Interpretation of the Reformation and its Antecedents. *1974. XVI, 271 S., Ln. DM 52,—*

In Vorbereitung:

Band 72 GERHARD PHILIPP WOLF, **Das neuere französische Lutherbild.**

Band 73 WOLFGANG STEIN, **Das kirchliche Amt bei Luther.**

VORTRÄGE

Die in der Reihenzählung nicht aufgeführten Bände und Vorträge dieser Reihen sind Veröffentlichungen der Abteilung für Universalgeschichte des gleichen Instituts.